Sound and Light: Teacher's

Contents in Brief

Teacher's Edition

See Program Component List on page ii

Student Edition

Prentice Hall Science Explorer

Series Tables of Contents

The Nature of Science and Technology

1. What Is Science?
2. The Work of Scientists
3. Technology and Engineering

Life Science

From Bacteria to Plants

1. Living Things
2. Viruses and Bacteria
3. Protists and Fungi
4. Introduction to Plants
5. Seed Plants

Animals

1. Sponges, Cnidarians, and Worms
2. Mollusks, Arthropods, and Echinoderms
3. Fishes, Amphibians, and Reptiles
4. Birds and Mammals
5. Animal Behavior

Cells and Heredity

1. Cell Structure and Function
2. Cell Processes and Energy
3. Genetics: The Science of Heredity
4. Modern Genetics
5. Changes Over Time

Human Biology and Health

1. Bones, Muscles, and Skin
2. Food and Digestion
3. Circulation
4. Respiration and Excretion
5. Fighting Disease
6. The Nervous System
7. The Endocrine System and Reproduction

Environmental Science

1. Populations and Communities
2. Ecosystems and Biomes
3. Living Resources
4. Land, Water, and Air Resources
5. Energy Resources

Earth Science

Inside Earth

1. Plate Tectonics
2. Earthquakes
3. Volcanoes
4. Minerals
5. Rocks

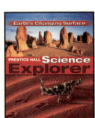

Earth's Changing Surface

1. Mapping Earth's Surface
2. Weathering and Soil Formation
3. Erosion and Deposition
4. A Trip Through Geologic Time

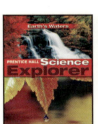

Earth's Waters

1. Earth: The Water Planet
2. Freshwater Resources
3. Ocean Motions
4. Ocean Zones

Weather and Climate

1. The Atmosphere
2. Weather Factors
3. Weather Patterns
4. Climate and Climate Change

Astronomy

1. Earth, Moon, and Sun
2. Exploring Space
3. The Solar System
4. Stars, Galaxies, and the Universe

Physical Science

Chemical Building Blocks

1. Introduction to Matter
2. Solids, Liquids, and Gases
3. Elements and the Periodic Table
4. Exploring Materials

Chemical Interactions

1. Atoms and Bonding
2. Chemical Reactions
3. Acids, Bases, and Solutions
4. Carbon Chemistry

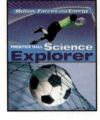

Motion, Forces, and Energy

1. Motion
2. Forces
3. Forces in Fluids
4. Work and Machines
5. Energy
6. Thermal Energy and Heat

Electricity and Magnetism

1. Magnetism
2. Electricity
3. Using Electricity and Magnetism
4. Electronics

Sound and Light

1. Characteristics of Waves
2. Sound
3. The Electromagnetic Spectrum
4. Light

Teacher's Edition

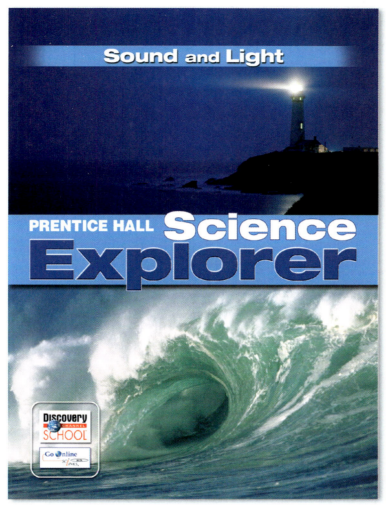

Sound and Light

PRENTICE HALL **Science Explorer**

PEARSON
Prentice Hall

Needham, Massachusetts
Upper Saddle River, New Jersey

ISBN 0-13-181134-7   1 2 3 4 5 6 7 8 9 10   08 07 06 05 04

Pacing Options

SCIENCE EXPLORER offers many aids to help you plan your instruction time, whether regular class periods or block scheduling. Section-by-section lesson plans for each chapter include suggested times for Student Edition activities. TeacherExpress™ and the Lab zone™ Easy Planner CD-ROM will help you manage your time electronically.

Pacing Chart

	PERIODS	BLOCKS		PERIODS	BLOCKS
Careers: Sonic Booms	1–2	$^1/_2$–1	**Chapter 4 Light**		
Chapter 1 Characteristics of Waves			Chapter 4 Project *Design and Build an Optical Instrument*	Ongoing	Ongoing
Chapter 1 Project *Over and Over and Over Again*	Ongoing	Ongoing	1 Light and Color	3–4	$1^1/_2$–2
1 What Are Waves?	2–3	1–1	2 Reflection and Mirrors	2–3	1–$1^1/_2$
2 Properties of Waves	3–4	$1^1/_2$–2	3 Refraction and Lenses	2–3	1–$1^1/_2$
3 Interactions of Waves	3–4	$1^1/_2$–2	4 Integrating Life Science: Seeing Light	1–2	$^1/_2$–1
4 Integrating Earth Science: Seismic Waves	1–2	$^1/_2$–1	5 Using Light	3–4	$1^1/_2$–2
Chapter 1 Review and Assessment	1–2	$^1/_2$–1	Chapter 4 Review and Assessment	1–2	$^1/_2$–1
Chapter 2 Sound			Interdisciplinary Exploration: The Magic of Movies	2–3	1–$1^1/_2$
Chapter 2 Project *Music to Your Ears*	Ongoing	Ongoing			
1 The Nature of Sound	2–3	1–$1^1/_2$			
2 Properties of Sound	2–3	1–$1^1/_2$			
3 Music	2–3	1–$1^1/_2$			
4 Integrating Life Science: How You Hear Sound	2–3	1–$1^1/_2$			
5 Using Sound	1–2	$^1/_2$–1			
Chapter 2 Review and Assessment	1–2	$^1/_2$–1			
Chapter 3 The Electromagnetic Spectrum					
Chapter 3 Project *You're on the Air*	Ongoing	Ongoing			
1 The Nature of Electromagnetic Waves	1–2	$^1/_2$–1			
2 Waves of the Electromagnetic Spectrum	3–4	$1^1/_2$–2			
3 Producing Visible Light	2–3	1–$1^1/_2$			
4 Tech & Design: Wireless Communication	3–4	$1^1/_2$–2			
Chapter 3 Review and Assessment	1–2	$^1/_2$–1			

Research-Based and Proven to Work

As the originator of the small book concept in middle school science, and as the nation's number one science publisher, Prentice Hall takes pride in the fact that we've always listened closely to teachers. In doing so, we've developed programs that effectively meet the needs of your classroom.

As we continue to listen, we realize that raising the achievement level of all students is the number one challenge facing teachers today. To assist you in meeting this latest challenge, Prentice Hall has combined the very best author team with solid research to create a program that meets your high standards and will ensure that no child is left behind.

With Prentice Hall, you can be confident that your students will not only be motivated, inspired, and excited to learn science, but that they will also achieve the success needed in today's environment of the No Child Left Behind (NCLB) legislation and testing reform.

On the following pages, you will read about the key elements found throughout *Science Explorer* that truly set this program apart and ensure success for you and your students.

> As we continue to listen, we realize that raising the achievement level of all students is the number one challenge facing teachers today.

A Science Program Backed by Research

In developing Prentice Hall *Science Explorer*, we used research studies as a central, guiding element. Research on *Science Explorer* indicated key elements of a textbook program that ensure students' success: support for reading and mathematics in science, consistent opportunities for inquiry, and an ongoing assessment strand. This research was conducted in phases and continues today.

1. Exploratory: Needs Assessment

Along with periodic surveys concerning state and national standards as well as curriculum issues and challenges, we conducted specific product development research, which included discussions with teachers and advisory panels, focus groups, and quantitative surveys. We explored the specific needs of teachers, students, and other educators regarding each book we developed in Prentice Hall *Science Explorer*.

2. Formative: Prototype Development and Field-Testing

During this phase of research, we worked to develop prototype materials. Then we tested the materials by field-testing with students and teachers and by performing qualitative and quantitative surveys. In our early prototype testing, we received feedback about our lesson structure. Results were channeled back into the program development for improvement.

3. Summative: Validation Research

Finally, we conducted and continue to conduct long-term research based on scientific, experimental designs under actual classroom conditions. This research identifies what works and what can be improved in the next revision of Prentice Hall *Science Explorer*. We also continue to monitor the program in the market. We talk to our users about what works, and then we begin the cycle over again. The next section contains highlights of this research.

A Science Program With Proven Results

In a year-long study in 2000–2001, students in six states using Prentice Hall *Science Explorer* outscored students using other science programs on a nationally normed standardized test.

The study investigated the effects of science textbook programs at the eighth-grade level. Twelve eighth-grade science classes with a total of 223 students participated in the study. The selected classes were of similar student ability levels.

Each class was tested at the beginning of the school year using the TerraNova CTBS Basic Battery Plus, and then retested at the end of the school year. The final results, shown in the graph, show a significant improvement in test scores from the pre-test to the post-test evaluation.

• All tests were scored by CTB/McGraw-Hill, the publisher of the TerraNova exam. Statistical analyses and conclusions were performed by an independent firm, Pulse Analytics, Inc.

In Japan, Lesson Study Research has been employed for a number of years as a tool for teachers to improve their curriculum. In April 2003, Prentice Hall adapted this methodology to focus on a lesson from this edition. Our goal was to test the effectiveness of lesson pedagogy and improve it while in the program development stage. In all three classrooms tested, student learning increased an average of 10 points from the pre- to the post-assessment.

• Detailed results of these studies can be obtained at **www.PHSchool.com/research.**

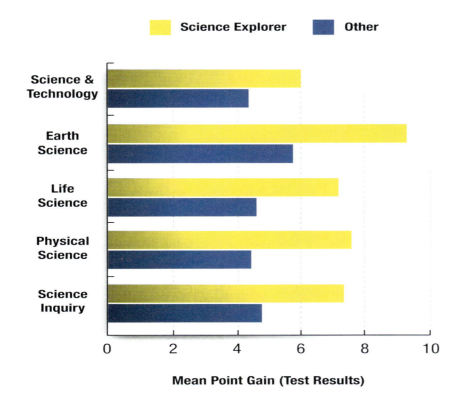

Mean Point Gain (Test Results)

Inquiry

Foundational Research: Inquiry in the Science Classroom

"How do I know if my students are inquiring?" "If students are busy doing lots of hands-on activities, are they using inquiry?" "What is inquiry, anyway?" If you're confused, you are not alone. Inquiry is the heart and soul of science education, with most of us in continuous pursuit of achieving it with our students!

Defining Science Inquiry

What is it? Simply put, inquiry is the intellectual side of science. It is thinking like a scientist—being inquisitive, asking why, and searching for answers. The National Science Education Content Standards define inquiry as the process in which students begin with a question, design an investigation, gather evidence, formulate an answer to the original question, and communicate the investigative process and results. Since it is often difficult to accomplish all this in one class period, the standards also acknowledge that at times students need to practice only one or two inquiry components.

Understanding Inquiry

The National Research Council in Inquiry and the National Science Education Standards (2000) identified several "essential features" of classroom inquiry. We have modified these essential features into questions to guide you in your quest for enhanced and more thoughtful student inquiry.

1. *Who asks the question?* In most curricula, these focusing questions are an element given in the materials. As a teacher you can look for labs that, at least on a periodic basis, allow students to pursue their own questions.

2. *Who designs the procedures?* To gain experience with the logic underlying experimentation, students need continuous practice with designing procedures. Some labs in which the primary target is content acquisition designate procedures. But others should ask students to do so.

3. *Who decides what data to collect?* Students need practice in determining the data to collect.

4. *Who formulates explanations based upon the data?* Students should be challenged to think—to analyze and draw conclusions based on their data, not just copy answers from the text materials.

5. *Who communicates and justifies the results?* Activities should push students not only to communicate but also to justify their answers. Activities also should be thoughtfully designed and interesting so that students want to share their results and argue about conclusions.

Making Time for Inquiry

One last question—Must each and every activity have students do all of this? The answer is an obvious and emphatic "No." You will find a great variety of activities in *Science Explorer*. Some activities focus on content acquisition, and thus they specify the question and most of the procedures. But many others stress in-depth inquiry from start to finish. Because inquiry is an intellectual pursuit, it cannot merely be characterized by keeping students busy and active. Too many students have a knack for being physically but not intellectually engaged in science. It is our job to help them engage intellectually.

Michael J. Padilla, Ph.D.
Program Author of *Science Explorer*
Professor of Science Education
University of Georgia
Athens, Georgia

"Because inquiry is an intellectual pursuit, it cannot merely be characterized by keeping students busy and active."

Evaluator's Checklist

Does your science program promote inquiry by—

✔ Enabling students to pursue their own questions

✔ Allowing students to design their own procedures

✔ Letting students determine what data are best to collect

✔ Challenging students to think critically

✔ Pushing students to justify their answers

Inquiry in *Science Explorer*

Science Explorer offers the most opportunities to get students to think like a scientist. By providing inquiry opportunities throughout the program, *Science Explorer* enables students to enhance their understanding by participating in the discovery.

Student Edition Inquiry

Six lab and activity options are included in every chapter, structured from directed to open-ended—providing you the flexibility to address all types of learners and accommodate your class time and equipment requirements. As Michael Padilla notes, some activities focus on content acquisition, and thus the question and most of the procedures are specified. But many others stress in-depth inquiry from start to finish. The graph below shows how, in general, inquiry levels are addressed in the Student Edition.

Science Explorer encourages students to develop inquiry skills across the spectrum from teacher-guided to open-ended. Even more opportunities for real-life applications of inquiry are included in Science & Society, Science & Technology, Careers in Science, and Interdisciplinary Exploration features.

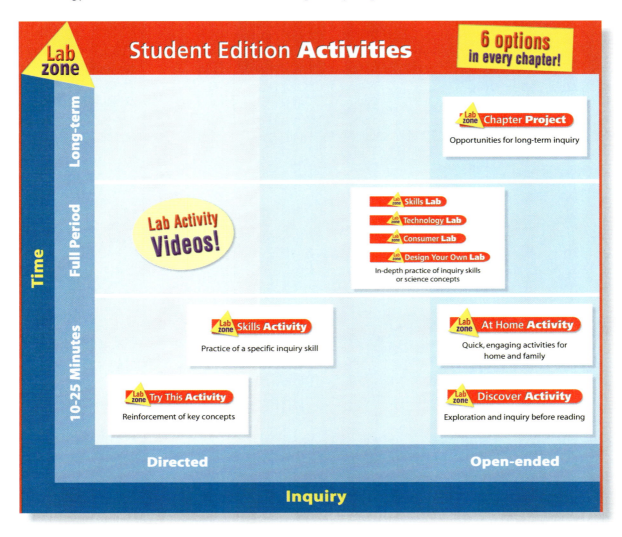

Inquiry Skills Chart

SCIENCE EXPLORER provides comprehensive teaching, practice, and assessment of science skills, with an emphasis on the process skills necessary for inquiry. This chart lists the skills covered in the program and cites the page numbers where each skill is covered.

Basic Process SKILLS				
	Student Text: Projects and Labs	Student Text: Activities	Student Text: Caption and Review Questions	Teacher's Edition: Extensions
Observing	5, 24–25, 53, 88–89, 97–99, 112, 124	6, 19, 22, 36, 46, 54, 85, 106, 113, 114, 119, 126	37, 72, 78, 115, 121	6, 9, 19, 21, 22, 49, 61, 72, 77, 79, 115, 121, 125, 127, 134
Inferring	88–89, 112	26, 55, 60, 70, 92	10, 15, 23, 41, 52, 56, 66, 87, 118, 140	38
Predicting	112, 124	11, 39, 45, 120	18, 23, 32, 47, 66, 93, 96, 102, 123	80
Classifying	5, 16	129, 130	29, 32, 66, 71, 81, 102, 118, 137, 140	18, 27
Making Models	24–25, 97–99	90	32	27, 44, 46, 72, 79, 93, 94, 116
Communicating	5, 16, 24–25, 35, 53, 57, 88–89, 97–99, 105, 112, 124	10, 23, 29, 41, 47, 52, 56, 59, 63, 65, 87, 95, 96, 111, 118, 123, 128, 135, 137	140	18, 133
Measuring				13
Calculating		8, 13, 15, 78, 92	15, 32, 47, 66, 81	14, 62
Creating Data Tables	24–25, 88–89, 124			
Graphing	69	28, 39	66	
Advanced Process SKILLS				
Posing Questions	105	84, 125		
Developing Hypothesis	16, 53	17, 109	12, 41	
Designing Experiments	16, 53, 89, 99, 112	62		

Advanced Process SKILLS (continued)

	Student Text: Projects and Labs	Student Text: Activities	Student Text: Caption and Review Questions	Teacher's Edition: Extensions
Controlling Variables	53, 124			
Forming Operational Definitions	97–99	42, 74		
Interpreting Data	5, 16, 69, 88–89, 124	39, 92, 120	29, 44, 66, 102	
Drawing Conclusions	53, 88–89, 97–99	48, 73, 76	38, 63, 111, 136	

Critical Thinking SKILLS

	Student Text: Projects and Labs	Student Text: Activities	Student Text: Caption and Review Questions	Teacher's Edition: Extensions
Comparing and Contrasting	16		9, 10, 15, 29, 32, 47, 52, 63, 66, 73, 96, 102, 107, 111, 118, 123, 128, 140	23, 48, 51, 85, 86, 114, 117
Applying Concepts	24–25, 35	10, 23, 29, 41, 47, 52, 56, 63, 87, 111, 123, 128	32, 41, 47, 108, 111, 140	14, 61
Interpreting Diagrams, Graphs, Photographs, and Maps			23, 27, 32, 40, 43, 56, 62, 63, 77, 91, 96, 109, 111, 117, 123, 131	
Relating Cause and Effect			23, 47, 52, 56, 73, 96, 102, 123, 127, 137, 140	
Making Generalizations			81, 87, 118, 140	
Making Judgments		59, 83	52, 56	
Problem Solving	57	59	14, 102, 140	

Informational Organizational SKILLS

	Student Text: Projects and Labs	Student Text: Activities	Student Text: Caption and Review Questions	Teacher's Edition: Extensions
Concept Maps			31, 65, 101	10, 29, 30, 64, 100, 138
Compare/Contrast Tables			139	81, 107
Venn Diagrams				91, 131
Flowcharts				
Cycle Diagrams				

The *Science Explorer* program provides additional teaching, reinforcement, and assessment of skills in the *Inquiry Skills Activities Book* and the *Integrated Science Laboratory Manual*.

A National Look at Science Education

Project 2061 was established by the American Association for the Advancement of Science (AAAS) as a long-term project to improve science education nationwide. A primary goal of Project 2061 is to define a "common core of learning"—the knowledge and skills we want all students to achieve. Project 2061 published *Science for All Americans* in 1989 and followed this with *Benchmarks for Science Literacy* in 1993. *Benchmarks* recommends what students should know and be able to do by the end of grades 2, 5, 8, and 12. Project 2061 clearly states that *Benchmarks* is not a curriculum but a tool for designing successful curricula.

The National Research Council (NRC) used *Science for All Americans* and *Benchmarks* to develop the National Science Education Standards (NSES), which were published in 1996. The NSES are organized into six categories (Content, Teaching, Assessment, Professional Development, Program, and System) to help schools establish the conditions necessary to achieve scientific literacy for all students.

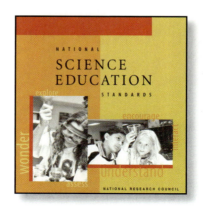

Michael Padilla, the program author of *Science Explorer,* guided one of six teams of teachers whose work led to the publication of *Benchmarks.* He also was a contributing writer of the National Science Education Standards. Under his guidance, *Science Explorer* has implemented these standards through its inquiry approach, a focus on student learning of important concepts and skills, and teacher support aligned with the NSES teaching standards.

Neither *Benchmarks* nor the NSES requires a single, uniform national curriculum, and in fact there is a great diversity nationwide in science curricula. The correlations that follow are designed to help you use the *Science Explorer* program to meet your particular curriculum needs.

Meeting the National Science Education Standards

CHARACTERISTICS OF WAVES

Science as Inquiry (Content Standard A)

● **Use appropriate tools and techniques to gather, analyze, and interpret data** Students investigate examples of periodic motion. Students investigate waves using spring toys. (*Chapter Project; Skills Lab—Wavy Motions*)

● **Develop descriptions, explanations, predictions, and models using evidence** Students make a model to study the interactions of waves. (*Skills Lab—Making Waves*)

● **Use mathematics in all aspects of scientific inquiry** The speed, wavelength, and frequency of a wave are mathematically related (*Properties of Waves*)

Physical Science (Content Standard B)

● **Transfer of energy** A wave is a disturbance that transfers energy from place to place. The basic properties of waves are amplitude, wavelength, frequency, and speed. Reflection, refraction, and diffraction can change a wave's direction. Waves produced by earthquakes are known as seismic waves. (*What Are Waves?; Properties of Waves; Skills Lab—Wavy Motion; Interactions of Waves; Skills Lab—Making Waves; Seismic Waves*)

Science and Technology (Content Standard E)

● **Understandings about science and technology** A seismograph records the ground movements caused by seismic waves. (*Seismic Waves*)

SOUND

Science as Inquiry (Content Standard A)

● **Design and conduct a scientific investigation** Students design and conduct an experiment to investigate pitch. (*Design Your Own Lab*)

Physical Science (Content Standard B)

● **Motions and forces** When a sound source moves, the frequency of the waves changes because the motion of the source adds to the motion of the waves. (*Properties of Sounds*)

● **Transfer of energy** Sound is a disturbance that travels through a medium as a longitudinal wave. Loudness and pitch are two properties of sound. Music is a set of notes that combine in patterns that are pleasing. (*The Nature of Sound; Properties of Sound; Music; Design Your Own Lab*)

A National Look at Science Education *(continued)*

Life Science (Content Standard C)

● **Structure and function in living systems** The function of the ear is to gather sound waves and transmit information about sound to the brain. *(How You Hear Sound)*

Science and Technology (Content Standard E)

● **Design a solution or product** Students design and build a simple musical instrument. Students design and build a hearing protection device. *(Chapter Project; Technology Lab)*

● **Understandings about science and technology** There are three basic groups of musical instruments: stringed, wind, and percussion. Ultrasound technologies, such as sonar and ultrasound imaging, are used to observe things that cannot be seen easily. *(Music; Using Sound)*

Science in Personal and Social Perspectives (Content Standard F)

● **Science and technology in society** Students consider the issues of noise pollution. *(Science and Society)*

THE ELECTROMAGNETIC SPECTRUM

Science as Inquiry (Content Standard A)

● **Use appropriate tools and techniques to gather, analyze, and interpret data** Students collect and analyze data about people's use of wireless communication devices. Students investigate which types of light bulbs provide the best illumination. *(Chapter Project; Consumer Lab)*

● **Develop descriptions, explanations, predictions, and models using evidence** Students build a device that can collect and convert radio signals. *(Skills Lab)*

Physical Science (Content Standard B)

● **Transfer of energy** An electromagnetic wave consists of vibrating electric and magnetic fields that move through space at the speed of light. The electromagnetic spectrum is made up of radio rays, infrared rays, visible light, ultraviolet rays, X-rays, and gamma rays. *(The Nature of Electromagnetic Waves; Waves of the Electromagnetic Spectrum; Skills Lab)*

Science and Technology (Content Standard E)

● **Understandings about science and technology** Each type of electromagnetic wave has properties that make it useful for certain purposes. Common types of light bulbs include incandescent, tungsten-halogen, fluorescent, vapor, and neon lights. Radio waves transmit signals for radio and television programs; cellular phones transmit and receive signals using high-frequency microwaves. *(Waves of the Electromagnetic Spectrum; Producing Visible Light; Consumer Lab; Wireless Communication; Skills Lab)*

Science in Personal and Social Perspectives (Content Standard F)

● **Science and technology in society** Students weigh the impact of microwave ovens. Developments in communication have turned the world into a global village. *(Technology and Society; Science and History)*

LIGHT

Science as Inquiry (Content Standard A)

● **Use appropriate tools and techniques to gather, analyze, and interpret data** Students investigate how the distance between an object and a convex lens affects the image formed. *(Skills Lab—Looking at Images)*

● **Develop descriptions, explanations, predictions, and models using evidence** Students investigate how color filters affect the appearance of objects in white light. *(Skills Lab—Changing Colors)*

Physical Science (Content Standard B)

● **Transfer of energy** When light strikes an object, the light can be reflected, transmitted, or absorbed. The two ways in which a surface can reflect light are regular reflection and diffuse reflection. When light rays enter a medium at an angle, the change of speed causes the rays to change direction. *(Light and Color; Reflection and Mirrors; Refraction and Lenses)*

Life Science (Content Standard C)

● **Structure and function in living systems** You see objects when a process occurs that involves both your eyes and your brain. *(Seeing Light)*

Science and Technology (Content Standard E)

● **Design a solution or product** Students design and build an optical instrument. *(Chapter Project)*

● **Understandings about science and technology** Plane, concave, and convex mirrors are used to produce different kinds of images. A lens is a curved piece of transparent material that is used to refract light. Concave and convex lenses are used to correct vision problems. Three common types of optical instruments are telescopes, microscopes, and cameras. The development of technologies that use light has changed the way we look at the world and beyond. *(Chapter Project; Reflection and Mirrors; Refraction and Lenses; Skills Lab—Looking at Images; Seeing Light; Using Light; Tech & Design in History)*

Note: To see how the benchmarks are supported by *SCIENCE EXPLORER,* go to **PHSchool.com.**

Reading Comprehension in the Science Classroom

Q&A

Q: Why are science texts often difficult for students to read and comprehend?

A: In general, science texts make complex literacy and knowledge demands on learners. They have a more technical vocabulary and a more demanding syntax, and place a greater emphasis on inferential reasoning.

Q: What does research say about facilitating comprehension?

A: Studies comparing novices and experts show that the conceptual organization of experts' knowledge is very different from that of novices. For example, experts emphasize core concepts when organizing knowledge, while novices focus on superficial details. To facilitate comprehension, effective teaching strategies should support and scaffold students as they build an understanding of the key concepts and concept relationships within a text unit.

Q: What strategies can teachers use to facilitate comprehension?

A: Three complementary strategies are very important in facilitating student comprehension of science texts. First, guide student interaction with the text using the built-in strategies. Second, organize the curriculum in terms of core concepts (e.g., the **Key Concepts** in each section). Third, develop visual representations of the relationships among the key concepts and vocabulary that can be referred to during instruction.

Nancy Romance, Ph.D.
Professor of Science Education
Florida Atlantic University
Fort Lauderdale, Florida

"Effective teaching strategies should support and scaffold students as they build an understanding of the key concepts and concept relationships within a text unit."

Reading Support in *Science Explorer*

The latest research emphasizes the importance of activating learners' prior knowledge and teaching them to distinguish core concepts from less important information. These skills are now more important than ever, because success in science requires students to read, understand, and connect complex terms and concepts.

Before students read—

Reading Preview introduces students to the key concepts and key terms they'll find in each section. The **Target Reading Skill** is identified and applied with a graphic organizer.

During the section—

Boldface Sentences identify each key concept and encourage students to focus on the big ideas of science.

Reading Checkpoints reinforce students' understanding by slowing them down to review after every concept is discussed.

Caption Questions draw students into the art and photos, helping them connect the content to the images.

After students read—

Section Assessment revisits the **Target Reading Skill** and encourages students to use the graphic organizer.

Each review question is scaffolded and models the way students think, by first easing them into a review and then challenging them with increasingly more difficult questions.

Evaluator's Checklist

Does your science program promote reading comprehension with—

- ✔ Text structured in an outline format and key concepts highlighted in boldface type
- ✔ Real-world applications to activate prior knowledge
- ✔ Key concepts, critical vocabulary, and a reading skill for every section
- ✔ Sample graphic organizers for each section
- ✔ Relevant photos and carefully constructed graphics with questions
- ✔ Reading checkpoints that appear in each section
- ✔ Scaffolded questions in section assessments

Math in the Science Classroom

Why should students concern themselves with mathematics in your science class?

Good science requires good data from which to draw conclusions. Technology enhances the ability to measure in a variety of ways. Often the scientist must measure large amounts of data, and thus an aim of analysis is to reduce the data to a summary that makes sense and is consistent with established norms of communication—i.e., mathematics.

Calculating measures of central tendency (e.g., mean, median, or mode), variability (e.g., range), and shape (graphic representations) can effectively reduce 500 data points to 3 without losing the essential characteristics of the data. Scientists understand that a trade-off exists between precision and richness as data are folded into categories, and so margins of error can be quantified in mathematical terms and factored into all scientific findings.

Mathematics is the language used by scientists to model change in the world. Understanding change is a vital part of the inquiry process. Mathematics serves as a common language to communicate across the sciences. Fields of scientific research that originated as separate disciplines are now integrated, such as happened with bioengineering. What do the sciences have in common? Each uses the language of mathematics to communicate about data and the process of data analysis. Recognizing this need, *Science Explorer* integrates mathematics practice throughout the program and gives students ample opportunity to hone their math skills.

Clearly, mathematics plays an important role in your science classroom!

William Tate, Ph.D.
Professor of Education and Applied Statistics and Computation
Washington University
St. Louis, Missouri

"Mathematics is the language used by scientists to model change in the world."

Integrated Math Support

In the Student Edition

The math instruction is based on principles derived from Prentice Hall's research-based mathematics program.

Sample Problems, Math Practice, Analyzing Data, and a Math Skills Handbook all help to provide practice at point of use, encouraging students to Read and Understand, Plan and Solve, and then Look Back and Check.

Color-coded variables aid student navigation and help reinforce their comprehension.

In the Teacher's Edition

Math teaching notes enable the science teacher to support math instruction and math objectives on high-stakes tests.

In the Guided Reading and Study Workbook

These unique worksheets help students master reading and enhance their study and math skills. Students can create a record of their work for study and review.

Evaluator's Checklist

Does your science program promote math skills by—

✔ Giving students opportunities to collect data

✔ Providing students opportunities to analyze data

✔ Enabling students to practice math skills

✔ Helping students solve equations by using color-coded variables

✔ Using sample problems to apply science concepts

Technology and Design

Technology and Design in the Science Classroom

Much of the world we live in is designed and made by humans. The buildings in which we live, the cars we drive, the medicines we take, and often the food we eat are products of technology. The knowledge and skills needed to understand the processes used to create these products should be a component of every student's basic literacy.

Some schools offer hands-on instruction on how technology development works through industrial arts curricula. Even then, there is a disconnect among science (understanding how nature works), mathematics (understanding data-driven models), and technology (understanding the human-made world). The link among these fields of study is the engineering design process—that process by which one identifies a human need and uses science knowledge and human ingenuity to create a technology to satisfy the need. Engineering gives students the problem-solving and design skills they will need to succeed in our sophisticated, three-dimensional, technological world.

As a complement to "science as inquiry," the National Science Education Standards (NRC, 1996) call for students at all age levels to develop the abilities related to "technology as design," including the ability to identify and frame a problem and then to design, implement, and evaluate a solution. At the 5–8 grade level, the standards call for students to be engaged in complex problem-solving and to learn more about how science and technology complement each other. It's also important for students to understand that there are often constraints involved in design as well as trade-offs and unintended consequences of technological solutions to problems.

As the *Standards for Technological Literacy* (ITEA, 2000) state, "Science and technology are like conjoined twins. While they have separate identities they must remain inextricably connected." Both sets of standards emphasize how progress in science leads to new developments in technology, while technological innovation in turn drives advances in science.

Ioannis Miaoulis, Ph.D.
President
Museum of Science
Boston, Massachusetts

"Engineering gives students the problem-solving and design skills they will need to succeed in our sophisticated, three-dimensional, technological world."

Evaluator's Checklist

Does your science program promote technology and design by—

✔ Incorporating technology and design concepts and skills into the science curriculum

✔ Giving students opportunities to identify and solve technological design problems

✔ Providing students opportunities to analyze the impact of technology on society

✔ Enabling students to practice technology and design skills

Technology and Design

Technology and Design in *Science Explorer*

How often do you hear your students ask: "Why do I need to learn this?" Connecting them to the world of technology and design in their everyday life is one way to help answer this question. It is also why so many state science curricula are now emphasizing technology and design concepts and skills.

Science Explorer makes a special effort to include a technology and design strand that encourages students to not only identify a need but to take what they learned in science and apply it to design a possible solution, build a prototype, test and evaluate the design, and/or troubleshoot the design. This strand also provides definitions of technology and engineering and discusses the similarities and differences between these endeavors and science. Students will learn to analyze the risks and benefits of a new technology and to consider the tradeoffs, such as safety, costs, efficiency, and appearance.

In the Student Edition

Integrated Technology & Design Sections

Sections throughout *Science Explorer* specifically integrate technology and design with the content of the text. For example, students not only learn how seismographs work but also learn what role seismographs play in society and how people use the data that are gathered.

Technology Labs

These labs help students gain experience in designing and building a device or product that meets a particular need or solves a problem. Students follow a design process of Research and Investigate, Design and Build, and Evaluate and Redesign.

Chapter Projects

Chapter Projects work hand-in-hand with the chapter content. Students design, build, and test based on real-world situations. They have the opportunity to apply the knowledge and skills learned to building a product.

Special Features

This technology and design strand is also reflected in Technology & Society and Science & Society features as well as Technology & History timelines. These highly visual features introduce a technology and its impact on society. For example, students learn how a hybrid car differs from a traditional car.

Assessment in the Science Curriculum

No Child Left Behind clearly challenges school districts across the nation to raise expectations for all students with testing of student achievement in science beginning in 2007–2008.

A primary goal of NCLB is to provide classroom teachers with better data from scientifically valid assessments in order to inform instructional planning and to identify students who are at risk and require intervention. It has been a common practice to teach a science lesson, administer a test, grade it, and move on. This practice is a thing of the past. With the spotlight now on improving student performance, it is essential to use assessment results as a way to identify student strengths and challenges. Providing student feedback and obtaining student input is a valuable, essential part of the assessment process.

Assessment is a never-ending cycle, as is shown in the following diagram. Although you may begin at any point in the assessment cycle, the basic process is the same.

An important assessment strategy is to ensure that students have ample opportunities to check their understanding of skills and concepts before moving on to the next topic. Checking for understanding also includes asking appropriate, probing questions with each example presented. This enables students and teachers to know whether the skills or concepts being introduced are actually understood.

Eileen Depka
Supervisor of Standards
and Assessment
Waukesha, Wisconsin

"Meeting the NCLB challenge will necessitate an integrated approach to assessment with a variety of assessment tools."

Implement the plan with a focus on gathering and using assessment information throughout.

Use a variety of assessment tools to gain information and strengthen student understanding.

Analyze assessment results to create a picture of student strengths and challenges.

Identify strategies to achieve the target, create a plan for implementation, and choose assessments tools.

Choose a target to create a focused path on which to proceed.

IMPLEMENT · ASSESS · ANALYZE · TARGET · STRATEGIZE

Evaluator's Checklist

Does your science program include assessments that—

✔ Are embedded before, during, and after lesson instruction
✔ Align to standards and to the instructional program
✔ Assess both skill acquisition and understanding
✔ Include meaningful rubrics to guide students
✔ Mirror the various formats of standardized tests

Assessment in *Science Explorer*

Science Explorer's remarkable range of strategies for checking progress will help teachers find the right opportunity for reaching all their students.

The assessment strategies in *Science Explorer* will help both students and teachers alike ensure student success in content mastery as well as high-stakes test performance. A wealth of opportunities built into the Student Edition help students monitor their own progress. Teachers are supported with ongoing assessment opportunities in the Teacher's Edition and an easy-to-use, editable test generator linked to content objectives. These integrated, ongoing assessment tools assure success.

Especially to support state and national testing objectives, Prentice Hall has developed test preparation materials that model the NCLB approach.

- **Diagnostic Assessment** tools provide in-depth analysis of strengths and weaknesses, areas of difficulty, and probable underlying causes that can help teachers make instructional decisions and plan intervention strategies.

- **Progress Monitoring** tools aligned with content objectives and state tests provide ongoing, longitudinal records of student achievement detailing individual student progress toward meeting end-of-year and end-of-schooling grade level, district, or state standards.

- **Outcomes** tools that mimic state and national tests show whether individual students have met the expected standards and can help a school system judge whether it has made adequate progress in improving its performance year by year.

Caption Questions enhance critical thinking skills

Reading Checkpoints reinforce students' understanding

Scaffolded Section Assessment Questions model the way students think

Comprehensive Chapter Reviews and Assessment provide opportunities for students to check their own understanding and practice valuable high-stakes test-taking skills

Exam*View*®, Computer Test Bank CD-ROM provides teachers access to thousands of modifiable test questions in English and Spanish

Test Preparation Blackline Masters and Student Workbook include diagnostic and prescription tools, progress-monitoring aids, and practice tests that help teachers focus on improving test scores.

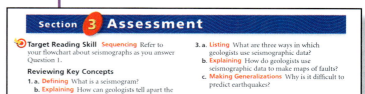

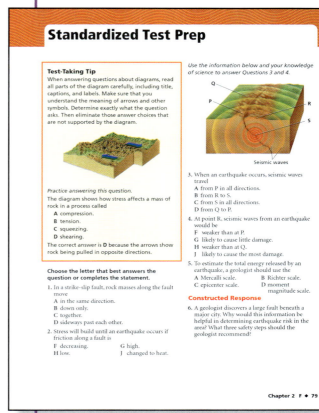

Master Materials List

SCIENCE EXPLORER offers an abundance of activity options in the Student Edition so you can pick and choose those that suit your needs. Prentice Hall has worked with Neo/SCI Corporation to develop Consumable Kits and Nonconsumable Kits that precisely match the needs of the SCIENCE EXPLORER labs. Use this Master Materials List or the Materials Ordering CD-ROM to help order your supplies. For more information on materials kits for this program, contact your local Prentice Hall sales representative or Neo/SCI Corporation at 1-800-526-6689 or www.neosci.com.

Neo SCI®
New ideas for teaching science

Consumable Materials

Description	Textbook Section(s)	Quantity per class	Description	Textbook Section(s)	Quantity per class
Balloon, large, pkg/10	3-4(DIS)	1	Modeling clay, white, 1 lb	1-3(Lab), 1-4(DIS), 3-1(DIS), 4-3(Lab)	5
Battery, D-cell	3-1(DIS), 3-1(TT), 4-1(Lab), 4-2(SA), 4-3(Lab)	5	Objects, yellow, red, and blue	4-1(Lab)	1
*Bottle, plastic, 1-L	1-3(TT), 2-3(Lab)	15	*Paper towel, roll	1-1(DIS), 1-3(SA), 1-3(Lab)	1
*Bottle, plastic, 2-L	2-3(Lab)	5	*Paper, sheet, white, ream	2-4(Lab), 3-2(DIS), 3-3(Lab), 4-3(DIS), 4-3(Lab), 4-4(DIS), 4-4(TT)	1
*Box, cardboard, medium-sized	3-2(DIS), 3-3(Lab)	10			
*Box, shoe	4-1(Lab)	5			
*Bulb, light, fluorescent	3-3(DIS), 3-3(SA)	5	*Paper, tracing, sheet	3-4(DIS)	5
Bulb, light, uncoated, 100W	3-3(DIS), 3-3(SA), 3-3(Lab)	5	Paper, wax, roll, 75 sq. ft.	3-3(Lab), 4-5(DIS)	1
Bulb, light, 60W	3-3(Lab)	5	*Pencil	1-1(DIS), 2-3(DIS), 2-4(Lab), 4-4(DIS)	15
Bulb, light, incandescent, variety	3-3(Lab)	5	*Pencils, colored, pkg/4	3-2(DIS), 3-3(SA)	5
Bulb, light, mini, pkg/10	4-3(Lab)	1	Pushpin, pkg/100	4-5(DIS)	1
*Can, metal	4-2(SA)	5	Rubber band, assorted, 1.5 oz	2-3(DIS), 4-5(DIS)	1
Cardboard, piece, 30 cm x 48 cm	3-4(Lab)	10	Sand, white, fine, 3 lb	1-4(DIS)	1
Cardboard, piece, white, 5" x 5"	2-5(SA), 4-1(DIS), 4-3(Lab)	15	Straw, drinking, pkg/50	1-3(TT), 1-3(SA), 2-2(SA), 2-3(Lab)	1
Cards, index, 5" x 8"	3-1(DIS)	20	String, ball	1-2(SA), 2-4(TT), 2-4(Lab), 3-1(DIS), 4-1(DIS)	1
Cellophane, blue, sheet	4-1(Lab)	5			
Cellophane, green, sheet	4-1(Lab)	5			
Cellophane, red, sheet	4-1(SA), 4-1(Lab)	10	Sugar, granulated, 454 g	3-2(TT)	1
Cellophane, yellow, sheet	4-1(SA)	5	Tape, masking, roll	1-2(SA), 2-5(DIS), 3-3(Lab), 3-4(Lab), 4-2(Lab), 4-3(Lab)	1
Cork	1-1(DIS), 1-3(Lab)	10			
Corn oil, 16 oz	3-2(TT)	1	*Tape, transparent, removable	4-1(Lab)	1
Cotton balls, bag	2-4(Lab)	1	Tube, cardboard, paper towel	2-5(SA), 3-4(Lab)	10
Cup, paper, 7 oz, pkg/50	4-2(SA), 4-5(DIS)	1	Wire, insulated, 160 m	3-4(Lab), 4-3(Lab)	1
Cup, plastic, 9 oz, pkg/50	3-1(TT)	1	*Wire, antenna, 160 m	3-4(Lab)	1
Dropper, plastic, pkg/10	1-3(Lab)	1			
Foil, aluminum, roll, 12" x 25'	3-4(Lab)	1			
*Glue, white, 4 oz	2-4(Lab)	1			
Markers (red, green, and blue)	4-1(DIS)	5			

KEY: CP: Chapter Project; DIS: Discover; SA: Skills Activity; TT: Try This; Lab: Skills, Consumer, Design Your Own, or Technology

* = School Supplied

Quantities based on five groups of six students per class.

Master Materials List

Nonconsumable Materials

Description	Textbook Section(s)	Quantity per class	Description	Textbook Section(s)	Quantity per class
Alligator clip	3-4(Lab), 4-3(Lab)	10	Nail	2-2(DIS)	10
Ball, tennis	1-3(DIS), 2-5(DIS)	5	Pan, aluminum, 12" x 11" x 2"	1-3(Lab), 1-1(DIS), 2-1(DIS)	5
Battery holder	4-3(Lab)	5	Prism, 25 mm x 50 mm	3-2(DIS)	5
Beaker, glass, 250-mL	3-2(TT)	5	*Radio	2-4(Lab)	1
Board, wooden, 1" x 4" x 8"	2-2(DIS)	5	Rope, 7/32" x 50'	1-2(DIS)	1
*Book	2-5(SA)	5	Ruler, 30-cm	1-3(Lab), 2-3(DIS), 2-3(Lab), 2-5(SA), 3-1(DIS), 4-1(DIS), 4-3(Lab)	5
*Bowl	2-1(DIS)	5			
Convex lens, focal length 15 cm	4-3(Lab)	5			
Crystal diode	3-4(Lab)	5	*Scissors	2-2(SA), 2-4(Lab), 3-3(Lab), 3-4(Lab), 4-1(DIS), 4-1(Lab)	5
*Earphones	3-4(Lab)	5			
Fabric, muslin	2-4(Lab)	5			
Film canister with lid	1-4(DIS)	25	Slide, projection	3-1(TT)	1
*Flag, American	4-1(SA)	1	*Slide projector	3-1(TT)	1
Flashlight	3-1(DIS), 3-1(TT), 4-1(Lab), 4-2(SA)	5	Socket, mini	3-3(Lab), 4-3(Lab)	5
*Foam, flexible, piece	2-4(Lab)	5	Spectroscope	3-3(SA)	5
Goggles, safety	3-3(DIS)	30	*Spoon, teaspoon, metal	2-4(TT)	5
Graduated cylinder, 250-mL	2-3(Lab)	5	*Stand, cardboard	4-3(Lab)	5
Hand lens, pkg/5	4-3(DIS), 4-5(TT)	2	*Stopwatch	1-2(SA), 2-5(DIS)	5
Headgear, variety	2-4(Lab)	30	String, guitar	2-2(DIS)	5
*Hole punch	3-1(DIS)	5	Tape measure	2-4(Lab)	5
*Hose, vacuum cleaner	2-2(TT)	5	Thermometer, 12", alcohol, −10°C to 110°C	3-2(TT)	5
*Lamp, table	3-3(Lab)	5	Toy, spring	1-2(Lab)	5
Meter stick, 1/2	1-2(Lab), 1-3(DIS), 2-5(DIS), 3-3(Lab), 4-3(Lab)	5	Tuning fork, 256 Hz	2-1(DIS)	5
			Washer, 1/2"	1-2(SA)	5
*Microwave	3-2(TT)	1	*Watch, ticking	2-5(SA)	5
Mirror, 7.5 cm x 12.5 cm	1-3(Lab), 4-2(Lab)	10	*Wire strippers	3-4(Lab)	5

KEY: CP: Chapter Project; **DIS:** Discover; **SA:** Skills Activity; **TT:** Try This; **Lab:** Skills, Consumer, Design Your Own, or Technology

* = School Supplied

Quantities based on five groups of six students per class.

Reviewers

Tufts University Content Reviewers

Faculty from Tufts University in Medford, Massachusetts, developed *Science Explorer* chapter projects and reviewed the student books.

Astier M. Almedom, Ph.D.
Department of Biology

Wayne Chudyk, Ph.D.
Department of Civil and Environmental Engineering

John L. Durant, Ph.D.
Department of Civil and Environmental Engineering

George S. Ellmore, Ph.D.
Department of Biology

David Kaplan, Ph.D.
Department of Biomedical Engineering

Samuel Kounaves, Ph.D.
Department of Chemistry

David H. Lee, Ph.D.
Department of Chemistry

Douglas Matson, Ph.D.
Department of Mechanical Engineering

Karen Panetta, Ph.D.
Department of Electrical Engineering and Computer Science

Jan A. Pechenik, Ph.D.
Department of Biology

John C. Ridge, Ph.D.
Department of Geology

William Waller, Ph.D.
Department of Astronomy

Content Reviewers

Paul Beale, Ph.D.
Department of Physics
University of Colorado
Boulder, Colorado

Jeff Bodart, Ph.D.
Chipola Junior College
Marianna, Florida

Michael Castellani, Ph.D.
Department of Chemistry
Marshall University
Huntington, West Virginia

Eugene Chiang, Ph.D.
Department of Astronomy
University of California – Berkeley
Berkeley, California

Charles C. Curtis, Ph.D.
Department of Physics
University of Arizona
Tucson, Arizona

Daniel Kirk-Davidoff, Ph.D.
Department of Meteorology
University of Maryland
College Park, Maryland

Diane T. Doser, Ph.D.
Department of Geological Sciences
University of Texas at El Paso
El Paso, Texas

R. E. Duhrkopf, Ph.D.
Department of Biology
Baylor University
Waco, Texas

Michael Hacker
Co-director, Center for Technological Literacy
Hofstra University
Hempstead, New York

Michael W. Hamburger, Ph.D.
Department of Geological Sciences
Indiana University
Bloomington, Indiana

Alice K. Hankla, Ph.D.
The Galloway School
Atlanta, Georgia

Donald C. Jackson, Ph.D.
Department of Molecular Pharmacology, Physiology, & Biotechnology
Brown University
Providence, Rhode Island

Jeremiah N. Jarrett, Ph.D.
Department of Biological Sciences
Central Connecticut State University
New Britain, Connecticut

David Lederman, Ph.D.
Department of Physics
West Virginia University
Morgantown, West Virginia

Becky Mansfield, Ph.D.
Department of Geography
Ohio State University
Columbus, Ohio

Elizabeth M. Martin, M.S.
Department of Chemistry and Biochemistry
College of Charleston
Charleston, South Carolina

Joe McCullough, Ph.D.
Department of Natural and Applied Sciences
Cabrillo College
Aptos, California

Robert J. Mellors, Ph.D.
Department of Geological Sciences
San Diego State University
San Diego, California

Joseph M. Moran, Ph.D.
American Meteorological Society
Washington, D.C.

David J. Morrissey, Ph.D.
Department of Chemistry
Michigan State University
East Lansing, Michigan

Philip A. Reed, Ph.D.
Department of Occupational & Technical Studies
Old Dominion University
Norfolk, Virginia

Scott M. Rochette, Ph.D.
Department of the Earth Sciences
State University of New York, College at Brockport
Brockport, New York

Laurence D. Rosenhein, Ph.D.
Department of Chemistry
Indiana State University
Terre Haute, Indiana

Ronald Sass, Ph.D.
Department of Biology and Chemistry
Rice University
Houston, Texas

George Schatz, Ph.D.
Department of Chemistry
Northwestern University
Evanston, Illinois

Sara Seager, Ph.D.
Carnegie Institution of Washington
Washington, D.C.

Robert M. Thornton, Ph.D.
Department of Biology
University of California
Davis, California

John R. Villarreal, Ph.D.
College of Science and Engineering
The University of Texas – Pan American
Edinburg, Texas

Kenneth Welty, Ph.D.
School of Education
University of Wisconsin–Stout
Stout, Wisconsin

Edward J. Zalisko, Ph.D.
Department of Biology
Blackburn College
Carlinville, Illinois

Teacher Reviewers

David R. Blakely
Arlington High School
Arlington, Massachusetts

Jane E. Callery
Two Rivers Magnet Middle
  School
East Hartford, Connecticut

Melissa Lynn Cook
Oakland Mills High School
Columbia, Maryland

James Fattic
Southside Middle School
Anderson, Indiana

Dan Gabel
Hoover Middle School
Rockville, Maryland

Wayne Goates
Eisenhower Middle School
Goddard, Kansas

Katherine Bobay Graser
Mint Hill Middle School
Charlotte, North Carolina

Darcy Hampton
Deal Junior High School
Washington, D.C.

Karen Kelly
Pierce Middle School
Waterford, Michigan

David Kelso
Manchester High School Central
Manchester, New Hampshire

Benigno Lopez, Jr.
Sleepy Hill Middle School
Lakeland, Florida

Angie L. Matamoros, Ph.D.
ALM Consulting, Inc.
Weston, Florida

Tim McCollum
Charleston Middle School
Charleston, Illinois

Bruce A. Mellin
Brooks School
North Andover, Massachusetts

Ella Jay Parfitt
Southeast Middle School
Baltimore, Maryland

Evelyn A. Pizzarello
Louis M. Klein Middle School
Harrison, New York

Kathleen M. Poe
Fletcher Middle School
Jacksonville, Florida

Shirley Rose
Lewis and Clark Middle School
Tulsa, Oklahoma

Linda Sandersen
Greenfield Middle School
Greenfield, Wisconsin

Mary E. Solan
Southwest Middle School
Charlotte, North Carolina

Mary Stewart
University of Tulsa
Tulsa, Oklahoma

Paul Swenson
Billings West High School
Billings, Montana

Thomas Vaughn
Arlington High School
Arlington, Massachusetts

Susan C. Zibell
Central Elementary
Simsbury, Connecticut

Safety Reviewers

W. H. Breazeale, Ph.D.
Department of Chemistry
College of Charleston
Charleston, South Carolina

Ruth Hathaway, Ph.D.
Hathaway Consulting
Cape Girardeau, Missouri

Douglas Mandt, M.S.
Science Education Consultant
Edgewood, Washington

Activity Field Testers

Nicki Bibbo
Witchcraft Heights School
Salem, Massachusetts

Rose-Marie Botting
Broward County Schools
Fort Lauderdale, Florida

Colleen Campos
Laredo Middle School
Aurora, Colorado

Elizabeth Chait
W. L. Chenery Middle School
Belmont, Massachusetts

Holly Estes
Hale Middle School
Stow, Massachusetts

Laura Hapgood
Plymouth Community
  Intermediate School
Plymouth, Massachusetts

Mary F. Lavin
Plymouth Community
  Intermediate School
Plymouth, Massachusetts

James MacNeil, Ph.D.
Cambridge, Massachusetts

Lauren Magruder
St. Michael's Country
  Day School
Newport, Rhode Island

Jeanne Maurand
Austin Preparatory School
Reading, Massachusetts

Joanne Jackson-Pelletier
Winman Junior High School
Warwick, Rhode Island

Warren Phillips
Plymouth Public Schools
Plymouth, Massachusetts

Carol Pirtle
Hale Middle School
Stow, Massachusetts

Kathleen M. Poe
Fletcher Middle School
Jacksonville, Florida

Cynthia B. Pope
Norfolk Public Schools
Norfolk, Virginia

Anne Scammell
Geneva Middle School
Geneva, New York

Karen Riley Sievers
Callanan Middle School
Des Moines, Iowa

David M. Smith
Eyer Middle School
Allentown, Pennsylvania

Gene Vitale
Parkland School
McHenry, Illinois

Contents

Sound and Light

Reference Section

VIDEO

Enhance understanding through dynamic video.

Preview Get motivated with this introduction to the chapter content.

Field Trip Explore a real-world story related to the chapter content.

Assessment Review content and take an assessment.

Web Links

Get connected to exciting Web resources in every lesson.

SC*I*NKS. NSTA Find Web links on topics relating to every section.

Active Art Interact with selected visuals from every chapter online.

Planet Diary® Explore news and natural phenomena through weekly reports.

Science News® Keep up to date with the latest science discoveries.

Experience the complete text-book online and on CD-ROM.

Activities Practice skills and learn content.

Videos Explore content and learn important lab skills.

Audio Support Hear key terms spoken and defined.

Self-Assessment Use instant feedback to help you track your progress.

Activities

Turning Down the Volume on Sonic Booms

Inquiry and Engineering

Engineer Christine Mann Darden conducts research on sonic booms. By reading about her work, students will gain insights about how research is done. They will read about how Dr. Darden plans and conducts her research. They will also learn about observing, measuring, and studying models as key elements of scientific research. The skills that Dr. Darden uses every day are the same inquiry skills that students need to become successful young scientists.

Build Background Knowledge

Knowledge About Sonic Booms Ask whether any students have ever heard a sonic boom. If any students have, encourage them to describe what they heard. If no students have heard a sonic boom, explain that it is a very loud bang, similar to a clap of thunder. Make students aware that Dr. Darden studies how the shape of aircraft determines the loudness of sonic booms. State that Dr. Darden is interested in making sonic booms quieter because she wants supersonic travel to become more common.

Introduce the Career

Before students read the feature, let them read the title, examine the pictures, and read the captions on their own. Then, ask: **What questions came into your mind as you looked at these pictures?** *(Students might suggest questions such as: "What is a sonic boom? What does supersonic mean? Why are they testing aircraft if they already know what sonic booms are?")* Point out to students that just as they have questions about what they are seeing, scientists also have questions about what they observe.

Careers in Science

Turning Down the Volume on Sonic Booms

A sleek white plane swoops high into the California sky. This F-5E navy jet has been specially modified for this test. Its nose tapers smoothly. Its underside curves. The plane reaches supersonic speed—a speed faster than the speed of sound. The aircraft breaks the sound barrier. Sensors on the ground and in nearby planes measure the sonic boom—the sudden, sharp BOOM made when a plane flies faster than sound.

Scientists hold their breath while another plane—an unmodified F-5E jet—flies the same course at supersonic speed. The two planes' sound patterns are different! The test demonstrates that the shape of a supersonic aircraft can reduce sonic booms.

Aeronautics engineer Christine Darden is a national expert on sonic booms. Her team at the National Aeronautics and Space Administration (NASA) has been looking for ways to soften sonic booms. They had predicted that changing the shape of an airplane could soften sonic booms. They had tested models. But this was the first actual test flight based on their work. Fifty years after the first supersonic flight, another significant discovery had been made.

x ◆ O

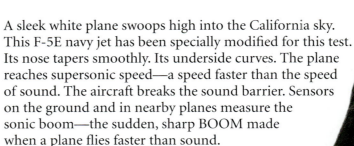

Career Path

Christine Mann Darden grew up in Monroe, North Carolina. She earned a Ph.D. in mechanical engineering at George Washington University in Washington, D.C. For more than 30 years, Dr. Darden was an aeronautical engineer at NASA's Langley Research Center in Hampton, Virginia. She is currently Assistant Director for Planning at Langley.

Background

Facts and Figures Engineering is the application of math and science knowledge to the effective use of materials and forces in nature. There are numerous branches of engineering, and the branches are interrelated. Therefore, an engineer specializing in any one field must have some understanding of the other fields. Aeronautical engineers, for example, must have some knowledge of airplane design, manufacture, and testing. They also must understand aerodynamics, structural engineering as it relates to building airplanes, and how jet engines work.

Aerospace engineers focus on craft that fly beyond Earth's atmosphere. They need to know about rocket engines, satellites, astronomy, gravity, and spacecraft design.

This modified F-5E fighter jet makes an historic test flight (above). Christine prepares to test a model of the F-5E in the supersonic wind tunnel (right). This tunnel at Langley Research Center is four feet by four feet.

Talking With
Dr. Christine Darden

Choosing Engineering

Christine's research in sonic booms is a long way from her first career as a math teacher. In the late 1960s, she taught near the NASA labs in Virginia. At the time, NASA was working on a program to send astronauts to the moon. Christine went to work for NASA as a mathematician.

She quickly became fascinated with the work of the NASA research engineers. "They were the ones who were working with the really tough challenges of the program," she says. "They were doing the interesting, hands-on work." At the time, there were few engineers in aerospace. Christine decided to get a degree in engineering. She has been at NASA studying supersonic aircraft ever since.

Breaking the Sound Barrier

The sound barrier was first broken in 1947. Since then, people have complained about sonic booms so much that the government has passed regulations. It's now against the law to fly most aircraft at supersonic speeds over the United States.

"If it is loud enough, a sonic boom can actually break windows and do damage to buildings," says Christine. "People find it very disturbing. Right now, the boom is one of the biggest obstacles to commercial supersonic air service." But what if scientists can find ways to lower the volume of sonic booms?

O ◆ 1

Background

Facts and Figures A wind tunnel is a device used to study how objects, such as airplanes and spacecraft behave when moving through air. In a wind tunnel, the object remains fixed while air is forced through the tunnel around it. Some wind tunnels are less than a meter across, while others are large enough to test small aircraft. For example, NASA has a wind tunnel in California that measures 24 meters by 37 meters. The larger the wind tunnel, the more power that is needed to force the air through it. As a result, supersonic testing usually is done in small tunnels using scale models. At supersonic speeds, air friction generates heat, so wind tunnels for researching supersonic speeds include heaters to simulate this heating.

Explore the Career

Choose from among the teaching strategies on these pages as you help your students explore the practical application of inquiry skills.

Discuss Ask: **What was Dr. Darden's first job at NASA?** *(She was a mathematician.)* **How did she become interested in engineering?** *(She became interested in the work of the NASA research engineers.)* **Why did she go back to school to get a degree in engineering when she already had a degree in mathematics?** *(Sample answer: She was not qualified to be an engineer and needed more training.)* Tell students that many people go back to school later in life to pursue a degree in another field after deciding that their initial career choice was not the best one for them.

Research Encourage interested students to research achievements in supersonic flight. For example, they might investigate how the sound barrier was first broken by the American test pilot Chuck Yeager flying a Bell X-1 rocket plane in 1947. They also might investigate more recent developments in supersonic flight, such as military aircraft that have exceeded Mach 3 (three times the speed of sound), including the MiG-25 Foxbat interceptor or the SR-71 spy plane. Another possible area of research is the Concorde, a commercial supersonic aircraft that flew regular trans-Atlantic flights until 2004. Invite students to share their research findings with the class.

Build Inquiry Skills Point out that Dr. Darden's team studies waves in water as well as waves in air. Ask: **Why do they study waves in water instead of just in air?** *(Sample answer: You can see waves in water, but you cannot readily see waves in air.)* Ask students if they have ever experimented with waves in water. If they have, urge them to share any insights they gained.

Demonstrate Make sure students know that the bow of a ship is the front of the ship. If possible, find a video clip of a ship moving through water that shows the waves caused by the bow. Alternatively, you can demonstrate the waves using a toy boat in a large pan of water. Relate the waves made by the boat in water to the waves made by an airplane in air.

A supersonic aircraft sends out shock waves that people hear as a sonic boom.

What Is a Sonic Boom?

You have probably heard the sound that is made when an airplane breaks the sound barrier. A sonic boom sounds like a clap of thunder or a sharp explosion high in the sky. Just what are you hearing?

"A sonic boom is a compression or pressure wave," Christine explains. "An airplane pushes a wave of air molecules ahead of it as it travels forward, just as a ship's bow pushes out a wave as it moves through the water. Those compressions travel outward from the plane as a shock wave of high pressure. When that shock wave reaches our ears, we hear it as a boom."

"Think of blowing up a balloon," Christine says. "With the balloon inflated, the air on the inside is much more compressed than the air on the outside. When the balloon pops, the compression immediately flies outward in the form of a shock wave."

"Christine's NASA team found that the shape of an aircraft determines the size of the sonic boom it creates."

2 ◆ O

How Do You Study Sound?

You can't see a sonic boom. So how do you research it? Christine's Sonic Boom Group at NASA investigated the distinctive "sound print" made by aircraft that fly faster than the speed of sound.

"Part of our work is coming up with new ways to observe and measure the phenomenon we're studying," says Christine. "For example, we know that all waves have similar properties. So we look at how waves behave in water to tell us something about how they behave in the air."

How Do You Test Aircraft?

One way to study how supersonic aircraft create sonic booms is to "fly" model aircraft in a high-speed wind tunnel. The scientists place the steel models in the tunnel. They observe how the models behave in winds moving at up to three times the speed of sound. (The speed of sound varies with altitude and temperature. At sea level on a 16°C day, the speed of sound is about 1,207 kilometers per hour.)

Instruments on the sides of the tunnel allow Christine to "hear" the sonic boom created by the model. By adding very fine smoke, she can even watch how the air moves over the plane. "We can actually see the shock wave," she says.

How Can Sonic Booms Be Softened?

Christine's NASA team found that the shape of an aircraft determines the size of the sonic boom it creates. They performed tests with computer programs, on actual supersonic jets, and in wind tunnels. Some experiments showed that angling the wings back sharply reduces the size of the shock wave and the loudness of the sonic boom. Another factor in softening the sonic boom was the overall shape of the plane, especially a sleek, narrow design.

But the same features that make planes quieter also make them harder to fly. "You could put a needle up there supersonically and you wouldn't get a sonic boom," explains Christine. "But you wouldn't have much of an airplane, either."

The test flights of the modified F-5E jet in 2003 took the research out of the laboratory and into the sky. The tests were a milestone in softening sonic booms. Someday, supersonic commercial jets may be allowed to fly across the United States.

Writing in Science

Career Link Christine's Sonic Boom Group at NASA tested the way that changes in an airplane's shape might affect a sonic boom. They set up experiments to test these changes. Now think of different-shaped boats moving through water—a kayak, a tugboat, and a rowboat. Predict the type of wave that each boat will make. In a paragraph, describe ways in which you could test your predictions.

Go Online
PHSchool.com

For: More on this career
Visit: PHSchool.com
Web Code: cgb-5000

Christine is shown here with the modified F-5E jet that she and her team designed.

O ◆ 3

Help Students Read

Monitor Understanding Check student's comprehension of the main ideas in the feature. Ask: **Why are supersonic jets not allowed to fly across the United States?** (*Supersonic jets cause sonic booms that can damage buildings and disturb people on the ground.*) **How are Dr. Darden and her group at NASA trying to overcome this restriction?** (*They are trying to design an aircraft with a shape that produces a softer sonic boom.*)

Inferring Point out the statement made by Dr. Darden on this page: "You could put a needle up there supersonically and you wouldn't get a sonic boom." Ask: **What was Dr. Darden implying about airplane shape and sonic booms in this statement?** (*Sample answer: She was implying that an airplane with a long, narrow shape would not produce a sonic boom.*)

Writing in Science

Writing Mode Exposition: How to
Scoring Rubric
4 Exceeds criteria; includes clearly stated, logical predictions and a thorough description of ingenious ways to test them
3 Meets criteria
2 Includes at least one prediction and a description of a way to test it but is too brief and/or contains some logical or factual errors
1 Includes a prediction and description of a test but is incomplete and/or contains serious logical or factual errors

For: More on this career
Visit: PHSchool.com
Web Code: cgb-5000

Students can do further research on this career and others that are related to the study of engineering.

Chapter at a Glance

PRENTICE HALL

TeacherEXPRESS™
Plan • Teach • Assess

  Chapter **Project** *Over and Over and Over Again*

Technology

Local Standards

All in One Teaching Resources

- Chapter Project Teacher Notes, pp. 38–39
- Chapter Project Student Overview, pp. 40–41
- Chapter Project Student Worksheets, pp. 42–43
- Chapter Project Scoring Rubric, p. 44

DISCOVERY CHANNEL SCHOOL
Video Preview

Section 1

2 periods
1 block

What Are Waves?

O.1.1.1 Explain what causes mechanical waves.

O.1.1.2 Describe two types of waves and how they can be represented.

Go Online
SCiLINKS™ NSTA

Section 2

3 periods
1 1/2 blocks

Properties of Waves

O.1.2.1 Describe the basic properties of waves.

O.1.2.2 Explain how a wave's speed is related to its wavelength and frequency.

Go Online
PHSchool.com

Section 3

4 periods
2 blocks

Interactions of Waves

O.1.3.1 Describe how reflection, refraction, and diffraction change a wave's direction.

O.1.3.2 State the different types of interference.

O.1.3.3 Explain how standing waves form.

Go Online
active art

Section 4

1 1/2 periods
1 block

Seismic Waves

O.1.4.1 Identify the types of seismic waves.

O.1.4.2 Explain how a seismograph works.

DISCOVERY CHANNEL SCHOOL
Video Field Trip

Go Online
SCiLINKS™ NSTA

Review and Assessment

All in One Teaching Resources

- Key Terms Review, p. 79
- Transparency O14
- Performance Assessment Teacher Notes, p. 87
- Performance Assessment Scoring Rubric, p. 88
- Performance Assessment Student Worksheet, p. 89
- Chapter Test, pp. 90–93

DISCOVERY CHANNEL SCHOOL
Video Assessment

Go Online
PHSchool.com

Test Preparation

Test Preparation Blackline Masters

Lab zone

Chapter Activities Planner

For more activities
LAB ZONE Easy Planner CD-ROM

Student Edition	Inquiry	Time	Materials	Skills	Resources
Chapter Project, p. 5	Open-Ended	Ongoing (1–2 weeks)	**All in One** Teaching Resources See p. 38	Observing, classifying, interpreting data, communicating	Lab zone Easy Planner **All in One** Teaching Resources Support pp. 38–39
Section 1					
Discover Activity, p. 6	Guided	10 minutes	Large shallow pan, water, a cork, paper towels	Observing	**Lab zone Easy Planner**
Section 2					
Discover Activity, p. 11	Guided	10 minutes	3 m of medium-weight rope	Predicting	**Lab zone Easy Planner**
Skills Activity, p. 13	Directed	10 minutes	Metal washer, 25 cm of string, tape, stopwatch	Calculating	**Lab zone Easy Planner**
Skills Lab, p. 16	Guided	40 minutes	Spring toy, meter stick	Comparing and contrasting, classifying	**Lab zone Easy Planner Lab Activity Video** **All in One** Teaching Resources Skills Lab: *Wavy Motions*, pp. 59–60
Section 3					
Discover Activity, p. 17	Guided	10 minutes	Ball, meter stick, water	Developing hypotheses	**Lab zone Easy Planner**
Skills Activity, p. 19	Directed	10 minutes	Drinking straw, piece of terry cloth or paper towel	Observing	**Lab zone Easy Planner**
Try This Activity, p. 22	Directed	10 minutes	Two identical empty bottles, two drinking straws, water	Observing	**Lab zone Easy Planner**
At-Home Activity, p. 23	Guided	Home		Making models	**Lab zone Easy Planner**
Skills Lab, pp. 24–25	Guided	40 minutes	Water, plastic dropper, metric ruler, paper towels, modeling clay, cork or other small floating object, ripple tank (aluminum foil lasagna pan with mirror at the bottom)	Observing, making models	**Lab zone Easy Planner Lab Activity Video** **All in One** Teaching Resources Skills Lab: *Making Waves*, pp. 69–71
Section 4					
Discover Activity, p. 26	Guided	10 minutes	5 empty plastic film canisters, sand, modeling clay	Inferring	**Lab zone Easy Planner**
Analyzing Data, p. 28	Directed	10 minutes		Predicting	**Lab zone Easy Planner**
At-Home Activity, p. 29	Open-Ended	Home		Observing	**Lab zone Easy Planner**

Section 1 What Are Waves?

 2 periods, 1 block

Objectives

O.1.1.1 Explain what causes mechanical waves.

O.1.1.2 Describe two types of waves and how they can be represented.

Local Standards

Key Terms

• wave • energy • medium • mechanical wave • vibration • transverse wave
• crest • trough • longitudinal wave • compression • rarefaction

Preteach

Build Background Knowledge

Students look for patterns in a periodic event that they observe in a video.

Lab zone Discover Activity *How Do Waves Travel?* **L1**

Targeted Print and Technology Resources

 **Teaching Resources**

L2 Reading Strategy Transparency
O1: *Using Prior Knowledge*

🔘 **Presentation-Pro CD-ROM**

Instruct

Waves and Energy Make a concept map to show that mechanical waves require a medium but electromagnetic waves do not.

Types of Waves Draw simple wave diagrams and challenge students to show how transverse and longitudinal waves differ.

Targeted Print and Technology Resources

 **Teaching Resources**

L2 Guided Reading, pp. 47–49
L2 Transparencies O2, O3, O4

www.SciLinks.org Web Code: scn-1511

🔘 **Student Edition on Audio CD**

Assess

Section Assessment Questions

🎯 Have students use their completed lists of what they know and learned to answer the questions.

Reteach

Students write a sentence correctly using the key terms *wave, vibration, energy,* and *medium.*

Targeted Print and Technology Resources

Teaching Resources

• Section Summary, p. 46
L1 Review and Reinforce, p. 50
L3 Enrich, p. 51

Section 2 Properties of Waves

 3 periods, 1 1/2 blocks

Objectives

O.1.2.1 Describe the basic properties of waves.

O.1.2.2 Explain how a wave's speed is related to its wavelength and frequency.

Local Standards

Key Terms

• amplitude • wavelength • frequency • hertz (Hz)

Preteach

Build Background Knowledge

Students name examples of waves they have seen and describe variations in the speed and size of the waves.

Discover Activity *Can You Change a Wave?* **L1**

Targeted Print and Technology Resources

All in One Teaching Resources

L2 Reading Strategy Transparency O5: *Outlining*

⊙ **Presentation-Pro CD-ROM**

Instruct

Amplitude Have students use Figure 5 to measure the amplitude of waves.

Wavelength Explain that the wavelength of a transverse wave is the distance between two crests or two troughs, and have students infer that the wavelength of a longitudinal wave is the distance between two compressions or two rarefactions.

Frequency Write the definition of *frequency* on the board, and underline and explain its key components.

Speed Explain that the speed of a wave is like the speed of a car, measured in units of distance/time.

Skills Lab *Wavy Motions* **L2**

Targeted Print and Technology Resources

All in One Teaching Resources

L2 Guided Reading, pp. 54–56
L2 Transparencies O6, O7
L2 Skills Lab: *Wavy Motions,* p. 59–60

▭ **Lab Activity Video/DVD**
Skills Lab: *Wavy Motions*

PHSchool.com Web Code: cgd-5012

⊙ **Student Edition on Audio CD**

Assess

Section Assessment Questions

⟳ Have students use their completed outlines to answer the questions.

Reteach

Students describe or define *amplitude, wavelength,* and *frequency.*

Targeted Print and Technology Resources

All in One Teaching Resources

• Section Summary, p. 53
L1 Review and Reinforce, p. 57
L3 Enrich, p. 58

Section 3 Interactions of Waves

 4 periods, 2 blocks

Objectives

O.1.3.1 Describe how reflection, refraction, and diffraction change a wave's direction.

O.1.3.2 State the different types of interference.

O.1.3.3 Explain how standing waves form.

Key Terms

• reflection • law of reflection • refraction • diffraction • interference
• constructive interference • destructive interference • standing wave • node
• antinode • resonance

Local Standards

Preteach

Build Background Knowledge

Students recall reflections they have seen in windows and pools, and explain why glass and water act like mirrors.

 **Discover Activity** *How Does a Ball Bounce?* **L2**

Targeted Print and Technology Resources

All in One Teaching Resources

L2 Reading Strategy Transparency O8: *Asking Questions*

 Presentation-Pro CD-ROM

Instruct

Reflection Use a mirror to introduce reflection, and explain that reflection occurs when waves strike a surface they cannot pass through.

Refraction Define *refraction*, and explain that refraction occurs when one side of a wave enters a new medium before the other side.

Diffraction Have students trace the path of waves in Figure 9 and note what happens to the waves when diffraction occurs.

Interference Make a table on the board that compares and contrasts constructive and destructive interference.

Standing Waves Use a diagram to help students understand how interference affects waves and produces standing waves.

 Skills Lab *Making Waves* **L2**

Targeted Print and Technology Resources

All in One Teaching Resources

L2 Guided Reading, pp. 63–66
L2 Transparencies O9, O10, O11, O12
L2 Skills Lab: *Making Waves,* p. 69–71

Lab Activity Video/DVD
Skills Lab: *Making Waves*

PHSchool.com Web Code: cgp-5013

 Student Edition on Audio CD

Assess

Section Assessment Questions

 Have students use their completed questions and answers to answer the questions.

Reteach

Students explain how reflection and refraction change light waves.

Targeted Print and Technology Resources

All in One Teaching Resources

• Section Summary, p. 62
L1 Review and Reinforce, p. 67
L3 Enrich, p. 68

Section 4 Seismic Waves

 1 1/2 periods, 1 block

Objectives

O.1.4.1 Identify the types of seismic waves.

O.1.4.2 Explain how a seismograph works.

Local Standards

Key Terms

• seismic wave • P wave • S wave • surface wave • tsunami • seismograph

---

Preteach

Build Background Knowledge

Students observe pictures of earthquake damage and infer that the damage is caused by vibrations of Earth's surface.

 **Discover Activity** *Can You Find the Sand?* **L2**

Targeted Print and Technology Resources

All in One Teaching Resources

L2 Reading Strategy: *Building Vocabulary*

⊙ **Presentation-Pro CD-ROM**

Instruct

Types of Seismic Waves Write the three types of seismic waves on the board, and compare and contrast their characteristics.

Detecting Seismic Waves Use an analogy to help students understand how seismographs detect seismic waves.

Targeted Print and Technology Resources

All in One Teaching Resources

L2 Guided Reading, pp. 74–76
L2 Transparency O13

www.SciLinks.org Web Code: scn-1514

Video Field Trip

⊙ **Student Edition on Audio CD**

Assess

Section Assessment Questions

Have students use their completed sentences to answer the questions.

Reteach

Students list properties of each type of seismic wave.

Targeted Print and Technology Resources

All in One Teaching Resources

• Section Summary, p. 73
L1 Review and Reinforce, p. 77
L3 Enrich, p. 78

Professional Development

Section 1 **What Are Waves?**

Torsional and Combination Waves There are three basic types of individual waves. Besides transverse and longitudinal waves, which are described in the text, there are also torsional waves. Torsional waves are produced by twisting a medium. For example, twisting several coils of a spring toy around the center of the toy results in a torsional wave traveling along the spring.

Some waves may be a combination of types. For example, waves at the surface of deep water are mainly transverse. However, closer to shore, where the water is shallower, the waves interact with the bottom and become partly longitudinal. As water depth decreases, the longitudinal part of the waves grows larger until it exceeds the transverse part.

Combination waves that travel along the surface between two mediums are called surface waves. For example, in the ocean, surface waves travel along the surface between water and air. In surface waves and other combination waves, particles of the medium have a circular motion, as shown in the figure.

Movement of a Particle in a Surface Wave

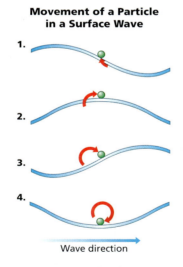

Wave direction

Section 2 **Properties of Waves**

Wave Period In addition to the wave properties described in the text, there is another wave property, called wave period. The period of a wave is the time it takes a particle of the medium to make one complete wave cycle. Period is measured in units of time, such as seconds or hours, and is often represented by the letter *T*. The period of a transverse wave can be found by measuring the time it takes for two consecutive crests or troughs to pass a stationary point.

Wave period is the inverse of wave frequency. This relationship can be expressed as:

$$\text{Period} = \frac{1}{\text{Frequency}}$$

Like frequency, wave period can be used to calculate wave speed:

$$\text{Speed} = \frac{\text{Wavelength}}{\text{Period}}$$

When surface waves travel from deep to shallow water, most of their properties change. For example, both speed and wavelength decrease. However, the time between consecutive crests remains the same, so the period does not change.

Help Students Read

Identifying Main Ideas
Finding Sentences That State Main Ideas

Strategy Help students identify main ideas about important concepts, such as wave amplitude. Have them find sentences in the text that best express the main ideas about the concept.

Example
1. Call students' attention to the text on wave amplitude in Section 2, *Properties of Waves.*
2. Have students read the material on amplitude and identify a few sentences that most completely and concisely express the main ideas about the amplitude of waves.
3. Call on several students to read aloud the sentences they have selected.
4. Ask the class if they agree with the choices, and have students read any other sentences they think are better choices.
5. With a show of hands, have the class select just three or four sentences that best express the main ideas about amplitude.
6. Have students state in their own words the main ideas expressed by the selected sentences.

See Section 2, *Properties of Waves*, for a script using the identifying main ideas strategy with students.

Section 3 Interactions of Waves

Factors Affecting Diffraction The amount of diffraction, or bending, that occurs when waves pass around a barrier or through a hole in a barrier generally depends on the ratio of the wavelength to the diameter of the barrier or hole. The greatest bending of a wave occurs when the diameter of the barrier or hole is equal to the wavelength. If the diameter is much larger or smaller than the wavelength, the diffraction is less and may be scarcely noticeable. The figure illustrates how wavelength and hole diameter affect diffraction.

Diffraction Patterns

Hole same size as the wavelength

Hole much larger than the wavelength

Hole much smaller than the wavelength

No waves

Section 4 Seismic Waves

Seismic Waves and Shadow Zones Seismic waves fall into two major types: body waves, which penetrate Earth, and surface waves, which travel along the surface. Body waves consist of P (primary) waves and S (secondary) waves, named for the order in which they arrive at a location some distance from the earthquake. Surface waves can be Rayleigh waves or Love waves, named for the two British scientists who discovered them.

P waves are also called compression waves, because they alternately compress and expand rock. They are sometimes called density waves, because the density of particles in the medium changes as the waves move through. P waves can travel as fast as 7.0 kilometers per second and are the most powerful seismic waves.

S waves are also called shear waves, because they shear, or cut, rock. They travel half as fast as P waves, or up to 3.5 kilometers per second. S waves travel more slowly because they are transverse waves and particles of medium move farther in transverse waves.

Shadow zones are areas on the opposite side of Earth from an earthquake where body waves do not reach. The waves cannot pass through some structures in Earth's interior or are refracted as they pass through. Scientists have studied data on shadow zones for more than a century to learn about Earth's interior. Around 1900, data on shadow zones helped a Croatian seismologist named Mohorovičić determined that there is a rocky surface layer, or crust, overlying more rigid rocks below the surface layer. The interface between the crust and mantle later became known as the Mohorovičić, or Moho, Discontinuity because of his work.

Over the next few decades, data on shadow zones were used to determine that Earth has a distinct central core with a radius of about 3,480 km. The inner core was also discovered and found to have a radius of about 1,216 km. In further studies of seismic waves, scientists determined that the outer core is liquid and the inner core is solid.

Address Misconceptions

Students may confuse tsunamis with tides, because tsunamis are sometimes called tidal waves. For a strategy for overcoming this misconception, see **Address Misconceptions** in Section 4, *Seismic Waves.*

interactive Textbook

- Complete student edition
- Video and audio
- Simulations and activities
- Section and chapter activities

Chapter 1

Characteristics of Waves

interactive Textbook

In this art, colored lights shine on waves moving along spinning ropes. ▶

4 ◆ 0

Lab zone   Chapter Project   L3

Objectives

This Chapter Project will give students a chance to identify examples of periodic motion and events and to apply wave concepts to describe them. After completing this Chapter Project, students will be able to

- observe and classify periodic motions or events
- interpret data about their frequency and duration
- communicate results to the class

Skills Focus

Observing, classifying, interpreting data, communicating

Project Time Line 1–2 weeks

 **Teaching Resources**

- Chapter Project Teacher Notes
- Chapter Project Worksheet 1
- Chapter Project Worksheet 2
- Chapter Project Scoring Rubric

Developing a Plan

Guide students in identifying and observing periodic motions and events, sketching or describing them, and recording data on their frequency, duration, and other properties. Then, have students apply chapter concepts to describe selected motions or events. Finally, give students the opportunity to present their observations and analyses to the class as a poster, display, or demonstration.

Possible Materials

Provide students with graph paper to sketch their observations and stopwatches to measure the frequency and duration of periodic events. Pictures from magazines and newspaper may be helpful to illustrate periodic motions and events. Provide poster board, markers, scissors, and tape for students to use in preparing their presentations.

Discovery
CHANNEL
SCHOOL

Characteristics of Waves
▶ Video Preview
Video Field Trip
Video Assessment

Characteristics of Waves

Show the Video Preview to introduce waves and their characteristics. Discussion question: **What is a tsunami?** *(A tsunami is an enormous wave caused by undersea or coastal earthquakes, volcanoes, or landslides.)*

Lab zone™ Chapter **Project**

Over and Over and Over Again

Some waves involve repeating patterns, or cycles. Any motion that repeats itself at regular intervals is called periodic motion. The hands moving on a clock, a child swinging on a swing, and a Ferris wheel going round and round are examples of periodic motion.

Your Goal To find examples of periodic motion and describe them

To complete this project you must

● identify examples of periodic motion or events that have periodic characteristics

● collect and organize data on the frequency and duration of each event

● present your findings as a poster, a display, or a demonstration

Plan It! With your group, brainstorm examples of objects or events that go back and forth or alternate from high to low, dark to light, loud to quiet, or crowded to uncrowded. Select at least two objects or events to observe. Record data such as how long it takes for the event to finish and start again or the highest and lowest point of the object's motion. Finally, organize your findings to present to your class.

Chapter 1 0 ◆ 5

Performance Assessment
The Chapter Project Scoring Rubric will help you evaluate how well students complete the Chapter Project. You may want to share the scoring rubric with your students so they will know what is expected. Students will be assessed on

● the thoroughness of their lists of periodic motions and events

● the accuracy of their observations and how well they organize their data

● their ability to apply wave concepts, such as amplitude, speed, and frequency, to their data

● the clarity and completeness of their presentations and written analyses
   Students can keep their data and analyses in their portfolios.

Launching the Project
To introduce the project, have students join hands in a circle and then raise and lower their arms to create a wave that goes around the circle. Have the class experiment making waves of different speeds, frequencies, and amplitudes. Point out that a wave is a regularly repeating pattern, or periodic

motion. Ask: **What other periodic motions or events can you think of?** *(Examples might include the motions of ocean tides, playground swings, hands on a clock, and the sun.)* Have students brainstorm a list of periodic motions and events they could include in this project.

Portfolio

Objectives

After this lesson, students will be able to

O.1.1.1 Explain what causes mechanical waves.

O.1.1.2 Describe two types of waves and how they can be represented.

Target Reading Skill 🎯

Using Prior Knowledge Explain that using prior knowledge helps students connect what they already know to what they are about to read.

Answers

Sample answer:

What You Know

1. Waves are high and low.
2. Waves move things up and down.

What You Learned

1. Mechanical waves can be transverse waves or longitudinal waves.
2. Transverse waves move the medium up and down or side to side, and they have crests and troughs.
3. Longitudinal waves move the medium back and forth, and they have compressions and rarefactions.

All in One Teaching Resources

• Transparency O1

Preteach

Build Background Knowledge   L2

Observing Periodic Events

Show a video of a periodic motion or event, such as waves breaking on a beach or a Ferris wheel in motion. Ask students to look for patterns in the motion or event. Tell students they will learn about the periodic motions of waves in this section.

Reading Preview

Key Concepts

• What causes mechanical waves?
• What are two types of waves and how are they classified?

Key Terms

• wave • energy • medium
• mechanical wave • vibration
• transverse wave • crest
• trough • longitudinal wave
• compression • rarefaction

🎯 Target Reading Skill

Using Prior Knowledge Before you read, look at the section headings and visuals to see what this section is about. Then write what you know about waves and energy in a graphic organizer like the one below. As you read, continue to write in what you learn.

What You Know
1. Waves are high and low.
2.

What You Learned
1.
2.

▼ **A motorboat making waves**

Lab zone Discover **Activity**

How Do Waves Travel?

1. Fill a shallow pan with about 3 cm of water.
2. With a pencil, touch the surface of the water at one end of the pan twice each second for about a minute.
3. Describe the pattern the waves make. Sketch a rough diagram of what you see.
4. Float a cork in the center of the pan. Repeat Step 2 and observe how the cork moves. Draw a diagram of what you see.

Think It Over
Observing How did the cork move in Step 4? How is its movement similar to the wave's movement? How is it different?

It was a long swim, but now you're resting on the swimming raft in the lake. You hear the water lapping gently against the raft as the sun warms your skin. Suddenly a motorboat zooms by. A few seconds later you're bobbing wildly up and down as the boat's waves hit the raft. Although the speedboat didn't touch the raft, its energy caused waves in the water. Then the waves moved the raft—and you!

You can see and feel the water waves when you're on a swimming raft. But did you know that many kinds of waves affect you every day? Sound is a wave. Sunlight is a different kind of wave. Light, sound, and water waves may seem very different, but they all are waves. What is a wave?

Lab zone Discover **Activity**

Skills Focus Observing

Materials large shallow pan, water, a cork, paper towels

Time 10 minutes

Tip You can carry out the activity as a demonstration by using a clear glass pan and placing it on an overhead projector. Images of the waves will be projected onto the screen.

L1 **Expected Outcome** Waves will spread across the surface of the water from the moving pencil.

Think It Over In Step 4, the cork bobbed up and down. The cork moves when the wave passes through it. However, the cork moves vertically, and the wave moves horizontally.

Waves and Energy

A **wave** is a disturbance that transfers energy from place to place. In science, **energy** is defined as the ability to do work. To understand waves, think about the swimming raft. A wave that disturbs the surface of the water also will disturb the raft. The wave's energy lifts the heavy raft as the wave passes under it. But the disturbance caused by the wave is temporary. After the wave passes, the water is calm again and the raft stops bobbing.

What Carries Waves? Most kinds of waves need something to travel through. Sound waves travel through air. Water waves travel along the surface of the water. A wave can even travel along a rope. The material through which a wave travels is called a **medium.** Gases (such as air), liquids (such as water), and solids (such as rope) all act as mediums. Waves that require a medium through which to travel are called **mechanical waves.**

But not all waves require a medium to travel through. Light from the sun, for example, can carry energy through empty space. If light could not travel through empty space, you could not even see the sun! Waves that can travel without a medium are called electromagnetic waves. You will learn more about electromagnetic waves in Chapter 3.

How Do Waves Transfer Energy? Although mechanical waves travel through a medium, they do not carry the medium with them. Look at the duck in Figure 1. When a wave travels under the duck, the duck moves up and down. But the duck does not travel with the wave. After the wave passes, the duck and the water return to where they started.

Why doesn't the medium travel along with the wave? All mediums are made of tiny particles. When a wave enters a medium, it transfers energy to the medium's particles. The particles bump into each other, passing the wave's energy along. To understand this, think about how food is passed at a table. You hand the food to the next person, who passes it to the next person, and so on. The food is transferred, but the people don't move. The food is like the wave's energy, and the people are like particles in a medium.

FIGURE 1
Motion of a Medium
Waves travel through water, but they do not carry the water (or the duck) with them. **Predicting** *If you add a sixth stage to the diagram, which earlier stage should it most resemble?*

Differentiated Instruction

English Learners/Beginning **L1**
Comprehension: Prior Knowledge
Have students think of familiar examples of waves, such as waves in a pond. Identify the medium in one example, and have students identify the mediums in the other examples. **learning modality: verbal**

English Learners/Intermediate **L2**
Vocabulary: Writing After students have read about waves and energy, list the key terms *wave, energy, medium*, and *vibration* on the board. Use a familiar word, such as *school*, in a sentence that reveals its meaning. *(Example: A school is a place where people go to learn.)* Then, ask students to write similar sentences using the key terms. **learning modality: verbal**

Waves and Energy

Teach Key Concepts **L2**
Waves, Energy, and Mediums
Focus Introduce the concept of *wave* by reading its definition.

Teach On the board, draw a concept map showing that waves can be either mechanical waves, which need a medium such as water, or electromagnetic waves, which do not need a medium.

Apply Ask students: **Are sound waves mechanical or electromagnetic?** *(Sound waves need a medium such as air or water, so they are mechanical.)* **learning modality: visual**

Lab zone Teacher **Demo** **L1**

Movement of Wave and Medium

Materials 2 m of cord, 20 cm of ribbon
Time 10 minutes

Focus Demonstrate how a mechanical wave moves its medium.

Teach Tie one end of the cord to a doorknob, and tie the ribbon to the middle of the cord so the ends of the ribbon hang down. Create a wave in the cord, and have students observe how the ribbon moves as the wave passes.

Apply Ask: **How does a mechanical wave move its medium?** *(Up and down)* **learning modality: visual**

Independent Practice **L2**
All in One Teaching Resources
• Guided Reading and Study Worksheet: *What Are Waves?*

◉ Student Edition on Audio CD

Monitor Progress _____ **L2**

Skills Check Ask students to use the terms *disturbance, medium* and *wave* to describe what happens when a pebble is dropped into a pond.

Answer
Figure 1 A sixth stage should most resemble the second stage.

Math Skill Angles

Focus Review right angles to help students visualize how particles move in a transverse wave.

Teach Challenge students to find right angles in the classroom.

Answers
1. Four right angles can fit in a circle.
2. Two right angles contain 180 degrees.

Types of Waves

Teach Key Concepts `L2`
Transverse and Longitudinal Waves

Focus Describe the movement of waves and particles in transverse and longitudinal waves.

Teach On the board, draw a sine curve to represent a transverse wave and a simple spring shape with areas of compression and rarefaction to represent a longitudinal wave. Then, have students add arrows to the diagrams to indicate the direction that the wave and particles of medium move in each type of wave.

Apply Tell students that sound waves are longitudinal. Ask: **In the sound waves that are moving from my mouth to your ears, in what direction are the particles of air moving?** (*Parallel to the sound waves*) **learning modality: verbal**

All in One Teaching Resources
• Transparency O2

Use Visuals: Figure 2 `L2`
Understanding Transverse Waves

Focus Use the figure to help students understand the characteristics of transverse waves.

Teach Challenge students to sketch similar drawings, making the crests closer together and farther apart, taller, and shorter. Ask Students to label the crests and troughs.

Apply Challenge students to provide examples of transverse waves in the every day world. **learning modality: visual**

Angles

An angle is formed when two lines meet at a point. Angles are measured in degrees, indicated by the symbol °. A circle has 360 degrees. A right angle is an angle that contains 90 degrees. Two lines that meet at a point to form a 90° angle are said to be perpendicular to each other.

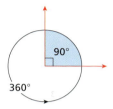

Practice Problems
1. Draw a circle on a piece of paper. How many right angles can you fit in the circle?
2. How many degrees do two right angles contain?

What Causes Waves? Energy always is required to make a wave. **Mechanical waves are produced when a source of energy causes a medium to vibrate.** A **vibration** is a repeated back-and-forth or up-and-down motion. When a vibration moves through a medium, a wave results.

Moving objects have energy. A moving object can transfer energy to a medium, producing waves. For example, you can make waves by dipping your finger in water. Your finger has energy because it is moving. When your finger touches the water, it transfers energy to the water and makes waves. In the same way, a motorboat slicing through calm water transfers energy to the water and makes waves.

Reading Checkpoint What is a vibration?

Types of Waves

Waves move through mediums in different ways. **Mechanical waves are classified by how they move. There are two types of mechanical waves: transverse waves and longitudinal waves.**

Transverse Waves When you make a wave on a rope, the wave moves from one end of the rope to the other. But the rope itself moves up and down or from side to side, at right angles to the direction in which the wave travels. Waves that move the medium at right angles to the direction in which the waves travel are called **transverse waves.** Transverse means "across." As a transverse wave moves, the particles of the medium move across, or at a right angle to, the direction of the wave.

In Figure 2, you can see that the red ribbon on the rope is first at a low point of the wave. Then it is at a high point. The high part of a transverse wave is called a **crest,** and the low part is called a **trough** (trawf).

FIGURE 2
Transverse Waves
A transverse wave moves the rope up and down in a direction perpendicular to the direction in which the wave travels.

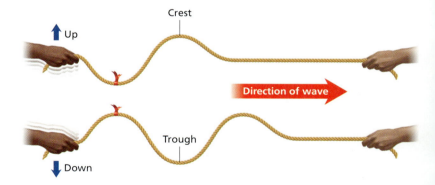

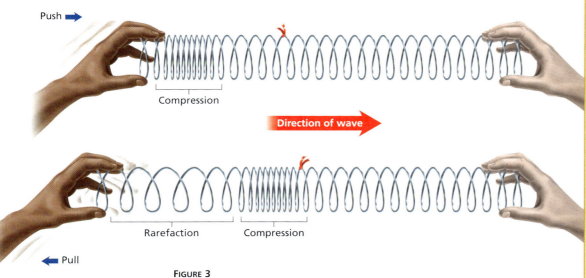

Push ➡

Compression

Direction of wave

Pull ⬅

Rarefaction   Compression

FIGURE 3
Longitudinal Waves
A longitudinal wave moves the coils of a spring toy back and forth in a direction parallel to the direction the wave travels. **Comparing and Contrasting** *How do the coils in a compression compare to the coils in a rarefaction?*

Longitudinal Waves Figure 3 shows a different kind of wave. If you stretch out a spring toy and push and pull one end, you can produce a longitudinal wave. **Longitudinal waves** (lawn juh TOO duh nul) move the medium parallel to the direction in which the waves travel. The coils in the spring move back and forth parallel to the wave motion.

Notice in Figure 3 that in some parts of the spring, the coils are close together. In other parts of the spring, the coils are more spread out. The parts where the coils are close together are called **compressions** (kum PRESH unz). The parts where the coils are spread out, or rarified, are called **rarefactions** (rair uh FAK shunz).

As compressions and rarefactions travel along the spring toy, each coil moves forward and then back. The energy travels from one end of the spring to the other, creating a wave. After the wave passes, each coil returns to the position where it started.

Sound is also a longitudinal wave. In air, sound waves cause air particles to move back and forth. In areas where the particles are pushed together, compressions form. In between the compressions, particles are spread out. These are rarefactions.

For: Links on waves
Visit: www.SciLinks.org
Web Code: scn-1511

━ **Differentiated Instruction** ━

Less Proficient Readers L1
Organizing Information Partner less proficient readers with more proficient readers. Ask the partners to work together to make a Venn diagram or compare/contrast table to summarize the similarities and differences between transverse and longitudinal waves. **learning modality: visual**

Less Proficient Readers L1
Taking Notes Have students listen to the **Student Edition on Audio CD.** Guide them in taking notes on the section as they listen. Tell them to write down any words, sentences, or ideas that help them understand or remember the material. **learning modality: verbal**

Use Visuals: Figure 3 L2
Understanding Longitudinal Waves
Focus Use the figure to help students understand how longitudinal waves differ from transverse waves.

Teach Point out how the longitudinal wave and individual coils in the toy move in the same direction in the figure. Help students recall how a rope moves perpendicular to a transverse wave passing through it.

Apply Have students answer the caption question. **learning modality: visual**

All in One Teaching Resources
• Transparency O3

 Build Inquiry L2

Observing Longitudinal Waves

Materials spring toy, 15 cm of ribbon
Time 10 minutes

Focus Show students how the spring toy can be used to make longitudinal waves.

Teach Have students tie the ribbon to a coil in the spring toy and then make longitudinal waves. Tell students to observe how the coil with the ribbon moves when the waves pass through it.

Apply Ask: **How do particles in a longitudinal wave move?** *(Parallel to the direction of the wave)* **learning modality: kinesthetic**

For: Links on waves
Visit: www.SciLinks.org
Web Code: scn-1511

Download a worksheet that will guide students' review of Internet resources on waves.

Monitor Progress ━━━━ L2

Drawing Have students draw diagrams of transverse and longitudinal waves using arrows to show the directions of waves and particles.

Answers
Figure 3 The coils in a compression are closer together than the coils in a rarefaction.

 Reading Checkpoint A vibration is a repeated back-and-forth or up-and-down motion.

Monitor Progress _____ **L2**

Answer

 Reading Checkpoint The rest position is drawn as a horizontal dashed line, showing the position of the medium before the wave disturbs it.

Assess

Reviewing Key Concepts

1. a. A wave that requires a medium to travel through **b.** Mechanical waves are produced when a source of energy causes a medium to vibrate. **c.** The wave moved past the dock.

2. a. Transverse and longitudinal **b.** Diagrams should look like a sine curve, with one of the high points labeled *crest* and one of the low points labeled *trough*. Sample answer: A crest is the tallest part of a wave, and a trough is the lowest part. **c.** A transverse wave moves a medium at right angles to the direction of the wave. A longitudinal wave moves the medium parallel to the direction of the wave.

All in One Teaching Resources

• Transparency 04

Reteach   **L1**

Ask students to write one or two sentences correctly using the key terms *wave, vibration, energy*, and *medium*.

Performance Assessment   **L2**

Skills Check Have students make a concept map that relates the following key terms: *mechanical wave, transverse wave, longitudinal wave, crest, trough, compression, rarefaction.*

All in One Teaching Resources

• Section Summary: *What Are Waves?*
• Review and Reinforcement: *What Are Waves?*
• Enrich: *What Are Waves?*

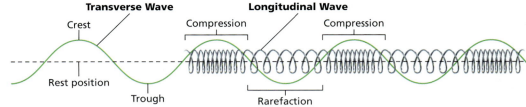

FIGURE 4
Representing Waves
The compressions of a longitudinal wave correspond to the crests of a transverse wave. The troughs correspond to rarefactions.

Representing Types of Waves You can use diagrams to represent transverse and longitudinal waves. Transverse waves like those on a rope are easy to draw. You can draw a transverse wave as shown in Figure 4. Think of the horizontal line as the position of the rope before it is disturbed. This position is called the rest position. As the wave passes, the rope moves above or below the rest position. Remember that the crests are the highest points of the wave and the troughs are the lowest points of the wave.

To draw longitudinal waves, think of the compressions in the spring toy as being similar to the crests of a transverse wave. The rarefactions in the spring toy are like the troughs of a transverse wave. By treating compressions as crests and rarefactions as troughs, you can draw longitudinal waves in the same way as transverse waves.

Reading Checkpoint How do you draw the rest position of a transverse wave?

Section 1 Assessment

Target Reading Skill **Using Prior Knowledge** Revise your graphic organizer about waves based on what you just learned in the section.

Reviewing Key Concepts

1. a. Defining What is a mechanical wave?
   b. Explaining How are mechanical waves produced?
   c. Inferring A wave moves a floating dock up and down several times, but then the dock stops moving. What happened to the wave?
2. a. Identifying What are the two types of mechanical waves?
   b. Describing Use a wave diagram to represent the crests and troughs of a wave. Then describe a crest and trough in your own words.

   c. Comparing and Contrasting How does a transverse wave move a medium? How does a longitudinal wave move a medium?

Writing in Science

Firsthand Account Suppose you are a particle of water in a lake. Describe what happens to you when a motorboat passes by. Be sure to use words like *vibration* and *crest* in your description.

10 ◆ O

Chapter Project

Keep Students on Track Check that students have listed several different periodic motions or events, including those that repeat in just seconds or minutes and others that repeat at longer intervals. Suggest they include examples that occur not only at home or school but also in the natural world. Remind students to describe or sketch each motion or event.

Writing in Science

Writing Mode Description
Scoring Rubric
4 Exceeds criteria; includes precise, sensory details in a complete description that correctly uses all relevant key terms
3 Meets criteria
2 Includes a few details and correctly uses some key terms but contains errors
1 Includes only a general description and/or fails to use key terms correctly

Reading Preview

Key Concepts
- What are the basic properties of waves?
- How is a wave's speed related to its wavelength and frequency?

Key Terms
- amplitude
- wavelength
- frequency
- hertz (Hz)

 Target Reading Skill

Outlining An outline shows the relationship between main ideas and supporting ideas. As you read, make an outline about the properties of waves that you can use for review. Use the red headings for the main ideas and the blue headings for the supporting ideas.

Properties of Waves
I. Amplitude
A. Amplitude of transverse waves
B.
II. Wavelength
III.

Lab zone · Discover **Activity**

Can You Change a Wave?

1. Lay a 3-meter-long rope on the floor. Hold one end of the rope. Have a partner hold the other end.
2. Flick your end left and right about once per second. Observe the waves.
3. Now flick your end about twice per second. Observe the waves.
4. Switch roles with your partner and repeat Steps 2 and 3.

Think It Over
Predicting What happened to the waves when you flicked the rope more often? Predict how the wave will change if you flick the rope less often than once per second. Try it.

One of the most elegant and graceful Olympic sports is rhythmic gymnastics. A ribbon dancer flicks a stick attached to a ribbon, making waves that travel down the ribbon. Some of the waves are longer, while others are shorter. The rate at which the gymnast flicks her hands affects both the length and shape of the waves in the ribbon.

This is just one of many different kinds of waves. Waves can carry a little energy or a lot. They can be short or long. They can be rare or frequent. They can travel fast or slow. All waves, however, share certain properties. **The basic properties of waves are amplitude, wavelength, frequency, and speed.**

A rhythmic gymnast ▲

Chapter 1 0 ◆ 11

Section 2
Properties of Waves

Objectives

After this lesson, students will be able to

O.1.2.1 Describe the basic properties of waves.

O.1.2.2 Explain how a wave's speed is related to its wavelength and frequency and calculate a wave's speed.

Target Reading Skill

Outlining Explain that using an outline format helps students organize information by main topic, subtopic, and details.

Answers

Properties of Waves
I. Amplitude
  A. Amplitude of transverse waves
  B. Amplitude of longitudinal waves
II. Wavelength
III. Frequency
IV. Speed

All in One Teaching Resources
- Transparency O5

Preteach

Build Background Knowledge   L2

Waves and Wavelike Motion
Ask students: **What are some examples of waves or wavelike motions you have seen?** (*Sample answer: Ocean waves, motion of a snake, ripples on water*) Have students describe different speeds or sizes of waves. Tell students they will learn more about properties of waves in this section.

Lab zone · Discover **Activity**

Skills Focus Predicting   L1

Materials 3 m of medium-weight rope

Time 10 minutes

Tips Before the activity, introduce the term *wavelength* to help students describe their experiences. Caution students not to flick the rope at one another. Students might perform the activity in the hall if more space is needed.

Expected Outcome Transverse waves will travel down the rope when it is flicked repeatedly at one end.

Think It Over The wavelength was shorter when the rope was flicked more often. The wavelength will be longer if the rope is flicked less often.

Amplitude

Teach Key Concepts L2
Introducing Amplitude

Focus Introduce amplitude as one of the four basic properties of waves.

Teach In Figure 5, have students measure the maximum distance the yellow, blue, and green ropes are displaced from their rest positions. Tell students this is the amplitude of the waves.

Apply Ask: **What units are used to measure amplitude?** (*Units of distance, such as centimeters*) **learning modality: kinesthetic**

Help Students Read L1
Identifying Main Ideas Refer to the Content Refresher in this chapter, which provides guidelines for using the Identifying Main Ideas strategy.

After students read the material on this page, ask: **Which sentences contain the most important information about amplitude?** (*Sample answer: The more energy a wave has, the greater its amplitude.*) Let several students read the sentences of their choice before taking a consensus on the best three or four sentences. Then, ask: **What are the main ideas expressed by these sentences?** (*Sample answer: Amplitude is determined by the amount of energy in a wave.*)

Independent Practice L2

All in One Teaching Resources
• Guided Reading and Study Worksheet: *Properties of Waves*

Student Edition on Audio CD

All in One Teaching Resources
• Transparency O6

Amplitude

Some crests are very high, while others are very low. The distance the medium rises depends on the amplitude of the wave. **Amplitude** is the maximum distance that the particles of the medium carrying the wave move away from their rest positions. For example, the amplitude of a water wave is the maximum distance a water particle moves above or below the surface level of calm water. You can increase the amplitude of a wave in a rope by moving your hand up and down a greater distance. To do this, you have to use more energy. This energy is transferred to the rope. Thus, the more energy a wave has, the greater its amplitude.

Amplitude of Transverse Waves As shown in Figure 5, the amplitude of a transverse wave is the maximum distance the medium moves up or down from its rest position. You can find the amplitude of a transverse wave by measuring the distance from the rest position to a crest or to a trough.

Amplitude of Longitudinal Waves The amplitude of a longitudinal wave is a measure of how compressed or rarefied the medium becomes. A high-energy wave causes more compression and rarefaction than a low-energy wave. When the compressions are dense, it means that the wave's amplitude is large.

FIGURE 5
Amplitude, Wavelength, and Frequency
The basic properties of all waves include amplitude, wavelength, and frequency.
Developing Hypotheses *How could you increase the amplitude of a wave in a rope? How could you increase the frequency?*

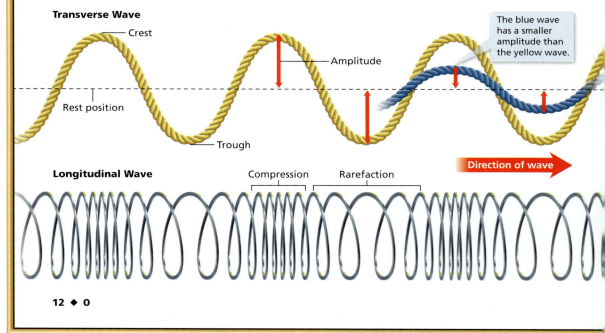

Transverse Wave
Crest
Amplitude
Rest position
Trough

The blue wave has a smaller amplitude than the yellow wave.

Direction of wave

Longitudinal Wave
Compression   Rarefaction

12 ◆ O

Wavelength

A wave travels a certain distance before it starts to repeat. The distance between two corresponding parts of a wave is its **wavelength.** You can find the wavelength of a transverse wave by measuring the distance from crest to crest, as shown in Figure 5. Or you could measure from trough to trough. The wavelength of a longitudinal wave is the distance between compressions.

Frequency

Wave **frequency** is the number of complete waves that pass a given point in a certain amount of time. For example, if you make waves on a rope so that one wave passes by every second, the frequency is 1 wave per second. How can you increase the frequency? Simply move your hand up and down more quickly, perhaps two or three times per second. To decrease the frequency, move your hand up and down more slowly.

Frequency is measured in units called **hertz** (Hz). A wave that occurs every second has a frequency of 1 Hz. If two waves pass you every second, then the frequency of the wave is 2 per second, or 2 hertz. The hertz was named after Heinrich Hertz, the German scientist who discovered radio waves.

 Reading Checkpoint In what unit is the frequency of a wave measured?

Lab zone **Skills Activity**

Calculating

Tie a metal washer to one end of a 25-cm long string. Tape the other end of the string to the edge of a table. Let the washer hang and then pull it about 10 cm to the side and release it. Measure the time it takes the washer to swing through 10 complete cycles. (In 1 cycle, the washer swings forward and back, returning to its starting point.) Calculate the frequency by dividing 10 cycles by the time interval.

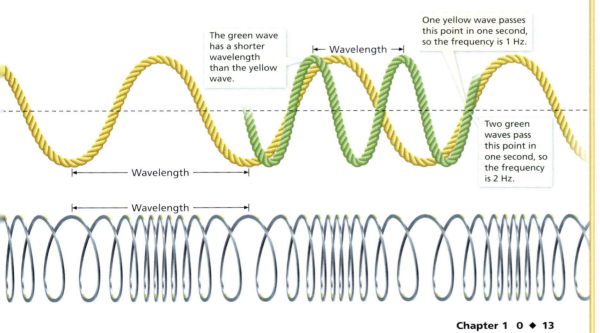

The green wave has a shorter wavelength than the yellow wave.

|← Wavelength →|

One yellow wave passes this point in one second, so the frequency is 1 Hz.

Two green waves pass this point in one second, so the frequency is 2 Hz.

|← Wavelength →|

|← Wavelength →|

Wavelength

Teach Key Concepts　　L2

Measuring Wavelength

Focus Define wavelength as the distance between corresponding parts of a wave.

Teach Explain that the wavelength of a transverse wave is the distance between two crests or two troughs.

Apply Ask: **What is the wavelength of a longitudinal wave?** *(The distance between two compressions or two rarefactions)*
learning modality: verbal

Frequency

Teach Key Concepts　　L2

Frequency of Waves

Focus Introduce wave frequency by reading its definition.

Teach Write the definition on the board, and underline *number, complete waves,* and *amount of time.* Explain that *number* refers to a simple count of the waves as they pass a point; a *complete wave* is the distance from one crest or trough to the next (a wavelength); and the *amount of time* is a measured time interval.

Apply Ask: **What is the frequency of a wave in which two complete waves pass a given point every second?** *(2 waves per second)*
learning modality: logical/mathematical

Lab zone **Skills Activity**

Skills Focus Calculating　　L3

Materials metal washer, 25 cm of string, tape, stopwatch

Time 10 minutes

Tip Make sure students swing the washer far enough for it to complete at least 10 cycles before coming to rest.

Expected Outcome It takes 10 seconds for the completion of 10 cycles. Dividing 10 cycles by 10 seconds gives a frequency of 1 Hz.

Extend Ask: **How could you change the activity to observe the effects of different conditions on frequency?** *(Sample answer: Use a longer string.)* **learning modality: kinesthetic**

Monitor Progress　　L2

Drawing Have students draw two longitudinal waves with different amplitudes.

Answers
Figure 5 You could increase amplitude by shaking the rope harder. You could increase frequency by shaking the rope faster.

 Reading Checkpoint Frequency is measured in hertz (Hz).

Speed

Teach Key Concepts L2
Calculating Wave Speed

Focus Introduce wave speed as the distance a wave travels in a given amount of time.

Teach Explain that the speed of a wave is like the speed of a car. It is given in units of distance/time. For example, a car's speed might be given in km/h and a wave's speed in m/s.

Apply Have students show how multiplying wavelength by frequency gives speed in units of distance/time. (*Sample answer: 10 cm × 2/s = 20 cm/s*) **learning modality: logical/mathematical**

Effect of Medium on Wave Speed L2

Materials metal and plastic spring toys

Time 10 minutes

Focus Challenge pairs of students to design an experiment, using the materials provided, to determine how different mediums affect the speed of longitudinal waves.

Teach Let students use the materials to test their designs. (*Students can compare the speed of waves in the metal and plastic spring toys.*)

Apply Ask: **How did the different mediums affect wave speed?** (*Sample answer: The waves were slower in the plastic spring toy.*) **learning modality: kinesthetic**

For: More on wave properties
Visit: PHSchool.com
Web Code: cgd-5012

Students can review wave properties in an online interactivity.

FIGURE 6
Speed of Waves
Light waves travel much faster than sound waves.
Problem Solving *Why do you see lightning before hearing thunder?*

Speed

Imagine watching a distant thunderstorm approach on a hot summer day. First you see a flash of lightning. A few seconds later you hear the thunder rumble. Even though the thunder occurs the instant the lightning flashes, the light and sound reach you seconds apart. This happens because light waves travel much faster than sound waves. In fact, light waves travel about a million times faster than sound waves!

Different waves travel at different speeds. The speed of a wave is how far the wave travels in a given length of time, or its distance divided by the time it took to travel that distance. **The speed, wavelength, and frequency of a wave are related to one another by a mathematical formula:**

$$\text{Speed} = \text{Wavelength} \times \text{Frequency}$$

If you know two of the quantities in the speed formula—speed, wavelength, and frequency—you can calculate the third quantity. For example, if you know a wave's speed and wavelength, you can calculate the frequency. If you know the speed and the frequency, you can calculate the wavelength.

$$\text{Frequency} = \frac{\text{Speed}}{\text{Wavelength}} \qquad \text{Wavelength} = \frac{\text{Speed}}{\text{Frequency}}$$

If a medium does not change, the speed of a wave is constant. For example, in air at a given temperature and pressure, all sound waves travel at the same speed. If speed is constant, what do you think will happen if the wave's frequency changes? If you multiply wavelength by frequency, you should always get the same speed. Therefore, if you increase the frequency of a wave, the wavelength must decrease.

Reading Checkpoint What is the speed of a wave?

Go Online
For: More on wave properties
Visit: PHSchool.com
Web Code: cgd-5012

14 ◆ O

Differentiated Instruction

Less Proficient Readers L1
Applying Concepts Students may develop a better grasp of the wave concepts of speed, wavelength, and frequency by solving more problems using the speed equation. Give students several examples of waves with different frequencies and wavelengths but with the same speed. For some of the waves, have students find the frequency; for others, have them find the wavelength. **learning modality: logical/mathematical**

Gifted and Talented L3
Applying Concepts Remind students that all sound waves have the same speed in a given medium at a fixed temperature and pressure. Then, challenge students to draw a graph that demonstrates the relationship between frequency and wavelength of sound waves. (*Students can label one axis "frequency" and the other axis "wavelength." The graph should be a curved line to show an inverse relationship between the two variables.*) **learning modality: logical/mathematical**

14 ● O

Math Sample Problem

Calculating Frequency

The speed of a wave on a rope is 50 cm/s and its wavelength is 10 cm. What is the wave's frequency?

1 **Read and Understand**
What information are you given?

Speed = **50 cm/s**
Wavelength = **10 cm**

2 **Plan and Solve**
What quantity are you trying to calculate?

The frequency of a wave = ▪Hz

What formula contains the given quantities and the unknown quantity?

$$\text{Frequency} = \frac{\text{Speed}}{\text{Wavelength}}$$

Perform the calculation.

$$\text{Frequency} = \frac{\text{Speed}}{\text{Wavelength}} = \frac{50 \text{ cm/s}}{10 \text{ cm}}$$

$$\text{Frequency} = \frac{5}{s} = 5 \text{ Hz}$$

3 **Look Back and Check**
Does your answer make sense?

The wave speed is 50 cm per second. Because the distance from crest to crest is 10 cm, 5 crests will pass a point every second.

Math Practice

1. A wave has a wavelength of 2 mm and a frequency of 3 Hz. At what speed does the wave travel?
2. The speed of a wave on a guitar string is 142 m/s and the frequency is 110 Hz. What is the wavelength of the wave?

Section 2 Assessment

🔸 **Target Reading Skill** **Outlining** Use the information in your outline to help you answer the questions below.

Reviewing Key Concepts

1. **a.** **Listing** What are four basic properties of waves?
   b. **Explaining** Which wave property is directly related to energy?
   c. **Comparing and Contrasting** Which wave properties are distances? Which are measured relative to time?
2. **a.** **Identifying** What formula relates speed, wavelength, and frequency?
   b. **Inferring** Two waves have the same wavelength and frequency. How do their speeds compare?
   c. **Calculating** A wave's frequency is 2 Hz and its wavelength is 4 m. What is the wave's speed?

Math Practice

3. **Calculating Frequency** A wave travels at 3 m/s along a spring toy. If the wavelength is 0.2 m, what is the wave's frequency?

Chapter 1 0 ◆ 15

Math Practice

Math Skill Calculating frequency
Answer
3. 15 Hz (3 m/s ÷ 0.2 m)

Lab zone Chapter Project

Keep Students on Track As students observe and record the amplitude, wavelength, and frequency of two of the periodic motions or events on their list, have them draw a diagram or graph of each motion or event and label all the properties in the drawing. Make sure students have used appropriate methods for measuring the properties.

Math Sample Problem

Math Skill Calculating frequency
Focus Remind students that the formula for speed is: Speed = Wavelength × Frequency.
Teach Show students how the formulas for frequency and wavelength can be derived from the formula for speed.

Answers
1. (2 mm)(3 Hz) = 6 mm/s
2. (142 m/s)/(110 Hz) = 1.3 m

All in One Teaching Resources
• Transparency O7

Monitor Progress _____ L2

Answers
Figure 6 You see lightning before hearing thunder because light waves travel much faster than sound waves.

✔ **Reading Checkpoint** The speed of a wave is the distance it travels divided by the time it took to travel that distance.

Assess

Reviewing Key Concepts

1. **a.** Amplitude, wavelength, frequency, and speed **b.** Amplitude is directly related to wave energy. **c.** Amplitude and wavelength are distances. Frequency and speed are relative to time.
2. **a.** Speed = Wavelength × Frequency **b.** The speeds must be the same. **c.** 8 m/s (4 m × 2 Hz).

Reteach L1
Call on students to describe or define wave amplitude, wavelength, and frequency.

Performance Assessment L2
Skills Check Have students calculate the speed of a wave that has a wavelength of 3 cm and a frequency of 10 Hz. (30 cm/s)

O ● 15

Wavy Motions L2

Prepare for Inquiry

Skills Objective
After this lab, students will be able to
- compare and contrast transverse and longitudinal waves
- classify transverse and longitudinal waves

 Prep Time 10 minutes
Class Time 40 minutes

Advance Planning
Obtain enough toys for each pair of students to share one.

Safety
Caution students that stretched springs, if suddenly released, can cause injury. Review the safety guidelines in Appendix A.

All in One Teaching Resources
- Lab Worksheet: *Wavy Motions*

Guide Inquiry

Introduce the Procedure
Before students begin, ask them to describe how they could use a spring toy to model waves. Then, with the help of a volunteer, show the class how to generate longitudinal and transverse waves with a spring toy.

Troubleshooting the Experiment
- Caution students not to overstretch the spring toy because it may lose its shape.
- Make sure students hold firmly onto the ends of the spring toys so they are not accidentally released.

Expected Outcome
Students use the spring toy to generate transverse and longitudinal waves. Increasing the rate at which they vibrate the end of the spring increases the frequency and decreases the wavelength of the waves.

Extend Inquiry

Design an Experiment Students can repeat the procedure using spring toys of different sizes, masses, or materials. Sample outcome: Spring toys with different masses need different amounts of force to stretch and create waves of a given amplitude.

Wavy Motions

Problem
How do waves travel in a spring toy?

Skills Focus
comparing and contrasting, classifying

Materials
- spring toy
- meter stick

Procedure
1. On a smooth floor, stretch the spring to about 3 meters. Hold one end while your partner holds the other end. Do not over-stretch the spring toy.
2. Pull a few coils of the spring toy to one side near one end of the spring.
3. Release the coils and observe the motion of the spring. What happens when the disturbance reaches your partner? Draw what you observe.
4. Have your partner move one end of the spring toy to the left and then to the right on the floor. Be certain that both ends of the spring are held securely. Draw a diagram of the wave you observe.
5. Repeat Step 4, increasing the rate at which you move the spring toy left and right. Record your observations.
6. Squeeze together several coils of the spring toy, making a compression.
7. Release the compressed section of the spring toy and observe the disturbance as it moves down the spring. Record your observations. Draw and label what you see.

Analyze and Conclude
1. **Comparing and Contrasting** Compare the waves generated in Steps 1–5 with the waves generated in Steps 6–7.
2. **Classifying** Were the waves generated in Steps 1–5 transverse or longitudinal? Explain your answer.
3. **Comparing and Contrasting** In Step 3 of the procedure, compare the original wave to the wave that came back.
4. **Classifying** Were the waves generated in Steps 6 and 7 transverse or longitudinal? Explain your answer.
5. **Interpreting Data** What happened to the wavelength and frequency when you increased the rate at which the spring toy moved left and right?
6. **Developing Hypotheses** How might you change the amplitude of the longitudinal waves you made?
7. **Communicating** Use your drawings to make a poster that explains your observations.

Design an Experiment
Obtain some different spring toys. Look for different sizes and materials, such as metal and plastic. Design an experiment to test whether the differences of the spring toys result in differences in the waves the springs make. Have your teacher approve your procedure before you carry out the experiment.

Analyze and Conclude

1. Steps 1–5, transverse waves; Steps 6–7, longitudinal waves

2. Transverse; movement of the medium was perpendicular to wave movement.

3. The reflected wave was inverted.

4. Longitudinal; movement of the medium was parallel to wave movement.

5. Wavelength decreased; frequency increased.

6. By moving your hand a greater distance

7. Students' posters should show how transverse and longitudinal waves differ in the direction the particles move relative to the direction of the wave.

Reading Preview

Key Concepts
- How do reflection, refraction, and diffraction change a wave's direction?
- What are the different types of interference?
- How do standing waves form?

Key Terms
- reflection • law of reflection
- refraction • diffraction
- interference
- constructive interference
- destructive interference
- standing wave • node
- antinode • resonance

Target Reading Skill

Asking Questions Before you read, preview the red headings. In a graphic organizer like the one below, ask a *what*, *how*, *when*, or *where* question for each heading. As you read, write the answers to your questions.

Interactions of Waves

Question	Answer
How are waves reflected?	Waves are reflected . . .

Lab zone Discover Activity

How Does a Ball Bounce?

1. Choose a spot at the base of a wall. From a distance of 1 m, roll a wet ball along the floor straight at the spot you chose. Watch the angle at which the ball bounces by looking at the path of moisture on the floor.
2. Wet the ball again. From a different position, roll the ball at the same spot, but at an angle to the wall. Again, observe the angle at which the ball bounces back.

Think It Over

Developing Hypotheses How do you think the angle at which the ball hits the wall is related to the angle at which the ball bounces back? Test your hypothesis.

You slip into the water in your snorkel gear. With your mask on, you can see clearly across the pool. As you start to swim, your flippers disturb the water, sending ripples moving outward in all directions. As each ripple hits the wall, it bounces off the wall and travels back toward you.

When water waves hit the side of a swimming pool, they bounce back because they cannot pass through the solid wall. Other kinds of waves may interact in a similar way when they hit the surface of a new medium. This type of interaction is called reflection.

Making waves in a pool ▶

0 ◆ 17

Lab zone Discover Activity

Skills Focus Developing hypotheses **L2**

Materials ball, meter stick, water

Time 10 minutes

Tip If your floor does not show the moisture path well, place paper on the floor for students to roll the wet ball over.

Expected Outcomes The ball will roll to the wall and bounce back, leaving a visible trail of moisture on the floor.

Think It Over The ball bounced back from the wall at the same angle that it hit the wall.

Section 3
Interactions of Waves

Objectives
After this lesson, students will be able to

O.1.3.1 Describe how reflection, refraction, and diffraction change a wave's direction.

O.1.3.2 Distinguish among the different types of interference.

O.1.3.3 Explain how standing waves form.

Target Reading Skill

Asking Questions Explain that when students ask questions about the headings, they are preparing themselves to better understand what they are about to read.

Answers
Sample questions and answers:

1. How are waves reflected? (Waves are reflected when they hit a surface through which they cannot pass and bounce back.)

2. What is refraction? (The bending of waves due to a change in speed)

3. When does diffraction occur? (When a wave moves around a barrier or through an opening in a barrier)

4. What is a standing wave? (A wave that appears to stand in one place, even though it is really two waves interfering)

All in One Teaching Resources
- Transparency O8

Preteach

Build Background Knowledge **L2**

Experience With Reflection
Help students recall occasions when they saw themselves reflected in a store window or pool of water. Ask: **Why do clear glass and still water act like mirrors?** (*Because they reflect light*) Tell students they will learn more about reflection and other wave interactions in this section.

Instruct

Reflection

Teach Key Concepts L2
Reflection of Waves

Focus Introduce the concept of reflection by holding up a large mirror. Tell students that they can see their faces in the mirror because light waves from their faces are reflected back from the mirror's shiny surface.

Teach Explain that all waves, not just light waves, are reflected whenever they hit a surface they cannot pass through.

Apply Ask: **How can you tell when sound waves are reflected back from a surface?** (*You can hear an echo.*) **learning modality: visual**

Reflecting Light Around a Barrier

Materials flashlight, small mirror

Time 15 minutes

Focus Tell students that light waves do not bend around barriers, such as walls. However, light waves can be reflected in such a way that they bounce around a barrier.

Teach Challenge students to design a plan for using a mirror to reflect the beam of a flashlight around a corner in a hallway. Have them make a sketch showing how they will place the mirror and the angle at which the beam of light will strike it. Let students try their plans.

Apply Ask: **What angles would not work well?** (*Angles much smaller or larger than 45°*) **learning modality: kinesthetic**

Independent Practice L2

All in One Teaching Resources

• Guided Reading and Study Worksheet: *Interactions of Waves*

Student Edition on Audio CD

All in One Teaching Resources

• Transparency O9

Reflection

When an object or a wave hits a surface through which it cannot pass, it bounces back. This interaction with a surface is called **reflection.** There are many examples of reflection in your everyday life. When you did the Discover Activity, you saw that the ball hit the wall and bounced back, or was reflected. When you looked in your mirror this morning, you used light that was reflected to see yourself. If you have ever shouted in an empty gym, the echo you heard was caused by sound waves that reflected off the gym walls.

All waves obey the law of reflection. To help you understand this law, look at Figure 7. In the photo, you see light reflected off the surface of the sunglasses. The diagram shows how the light waves travel to make the reflection. The arrow labeled *Incoming wave* represents a wave moving toward the surface at an angle. The arrow labeled *Reflected wave* represents the wave that bounces off the surface at an angle. The dashed line labeled *Normal* is drawn perpendicular to the surface at the point where the incoming wave strikes the surface. The angle of incidence is the angle between the incoming wave and the normal. The angle of reflection is the angle between the reflected wave and the normal line. The **law of reflection** states that the angle of incidence equals the angle of reflection.

Reading Checkpoint What is reflection?

FIGURE 7
Law of Reflection
The angle of incidence equals the angle of reflection. All waves obey this law, including the light waves reflected from these sunglasses.
Predicting *What happens to the angle of reflection if the angle of incidence increases?*

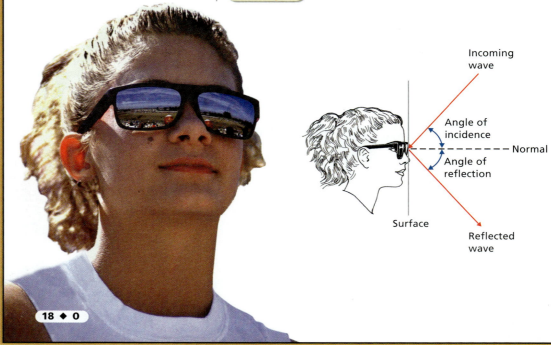

Differentiated Instruction

Gifted and Talented L3
Communicating How Rainbows Form
Challenge students to research how and why refraction of white light causes the light to separate into a rainbow of colored light. After researching the problem, students can make an illustrated poster to explain the formation of rainbows to the class. **learning modality: visual**

Special Needs L1
Classifying Wave Interactions Pair special needs students with other students. Have each pair develop a table that classifies wave interactions. For each type of wave interaction, the table should indicate the conditions under which it occurs, how it affects the waves, and an example of when it occurs. **learning modality: visual**

FIGURE 8
Refraction of Light Waves
Light bends when it enters water at an angle
because one side of each wave slows down
before the other side does.

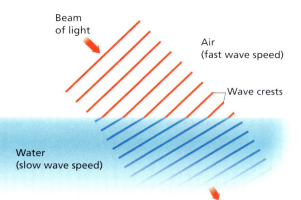

Beam of light

Air (fast wave speed)

Wave crests

Water (slow wave speed)

Refraction

Have you ever been riding a skateboard and gone off the sidewalk onto grass? If so, you know it's hard to keep moving in a straight line. The front wheel on the side moving onto the grass slows down. The front wheel still on the sidewalk continues to move fast. The difference in the speeds of the two front wheels causes the skateboard to change direction.

What Causes Refraction? Like the skateboard that changes direction, changes in speed can cause waves to change direction, as shown in Figure 8. **When a wave enters a new medium at an angle, one side of the wave changes speed before the other side, causing the wave to bend.** The bending of waves due to a change in speed is called **refraction.**

When Does Refraction Occur? A wave does not always bend when it enters a new medium. Bending occurs only when the wave enters the new medium at an angle. Then one side of the wave enters the medium first. This side changes speed, but the other side still travels at its original speed. Bending occurs because the two sides of the wave travel at different speeds.

Even if you don't skateboard, you have probably seen refraction in daily life. Have you ever had trouble grabbing something underwater? Have you ever seen a rainbow? Light can bend when it passes from water into air, making an underwater object appear closer than it really is. When you reach for the object, you miss it. When white light enters water, different colors in the light bend by different amounts. The white light separates into the colors you see in a rainbow.

 Reading Checkpoint · When does refraction occur?

Lab zone Skills Activity

Observing

You can simulate what happens as waves move from one medium to another.

1. Roll a drinking straw from a smooth tabletop straight onto a thin piece of terry cloth or a paper towel. Describe how the straw's motion changes as it leaves the smooth surface.
2. Repeat Step 1, but roll the straw at an angle to the cloth or paper.

Describe what happens as each side of the straw hits the cloth or paper. How are your results similar to what happens when waves are refracted?

Lab zone Skills Activity

Skills Focus Observing L2

Materials drinking straw, piece of terry cloth or paper towel

Time 10 minutes

Tips Demonstrate rolling the straw along the tabletop. Push or blow on the straw so that it rolls by itself. It may help to tape the cloth or towel in place so it does not move if students blow on it.

Expected Outcome The side of the straw that hits the piece of terry cloth or paper towel first slows down first, causing the straw to turn.

Extend Students can experiment with different materials to determine which causes the greatest refraction of the rolling straw. **learning modality: kinesthetic**

Refraction

Teach Key Concepts L2
Refraction of Waves

Focus Define refraction as the bending of a wave due to a change in speed when the wave enters a new medium.

Teach Explain that refraction occurs only when one side of the wave enters the new medium and changes speed before the other side. The wave bends as the two sides of the wave travel at different speeds.

Apply Ask: **What characteristics must a new medium have to cause refraction?** (*It must allow waves to pass through but at a different speed than the original medium.*)
learning modality: verbal

Use Visuals: Figure 8 L2
Observing Refraction of Light

Focus Have students observe the refraction of light waves in Figure 8.

Teach Point out how the light enters the water at an angle, so the side of the wave entering the water first slows down while the other side maintains its original speed.

Apply Ask: **Would the light be refracted if it entered the water at a 90° angle?** (*No, because both sides would enter the water and slow down at the same time*) **learning modality: visual**

All in One Teaching Resources

• Transparency O10

Monitor Progress L2

Oral Presentation Ask students to explain the difference between reflection and refraction.

Answers
Figure 7 The angle of reflection increases.

Reading Checkpoint · Reflection is the interaction in which a wave bounces off a surface through which it cannot pass.

Reading Checkpoint · Refraction occurs when a wave enters a new medium at an angle and one side of the wave changes speed before the other side, causing the wave to bend.

Diffraction

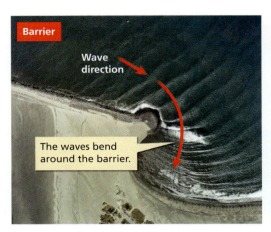

Barrier · Wave direction · The waves bend around the barrier.

Narrow Opening · Wave direction · The waves spread out after passing through the narrow opening.

FIGURE 9
Diffraction of Water Waves
Waves diffract when they move around a barrier or pass through an opening. As a wave passes a barrier, it bends around the barrier. After a wave goes through a narrow opening, it spreads out.

Diffraction

Sometimes waves bend around a barrier or pass through a hole. **When a wave moves around a barrier or through an opening in a barrier, it bends and spreads out.** These wave interactions are called **diffraction.** Figure 9 shows how waves bend and spread by diffraction.

Interference

Have you ever seen soccer balls collide in a practice drill? The balls bounce off each other because they cannot be in the same place at the same time. Surprisingly, this is not true of waves. Unlike two balls, two waves can overlap when they meet. **Interference** is the interaction between waves that meet. **There are two types of interference: constructive and destructive.**

Constructive Interference The interference that occurs when waves combine to make a wave with a larger amplitude is called **constructive interference.** You can think of constructive interference as waves "helping each other," or adding their energies. When the crests of two waves overlap, they make a higher crest. When the troughs of two waves overlap, they make a deeper trough. In both cases, the amplitude increases.

Figure 10 shows how constructive interference can occur when two waves travel toward each other. When the crests from each wave meet, constructive interference makes a higher crest in the area of overlap. The amplitude of this crest is the sum of the amplitudes of the two original crests. After the waves pass through each other, they continue on as if they had never met.

 Reading Checkpoint What is constructive interference?

Destructive Interference The interference that occurs when two waves combine to make a wave with a smaller amplitude is called **destructive interference.** You can think of destructive interference as waves subtracting their energies.

Destructive interference occurs when the crest of one wave overlaps the trough of another wave. If the crest has a larger amplitude than the trough, the crest "wins" and part of it remains. If the original trough had a larger amplitude, the result is a trough. If the original waves had equal amplitudes, then the crest and trough can completely cancel as shown in Figure 10.

Go Online
active art

For: Wave Interference activity
Visit: PHSchool.com
Web Code: cgp-5013

FIGURE 10
Wave Interference
Interference can be constructive or destructive.
Interpreting Diagrams *What does the black dotted line represent in the diagram below?*

Constructive Interference

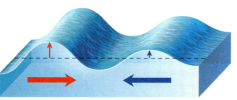

① Two waves approach each other. The wave on the left has a higher amplitude.

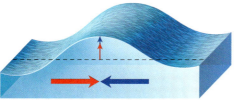

② The crest's new amplitude is the sum of the amplitudes of the original crests.

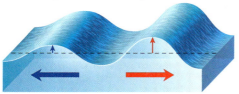

③ The waves continue as if they had not met.

Destructive Interference

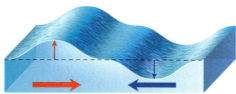

① Two waves approach each other. The waves have equal amplitudes.

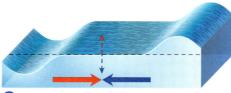

② A crest meets a trough. In the area of overlap, the waves cancel completely.

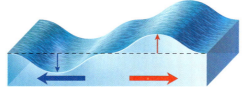

③ The waves continue as if they had not met.

Chapter 1 0 ◆ 21

 Build Inquiry L2

Observing Interference

Materials 1–2 m of rope
Time 15 minutes

Focus Remind students that interference occurs when two waves meet.

Teach Have pairs of students create interference by sending a single pulse through a rope from both ends. First, have both students send upright waves. Then, have one of the students send an inverted wave. Remind students that constructive interference occurs when two crests meet and destructive interference occurs when a crest meets a trough.

Apply Ask: **How is the amplitude of waves affected by constructive interference?** *(It increases.)* **By destructive interference?** *(It decreases.)* **learning modality: kinesthetic**

Go Online
active art

For: Wave Interference activity
Visit: PHSchool.com
Web Code: cgp-5013

Students can investigate the wave interference active art online.

All in ▼ **Teaching Resources**
• Transparency O11

Differentiated Instruction

English Learners/Beginning L1
Vocabulary: Word Analysis On the board, write *constructive* and *destructive* and draw vertical lines to separate *con-* and *de-* from *-struct*. Say that *-struct* means "building," *con-* means "together," and *de-* means "do the opposite." Ask: **What does constructive mean?** *(Building together)* **Destructive?** *(Doing the opposite of building)* **learning modality: verbal**

English Learners/Intermediate L2
Comprehension: Use Visuals Have students identify similarities and differences between the two types of interference shown in Figure 10. Then, based on their observations, have them make a table comparing and contrasting the two types of interference. **learning modality: visual**

Monitor Progress L2

Writing Tell students to describe constructive and destructive interference between waves of different amplitudes.

Answers
Figure 10 The black dotted line represents the rest position of the wave.

✓ **Reading Checkpoint** Constructive interference is interference that occurs when waves combine to make a wave with a larger amplitude.

O ● 21

Standing Waves

FIGURE 11
Standing Waves
These photos show standing waves in vibrating elastic strings. The photographer used a bright flashing light called a strobe to "stop" the motion.

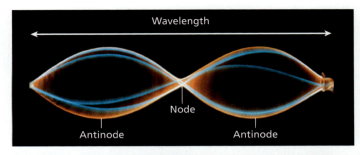

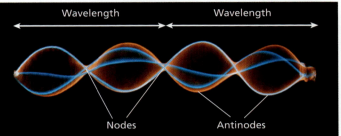

Teach Key Concepts `L2`

Understanding Standing Waves

Focus Say that a standing wave is a wave that appears to stand in one place. Explain that this is due to wave both constructive and destructive interference.

Teach On the board, write *Destructive Interference, Nodes, Constructive Interference, Antinodes.* Link the first two terms with an arrow. Explain that destructive interference causes nodes, which are points of zero amplitude. Then, link the second two terms with an arrow. Explain that constructive interference causes antinodes, which are points of maximum amplitude. State that nodes are like the troughs of a transverse wave and antinodes are like the crests of a transverse wave.

Apply Remind students that crests have more energy than troughs. Then, ask: **Which parts of a standing wave have more energy, nodes or antinodes?** *(Antinodes)* **learning modality: visual**

Teacher **Demo**

Observing Resonance `L2`

Materials thin crystal drinking glass, water

Time 10 minutes

Focus Tell students that objects have a natural frequency of vibration. When external vibrations match an object's natural frequency, it results in resonance, or an increase in the amplitude of standing waves.

Teach Wet your index finger with water and begin to move your finger around the rim of the glass. Increase the speed of your finger until the glass begins to "hum."

Apply Ask: **What causes the glass to hum?** *(Resonance caused by your finger moving at the same frequency as the natural frequency of the glass)* **learning modality: visual**

All in One Teaching Resources

• Transparency O12

Try This **Activity**

Interfering Waves

1. Place two identical empty bottles near each other. Using a straw, blow gently across the top of one bottle until you hear a sound. Describe the sound.
2. Using two straws, blow across the tops of both bottles at the same time. Describe what you hear.
3. Add a few drops of water to one bottle. Blow across the top of each bottle and note any differences in the sound.
4. Using two straws, blow across the tops of both bottles at the same time.

Observing Describe the sound you heard in Step 4. How did it differ from the sounds you heard in the other steps?

Standing Waves

If you tie a rope to a doorknob and continuously shake the free end, waves will travel down the rope, reflect at the end, and come back. The reflected waves will meet the incoming waves. When the waves meet, interference occurs.

If the incoming wave and a reflected wave have just the right frequency, they produce a combined wave that appears to be standing still. This combined wave is called a standing wave. A **standing wave** is a wave that appears to stand in one place, even though it is really two waves interfering as they pass through each other.

Nodes and Antinodes In a standing wave, destructive interference produces points with an amplitude of zero, as shown in Figure 11. These points of zero amplitude on a standing wave are called **nodes.** The nodes are always evenly spaced along the wave. At points in the standing wave where constructive interference occurs, the amplitude is greater than zero. The points of maximum amplitude on a standing wave are called **antinodes.** These are also the points of maximum energy on the wave. The antinodes always occur halfway between two nodes.

Try This **Activity**

Skills Focus Observing `L1`

Materials two identical empty bottles, two drinking straws, water

Time 10 minutes

Tip Students may need to practice until they can consistently produce a sound with a straw and bottle.

Expected Outcome When both bottles are empty, there is resonance because the bottles have the same frequency. After water is added to one of the bottles, students hear beats because there is an alternating pattern of constructive and destructive interference due to the higher frequency of the bottle with added water.

Extend Have students add water to the empty bottle until there is resonance at the higher frequency. **learning modality: kinesthetic**

Resonance Have you ever pushed a child on a swing? At first, it is difficult to push the swing. But once you get it going, you need only push gently to keep it going. This is because the swing has a natural frequency. Even small pushes that are in rhythm with the swing's natural frequency produce large increases in the swing's amplitude.

Most objects have at least one natural frequency of vibration. Standing waves occur in an object when it vibrates at a natural frequency. If a nearby object vibrates at the same frequency, it can cause resonance. **Resonance** is an increase in the amplitude of a vibration that occurs when external vibrations match an object's natural frequency.

Resonance can be useful. For example, musical instruments use resonance to produce stronger, clearer sounds. But sometimes resonance can be harmful. Figure 12 shows Mexico City after an earthquake in 1985. Mexico City is built on a layer of clay. The frequency of the earthquake waves matched the natural frequency of the clay, so resonance occurred. City buildings 8 to 18 stories high had the same natural frequency. Due to resonance, these buildings had the most damage. Both shorter and taller buildings were left standing because their natural frequency did not match the natural frequency of the clay.

 Reading Checkpoint How can resonance be useful?

FIGURE 12
Destructive Power of Resonance
In the 1985 earthquake in Mexico City, resonance caused the greatest damage to buildings between 8 and 18 stories tall.
Inferring Why did taller buildings survive the earthquake?

Section 3 Assessment

Target Reading Skill **Asking Questions** Use the answers to the questions you wrote about the headings to help you answer the questions below.

Reviewing Key Concepts

1. **a. Listing** What are three ways that waves change direction?
   b. Summarizing How does a wave change direction when it bounces off a surface?
   c. Relating Cause and Effect How does a change in speed cause a wave to change direction?
2. **a. Identifying** What are two types of interference?
   b. Interpreting Diagrams Look at Figure 10. What determines the amplitude of the wave produced by interference?

   c. Predicting Wave A has the same amplitude as wave B. What will happen when a crest of wave A meets a trough of wave B? Explain.
3. **a. Defining** What is a standing wave?
   b. Explaining How do nodes and antinodes form in a standing wave?

Lab zone **At-Home Activity**

Waves in a Sink With your parent's permission, fill the kitchen sink with water to a depth of about 10 cm. Dip your finger into the water repeatedly to make waves. Demonstrate reflection, diffraction, and interference for your family members.

Lab zone **At-Home Activity**

Waves in a Sink **L2** Suggest that students first use a floating cork to show the difference between the wave and the medium. Also, suggest that they describe each wave interaction before demonstrating it to family members. Allow a few students to show the class how they demonstrated wave interactions at home.

Monitor Progress **L2**

Answers
Figure 12 Taller buildings survived the earthquake because their natural frequency did not match the natural frequency of the clay and resonance did not occur.

✓ **Reading Checkpoint** Resonance can produce stronger, clearer sounds in musical instruments.

Assess

Reviewing Key Concepts

1. a. Reflection, refraction, and diffraction **b.** The angle of reflection equals the angle of incidence. **c.** When a wave enters a new medium at an angle, one side of the wave changes speed before the other side, causing the wave to bend.
2. a. Constructive interference and destructive interference **b.** The height of the crest is the sum of the amplitudes of the interfering crests. **c.** The crest and trough will cancel as the waves add their amplitudes at this point.
3. a. A wave that appears to stand in one place, even though it is really two waves interfering as they pass through each other **b.** Destructive interference produces nodes. Constructive interference produces antinodes.

Reteach **L1**

Write the words *reflection* and *refraction* on the board. Call on students to explain how each process changes light waves. Call on other students to correct any errors.

Performance Assessment **L2**
Writing Have students write a paragraph comparing and contrasting constructive and destructive interference.
Students can save their paragraphs in their portfolios. **Portfolio**

All in One Teaching Resources
• Section Summary: *Interactions of Waves*
• Review and Reinforcement: *Interactions of Waves*
• Enrich: *Interactions of Waves*

Skills Lab

Making Waves   L2

Prepare for Inquiry

Skills Objectives
After this lab, students will be able to
- model wave behavior
- observe waves under varying conditions
- control variables to produce waves with different properties
- interpret data and draw conclusions about wave behavior

Prep Time 30 minutes

Class Time 40 minutes

Advance Planning
Prepare the ripple tanks and have the other materials available.

Safety
Tell students to clean up all spills immediately and to be careful handling wet mirrors. Review the safety guidelines in Appendix A.

All in One Teaching Resources
- Lab Worksheet: *Making Waves*

Guide Inquiry

Invitation
Show a video of ocean waves or have students discuss waves they have seen. Ask them to describe the size of the waves and what happened when the waves met.

Introduce the Procedure
Tell students they will observe waves they make in a ripple tank. Show them a ripple tank filled with water and demonstrate how to generate waves. Call their attention to the reflection of the waves that they can see in the mirror on the bottom of the tank.

Skills Lab

Making Waves

Problem
How do water waves interact with each other and with solid objects in their paths?

Skills Focus
observing, making models

Materials
- water
- plastic dropper
- metric ruler
- paper towels
- modeling clay
- cork or other small floating object
- ripple tank (aluminum foil lasagna pan with mirror at the bottom)

Procedure
1. Fill the pan with water to a depth of 1.5 cm. Let the water come to rest. Make a data table like the one shown in your text.
2. Fill a plastic dropper with water. Then release a drop of water from a height of about 10 cm above the center of the ripple tank. Observe the reflection of the waves that form and record your observations.
3. Predict how placing a paper towel across one end of the ripple tank will affect the reflection of the waves. Record your prediction in your notebook.
4. Drape a paper towel across one end of the ripple tank so it hangs in the water. Repeat Step 2, and record your observations of the waves.
5. Remove the paper towel and place a stick of modeling clay in the water near the center of the ripple tank.

Data Table		
Type of Barrier	Observations Without Cork	Observations With Cork

6. From a height of about 10 cm, release a drop of water into the ripple tank halfway between the clay and one of the short walls. Record your observations.
7. Place the clay in a different position so that the waves strike it at an angle. Then repeat Step 6.
8. Place two sticks of clay end-to-end across the width of the tank. Adjust the clay so that there is a gap of about 2 cm between the ends of the two pieces. Repeat Step 6. Now change the angle of the barrier in the tank. Again repeat Step 6, and watch to see if the waves interact with the barrier any differently.

Troubleshooting the Experiment
- Point out the weaker reflected waves so students do not overlook them.
- Make sure students can correctly identify the crests and troughs of the waves.

Expected Outcome
Students can control wave amplitude, frequency, and wavelength by changing the methods they use to produce the waves. Students can also model, observe, and describe different types of wave interactions.

24 ◆ O

9. Cut the two pieces of clay in half. Use the pieces to make a barrier with three 2-cm gaps. Then repeat Step 6.

10. Remove all the clay and add a small floating object, such as a cork, to the water. Then repeat Steps 2–9 with the floating object. Observe and record what happens to the cork in each step.

11. Once you have finished all of the trials, clean and dry your work area.

Analyze and Conclude

1. **Observing** How are the waves affected by the paper towel hanging in the water?

2. **Observing** What happens when the waves strike a barrier head on? When they strike it at an angle?

3. **Observing** What happens when the waves strike a barrier with a gap in it? With three gaps in it?

4. **Making Models** What did the paper towel represent? What did the cork represent?

5. **Applying Concepts** How does the behavior of waves in your model compare to the behavior of waves in a harbor?

6. **Communicating** Evaluate your model. Write a paragraph about the ways your model represents a real situation. Then write a paragraph about your model's limitations.

More to Explore

Predict what would happen if you could send a steady train of uniform waves the length of the ripple tank for an extended time. Use a plastic bottle with a pinhole in the bottom to make a dropper that will help to test your prediction. Get permission from your teacher to try out your dropper device.

Analyze and Conclude

1. The wet paper towel absorbs the wave's energy. Either there is no reflected wave or the reflected wave is much weaker than the original wave.

2. When waves strike a barrier head on, the waves are reflected straight back, meeting the incoming waves and causing interference. When waves strike a barrier at some other angle, the waves are reflected back at the same angle but in the opposite direction.

3. Diffraction occurs when a wave hits a barrier with a gap in it. Part of the wave passes through the gap and spreads throughout the water on the other side of the barrier. The rest of the wave is reflected back from the barrier. When a wave hits a barrier with three gaps, three sections of the incoming wave pass through the barrier, and three small waves spread throughout the water on the other side of the barrier, growing wider and wider.

4. The paper towel represented a shoreline of sand or vegetation, materials that absorb some of the wave's energy. The cork represented an object floating in the water, such as a buoy, boat, or person.

5. The behavior of waves in the model is similar to the behavior of waves in a harbor. The waves in a harbor, however, would have more complex interactions.

6. Answers will vary. Ways the model represents a real situation might include the types of wave interactions. Limitations might include the small size of the water surface and the absence of currents and other water disturbances.

Extend Inquiry

More to Explore Students may predict that standing waves would occur. Sending uniform waves at a regular frequency makes it easier to observe wave properties and interactions. Students can increase the size of the hole in the bottle to produce more frequent waves and observe how this affects other wave properties.

Seismic Waves

Objectives

After completing this lesson, students will be able to

O.1.4.1 Identify the types of seismic waves.

O.1.4.2 Explain how a seismograph works.

Target Reading Skill

Building Vocabulary Explain that knowing the definitions of key-concept words helps students understand what they read.

Answers

Sample answers:

1. A seismic wave is produced by an earthquake.

2. A P wave is a longitudinal seismic wave.

3. An S wave is a transverse seismic wave.

4. A surface wave is a combination of a longitudinal wave and a transverse wave that travels along the surface of a medium.

5. A tsunami is a huge surface wave on the ocean caused by an underwater earthquake.

6. A seismograph is an instrument used to detect and measure earthquake waves.

Preteach

Build Background Knowledge `L2`

Viewing Earthquake Damage

Show students a video clip or photograph that depicts damage caused by an earthquake. Ask: **What causes the buildings and roads to break apart and collapse?** *(Sample answer: Vibrations of Earth's surface)* Tell students they will learn more about the vibrations caused by earthquakes in this section.

For: Links on seismic waves
Visit: www.SciLinks.org
Web Code: scn-1514

Download a worksheet that will guide students' review of Internet resources on seismic waves.

Reading Preview

Key Concepts

- What are the types of seismic waves?
- How does a seismograph work?

Key Terms

- seismic wave • P wave
- S wave • surface wave
- tsunami • seismograph

Target Reading Skill

Building Vocabulary Using a word in a sentence helps you think about how to best explain the word. As you read, carefully note the definition of each Key Term. Also note other details in the paragraph that contains the definition. Use all this information to write a sentence using the Key Term.

Earthquake damage in Chile in 1960 ▼

Lab zone Discover Activity

Can You Find the Sand?

1. Fill a plastic film canister with sand and replace the lid.
2. Place the canister on a table with four identical but empty canisters. Mix them around so that a classmate does not know which canister is which.
3. With your fist, pound on the table a few times. Ask your classmate which canister contains the sand.
4. Then stick each canister to the table with some modeling clay. Pound on the table again. Can your classmate tell which canister contains sand?

Think It Over

Inferring Pounding on a table makes waves. Why might the canister with sand respond differently from the empty canisters?

On May 22, 1960, a massive earthquake occurred under the Pacific Ocean about 120 km west of Chile. Traveling underground faster than the speed of sound, earthquake waves hit the coast in less than a minute. Buildings were demolished as the waves shook the ground. But the destruction wasn't finished. The earthquake sent water waves speeding toward the shore at almost 700 km/h. When the waves struck the shore, floods and mudslides killed many people who had survived the first wave of damage. For several more days, earthquakes occurred again and again. All told, thousands of people died and more than 2 million people in Chile were left homeless.

26 ◆ O

Lab zone Discover Activity

Skills Focus Inferring `L2`

Materials 5 empty plastic film canisters, sand, modeling clay

Time 10 minutes

Tip Remind students to tightly fasten the lid on the canister of sand.

Expected Outcome When the canisters are not stuck to the table with clay, the canister of sand moves less than the other canisters as the table is pounded. When the canisters are stuck to the table with clay, none of the canisters moves as the table is pounded.

Think It Over The canister that contains the sand is heavier, so it requires more energy to move than the empty canisters.

FIGURE 13
Seismic Waves
Seismic waves include P waves, S waves, and surface waves. **Interpreting Diagrams** *Which kind of seismic wave travels through Earth's core?*

Earthquake

Key
→ P waves
→ S waves
→ Surface waves

Core

Liquid outer core

Types of Seismic Waves

An earthquake occurs when rock beneath Earth's surface moves. This rock moves because forces deep inside Earth create stress or pressure in the rock. When the pressure in the rock builds up enough, the rock breaks or changes shape, releasing energy in the form of waves. The waves produced by earthquakes are called **seismic waves.** (The word seismic comes from the Greek word *seismos,* which means "earthquake.")

Seismic waves ripple out in all directions from the point where the earthquake occurred. As the waves move, they carry energy through Earth. The waves can travel from one side of Earth to the other. **Seismic waves include P waves, S waves, and surface waves.** Figure 13 shows how each kind of wave travels through Earth.

P Waves Some seismic waves are longitudinal waves. Longitudinal seismic waves are known as **P waves,** or primary waves. They are called primary waves because they move faster than other seismic waves and so arrive at distant points before other seismic waves. P waves are made up of compressions and rarefactions of rock inside Earth. These waves compress and expand the ground like a spring toy as they move through it.

S Waves Other seismic waves are transverse waves with crests and troughs. Transverse seismic waves are known as **S waves,** or secondary waves. S waves shake the ground up and down and side to side as they move through it. They cannot travel through liquids. Because part of Earth's core is liquid, S waves do not travel directly through Earth like P waves. Therefore, S waves cannot be detected on the side of Earth opposite an earthquake. Scientists on the side of Earth opposite the earthquake detect mainly P waves.

Characteristics of Waves

Video Preview
▶ Video Field Trip
Video Assessment

Go **O**nline
SciLINKS NSTA

For: Links on seismic waves
Visit: www.SciLinks.org
Web Code: scn-1514

Chapter 1 O ◆ 27

Instruct

Types of Seismic Waves

Teach Key Concepts [L2]

P Waves, S Waves, and Surface Waves

Focus Introduce seismic waves as waves in the ground that are caused by earthquakes.

Teach Write the three types of seismic waves on the board. Explain that both P waves and S waves penetrate inside Earth but surface waves just travel on the surface.

Apply Ask: **Are seismic waves mechanical or electromagnetic?** *(Mechanical; they travel through a medium.)* **learning modality: verbal**

All in One Teaching Resources
Transparency O13

Video Field Trip

Characteristics of Waves

Show the Video Field Trip to let students experience tsunamis and understand wave characteristics. Discussion question: **How does the wavelength of a tsunami compare with the wavelength of regular ocean waves?** *(The wavelength of a tsunami is much greater. Regular ocean waves usually have wavelengths between 40 and 400 m long; tsunamis typically have wavelengths between 100 and 700 km long.)*

Independent Practice [L2]

All in One Teaching Resources

• Guided Reading and Study Worksheet: *Seismic Waves*

 Student Edition on Audio CD

Monitor Progress [L2]

Writing Have students describe the three types of seismic waves.

Answer
Figure 13 P waves travel through Earth's core.

Differentiated Instruction

Less Proficient Readers [L1]
Classifying Seismic Waves Have students read about P waves and S waves, focusing on their similarities and differences. Then, help students create a Venn diagram showing at least one similarity and one difference. *(Sample answer: Both are seismic waves; P waves are longitudinal, S waves are transverse.)* **learning modality: visual**

Special Needs [L1]
Modeling P Waves and S Waves Relate P waves and S waves to waves with which students are already familiar. Explain that P waves are longitudinal, like the waves that travel through a spring toy, and S waves are transverse, like the waves that travel through a rope. **learning modality: verbal**

Math ▶ Analyzing Data

Math Skill Making and interpreting graphs

Focus Remind students that a tsunami is a huge ocean wave that may be caused by an underwater earthquake.

Teach Explain that a tsunami can be detected by ocean buoys. Point out that the graph plots the time at which the tsunami's first waves arrive at each distance from the epicenter.

Answers
1. Distance and time
2. In 2 hours, the tsunami travels 1,500 km; in 4 hours, it travels 3,000 km.
3. 7 hours

Help Students Read   L1
Using Prior Knowledge Before students read about surface waves, tell them that surface waves are a combination of P waves and S waves that have reached the surface. Remind students that P waves are longitudinal and S waves are transverse. Help them recall the movement of transverse and longitudinal waves. Then, have them predict how surface waves move.

🚩 Address Misconceptions   L1
Tsunamis: Waves or Tides?

Focus Tsunamis are sometimes referred to as tidal waves and may be confused with tides.

Teach Tell students that tsunamis are waves, not tides. Explain that tides are the alternate rising and falling of the ocean surface that occur everyday around the world due to the gravitational pull of the sun and moon. Tsunamis, on the other hand, are huge waves that occasionally occur because of ocean disturbances, such as earthquakes on the ocean floor.

Apply Ask: **Are tides periodic events? Why or why not?** *(Yes, because they keep occurring at regular intervals)* **learning modality: verbal**

Math ▶ Analyzing Data

Motion of a Tsunami
This graph shows the rate at which a tsunami moves across the Pacific Ocean. Use the data plotted on the graph to answer the following questions.

1. **Reading Graphs** What two variables are plotted on the graph?
2. **Interpreting Data** How far does the tsunami travel in two hours? In four hours?
3. **Predicting** Easter Island is 3,700 kilometers from the earthquake. How many hours would it take the tsunami to reach Easter Island?

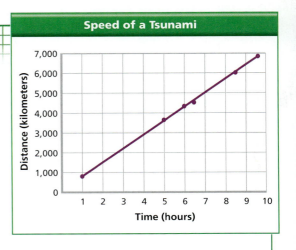

FIGURE 14
This map shows the progress of the 1960 tsunami caused by an earthquake in Chile. **Classifying** *What type of wave interference—constructive or destructive—causes tsunamis?*

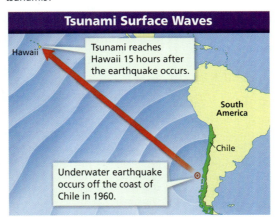

Surface Waves When P waves and S waves reach Earth's surface, they can create surface waves. A **surface wave** is a combination of a longitudinal wave and a transverse wave that travels along the surface of a medium. Surface waves produced by earthquakes move more slowly than P waves and S waves. However, they can cause the most severe ground movements. They combine up-and-down and side-to-side motions, making the ground roll like ocean waves.

Earthquakes that occur underwater, like the one off the coast of Chile in 1960, can produce huge surface waves on the ocean called **tsunamis** (tsoo NAH meez). Tsunamis come in all sizes, from 2 centimeters to 20 meters tall. They can travel thousands of kilometers across the ocean. In the deep ocean, the larger waves are only about 1 meter high. But as they near land, tsunamis slow down in the shallow water. The waves in the back catch up with those in the front and pile on top. Tsunamis caused by the 1960 earthquake in Chile traveled 10,000 kilometers across the Pacific Ocean to Hawaii. The waves that crashed over the coast in Hilo, Hawaii, were almost 11 meters high. The tsunamis killed 61 people and caused about $75 million dollars in home and property damage.

 How are tsunamis produced?

Detecting Seismic Waves

To detect and measure earthquake waves, scientists use instruments called **seismographs** (SYZ muh grafs). **A seismograph records the ground movements caused by seismic waves as they move through Earth.**

The frame of the seismograph is attached to the ground, so the frame shakes when seismic waves arrive. Seismographs used to have pens attached to the frame that made wiggly lines on a roll of paper as the ground shook. Now scientists use electronic seismographs to record data about Earth's motion.

Because P waves travel through Earth faster than S waves, P waves arrive at seismographs before S waves. By measuring the time between the arrival of the P waves and the arrival of the S waves, scientists can tell how far away the earthquake was. By comparing readings from at least three seismographs located at different places on Earth, scientists can tell where the earthquake occurred.

To find oil, water, and other valuable resources, geologists set off explosives at Earth's surface. Seismic waves from the explosions reflect from structures under the ground. Geologists then use seismograph data to locate the underground resources.

FIGURE 15
Seismologist Studying Data
A scientist studies the arrival time of seismic waves on the printout from a seismograph.

Section 4 Assessment

🌀 **Target Reading Skill** **Building Vocabulary** Use your sentences about seismic waves to help you answer the questions below.

Reviewing Key Concepts

1. a. Identifying What are three types of seismic waves?
b. Classifying Which seismic waves are transverse waves? Which are longitudinal waves?
c. Comparing and Contrasting Why do seismic waves that travel along Earth's surface cause more damage than other seismic waves?
2. a. Defining What is a seismograph?
b. Explaining How does a seismograph work?

c. Interpreting Data S waves arrive in Los Angeles 3 minutes after P waves. In Dallas, S waves arrive 1 minute after P waves. Which city is closer to the earthquake? Explain your answer.

Lab zone At-Home **Activity**

Sounds Solid Explore how waves travel through different solids. Have a family member or friend tap one end of a table with a spoon. Now put your ear to the table and listen again. What difference do you notice? Repeat the tapping on various surfaces around your home. What observations have you made?

Lab zone At-Home **Activity**

Sounds Solid L1 Suggest that students gently tap a variety of surfaces, such as wood, glass, and metal. They can record their observations in a table and share them with the class. (*The tapping sounds louder with your ear on the surface. The sound is loudest through metal, less loud through glass, and least loud through wood.*)

Detecting Seismic Waves

Teach Key Concepts   L2
Seismographs

Focus State that seismic waves are detected with seismographs.

Teach Have students imagine trying to draw a straight line while riding on a bumpy road. Say that seismographs react to seismic waves in a similar way.

Apply Ask: **How do you think a high-amplitude seismic wave would affect a seismograph?** (*It would cause a spike in the line.*) **learning modality: verbal**

Monitor Progress _____   L2

Answers
Figure 15 Tsunamis are caused by constructive interference.

 Reading Checkpoint   Tsunamis are produced by underwater earthquakes.

Assess

Reviewing Key Concepts

1. a. P waves, S waves, and surface waves
b. S waves are transverse waves, and P waves are longitudinal waves. **c.** Surface waves combine up-and-down and side-to-side motions, making the ground roll.
2. a. An instrument used to detect and measure earthquake waves **b.** Its frame is attached to the ground, so it shakes when seismic waves arrive. The vibrations are recorded electronically or by a pen that vibrates on paper. **c.** Dallas is closer. The closer you are to the source of the waves, the shorter the delay in arrival time of S waves after P waves.

Reteach   L1

Ask students to list properties of each type of seismic wave.

Performance Assessment   L2
Skills Check Have students create a concept map of seismic waves.

All in One Teaching Resources

• Section Summary: *Seismic Waves*
• Review and Reinforcement: *Seismic Waves*
• Enrich: *Seismic Waves*

Interactive Textbook

- Complete student edition
- Section and chapter self-assessments
- Assessment reports for teachers

Help Students Read
Building Vocabulary

Words in Context Choose several key terms from the chapter. For each term, have students write a sentence that uses the term correctly. *(Example: Vibration: A wave is caused by a vibration.)*

Word/Part Analysis Tell students that the words *compression* and *rarefaction* are the noun forms of the verbs *compress* and *rarefy*. Explain that many verbs can be changed to nouns by adding *-ion*. For example, the verbs *act* and *satisfy* can be changed to the nouns *action* and *satisfaction*. Say that compress means "to squeeze together" and rarefy means "to spread apart." Ask: **In the context of waves, what does compression mean?** *(Part of a longitudinal wave where the medium is squeezed together)* **Rarefaction?** *(Part of a longitudinal wave where the medium is spread apart)*

Connecting Concepts
Concept Maps Help students develop one way to show how the information in this chapter is related. Waves, including seismic waves, exhibit properties such as amplitude and interact in processes such as reflection. Have students brainstorm to identify the key concepts, key terms, details, and examples. Then, write each one on a self-sticking note and attach it at random on chart paper or on the board.

Tell students that this concept map will be organized in hierarchical order and to begin at the top with the key concepts. Ask students these questions to guide them in categorizing the information on the self-sticking notes: **What are the properties of waves? How do waves interact?**

① What Are Waves?
Key Concepts
- Mechanical waves are produced when a source of energy causes a medium to vibrate.
- Mechanical waves are classified by how they move. There are two types of mechanical waves: transverse waves and longitudinal waves.

Key Terms
wave
energy
medium
mechanical wave
vibration
transverse wave

crest
trough
longitudinal wave
compression
rarefaction

② Properties of Waves
Key Concepts
- The basic properties of waves are amplitude, wavelength, frequency, and speed.
- The speed, wavelength, and frequency of a wave are related to one another by a mathematical formula:

$$\text{Speed} = \text{Wavelength} \times \text{Frequency}$$

Key Terms
amplitude
wavelength
frequency
hertz (Hz)

③ Interactions of Waves
Key Concepts
- When an object or a wave hits a surface through which it cannot pass, it bounces back.
- When a wave enters a new medium at an angle, one side of the wave changes speed before the other side, causing the wave to bend.
- When a wave moves around a barrier or through an opening in a barrier, it bends and spreads out.
- There are two types of interference: constructive and destructive.
- If the incoming wave and a reflected wave have just the right frequency, they produce a combined wave that appears to be standing still.

Key Terms
reflection
law of reflection
refraction
diffraction
interference
constructive interference
destructive interference
standing wave
node
antinode
resonance

④ Seismic Waves
Key Concepts
- Seismic waves include P waves, S waves, and surface waves.
- A seismograph records the ground movements caused by seismic waves as they move through Earth.

Key Terms
seismic wave
P wave
S wave
surface wave
tsunami
seismograph

30 ◆ O

Prompt students by using connecting words or phrases, such as "are caused by," "can be," "are characterized by," and "include," to indicate the basis for the organization of the map. The phrases should form a sentence between or among a set of concepts.

Answer Accept logical presentations by students.

All in One Teaching Resources
- Key Terms Review: *Characteristics of Waves*
- Connecting Concepts: *Characteristics of Waves*

Review and Assessment

Organizing Information

Concept Mapping Copy the concept map about waves onto a sheet of paper. Then complete it and add a title. (For more on Concept Mapping, see the Skills Handbook.)

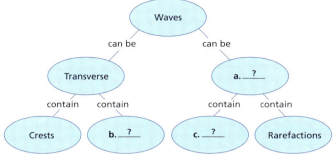

Waves

can be / can be

Transverse — a. ___?___

contain — contain | contain — contain

Crests — b. ___?___ | c. ___?___ — Rarefactions

Reviewing Key Terms

Choose the letter of the best answer.

1. A wave transfers
   a. energy.   b. particles.
   c. water.   d. air.

2. A wave that moves the medium in the same direction that the wave travels is a
   a. transverse wave.   b. longitudinal wave.
   c. standing wave.   d. mechanical wave.

3. The distance between one crest and the next crest is the wave's
   a. amplitude.   b. wavelength.
   c. frequency.   d. speed.

4. The number of complete waves that pass a point in a certain amount of time is a wave's
   a. amplitude.   b. frequency.
   c. wavelength.   d. speed.

5. The bending of a wave due to a change in its speed is
   a. interference.   b. reflection.
   c. diffraction.   d. refraction.

6. The interaction between waves that meet is
   a. reflection.   b. diffraction.
   c. refraction.   d. interference.

7. A point of zero amplitude on a standing wave is called a
   a. crest.   b. node.
   c. trough.   d. antinode.

8. Seismic waves that do not travel through liquids are
   a. P waves.   b. surface waves.
   c. S waves.   d. tsunamis.

Writing in Science

Research Report Write an article for a boating magazine about tsunamis. Include details about what causes them and why they are dangerous. Explain what is being done to help reduce damage from tsunamis.

Discovery CHANNEL SCHOOL

Characteristics of Waves
Video Preview
Video Field Trip
▶ Video Assessment

Chapter 1 0 ◆ 31

Review and Assessment

Organizing Information
a. Longitudinal
b. Troughs
c. Compressions

Reviewing Key Terms
1. a **2.** b **3.** b **4.** b **5.** d **6.** d
7. b **8.** c

Writing in Science

Writing Mode Interview
Scoring Rubric
4 Exceeds criteria; includes five or more significant questions answered with vivid, first-person descriptions that show an in-depth understanding of tsunamis
3 Meets criteria
2 Includes some irrelevant questions and/or the answers are too general or contain errors
1 Includes only a vague description and/or fails to show an understanding of tsunamis

Discovery CHANNEL SCHOOL
Video Assessment

Characteristics of Waves

Show the Video Assessment to review chapter content and as a prompt for the writing assignment. Discussion questions: **How are tsunami waves formed?** *(Tsunamis are enormous waves caused by the energy released during underwater or coastal earthquakes, volcanoes, or landslides.)* **In what ways are tsunami waves the same as typical ocean waves?** *(Like typical ocean waves, tsunami waves are made of a series of crests and troughs.)*

Go Online
PHSchool.com
For: Self-assessment
Visit: PHSchool.com
Web Code: cfa-5010

Students can take a practice test online that is automatically scored.

All in One Teaching Resources

- Transparency O14
- Chapter Test
- Performance Assessment Teacher Notes
- Performance Assessment Student Worksheet
- Performance Assessment Scoring Rubric

ExamView® Computer Test Bank CD-ROM

Checking Concepts

9. Transverse waves move the medium at a right angle to the wave direction, whereas longitudinal waves move the medium parallel to the wave direction. Diagrams should show the direction of the wave and the motion of particles in the medium. They could also include labels for crests, troughs, compressions, rarefactions, wavelength, and amplitude.

10. Measure from the rest position up to a crest or from the rest position down to a trough.

11. Measure the time it takes for a wave crest to travel a measured distance. Then, divide the distance by the time.

12. The angle of incidence is the same as the angle of reflection, or 55°.

13. In diffraction around a barrier, the wave bends toward the barrier. In diffraction through an opening, the wave bends outward and spreads out.

14. S waves do not travel through Earth's liquid outer core, so these waves are not detected on the side of Earth opposite from the earthquake.

Math Practice

15. Students should draw and label a right angle between the direction the wave moves and the direction particles of the medium move.

16. Speed = 0.1 m × 20 Hz = 2 m/s

17. Wavelength = 330 m/s ÷ 660 Hz = 0.5 m

Thinking Critically

18. The water just moves up and down from its rest position, so it does not move across the lake with the wave.

19. a. Wave A **b.** Wave B **c.** Wave A

20. Diagrams should show a crest that is 1.5 times higher than the crest of the taller original wave. The result is due to constructive interference, in which the amplitudes of the two waves add together.

21. The stiff wheel travels more slowly than the wheel on the other side, so the shopping cart will follow a curved path, similar to a wave that changes speed when it enters a new medium at an angle.

Checking Concepts

9. Explain the difference between transverse and longitudinal waves. Use diagrams to illustrate your explanation.

10. How can you measure the amplitude of a transverse wave?

11. Describe how to measure the speed of a wave.

12. What is the angle of incidence if a reflected wave bounces off a mirror with an angle of reflection equal to 55°?

13. Describe the two types of diffraction.

14. Explain why S waves cannot be detected everywhere on Earth after an earthquake.

Math Practice

15. Angles Label a 90° angle on a transverse wave.

16. Calculating Speed A wave in a spring has a wavelength of 0.1 m and a frequency of 20 Hz. What is the wave's speed?

17. Calculating Wavelength A sound wave has a frequency of 660 Hz and its speed is 330 m/s. What is its wavelength?

Thinking Critically

18. Applying Concepts Suppose ripples move from one side of a lake to the other. Does the water move across the lake? Explain.

19. Comparing and Contrasting The waves shown below travel at the same speed.
a. Which wave has the higher frequency?
b. Which has the longer wavelength?
c. Which has the greater amplitude?

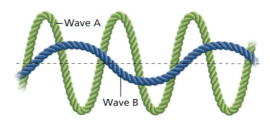
—Wave A
Wave B

32 ◆ O

20. Predicting One wave has an amplitude of 2m, and a second wave has an amplitude of 1m. At a given time, crests from each wave meet. Draw a diagram and describe the result.

21. Making Models If you push a shopping cart that has a stiff or damaged wheel, it is difficult to steer the cart in a straight line. Explain how this is similar to refraction of a wave as it enters a new medium.

Applying Skills

Use the illustration below to answer Questions 22–25.

The wave in the illustration is a giant ocean wave produced by an underwater earthquake.

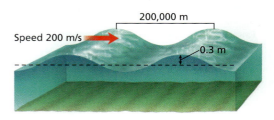
200,000 m
Speed 200 m/s
0.3 m

22. Classifying What kind of wave is shown in the diagram?

23. Interpreting Diagrams What is the amplitude of the wave? What is its speed?

24. Calculating Find the frequency of the wave.

25. Calculating How long would it take this wave to travel 5,000 km?

Lab zone Chapter **Project**

Performance Assessment Share your examples of periodic motion with your classmates. On your display, highlight the repeating patterns and the frequency of each example. Point out interesting connections. For example, track-and-field practice involves repetitions, as do other sports. Which examples involve waves moving through a medium?

Lab zone Chapter **Project**   L3

Performance Assessment In their presentations, be sure that students classify any waves as transverse, longitudinal, or surface waves. Also, be sure that they identify the mediums. After all the presentations, have students compare their observations and discuss their findings.

Standardized Test Prep

Choose the letter of the best answer.

1. The speed of a wave in a spring is 3 m/s. If the wavelength is 0.1 m, what is the frequency?
  A 30 Hz
  B 0.3 Hz
  C 30 m/s
  D 0.3 m/s

2. A wave enters a new medium. The wave
  F slows down and bends.
  G speeds up and bends.
  H may slow down or speed up.
  J must always bend.

3. During a storm, a TV reporter says that the ocean waves are 3 meters high. This reported distance equals the distance
  A from one crest to the next crest.
  B from one trough to the next trough.
  C from a crest to a trough.
  D from a crest to the level of calm water.

4. Two waves move in opposite directions as shown in the diagram below. What will be the height of the crest produced when the crests from each wave meet?
  F 20 cm
  G 35 cm
  H 15 cm
  J 5 cm

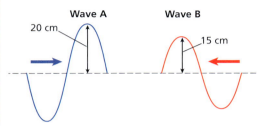

5. In an experiment, you and a friend stand at opposite ends of a football field. Your friend pops an inflated balloon while you observe. Which of the following is a testable hypothesis?
  A If sound travels much faster than light, you will hear the balloon pop before you see it pop.
  B If light travels much faster than sound, you will see the balloon pop before you hear it.
  C If sound and light travel at the same speed, you will see and hear the balloon pop at the same time.
  D all of the above

Constructed Response

6. A large rock is tossed into a pond to produce a water wave. Explain how you know that the wave transfers energy but not matter across the pond.

Applying Skills
22. Tsunami
23. Amplitude is 0.3 m. Speed is 200 m/s.
24. Frequency $= \dfrac{Speed}{Wavelength}$

200 m/s ÷ 200,000 m = 0.001 Hz

25. Time $= \dfrac{Distance}{Speed}$

5,000,000 m ÷ 200 m/s = 25,000 s (about 7 hr)

Standardized Test Prep

1. A **2.** H **3.** D **4.** G **5.** D
6. Sample answer: I know the wave transfers energy because it can move an object like a duck that is floating in the water. But the wave will not push the duck across the pond, so it does not transfer matter.

Chapter at a Glance

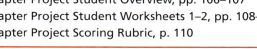 **Chapter Project** *Music to Your Ears*

All in One Teaching Resources

- Chapter Project Teacher Notes, pp. 104–105
- Chapter Project Student Overview, pp. 106–107
- Chapter Project Student Worksheets 1–2, pp. 108–109
- Chapter Project Scoring Rubric, p. 110

PRENTICE HALL
TeacherEXPRESS™
Plan • Teach • Assess

Technology

Local Standards

Section 1

3 periods
1 1/2 blocks

The Nature of Sound

O.2.1.1 Define sound.
O.2.1.2 Explain how sound waves interact.
O.2.1.3 Identify factors that affect the speed of sound.

Go Online
SciLINKS
NSTA

Section 2

3 periods
1 1/2 blocks

Properties of Sound

O.2.2.1 Identify factors that affect the loudness of a sound.
O.2.2.2 State what the pitch of a sound depends on.
O.2.2.3 Explain what causes the Doppler effect.

Go Online
PHSchool.com

Section 3

3 periods
1 1/2 blocks

Music

O.2.3.1 Identify what determines the sound quality of a musical instrument.
O.2.3.2 Name the basic groups of musical instruments.
O.2.3.3 Describe how acoustics is used in concert hall design.

Go Online
active art

Section 4

3 periods
1 1/2 blocks

How You Hear Sound

O.2.4.1 Describe the function of each section of the ear.
O.2.4.2 Identify what causes hearing loss.

Go Online
PHSchool.com

Section 5

2 periods
1 block

Using Sound

O.2.5.1 Explain why some animals use echolocation.
O.2.5.2 State the uses of ultrasound technologies.

Discovery CHANNEL SCHOOL
Video Field Trip

Go Online
PHSchool.com

Review and Assessment

All in One Teaching Resources

- Key Terms Review, p. 150
- Transparency O27
- Performance Assessment Teacher Notes, p. 157
- Performance Assessment Scoring Rubric, p. 158
- Performance Assessment Student Worksheet, p. 159
- Chapter Test, pp. 160–163

Discovery CHANNEL SCHOOL
Video Assessment

Go Online
PHSchool.com

Test Preparation

Test Preparation Blackline Masters

Chapter Activities Planner

For more activities

LAB ZONE Easy Planner CD-ROM

Student Edition	Inquiry	Time	Materials	Skills	Resources
Chapter Project, p. 35	Open-Ended	Ongoing (2–3 weeks)	**All in One** Teaching Resources See page 104	Applying concepts, controlling variables, communicating	Lab zone Easy Planner **All in One** Teaching Resources Support pp. 104–105
Section 1					
Discover Activity, p. 36	Guided	10 minutes	Bowl, water, tuning fork	Observing	**Lab zone Easy Planner**
At-Home Activity, p. 41	Guided	Home		Observing, applying concepts	**Lab zone Easy Planner**
Section 2					
Discover Activity, p. 42	Guided	10 minutes	Wooden board with two nails and guitar string	Forming operational definitions	**Lab zone Easy Planner**
Skills Activity, p. 45	Directed	10 minutes	Drinking straw, scissors	Predicting	**Lab zone Easy Planner**
Try This Activity, p. 46	Directed	10 minutes	Flexible plastic tube or vacuum cleaner hose	Observing	**Lab zone Easy Planner**
At-Home Activity, p. 47	Guided	Home		Observing, applying concepts	**Lab zone Easy Planner**
Section 3					
Discover Activity, p. 48	Guided	15 minutes	2 rubber bands of different thicknesses, 30-cm ruler, pencil	Developing hypotheses	**Lab zone Easy Planner**
Design Your Own Lab, p. 53	Open-Ended	40 minutes	1-L soda bottle, 2-L soda bottle, 250-mL graduated cylinder, metric ruler, straw, water	Developing hypotheses, controlling variables, designing experiments	**Lab zone Easy Planner Lab Activity Video** Design Your Own Lab: *Changing Pitch*, pp. 132–134
Section 4					
Discover Activity, p. 54	Guided	10 minutes		Observing	**Lab zone Easy Planner**
Try This Activity, p. 55	Directed	15 minutes	2 strings about 40 cm long, metal spoon	Inferring	**Lab zone Easy Planner**
At-Home Activity, p. 56	Guided	Home		Comparing and contrasting	**Lab zone Easy Planner**
Technology Lab, p. 57	Guided	40 minutes	Sound source (radio, tape player, or CD player), soundproofing materials, tape measure, scissors, string, pencil, different types of headgear, glue	Designing a solution, evaluating the design	**Lab zone Easy Planner Lab Activity Video** **All in One** Teaching Resources Technology Lab: *Design and Build Hearing Protectors*, pp. 141–142
Section 5					
Discover Activity, p. 60	Guided	10 minutes	Meter stick, masking tape, soft ball, stopwatch	Inferring	**Lab zone Easy Planner**
Skills Activity, p. 62	Directed	15 minutes	Square piece of cardboard, 2 cardboard tubes, metric ruler,	Designing experiments	**Lab zone Easy Planner**

Section 1 The Nature of Sound

 3 periods, 1 1/2 blocks

Objectives

O.2.1.1 Define sound.

O.2.1.2 Explain how sound waves interact.

O.2.1.3 Identify factors that affect the speed of sound.

Key Terms

• echo • elasticity • density

Local Standards

Preteach

Build Background Knowledge

Students use just their hands to make a sound and then explain what caused the sound.

 **Discover Activity** *What Is Sound?* L1

Targeted Print and Technology Resources

All in One Teaching Resources

L2 Reading Strategy Transparency O15: Identifying Main Ideas

⊙ **Presentation-Pro CD-ROM**

Instruct

Sound Waves Guide students in identifying the vibrations that begin particular sounds.

Interactions of Sound Waves Help students apply what they already know about reflection to the reflection of sound.

The Speed of Sound Put the speed of sound in context by comparing it with the speed of light.

Targeted Print and Technology Resources

All in One Teaching Resources

L2 Guided Reading, pp. 113–115

L2 Transparencies O16, O17, O18

www.SciLinks.org Web Code: scn-1521

⊙ **Student Edition on Audio CD**

Assess

Section Assessment Questions

Have students use their completed graphic organizers to answer the questions.

Reteach

Students apply section concepts to answer the riddle that opens the section.

Targeted Print and Technology Resources

All in One Teaching Resources

• Section Summary, p. 112

L1 Review and Reinforce, p. 116

L3 Enrich, p. 117

Section 2 Properties of Sound

3 periods, 1 1/2 blocks

ABILITY LEVELS
L1 Basic to Average
L2 For All Students
L3 Average to Advanced

Objectives

O.2.2.1 Identify factors that affect the loudness of sound.
O.2.2.2 State what the pitch of a sound depends on.
O.2.2.3 Explain what causes the Doppler effect.

Local Standards

Key Terms

• loudness • intensity • decibel (dB) • pitch • ultrasound • infrasound • larynx
• Doppler effect

Preteach

Build Background Knowledge

Students experience loudness, a property of sound, by becoming very quiet and then making a loud noise in unison.

 **Discover Activity** *How Does Amplitude Affect Loudness?* **L2**

Targeted Print and Technology Resources

 Teaching Resources
L2 Reading Strategy Transparency O19: Outlining

O **Presentation-Pro CD-ROM**

Instruct

Loudness Introduce loudness as the perception of the energy in sound by pointing out how loud sounds are associated with more powerful energy sources.

Pitch Explain, and have a volunteer demonstrate, sounds of different pitches.

The Doppler Effect Use Figure 12 to explain the Doppler effect.

Targeted Print and Technology Resources

 **Teaching Resources**
L2 Guided Reading, pp. 120–122
L2 Transparencies O20, O21

PHSchool.com Web Code: cgd-5022

O **Student Edition on Audio CD**

Assess

Section Assessment Questions

Have students use their completed outlines to answer the questions.

Reteach

Students identify key terms based on their definitions.

Targeted Print and Technology Resources

Teaching Resources
• Section Summary, p. 119
L1 Review and Reinforce, p. 123
L3 Enrich, p. 124

Section 3 Music

 3 periods, 1 1/2 blocks

Objectives

O.2.3.1 Identify what determines the sound quality of a musical instrument.

O.2.3.2 Name the basic groups of musical instruments.

O.2.3.3 Describe how acoustics is used in concert hall design.

Local Standards

Key Terms

• music • fundamental tone • overtone • acoustics • reverberation

---

Preteach

Build Background Knowledge

Students demonstrate how the same note at the same volume sounds different on different musical instruments.

 **Discover Activity** *How Can You Change Pitch?* L2

Targeted Print and Technology Resources

All in One Teaching Resources

L2 Reading Strategy Transparency O22: Previewing Visuals

⊙ **Presentation-Pro CD-ROM**

Instruct

Sound Quality Explain how sound quality depends on natural frequencies of vibration, and ask students to identify factors that might account for differences in natural frequencies.

Groups of Musical Instruments Challenge students to name musical instruments, and create a table on the board to classify the instruments in the three groups.

Acoustics Have students apply what they already know about interference to predict how sound might be affected by destructive and constructive interference.

 **Design Your Own Lab** *Changing Pitch* L2

Targeted Print and Technology Resources

All in One Teaching Resources

L2 Guided Reading, pp. 127–129
L2 Transparency O23
L2 Design Your Own Lab: *Changing Pitch*, pp. 132–134

📼 **Lab Activity Video/DVD**
Design Your Own Lab: *Changing Pitch*

PHSchool.com Web Code: cgp-5023

⊙ **Student Edition on Audio CD**

Assess

Section Assessment Questions

Have students use their questions and answers to answer the questions.

Reteach

Students explain how instruments in each of the three groups produce sound.

Targeted Print and Technology Resources

All in One Teaching Resources

• Section Summary, p. 126
L1 Review and Reinforce, p. 130
L3 Enrich, p. 131

Section 4 **How You Hear Sound**

 3 periods, 1 1/2 blocks

ABILITY LEVELS
L1 Basic to Average
L2 For All Students
L3 Average to Advanced

Objectives
O.2.4.1 Describe the function of each section of the ear.
O.2.4.2 Identify what causes hearing loss.

Local Standards

Key Terms
• ear canal • eardrum • cochlea

Preteach

Build Background Knowledge
Students explain how they could better hear a sound across a long distance as an introduction to the function of the outer ear.

 *Where Is the Sound Coming From?* **L1**

Targeted Print and Technology Resources

All in One Teaching Resources
L2 Reading Strategy Transparency
O24: Sequencing

⊙ **Presentation-Pro CD-ROM**

Instruct

The Human Ear Make a table on the board classifying each of the structures of the ear in its correct section of the ear.

Hearing Loss State the causes of hearing loss, and have students identify which causes might be prevented.

 *Design and Build Hearing Protectors* **L2**

Targeted Print and Technology Resources

All in One Teaching Resources
L2 Guided Reading, pp. 137–138
L2 Transparency O25
L2 Technology Lab: *Design and Build Hearing Protectors*, pp. 141–142

📼 **Lab Activity Video/DVD**
Technology Lab: *Design and Build Hearing Protectors*

⊙ **Student Edition on Audio CD**

Assess

Section Assessment Questions
↺ Have students use their completed flowcharts to answer the questions.

Reteach
Students write the name of each structure of the ear on an index card, shuffle the cards, and arrange them in the order sound travels through the ear.

Targeted Print and Technology Resources

All in One Teaching Resources
• Section Summary, p. 136
L1 Review and Reinforce, p. 139
L3 Enrich, p. 140

Section 5 **Using Sound**

 2 periods, 1 block

ABILITY LEVELS
L1 Basic to Average
L2 For All Students
L3 Average to Advanced

Objectives

O.2.5.1 Explain why some animals use echolocation.
O.2.5.2 State the uses of ultrasound technologies.

Local Standards

Key Terms

• echolocation • sonar • sonogram

Preteach

Build Background Knowledge

Students predict when an echo would occur and identify its cause as the reflection of sound waves.

 **Discover Activity** *How Can You Use Time to Measure* **L2** *Distance?*

Targeted Print and Technology Resources

All in One Teaching Resources

L2 Reading Strategy Transparency O26: Comparing and Contrasting

◉ **Presentation-Pro CD-ROM**

Instruct

Echolocation Create a simple diagram to show how sound waves are reflected from an object in echolocation.

Ultrasound Technologies Introduce sonar by comparing and contrasting it with radar, with which students will be more familiar.

Targeted Print and Technology Resources

All in One Teaching Resources

L2 Guided Reading, pp. 145–147

PHSchool.com Web Code: cgd-5025

Video Field Trip

◉ **Student Edition on Audio CD**

Assess

Section Assessment Questions

↪ Have students use their completed compare/contrast tables to answer the questions.

Reteach

Students define each of the key terms.

Targeted Print and Technology Resources

All in One Teaching Resources

• Section Summary, p. 144
L1 Review and Reinforce, p. 148
L3 Enrich, p. 149

Chapter 2 **Content Refresher**

Section 1 **The Nature of Sound**

Speed of Sound The speed of sound waves, like other mechanical waves, is the product of wavelength and frequency. Speed is the same for all sound waves under the same conditions, regardless of differences in wavelength and frequency. For example, the musical note A above middle C has a wavelength of 78 cm and a frequency of 440 Hz. The note A below middle C has a wavelength of 156 cm and a frequency of 220 Hz. The product of wavelength and frequency for both notes is the same: about 34,320 cm/s (343 m/s).

Conditions that affect the speed of sound include the density, elasticity, and temperature of the medium. In mathematical terms, the speed of sound varies inversely as the square root of the medium's density:

$$\text{Speed is proportional to } \frac{1}{\sqrt{\text{Density}}}$$

For example, carbon dioxide is denser than air, so sound travels more slowly in carbon dioxide than in air. On the other hand, helium is less dense than air, so sound travels more quickly in helium.

The relationship between the speed of sound and the elasticity of the medium can also be expressed mathematically. For materials in the same state of matter, speed of sound varies directly as the square root of elasticity:

$$\text{Speed is proportional to } \sqrt{\text{Elasticity}}$$

For example, steel is more elastic than copper, so the speed of sound in steel (about 4,880 m/s) is greater than the speed of sound in copper (about 3,350 m/s).

In gases, temperature affects the speed of sounds because the density of a gas varies with temperature. As temperature decreases, speed of sound decreases.

Help Students Read

Making Inferences

Inferring How Sound Waves Interact

Strategy Making inferences is a science process skill, but it can also be used to support reading comprehension. Before students read about sound waves, challenge them to infer the interactions of sound waves from their general knowledge of waves, based on Chapter 1.

Example

1. Remind students that sound waves are longitudinal mechanical waves that alternately compress and rarefy a medium such as air.

2. Guide students in recalling the ways in which waves interact. Have them describe what happens to waves that strike a barrier they cannot pass through. If students cannot correctly describe the reflection of waves, have them reread the relevant part of Chapter 1.

3. In a similar way, help students recall the other interactions of waves, including refraction, diffraction, and wave interference. For each type of interaction, have students describe what happens to the waves. If students cannot correctly describe the wave interactions, have them reread the relevant parts of Chapter 1.

4. After the class discussion of sound wave interactions, encourage students to draw diagrams illustrating the ways in which sound waves interact. When they read about these interactions in Chapter 2, they can make any necessary corrections in, and add more details to, their drawings.

See Section 1, *The Nature of Sound*, for a script for using the making inferences strategy with students.

Section 2 Properties of Sound

Frequency and Intensity Two important properties of sound waves are frequency and intensity. The frequency of sound waves determines pitch. Sounds with the same pitch can be produced in different ways. For example, some sirens produce sound by blasting air through a rotating gear that interrupts the air stream to cause vibrations. A gear with 44 teeth rotating at 10 revolutions per second causes 440 vibrations per second. This produces a sound with a frequency of 440 Hz. A piano string that produces the musical note A above middle C also vibrates at 440 Hz when it is struck. Thus, the siren and piano illustrate two different ways to produce a note with the same pitch.

Address Misconceptions

Students may think that the frequency of vibrations in a guitar string will increase if they pluck the string faster. For a strategy for overcoming this misconception, see **Address Misconceptions** in Section 2, *Properties of Sound.*

The intensity of a sound determines the loudness of the sound. Intensity can be defined as the average rate of flow of energy per unit area perpendicular to the direction of the sound waves. Mathematically, the intensity of sound varies inversely as the square of the distance from the sound source, or:

$$\text{Intensity is proportional to } \frac{1}{\text{Distance}^2}$$

This relationship between intensity and distance is also shown in the graph. Consider thunder as an example. The sound is four times as intense at a distance of 1 kilometer from the lightning bolt as it is at a distance of 2 kilometers.

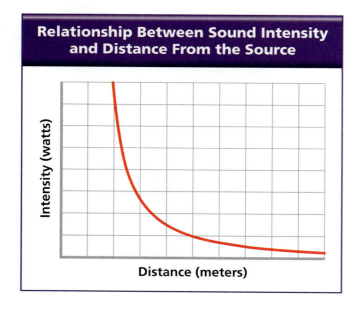

Relationship Between Sound Intensity and Distance From the Source

The inverse-square law is usually just an approximation of how the actual intensity of sound varies with distance from the sound source. This is because physical properties of the air—such as temperature, pressure and humidity—affect how air scatters and dampens sound waves, and these factors also reduce intensity.

Section 3 Music

Music, Speech, and Noise Music, speech, and noise are all types of sounds in which pure tones of a single frequency are seldom heard. Each note in music contains a fundamental tone of a certain frequency, and also higher tones, called overtones, that are multiples of the frequency of the fundamental tone. For example, as shown in the figure, middle C has a frequency of 262 Hz. Its overtones can include notes with frequencies of 524 Hz (1 octave, or eight notes, above middle C), 786 Hz (2 octaves above middle C), and so on. Overtones are also called harmonics of the fundamental tone.

Fundamental Tones and Overtones of Middle C

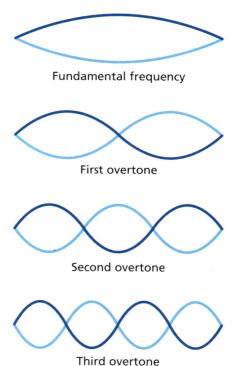

Fundamental frequency

First overtone

Second overtone

Third overtone

Speech, like music, contains a complex mixture of sounds. Only some of the sounds that make up speech are in harmonic relation to one another. As a result, talking does not sound as musical as singing. Noise consists of a mixture of sounds of many different frequencies but few if any harmonics. Like white light, which is a mixture of all different frequencies and colors of light, noise is a mixture of many different frequencies and pitches of sound. Different noises can be distinguished from one another mainly because they have different amplitude, or loudness, at various frequencies. These differences allow you to distinguish between the noise of a lawn mower, for example, and the noise of a chain saw.

Section 4 How You Hear Sound

Noise Pollution and Hearing Noise pollution is a relatively recent problem that developed as much of the world became urban and industrial. If you compare the sound level of different noises, it is easy to see why noise has become such a problem. The sound level of rustling leaves is about 10 decibels, and conversation is generally carried on at about 50 decibels. The noise generated by loud music, on the other hand, is likely to be at least 90 decibels. The decibel levels of some other sounds are shown in the graph. Because decibels are on a logarithmic scale, each ten-point increase in decibel rating reflects a tenfold increase in loudness. Thus, loud music generates noise that is about 10,000 times louder than conversation.

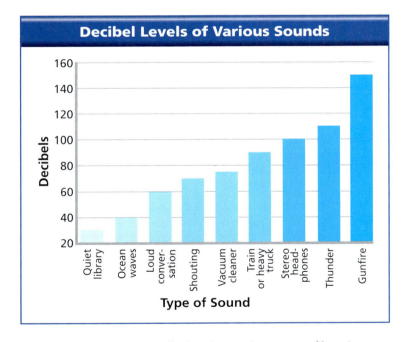

Decibel Levels of Various Sounds

Exposure to noise pollution is a major cause of hearing loss. Repeated loud noises permanently damage the delicate hair cells lining the cochlea, the structure in the inner ear that converts sound waves to electrical impulses that can be interpreted by the brain. Loud noise also contributes to cardiovascular problems and nervous disorders because it is very stressful. Noise pollution harms other animals as well as humans. For example, in Alaska, noise from airplanes reduces the chances that caribou calves will survive. Some scientists also think that increasing noise levels in the oceans may confuse whales and dolphins, some of which use sound waves for navigation and finding food.

Section 5 Using Sound

Echolocation and Ultrasound Imaging Echolocation and ultrasound imaging are two general ways that sound waves can be used. In echolocation, animals produce sounds and then interpret the echoes in order to navigate, avoid obstacles, and find food without relying on vision. Echolocation can be used to determine an object's distance and size and whether it is moving away from or toward the listener. The information from echolocation can be very precise. For example, orca, or killer whales, can use echolocation to distinguish between cod and salmon, and bats can use echolocation to avoid very fine wires in their flight path. Other animals that use echolocation include dolphins, porpoises, some birds, and shrews.

People use echolocation in the technology called sonar. In sonar, echoes from underwater sound waves are interpreted to determine the size and location of underwater objects. This use of sound waves was invented in the early 1900s and has been improved since then. Sonar technology was used in World War I to detect enemy submarines. Today, it is used to measure water depth, map the ocean floor, and track schools of fish.

Echolocation is also the basis of ultrasound imaging. This is a medical technology in which ultrasound waves are reflected off internal body tissues and structures. Information from the reflected waves is converted into detailed computer images of the inside of the body. The images may be photographs or videos. The best known application of ultrasound imaging is viewing a fetus in the womb. It can be used to determine the gender of the fetus and detect medical conditions or problems in development. Ultrasound examination of the heart, which is called echocardiography, can be used to detect heart defects, coronary artery disease, and other heart problems. Ultrasound waves can also be used to break up kidney stones into fragments small enough to pass through the urinary tract and out of the body. This painless procedure allows patients to avoid surgery.

Interactive Textbook
- Complete student edition
- Video and audio
- Simulations and activities
- Section and chapter activities

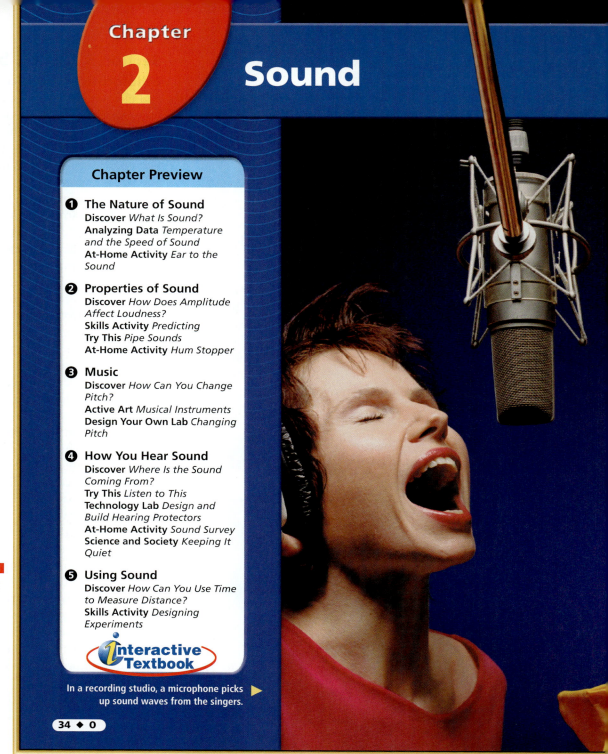

Chapter

2

Sound

Interactive Textbook

In a recording studio, a microphone picks up sound waves from the singers. ▶

34 ◆ O

Lab zone **Chapter Project**

Objectives **L3**

Students will apply what they learn about sound to design, build, and play simple musical instruments. After completing this Chapter Project, students will be able to
- apply chapter concepts to design musical instruments
- control variables as they construct and modify their instruments
- communicate their design and testing processes and perform on their instruments

Skills Focus
Applying concepts, controlling variables, communicating

Project Time Line 2 to 3 weeks

All in One **Teaching Resources**
- Chapter Project Teacher Notes
- Chapter Project Worksheet 1
- Chapter Project Worksheet 2
- Chapter Project Scoring Rubric

Developing a Plan
On the first day of the project, encourage students to describe and compare different types of musical instruments. Have students spend the next few days formulating designs and compiling lists of possible materials. Allow a week for students to design and construct their instruments. Tell students to test and modify their instruments while they learn to play a simple tune. On the final day or two, allow students to perform and present their design/redesign processes.

Possible Materials
Materials for constructing instruments will vary. You may give students a list of suitable materials and have them design instruments using only those materials. Alternatively, you may provide a range of materials from which students can choose or allow students to provide their own materials. Materials might include rubber bands, string, cardboard boxes, boards, nails, sections of plastic pipe, plastic bottles, wooden spoons, and dowels.

- ▶ Video Preview
- Video Field Trip
- Video Assessment

Lab zone™ Chapter **Project**

Music to Your Ears

In this chapter you will investigate the properties of sound. You will learn how sound is produced by different objects, including musical instruments. As you work through the chapter, you will gather enough knowledge to create a musical instrument of your own.

Your Goal To design, build, and play a simple musical instrument

Your musical instrument must
- be made of materials that are approved by your teacher
- be able to play a simple tune or rhythm
- be built and used following the safety guidelines in Appendix A

Plan It! Begin by discussing different kinds of instruments with your classmates. What instruments are common in your favorite type of music? Which type of instrument would you like to build? Make a list of materials you could use to build your instrument. Then, design and sketch your instrument. After your teacher approves your design, build your instrument and test it by playing a simple tune.

Chapter 2 O ◆ 35

Video Preview

Sound

Show the Video Preview to introduce the chapter and provide an overview of chapter content. Discussion question: **Why do submarine operators use sonar?** *(To detect objects or obstacles they cannot see under water)*

Performance Assessment

The Chapter Project Scoring Rubric will help you evaluate how well students complete the Chapter Project. You may want to share the scoring rubric with your students so they will know what is expected. Students will be assessed on
- the thoroughness and originality of their designs and the appropriateness of their construction materials
- how well they apply chapter concepts in the design, construction, and modification of their instruments
- how well they modify their instruments based on the results of their tests
- the clarity and organization of their presentations and how successfully their instruments can produce a tune

Students can keep their revised design plans in their portfolios.

Portfolio

Possible Shortcuts

To save time, allow students to work in small groups.

Launching the Project

To introduce the project, play a recording or video of people playing unusual musical instruments. Have students discuss the sounds produced by the instruments and compare them with the sounds produced by more familiar instruments. Encourage students to recall different styles of music and the instruments that are used to create them. Finally, have students brainstorm a list of instrument types they could create in this project.

Objectives

After this lesson, students will be able to

O.2.1.1 Define sound and explain what causes sound and how it travels.

O.2.1.2 Describe how sound waves interact.

O.2.1.3 Identify factors that affect the speed of sound.

Target Reading Skill 🔄

Identifying Main Ideas Explain that identifying main ideas and details helps students sort the facts from the information into groups. Each group can have a main topic, subtopics, and details.

Answers

Sample graphic organizer:

Main Idea: Sound waves interact with objects and with other sound waves.

Detail: Reflection occurs when sound waves strike a surface.

Detail: Sound waves can diffract around corners and through openings.

Detail: The interference of sound waves can be constructive or destructive.

All in One Teaching Resources

• Transparency O15

Preteach

Build Background Knowledge　　　L2

Making Sound Waves

Direct students to make a sound using just their hands. *(Students can clap their hands, tap their desk, or snap their fingers.)* Ask: **What caused the sound that you made?** *(The impact created by the hands or fingers caused the sound. Some students may say the impact caused the air to vibrate, thereby producing sound waves.)* Tell students they will learn about sound and sound waves in this section.

Reading Preview

Key Concepts

• What is sound?
• How do sound waves interact?
• What factors affect the speed of sound?

Key Terms

• echo • elasticity • density

🔄 Target Reading Skill

Identifying Main Ideas As you read the Interactions of Sound Waves section, write the main idea—the biggest or most important idea—in a graphic organizer like the one below. Then write three supporting details that further explain the main idea.

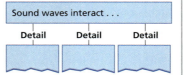

Main Idea

Sound waves interact . . .

Detail	Detail	Detail

Lab zone　Discover **Activity**

What Is Sound?

1. Fill a bowl with water.
2. Tap a tuning fork against the sole of your shoe. Place the tip of one of the prongs in the water. What do you see?
3. Tap the tuning fork again. Predict what will happen when you hold it near your ear. What do you hear?

Think It Over

Observing How are your observations related to the sound you hear? What might change if you use a different tuning fork?

Here is an old riddle: If a tree falls in a forest and no one hears it, does the tree make a sound? To answer the riddle, you must decide what the word "sound" means. If sound is something that a person must hear, then the tree makes no sound. If sound can happen whether a person hears it or not, then the tree makes a sound.

Sound Waves

To a scientist, a falling tree makes a sound whether someone hears it or not. When a tree crashes down, the energy with which it strikes the ground causes a disturbance. Particles in the ground and the air begin to vibrate, or move back and forth. The vibrations create a sound wave as the energy travels through the two mediums. **Sound is a disturbance that travels through a medium as a longitudinal wave.**

A falling tree ▶

Lab zone　Discover **Activity**

Skills Focus Observing　　L1

Materials bowl, water, tuning fork

Time 10 minutes

Tips Lower-frequency tuning forks make waves that are easier to see. Point out the prongs of the tuning fork if students are unsure which parts they are.

Expected Outcome Students will see tiny ripples when the prong is dipped in the water. When they hold the tuning fork up to their ear, they will hear the tuning fork hum.

Think It Over Ripples are caused by vibrations of the tuning fork, which also produce the sound students hear. Different tuning forks may produce waves with different characteristics.

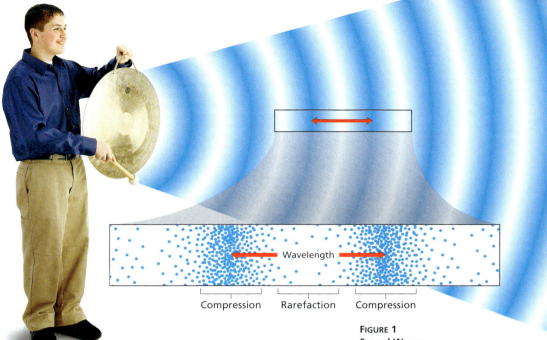

Making Sound Waves A sound wave begins with a vibration. Look at the metal gong shown in Figure 1. When the gong is struck, it vibrates rapidly. The vibrations disturb nearby air particles. Each time the gong moves to the right, it pushes air particles together, creating a compression. When the gong moves to the left, the air particles bounce back and spread out, creating a rarefaction. These compressions and rarefactions travel through the air as longitudinal waves.

How Sound Travels Like other mechanical waves, sound waves carry energy through a medium without moving the particles of the medium along. Each particle of the medium vibrates as the disturbance passes. When the disturbance reaches your ears, you hear the sound.

A common medium for sound is air. But sound can travel through solids and liquids, too. For example, when you knock on a solid wood door, the particles in the wood vibrate. The vibrations make sound waves that travel through the door. When the waves reach the other side of the door, they make sound waves in the air on the far side.

 Reading Checkpoint What are three types of mediums that sound can travel through?

FIGURE 1
Sound Waves
As a gong vibrates, it creates sound waves that travel through the air. **Observing** *What do you observe about the spacing of particles in a compression?*

Go Online
SciLINKS NSTA

For: Links on sound
Visit: www.SciLinks.org
Web Code: scn-1521

Chapter 2 O ◆ **37**

Instruct

Sound Waves

Teach Key Concepts L2
Making Sound

Focus Tell students that all sound waves begin with a vibration.

Teach Ask: **What are some sounds and how do they begin?** *(Sample answer: A drumbeat begins with a vibrating drumhead. A guitar sound begins with a vibrating string.)*

Apply Ask: **In what direction do air particles move when they vibrate in a sound wave?** *(Parallel to the direction of the wave)* **learning modality: verbal**

Lab zone **Teacher Demo** L2

Observing Sound Vibrations

Focus Help students visualize how sound waves move air particles.

Teach Sprinkle sand on a drumhead. Ask: **What do you observe when the drumhead is tapped?** *(The sand vibrates)*

Apply Ask: **How are air molecules near the drumhead similar to the sand particles?** *(They move when the drumhead is tapped.)*

Go Online
SciLINKS NSTA

For: Links on sound
Visit: www.SciLinks.org
Web Code: scn-1521

Download a worksheet that will guide students' review of Internet resources on sound.

All in One Teaching Resources
• Transparency O16

Independent Practice L2
All in One Teaching Resources
• Guided Reading and Study Worksheet: *The Nature of Sound*

 **Student Edition on Audio CD**

Monitor Progress L2
Answers
Figure 1 The particles are spaced closely.
Reading Checkpoint Gases, liquids, and solids

O ● **37**

Interactions of Sound Waves

Teach Key Concepts
Reflection of Sound Waves

Focus Introduce sound wave interactions with the familiar example of reflection of sound waves and echoes.

Teach Remind students that mechanical waves are reflected from surfaces they cannot pass through. Help students apply what they already know about reflection to sound. Ask: **What are examples of surfaces that readily reflect sound waves?** *(Sample answer: Rock walls, walls of high-rise buildings)* **How does reflection of sound waves affect the sound that you hear?** *(It causes echoes.)*

Apply Ask: **What are some everyday examples of reflected sound waves?** *(Any type of echo, such a shouts in a gym or thunder in the mountains)* **learning modality: verbal**

All in One Teaching Resources
Transparencies O17, O18

Help Students Read
Making Inferences Refer to the Content Refresher in this chapter, which provides guidelines for using the Making Inferences strategy.

Help students infer interactions of sound waves. Ask: **Based on your knowledge of waves, what happens to sound waves that strike a barrier they cannot pass through?** *(They bounce back, or reflect.)* **What happens to sound waves near the edge of a barrier or at a hole in a barrier?** *(They bend.)* **What happens when sound waves meet?** *(They can interfere constructively or destructively.)*

FIGURE 2
Reflection of Sound
Clapping your hands in a gym produces an echo when sound waves reflect off the wall.
Drawing Conclusions *What kind of material is the wall made of?*

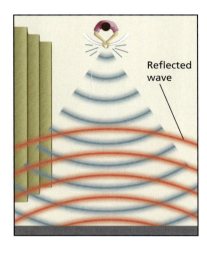

Reflected wave

Interactions of Sound Waves

Sound waves interact with the surfaces they contact and with each other. **Sound waves reflect off objects, diffract through narrow openings and around barriers, and interfere with each other.**

Reflection Sound waves may reflect when they hit a surface. A reflected sound wave is called an **echo.** In general, the harder and smoother the surface, the stronger the reflection. Look at Figure 2. When you clap your hands in a gym, you hear an echo because the hard surfaces—wood, brick, and metal—reflect sound directly back at you. But you don't always hear an echo in a room. In many rooms, there are soft materials that absorb most of the sound that strikes them.

Diffraction Have you ever wondered why you can hear your friends talking in a classroom before you walk through the doorway? You hear them because sound waves do not always travel in a straight line. Figure 3 shows how sound waves can diffract through openings such as doorways.

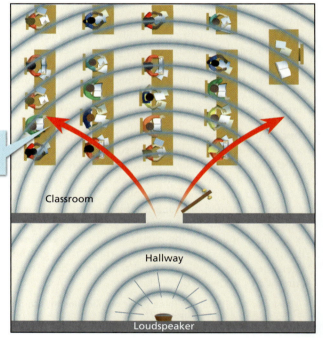

Sound waves spread out after passing through a doorway.

Classroom

FIGURE 3
Diffraction of Sound
Sound waves can spread out after passing through a doorway, and can bend around a corner.

Hallway

Loudspeaker

Sound waves can also diffract, or bend, around corners. This is why you can hear someone who is talking in the hallway before you come around the corner. The person's sound waves bend around the corner. Then they spread out so you can hear them even though you cannot see who is talking. Remember this the next time you want to tell a secret!

Interference Sound waves may meet and interact with each other. Recall from Chapter 1 that this interaction is called interference. The interference that occurs when sound waves meet can be constructive or destructive. In Section 3, you will learn how interference affects the sound of musical instruments.

 Reading Checkpoint What are two ways that sound waves diffract?

The Speed of Sound

Have you ever wondered why the different sounds from musicians and singers at a concert all reach your ears at the same time? It happens because the sounds travel through air at the same speed. At room temperature, about 20°C, sound travels through air at about 343 m/s. This speed is much faster than most jet planes travel through the air!

The speed of sound is not always 343 m/s. Sound waves travel at different speeds in different mediums. Figure 4 shows the speed of sound in different mediums. **The speed of sound depends on the elasticity, density, and temperature of the medium the sound travels through.**

Speed of Sound	
Medium	**Speed (m/s)**
Gases	
Air (0°C)	331
Air (20°C)	343
Liquids (30°C)	
Fresh water	1,509
Salt water	1,546
Solids (25°C)	
Lead	1,210
Cast iron	4,480
Aluminum	5,000
Glass	5,170

FIGURE 4
The speed of sound depends on the medium it travels through.

Math ▶ Analyzing Data

Temperature and the Speed of Sound

The speed of sound in dry air changes as the temperature changes. The graph shows data for the speed of sound in air at temperatures from −10°C to 20°C.

1. **Reading Graphs** What is the speed of sound in air at −10°C?
2. **Interpreting Data** Does the speed of sound increase or decrease as temperature increases?
3. **Predicting** What might be the speed of sound at 30°C?

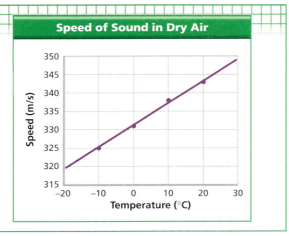

Speed of Sound in Dry Air

Chapter 2 O ◆ 39

The Speed of Sound

Teach Key Concepts   L2
Putting the Speed of Sound in Context

Focus State that sound travels faster than a jet plane at take off but not as fast as light.

Teach Ask: **Can you think of a situation in which you saw a distant action before you heard it?** *(Sample answer: Seeing the smoke from a starting gun before hearing the gun fire at the start of a race; seeing fireworks before hearing them.)* Explain that each action is seen before the sound is heard because sound travels more slowly than light.

Apply Ask: **Why do you usually hear thunder after you see lightning?** *(Because sound travels more slowly than light)*
learning modality: verbal

Math ▶ Analyzing Data

Math Skill Making and interpreting graphs

Focus Tell students that the speed of sound through dry air depends on the temperature of the air.

Teach Call students' attention to the graph. Explain that a line graph is one way to show the relationship between two variables, such as air temperature and speed of sound. Ask: **Which variable does each axis represent?** *(The x-axis represents air temperature, and the y-axis represents the speed of sound.)*

Answers
1. The speed at −10°C is 325 m/s.
2. The speed of sound increases as air temperature increases.
3. At 30°, the speed of sound might be 349 m/s.

Differentiated Instruction

Special Needs   L1
Feeling Sound Waves Give students a chance to feel sound waves traveling through a solid object. Have students place their hands on a guitar or piano as the instrument is played. The harder it is played, the more easily the vibrations can be felt. Explain to students that the vibrations they feel are sound waves that travel through a solid. **learning modality: kinesthetic**

Gifted and Talented   L3
Properties of Sound Waves Have students research values for the speed, frequency, and wavelength of sound waves through different mediums. Then, have them draw graphs to show how the variables change and also how the three variables are related to one another. Invite students to share their graphs with the class. **learning modality: logical/mathematical**

Monitor Progress   L2

Oral Presentation Call on students to identify factors that affect the speed of sound.

Answers
Figure 2 The wall is made of hard, smooth material that reflects sound waves.

 **Reading Checkpoint** Two ways sound waves diffract are through openings and around barriers.

Help Students Read

Vocabulary: Word/Part Analysis The term *elasticity* may be unfamiliar to students. Tell them that the word is a noun containing the adjective *elastic*. Explain that adding *-ity* to some adjectives changes them to nouns. Give students another example, such as scarce/scarcity. Say that scarce means "rare" or "few in number," and scarcity means "the state or condition of being rare or few in number." Ask: **If elastic means "springy," what does elasticity mean?** *(The state or condition of being springy)* Explain that elastic materials have the ability to bounce back after being disturbed.

Teacher **Demo**   L1

Demonstrating Density

Focus Remind students that the speed of sound waves depends in part on the density of the medium and that density is mass divided by volume.

Teach Demonstrate the concept of density with a slice of bread. Squeeze the bread into a ball that is smaller in size than the original slice. Point out that the same amount of bread is in the ball, but it now takes up less space. Ask: **Did the mass of the bread change?** *(No)* **Did the volume change?** *(Yes, the bread got smaller.)*

Apply Ask: **How did the density of the bread change?** *(It increased.)*

FIGURE 5
Modeling Elasticity
You can model elasticity by representing the particles in a medium as being held together by springs.

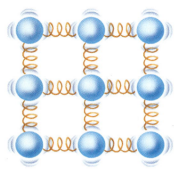

Elasticity If you stretch a rubber band and then let it go, it returns to its original shape. However, when you stretch modeling clay and then let it go, it stays stretched. Rubber bands are more elastic than modeling clay. **Elasticity** is the ability of a material to bounce back after being disturbed.

The elasticity of a medium depends on how well the medium's particles bounce back after being disturbed. To understand this idea, look at Figure 5. In this model, the particles of a medium are linked by springs. If one particle is disturbed, it is pulled back to its original position. In an elastic medium, such as a rubber band, the particles bounce back quickly. But in a less elastic medium, the particles bounce back slowly.

The more elastic a medium, the faster sound travels in it. Sounds can travel well in solids, which are usually more elastic than liquids or gases. The particles of a solid do not move very far, so they bounce back and forth quickly as the compressions and rarefactions of the sound waves pass by. Most liquids are not very elastic. Sound does not travel as well in liquids as it does in solids. Gases generally are not very elastic. Sound travels slowly in gases.

Density The speed of sound also depends on the density of a medium. **Density** is how much matter, or mass, there is in a given amount of space, or volume. The denser the medium, the more mass it has in a given volume. Figure 6 shows two cubes that have the same volume. The brass cube is denser because it has more mass in a given volume.

In materials in the same state of matter—solid, liquid, or gas—sound travels more slowly in denser mediums. The particles of a dense material do not move as quickly as those of a less dense material. Sound travels more slowly in dense metals, such as lead or silver, than in iron or steel.

FIGURE 6
Comparing Density
The volumes of these cubes are the same, but the brass cube has more mass.
Interpreting Photographs *Which cube has a greater density: brass or aluminum?*

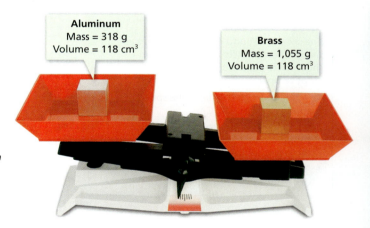

Aluminum
Mass = 318 g
Volume = 118 cm^3

Brass
Mass = 1,055 g
Volume = 118 cm^3

Temperature In a given medium, sound travels more slowly at lower temperatures than at higher temperatures. Why? At a low temperature, the particles of a medium move more slowly than at a high temperature. So, they are more difficult to move, and return to their original positions more slowly. For example, at 20°C, the speed of sound in air is about 343 m/s. But at 0°C, the speed of sound is about 330 m/s.

At higher altitudes, the air is colder than at lower altitudes, so sound travels more slowly at higher altitudes. On October 14, 1947, Captain Chuck Yeager of the United States Air Force used this knowledge to fly faster than the speed of sound.

To fly faster than the speed of sound, Captain Yeager flew his plane to an altitude of more than 12,000 meters. Here, the air temperature was −59°C. The speed of sound at this temperature is only about 293 m/s. At 12,000 meters, Captain Yeager accelerated his plane to a record-breaking 312 m/s. By doing this, he became the first person to "break the sound barrier."

 Reading Checkpoint How does temperature affect the speed of sound?

FIGURE 7
Breaking the Sound Barrier
On October 14, 1947, Captain Chuck Yeager became the first person to fly a plane faster than the speed of sound.

Section 1 Assessment

Target Reading Skill Identifying Main Ideas Use your graphic organizer to help you answer Question 2 below.

Reviewing Key Concepts

1. **a. Reviewing** What is sound?
   b. Explaining How is a sound wave produced?
   c. Sequencing Explain how a ringing telephone can be heard through a closed door.
2. **a. Listing** What are three ways that sound waves can interact?
   b. Applying Concepts Explain why you can hear a teacher through the closed door of a classroom.
   c. Inferring At a scenic overlook, you can hear an echo only if you shout in one particular direction. Explain why.
3. **a. Identifying** What property describes how a material bounces back after being disturbed?
   b. Summarizing What three properties of a medium affect the speed of sound?
   c. Developing Hypotheses Steel is denser than plastic, yet sound travels faster in steel than in plastic. Develop a hypothesis to explain why.

Lab zone At-Home Activity

Ear to the Sound Find a long metal fence or water pipe. **CAUTION:** *Beware of sharp edges and rust.* Put one ear to one end of the pipe while a family member taps on the other end. In which ear do you hear the sound first? Explain your answer to your family members. What accounts for the difference?

Chapter 2 O ◆ 41

Lab zone At-Home Activity

Ear to the Sound L2 The effect will be most noticeable if the pipe is at least 25 m long. Students will hear the sound first through the ear closest to the pipe and a little later through the other ear. Students might explain the outcome by saying that sound travels faster through metal than air because metal is much more elastic than air.

Objectives

After this lesson, students will be able to

O.2.2.1 Identify factors that affect the loudness of sound.

O.2.2.2 State what the pitch of a sound depends on.

O.2.2.3 Explain what causes the Doppler effect.

Target Reading Skill

Outlining Explain that using an outline format helps students organize information by main topic, subtopic, and details.

Answers

Properties of Sound
- I. Loudness
  - A. Energy of a sound source
  - B. Distance from a sound source
  - C. Measuring loudness
- II. Pitch
  - A. Pitch and frequency
  - B. Changing pitch
- III. Doppler effect
  - A. What causes the Doppler effect?
  - B. What causes shock waves?

All in One Teaching Resources
- Transparency O19

Preteach

Build Background Knowledge L2

Experience With Loudness

Ask: **Which is louder, the sound of a whisper in your ear or the sound of a distant airplane in the sky?** (*Students may say the whisper is louder.*) Explain that distance from the sound source is one factor that affects the loudness of sound. State that loudness is one of the properties of sound students will learn about in this section.

Section

2

Properties of Sound

Reading Preview

Key Concepts
- What factors affect the loudness of a sound?
- What does the pitch of a sound depend on?
- What causes the Doppler effect?

Key Terms
- loudness • intensity
- decibel (dB) • pitch
- ultrasound • infrasound
- larynx • Doppler effect

Target Reading Skill

Outlining An outline shows the relationship between main ideas and supporting ideas. As you read, make an outline about the properties of sound. Use the red headings for the main ideas and the blue headings for the supporting ideas.

Properties of Sound
I. Loudness
A. Energy of a sound source
B.
C.
II. Pitch
A.

Lab zone Discover **Activity**

How Does Amplitude Affect Loudness?

1. Your teacher will give you a wooden board with two nails in it. Attach a guitar string to the nails by wrapping each end tightly around a nail and tying a knot.

2. Hold the string near the middle. Pull it about 1 cm to one side. This distance is the amplitude of vibration. Let it go. How far does the string move to the other side? Describe the sound you hear.

3. Repeat Step 2 four more times. Each time, pull the string back a greater distance. Describe how the sound changes each time.

Think It Over

Forming Operational Definitions How would you define the amplitude of the vibration? What effect did changing the amplitude have on the sound?

Suppose that you and a friend are talking on a sidewalk and a noisy truck pulls up next to you and stops, leaving its motor running. What would you do? You might talk louder, almost shout, so your friend can hear you. You might lean closer and speak into your friend's ear so you don't have to raise your voice. Or you might walk away from the noisy truck so it's not as loud.

Loudness

Loudness is an important property of sound. **Loudness** describes your perception of the energy of a sound. In other words, loudness describes what you hear. You probably already know a lot about loudness. For example, you know that your voice is much louder when you shout than when you speak softly. The closer you are to a sound, the louder it is. Also, a whisper in your ear can be just as loud as a shout from a block away. **The loudness of a sound depends on two factors: the amount of energy it takes to make the sound and the distance from the source of the sound.**

Lab zone Discover **Activity**

Skills Focus Forming operational definitions

Materials wooden board, two nails, guitar string

Time 10 minutes

Tips Pound two nails into the board and wrap the guitar string tightly and securely around them, as shown in the picture.

L2 Have students use graph paper or a metric ruler to measure amplitude.

Expected Outcome The farther the string is pulled, the louder the sound.

Think It Over The amplitude of a vibration is the distance that the string moves to either side of its resting position. As amplitude increased, the sound became louder.

Energy of a Sound Source In general, the greater the energy used to make a sound, the louder the sound. If you did the Discover activity, you may have noticed this. The more energy you used to pull the guitar string back, the louder the sound when you let the string go. This happened because the more energy you used to pull the string, the greater the amplitude of the string's vibration. A string vibrating with a large amplitude produces a sound wave with a large amplitude. Recall that the greater the amplitude of a wave, the more energy the wave has. So, the larger the amplitude of the sound wave, the more energy it has and the louder it sounds.

Distance From a Sound Source If your friend is speaking in a normal voice and you lean in closer, your friend's voice sounds louder. Loudness increases the closer you are to a sound source. But why?

Imagine ripples spreading out in circles after you toss a pebble into a pond. In a similar way, a sound wave spreads out from its source. Close to the sound source, the sound wave covers a small area, as you can see in Figure 8. As the wave travels away from its source, it covers more area. The total energy of the wave, however, stays the same whether it is close to the source or far from it. Therefore, the closer the sound wave is to its source, the more energy it has in a given area. The amount of energy a sound wave carries per second through a unit area is its **intensity.** A sound wave of greater intensity sounds louder. As you move away from a sound source, loudness decreases because the intensity decreases.

For: More on the properties of sound
Visit: PHSchool.com
Web Code: cgd-5022

FIGURE 8
Intensity and Distance
Because sound waves spread out, intensity decreases with distance from the source.
Interpreting Diagrams *How does the intensity at 3 meters compare to the intensity at 2 meters?*

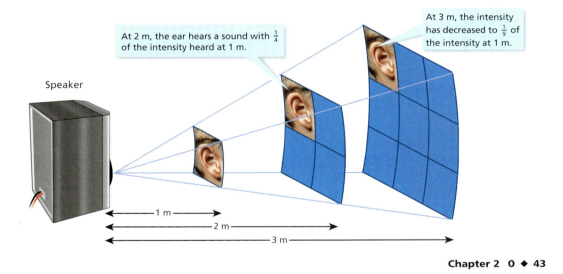

At 3 m, the intensity has decreased to $\frac{1}{9}$ of the intensity at 1 m.

At 2 m, the ear hears a sound with $\frac{1}{4}$ of the intensity heard at 1 m.

Speaker

1 m
2 m
3 m

Chapter 2 O ◆ 43

Instruct

Loudness

Teach Key Concepts [L2]
Loudness and Energy

Focus Introduce loudness as the perception of the energy in sound.

Teach Ask: **What are some things that sound loud?** *(Sample answer: Fans shouting at a basketball game)* **What are some things that sound soft?** *(Sample answer: Falling leaves)* Point out how the loud sounds are associated with more energy.

Apply Ask: **How are loudness and energy related?** *(The greater the energy of the sound source, the louder the sound.)* **learning modality: verbal**

For: More on the properties of sound
Visit: PHSchool.com
Web Code: cgd-5022

Students can review properties of sound in an online interactivity.

All in One Teaching Resources
• Transparency O20

Independent Practice [L2]
All in One Teaching Resources
• Guided Reading and Study Worksheet: *Properties of Sound*

🔘 **Student Edition on Audio CD**

Differentiated Instruction

Less Proficient Readers [L1]
Identifying Supporting Ideas Have students listen to this section on the **Student Edition on Audio CD**. As they listen, they can identify supporting ideas and add them under the appropriate headings and subheadings in their section outline. **learning modality: verbal**

Gifted and Talented [L3]
Researching Decibel Ratings Challenge students to research the decibel ratings of several sounds other than those listed in Figure 9. Examples might include tornado sirens and car horns. Tell students to add the sounds and their decibel ratings to an expanded table, based on Figure 9. Make copies of the table to share with the class. **learning modality: visual**

Monitor Progress [L2]

Writing Have students describe how energy and distance are related to the loudness of sound.

Answer
Figure 8 The intensity at 3 m is a little less than half the intensity at 2 m.

Modeling Sound Intensity and Distance

Materials 14 index cards, 108 grains of rice

Time 15 minutes

Focus Point out how sound intensity and distance are related in Figure 8.

Teach Have students use the materials to model the relationship shown in the figure. *(Sets of 1, 4, and 9 index cards can represent the area the sound waves cover at increasing distances from the sound source. An equal number of grains of rice (36) spread out over each set of cards can represent the energy of sound, which stays the same at each distance from the source but becomes more spread out.)*

Apply Ask students to explain which parts of their model represent energy and which parts represent area. **learning modality: kinesthetic**

Integrating Health Science L2

Many students use headphones to listen to music. Tell them that using headphones at high volume can be as damaging to their ears as listening to the roar of a chain saw. Add that a common symptom of hearing damage is ringing in the ears, which is called *tinnitus*. Tinnitus is thought to be due to signals from the brain that are sent out in response to damage to the nerves and structures of the ear. **learning modality: verbal**

Pitch

Teach Key Concepts L2

Pitch and Frequency

Focus Remind students that the frequency of a wave is the number of vibrations that occur per second.

Teach State that the frequency of a sound wave determines how high or low it is. Ask: **What do you call how high or low a sound is?** *(Its pitch)* Explain that high frequencies produce high-pitch sounds and low frequencies produce low-pitch sounds.

Apply Have a volunteer sing a high note followed by a low note. Ask: **Which note was caused by a higher frequency sound wave?** *(The higher-pitch note)* **learning modality: verbal**

Measuring Loudness	
Sound	**Loudness (dB)**
Rustling leaves	10
Whisper	15–20
Very soft music	20–30
Normal conversation	40–50
Heavy street traffic	60–70
Loud music	90–100
Rock concert	110–120
Jackhammer	120
Jet plane at takeoff	120–160

FIGURE 9
Some sounds are so soft that you can barely hear them. Others are so loud that they can damage your ears. **Interpreting Data** *Which sounds louder, a rock concert or a jet plane at takeoff?*

Measuring Loudness The loudness of different sounds is compared using a unit called the **decibel (dB).** Figure 9 shows the loudness of some familiar sounds. The loudness of a sound you can barely hear is about 0 dB. Each 10-dB increase in loudness represents a tenfold increase in the intensity of the sound. For example, soft music at 30 dB sounds ten times louder than a 20-dB whisper. The 30-dB music is 100 times louder than the 10-dB sound of rustling leaves. Sounds louder than 100 dB can cause damage to your ears, especially if you listen to those sounds for long periods of time.

 Reading Checkpoint What is a decibel?

Pitch

Pitch is another property of sound you may already know a lot about. Have you ever described someone's voice as "high-pitched" or "low-pitched?" The **pitch** of a sound is a description of how high or low the sound seems to a person. **The pitch of a sound that you hear depends on the frequency of the sound wave.**

Pitch and Frequency Sound waves with a high frequency have a high pitch. Sound waves with a low frequency have a low pitch. Frequency is measured in hertz (Hz). For example, a frequency of 50 Hz means 50 vibrations per second. Look at Figure 10. A bass singer can produce frequencies lower than 80 Hz. A trained soprano voice can produce frequencies higher than 1,000 Hz.

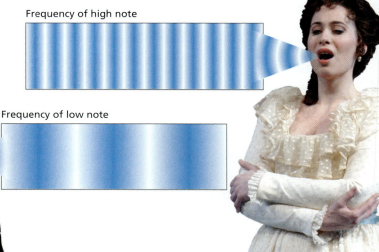

FIGURE 10
Pitch Depends on Frequency
The bass singer below sings low notes, and the soprano singer on the right sings high notes.

Frequency of high note

Frequency of low note

Most people can hear sounds with frequencies between 20 Hz and 20,000 Hz. Sound waves with frequencies above the normal human range of hearing are called **ultrasound.** The prefix *ultra-* means "beyond." Sounds with frequencies below the human range of hearing are called **infrasound.** The prefix *infra-* means "below." People cannot hear either ultrasound waves or infrasound waves.

Changing Pitch Pitch is an important property of music because music usually uses specific pitches called notes. To sing or play a musical instrument, you must change pitch often.

When you sing, you change pitch using your vocal cords. Your vocal cords are located in your voice box, or **larynx,** as shown in Figure 11. When you speak or sing, air from your lungs is forced up the trachea, or windpipe. Air then rushes past your vocal cords, making them vibrate. This produces sound waves. Your vocal cords are able to vibrate more than 1,000 times per second!

To sing different notes, you use muscles in your throat to stretch and relax your vocal cords. When your vocal cords stretch, they vibrate more quickly as the air rushes by them. This creates higher-frequency sound waves that have higher pitches. When your vocal cords relax, lower-frequency sound waves with lower pitches are produced.

With musical instruments, you change pitch in different ways depending on the instrument. For example, you can change the pitch of a guitar string by turning a knob to loosen or tighten the string. A tighter guitar string produces a higher frequency, which you hear as a note with higher pitch.

 Reading Checkpoint Where are your vocal cords located?

FIGURE 11
The Human Voice
When a person speaks or sings, the vocal cords vibrate. The vibrations produce sound waves in the air.

Sound Sound waves produced by the vibrating vocal cords come out through the mouth.

Vocal Cords The vocal cords inside the larynx vibrate as air rushes past them.

Lungs Air from the lungs rushes up the trachea.

Trachea

 O ◆ 45

 **Skills Activity**

Predicting

1. Flatten one end of a drinking straw and cut the end to form a point.
2. Blow through the straw. Describe what you hear.
3. Predict what changes you would hear if you shortened the straw by cutting off some of the straight end. Test your prediction by making two new straws of different lengths.

Lab zone Skills Activity

Skills Focus Predicting

Materials drinking straw, scissors

Time 10 minutes

Tips Caution students to use care when handling the scissors. Do not allow them to share straws, and have them dispose of straws in a trash can following the activity. Students must make at least two cuts to test their prediction.

Predicting Students may predict correctly that the sound produced by a shorter straw has a higher pitch than the sound produced by a longer straw.

Extend Have students compare the pitches of sounds made by blowing through straws that have equal lengths but different diameters, such as a hollow coffee stirrer and a soda straw. **learning modality: kinesthetic**

Address Misconceptions L2

Two Different Frequencies

Focus Students may confuse the frequency of vibrations in a guitar string with the frequency at which the string is plucked.

Teach Ask volunteers to take turns plucking a guitar string at different rates. Have the class listen to the sounds produced.

Apply Ask: **Why can't you make a guitar string produce a higher-pitch sound by plucking it faster?** (*Because the string still vibrates at the same frequency*) **learning modality: kinesthetic**

Use Visuals: Figure 11 L1

Vocal Cords

Focus Point out the location of the larynx in the figure. Explain that the larynx contains the vocal cords, which vibrate to produce sound waves.

Teach Have students place their fingers on their neck, as the girl in the photograph is doing. Then, tell students to hum. Ask: **What do you feel moving in your neck?** (*Vibrations of the vocal cords*) Tell students to hum at a low pitch and then a high pitch. Then, ask: **What difference do you feel in your vocal cords when you change the pitch?** (*Sample answer: The vibrations feel like they are coming from a different part of the vocal cords.*)

Extend Ask: **How do you think you raise the pitch of sounds produced by the vocal cords?** (*Some students may correctly infer that pitch is raised by increasing the tension of the vocal cords.*) **learning modality: kinesthetic**

Monitor Progress _____ L2

Oral Presentation Call on students to explain how pitch and frequency are related.

Answers
Figure 9 A jet plane at takeoff sounds louder than a rock concert.

Reading Checkpoint A decibel is the unit used for loudness of sound.

Reading Checkpoint Your vocal cords are located in your larynx, which is in your throat.

The Doppler Effect

Teach Key Concepts

Visualizing the Doppler Effect

Focus Have students look at Figure 12, which shows the Doppler effect. Say that the Doppler effect occurs when the source of a sound is moving relative to the listener.

Teach Ask: **What is the source of sound in the figure?** *(The siren on the firetruck)* **As the truck moves forward, what happens to the sound waves in front of the truck?** *(They bunch up.)* **How does this affect the frequency of the sound waves in front of the truck?** *(It makes the frequency higher.)* **How does this affect the pitch of the sound for people the truck is approaching?** *(It makes the pitch higher.)* Explain that the opposite occurs in behind the truck.

Apply Ask: **What are other situations in which the Doppler effect might occur?** *(Sample answer: The sound of a car horn as the car moves toward or away from the listener)* **learning modality: visual**

Teacher **Demo**

Modeling the Doppler Effect

Materials large pan, tuning fork, water

Time 10 minutes

Focus Say that you will model the Doppler effect with a tuning fork in water.

Teach Fill the pan with water. Strike a tuning fork and place one prong in the water about 10 cm from the edge of the pan. Slowly bring the prong toward the edge of the pan. Ask: **What happens to the waves as the prong approaches the side of the pan?** *(The waves in front of it get closer together.)*

Apply Ask: **What wave properties change in the Doppler effect?** *(Frequency and wavelength)* **learning modality: visual**

All in One Teaching Resources

• Transparency O21

 Lab zone Try This **Activity**

Pipe Sounds

1. Find an open space without objects or people nearby.
2. Hold the end of a flexible plastic tube firmly (a vacuum cleaner hose works well). Swing the tube in a circle over your head to produce a sound.
3. Keeping the speed steady, listen to the sound. Have a partner stand at a safe distance and listen at the same time.

Observing Describe the sound you heard. How is it different from the sound your partner heard? Explain the difference.

FIGURE 12
The Doppler Effect
As the firetruck speeds by, the observers hear a change in the pitch of the siren.
Applying Concepts *How could you describe the pitch heard by the firefighter?*

People behind the firetruck hear a lower pitch than the firefighters in the truck hear.

People standing in front of the firetruck hear a higher pitch than the firefighters in the truck hear.

FIRE DEPARTMENT

The Doppler Effect

If you listen carefully to the siren of a firetruck on its way to a fire, you will notice something surprising. As the truck goes by you, the pitch of the siren drops. But the pitch of the siren stays constant for the firefighters in the truck. The siren's pitch changes only if it is moving toward or away from a listener.

The change in frequency of a wave as its source moves in relation to an observer is called the **Doppler effect.** If the waves are sound waves, the change in frequency is heard as a change in pitch. The Doppler effect is named after the Austrian scientist Christian Doppler (1803–1853).

What Causes the Doppler Effect? Figure 12 shows how sound waves from a moving source behave. When the source moves toward a listener, the frequency of the waves is higher than it would be if the source were stationary. **When a sound source moves, the frequency of the waves changes because the motion of the source adds to the motion of the waves.**

To understand why the frequency changes, imagine that you are standing still and throwing tennis balls at a wall in front of you. If you throw one ball each second the balls hit the wall at a rate of one per second. Now suppose you walk toward the wall while still throwing one ball per second. Because each ball has a shorter distance to travel than the one before, each takes less time to get there. The balls hit the wall more often than one per second, so the frequency is higher. On the other hand, if you throw balls at the wall as you back away, each ball has farther to travel and the frequency is lower.

Try This **Activity**

Skills Focus Observing

Materials flexible plastic tube or vacuum cleaner hose

Time 10 minutes

Tips Tubes may be found at a vacuum cleaner supply store, or you may use small plastic tubes that are sold as noise-making toys. Warn students to be careful when swinging the tubes.

Expected Outcome The student swinging the tube hears a humming sound with a constant pitch. The partner hears a humming sound with a pitch that rises and falls as the tube approaches and recedes. Students may say that the source of sound was moving relative to the partner but not relative to the student swinging the tube. **learning modality: kinesthetic**

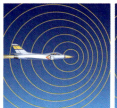
❶ Slower than the speed of sound

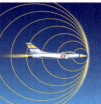
❷ Aproaching the speed of sound

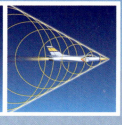
❸ Faster than the speed of sound

What Causes Shock Waves? At high speed, the Doppler effect can be spectacular. Look at Figure 13. When the plane travels almost as fast as the speed of sound, the sound waves pile up in front of the plane. This pile-up is the "sound barrier." As the plane flies faster than the speed of sound, it moves through the barrier. A shock wave forms as the sound waves overlap. The shock wave releases a huge amount of energy. People nearby hear a loud noise called a sonic boom when the shock wave passes by them.

Reading Checkpoint What is a shock wave?

FIGURE 13
Breaking the Sound Barrier
When a plane goes faster than the speed of sound, a shock wave is produced. The photo on the right shows how sudden changes in pressure at this speed can cause a small cloud to form.

Section 2 Assessment

🎯 **Target Reading Skill** Outlining Use the information in your outline about the properties of sound to help you answer the questions below.

Reviewing Key Concepts

1. **a. Identifying** What two factors affect the loudness of a sound?
   b. Applying Concepts Why does moving away from a radio affect the loudness you hear?
   c. Calculating A band plays music at 60 dB and then changes to a rock song at 80 dB. How many times louder is the rock song?
2. **a. Reviewing** What determines the pitch of a sound?
   b. Comparing and Contrasting How are high-pitch sounds different from low-pitch sounds?
   c. Explaining How do your vocal cords produce different pitches?
3. **a. Summarizing** What is the Doppler effect?
   b. Relating Cause and Effect What causes the Doppler effect?
   c. Predicting Would you hear a change in pitch if you are on a moving train and the train's whistle blows? Explain.

Lab zone At-Home Activity

Hum Stopper When listening to a cat's heart, a veterinarian will cover the cat's nostrils to keep the cat from purring. At home, ask family members to hum with their lips closed. Then ask them to cover both of their nostrils while humming. Use Figure 11 to explain what happened.

Chapter 2 O ◆ 47

Lab zone At-Home Activity

Hum Stopper L2 When you hum, your mouth is closed, so air can exit only through your nostrils. If you cover your nostrils, no air can escape. Without air moving past your vocal cords, the humming sound stops.

Lab zone Chapter Project

Keep Students on Track Have students apply section concepts to plan how they can change the pitch of sounds produced by their instruments. Tell them to modify their designs as necessary to allow control of pitch.

Objectives

After this lesson, students will be able to

O.2.3.1 Identify what determines the sound quality of a musical instrument.

O.2.3.2 Name the basic groups of musical instruments.

O.2.3.3 Describe how acoustics is used in concert hall design.

Target Reading Skill

Previewing Visuals Explain that looking at the visuals before they read helps students activate prior knowledge and predict what they are about to read.

Answers

Sample questions and answers:

Musical Instruments

How is pitch changed in each type of instrument? (*By changing the frequency of the vibrations*) **How is loudness changed in each type of instrument?** (*By changing the energy of the vibrations*)

All in One Teaching Resources

• Transparency O22

Preteach

Build Background Knowledge   L2

Comparing Instrumental Sounds

Ask students who play different musical instruments to bring their instruments to class. Have each student play the same note at the same volume. Call on students in the class to describe how the different instruments sound. Ask: **What do you think causes the instruments to sound different from one another?** (*Students might say construction materials, size, and shape.*)

Reading Preview

Key Concepts

• What determines the sound quality of a musical instrument?
• What are the basic groups of musical instruments?
• How is acoustics used in concert hall design?

Key Terms

• music • fundamental tone
• overtone • acoustics
• reverberation

Target Reading Skill

Previewing Visuals When you preview, you look ahead at the material to be read. Preview Figure 15. Then write two questions that you have about the diagrams in a graphic organizer like the one below. As you read, answer your questions.

Musical Instruments

Q. How is pitch changed in each type of instrument?
A.
Q.

Lab zone Discover Activity

How Can You Change Pitch?

1. Wrap two rubber bands of different thickness lengthwise around a 30-cm plastic ruler. The bands should not touch each other.
2. Place a pencil under the bands at the 10-cm mark.
3. Pluck each band. How are the sounds different?
4. Move the pencil to the 15-cm mark and repeat Step 3.

Think It Over

Drawing Conclusions Why are the sounds you made in Step 4 different from the sounds in Step 3?

You are late. When you arrive at your orchestra rehearsal, your friends are already tuning up. With all the instruments playing different notes, it sounds like noise! You quickly pull out your instrument and take your seat. Then the music starts, and everything changes. What makes noise and music different? The answer is in the way sound waves combine.

Orchestra rehearsal ▶

Lab zone Discover Activity

Skills Focus Developing hypotheses   L2

Materials 2 rubber bands of different thicknesses, 30-cm ruler, pencil

Time 15 minutes

Tips Rubber bands that are too thick will not stretch enough. Caution students to avoid launching the rubber bands with the rulers.

Expected Outcome Because they have different thicknesses, the rubber bands will have different natural frequencies and produce sounds of different pitches. When the pencil is moved from the 5-cm mark to the 15-cm mark, the pitch becomes higher.

Think It Over In Step 4, the pitch is higher because the part of the rubber band that is vibrating is shorter.

Sound Quality

Most people agree on what is or is not music. **Music** is a set of notes that combine in patterns that are pleasing. Noise, on the other hand, has no pleasing patterns. When you describe a sound as pleasant or unpleasant, you are describing sound quality. The sound quality of music depends on the instruments making the music. **The sound quality of musical instruments results from blending a fundamental tone with its overtones. Resonance also plays a role in the sound quality.**

Fundamental Tones and Overtones In Chapter 1, you learned that standing waves occur when waves with just the right frequency interfere as they reflect back and forth. Standing waves occur in musical instruments when they are played. In a guitar, for example, standing waves occur in a vibrating string. In a trumpet, standing waves occur in a column of vibrating air.

A standing wave can occur only at specific frequencies that are called natural frequencies. Every object has its own natural frequencies. The lowest natural frequency of an object is called the **fundamental tone.** The object's higher natural frequencies are called **overtones.** Overtones have frequencies that are two, three, or more times the frequency of the fundamental tone. Look at Figure 14 to see how the natural frequencies of a guitar string add together to produce a unique sound.

The fundamental tone determines what note you hear. For example, when a guitar and a trumpet play middle C, they both produce waves with a frequency of 262 Hz. But each instrument produces different overtones, so the blending of the fundamental tones and overtones produces different sound qualities.

Resonance Resonance affects the sound quality of a musical instrument by increasing the loudness of certain overtones. Recall that resonance occurs when one object causes a nearby object to vibrate at a natural frequency. A musical instrument is designed so that a part of it will resonate with the overtones it produces. In a guitar, for example, the vibrating strings cause the guitar's hollow body to resonate. The shape and material of the guitar determine which overtones are loudest.

 Reading Checkpoint What are overtones?

FIGURE 14
Sound Quality
A guitar string can resonate at several frequencies that combine to produce a unique sound quality.
Interpreting Data *What determines the resulting wave?*

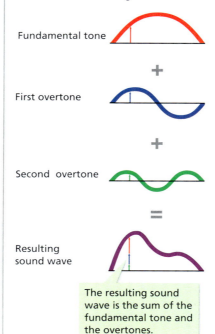

Fundamental tone

+

First overtone

+

Second overtone

=

Resulting sound wave

The resulting sound wave is the sum of the fundamental tone and the overtones.

Groups of Musical Instruments

Teach Key Concepts L2
Musical Instrument Groups

Focus Introduce the three groups of musical instruments.

Teach Have students read the caption and labels of Figure 15. Write the terms *Strings, Winds,* and *Percussion* on the board. Challenge students to brainstorm the names of different instruments, including both band and orchestra instruments. Tell them to try to think of other instruments besides the examples shown in the figure. As students name the instruments, write them under the appropriate headings. *(Sample answer: Strings include banjo, guitar, violin, cello, piano, harpsichord, harp; winds include harmonica, flute, oboe, bassoon, clarinet, saxophone, trumpet, trombone, and tuba; percussion include snare drum, cymbal, base drum, tympani, castanet, xylophone, and bell.)*

Extend The *active art* will show students how musical instruments in the three groups produce sounds and change pitch and loudness. **learning modality: visual**

Go Online *active art*

For: Musical instruments activity
Visit: PHSchool.com
Web Code: cgp-5023

Students can interact with the art of musical instruments online.

Lab zone Build **Inquiry** L1

Applying Concepts

Materials whistle

Time 10 minutes

Focus Have students apply their knowledge about musical instruments as they examine a whistle.

Teach Blow into a whistle, and have students evaluate its pitch. Ask: **Does a whistle make sound waves with a high or low frequency? How can you tell?** *(It has a high pitch, so it makes sound waves with a high frequency.)* **In which group of musical instruments would you classify a whistle? Why?** *(A whistle is a wind instrument,* *because movement of air through or across the mouthpiece causes the air inside the whistle to vibrate.)*

Apply Challenge students to explain how the size of a whistle is related to the frequency of the sound waves it produces. *(Because a whistle is small, the column of vibrating air is short, and a short air column produces high frequency sound waves.)*
learning modality: kinesthetic

Go Online *active art*

For: Musical Instruments activity
Visit: PHSchool.com
Web Code: cgp-5023

FIGURE 15
Musical Instruments
A musician controls the vibrations of a musical instrument to change pitch and loudness. **Classifying** *How would you classify a tuba, a tambourine, and a banjo?*

Wind Instrument: Clarinet
Loudness is controlled by how hard the musician blows.

Stringed Instrument: Violin
Loudness is increased by the musician pressing the bow harder against the strings.

Pitch depends on the length and thickness of the strings, the material they are made of, and how tightly the strings are stretched. A short string produces a high pitch, and a longer string produces a lower pitch.

Groups of Musical Instruments

How does a musician control the sounds produced by a musical instrument? To control pitch, the musician changes the fundamental tones produced by the instrument. To control loudness, the musician changes the energy of the vibrations. The way that pitch and loudness are controlled varies among the groups of instruments, as shown in Figure 15. **There are three basic groups of musical instruments: stringed instruments, wind instruments, and percussion instruments.**

Stringed Instruments The guitar and the violin are stringed instruments. The strings of these instruments produce sound by vibrating when they are strummed or rubbed with a bow. Their loudness is increased by resonance when the instrument's hollow body vibrates as the strings vibrate. The pitch of each string depends on four factors: its length and thickness, the material it is made from, and how tightly it is stretched. An instrument with long strings, such as a cello, produces lower notes than an instrument with short strings, such as a violin.

Percussion Instrument: Drum
Loudness is controlled by how hard the musician strikes the drum.

Pitch depends on the length of the air column, which can be changed by covering different holes. A short air column produces a high pitch, and a longer column produces a lower pitch.

Pitch depends on the size of the drum head, the material, and the tension in the drum head. A smaller drum produces a higher pitch

Wind Instruments Wind instruments include brass instruments, such as trumpets, and woodwind instruments, such as clarinets. Brass instruments produce sound when a musician's lips vibrate against the mouthpiece, causing the air column in the instrument to vibrate. Woodwinds usually contain a thin, flexible strip of material called a reed. A woodwind produces sound when the reed vibrates, causing the instrument's air column to vibrate. In wind instruments, the length of the vibrating air column determines the note that you hear. A tuba, which has a long air column, produces lower notes than a flute, which has a short air column.

Percussion Instruments Percussion instruments include drums, bells, cymbals, and xylophones. These instruments vibrate when struck. The pitch of a drum depends on its size, the material it is made of, and the tension in the drumhead. A large drum produces lower pitches than a small drum.

 What are four examples of percussion instruments?

Chapter 2   O ◆ 51

Lab zone **Teacher Demo**   **L2**

Controlling Pitch in Strings

Materials guitar
Time 10 minutes

Focus Show students how pitch is controlled in a stringed instrument.

Teach Have students examine the strings of a guitar. Point out that all the strings are the same length. Pluck one string after another, and have students listen for the differences in pitch. Ask: **Why do the strings produce sounds with different pitches if they are all the same length?** *(The strings differ in thickness and tension.)* Demonstrate how the pitch of each string can be raised by tightening it. Explain that this is done to tune the strings relative to one another and to other instruments.

Extend Ask: **What is another way to change the pitch of a guitar string?** *(Shorten the part of the string that vibrates by pressing it against a fret on the neck of the guitar.)* Demonstrate how this changes the pitch of a string. **learning modality: visual**

Help Students Read   **L1**
Comparing and Contrasting Have students make a table summarizing the most important points about the three different groups of musical instruments, using as column heads *Instrument Group, Examples, How Sound Is Produced, How Pitch Is Changed, How Loudness Is Changed*. Tell them to use information from the text and from Figure 5. Then, have students use their tables to identify similarities and differences among the three types. *(Sample answer: All three types produce sounds by making something vibrate, but they differ in what vibrates and how it is made to vibrate.)*

Differentiated Instruction

English Learners/Beginning   **L1**
Comprehension: Link to Visual Guide students in using Figure 15 to learn about the three groups of musical instruments. Explain the labels in the figure, and point out the relevant parts of the pictured instruments. Also, explain how pitch is generally controlled in instruments belonging to each group. **learning modality: visual**

English Learners/Intermediate   **L2**
Comprehension: Ask Questions After students have read the information on groups of musical instruments, ask them to explain in their own words how loudness is controlled in instruments belonging to each group. If students make any errors, direct them to reread the relevant labels in Figure 15. **learning modality: verbal**

Monitor Progress   **L2**

Skills Check Name several different musical instruments. Challenge students to classify each instrument by group.

Answers
Figure 15 A tuba is a wind instrument, a tambourine is a percussion instrument, and a banjo is a stringed instrument.

 Drums, bells, cymbals, and xylophones

O ● 51

Acoustics

Teach Key Concepts　L2
Wave Interference Affects Sound

Focus State that wave interference in sound waves affects sounds.

Teach Ask: **How do you think destructive and constructive interference affect sound?** (*Destructive interference diminishes or dampens sound. Constructive interference increases loudness and may distort sound.*)

Apply Have students explain how their inferences might be applied in the design of a concert hall. **learning modality: verbal**

Monitor Progress _____　L2

Answers
Figure 16 Reflect sound downward

Assess

Reviewing Key Concepts

1. a. Sound quality results from the blending of a fundamental tone with its overtones. **b.** By increasing the loudness of certain overtones
2. a. Stringed, wind, and percussion instruments **b.** For strings, change the length or tension of a string; for winds, change the length of the air column; for percussion, strike a surface that has a different tension or size. **c.** In a guitar: by plucking the strings harder; In a drum: by striking the drumhead harder.
3. a. The study of how sounds interact with each other and the environment **b.** Curved hard surfaces reflect sound waves and direct them to different parts of the hall. Soft surfaces absorb sound waves and reduce reverberation. **c.** With too little reverberation, instruments would sound thin and distant.

Reteach　L1
Call on students to explain how instruments in each of the three groups produce sound.

Performance Assessment　L2
Writing Have students describe how acoustics is used in concert hall design.

All in One Teaching Resources
- Section Summary: *Music*
- Review and Reinforcement: *Music*
- Enrich: *Music*

Keep Students on Track Have students experiment with different materials and

FIGURE 16
Concert Hall Acoustics
Surfaces in concert halls are designed with a variety of materials and shapes.
Inferring *What might be the purpose of the curved panels near the ceiling?*

Acoustics

Your surroundings affect the musical sounds that you hear at a concert. To understand this, compare the sound of your voice in different places—in class, outdoors, or in a gym. The differences you hear are due to the different ways that sounds interact. **Acoustics** is the study of how sounds interact with each other and the environment.

Sound waves can interfere with each other. Constructive interference may distort sound, while destructive interference can produce "dead spots" where loudness is reduced. Sound waves interact with the environment, also. For example, if you clap your hands in a gym, you hear echoes after you clap because sound waves reflect back and forth off the hard surfaces. This is **reverberation,** in which the echoes of a sound are heard after the sound source stops producing sound waves. The sound from a handclap can take more than a second to die out in a gym.

Acoustics is used in the design of concert halls to control reverberation and interference. Curved hard surfaces are used to direct sound waves to different parts of the concert hall. Soft surfaces absorb sound waves, reducing reverberation. But some reverberation is desirable. With too little reverberation, instruments would sound thin and distant. With too much reverberation, reflected waves interfere and individual notes become hard to pick out.

Section 3 Assessment

Target Reading Skill **Previewing Visuals** Refer to your questions and answers about Figure 15 to help you answer Question 2 below.

Reviewing Key Concepts
1. a. Describing How do overtones affect the sound quality of a musical instrument?
　b. Explaining How does resonance affect the sound quality of a musical instrument?
2. a. Listing What are the three groups of musical instruments?
　b. Summarizing How is pitch controlled in each group of musical instruments?
　c. Comparing and Contrasting How is loudness increased in a drum and in a guitar?

3. a. Defining What is acoustics?
　b. Relating Cause and Effect How is acoustics used in the design of concert halls?
　c. Making Judgments Why is some reverberation desirable in a concert hall?

Writing in Science

Explanation A friend e-mails you and asks how your new guitar produces music. Write an e-mail that answers your friend's question. Be sure to explain how you can change pitch, and why the guitar has a hollow body.

52 ◆ O

Lab zone Chapter **Project**

ways to vary pitch and loudness. Ask them to organize their observations in data tables so they can generalize about the sounds produced by different designs and materials.

Writing in Science

Writing Mode Exposition/How-To
Scoring Rubric
4 Exceeds criteria; includes a lucid, complete, and highly accurate explanation for the question
3 Meets criteria
2 Includes an explanation but contains some errors
1 Includes only a vague description and/or contains serious errors

Changing Pitch

Problem

When you blow across the mouth of a bottle, you can play a "note." What determines the pitch you hear?

Skills Focus

developing hypotheses, controlling variables, designing experiments

Suggested Materials

- 1-L soda bottle   • 2-L soda bottle
- 250-mL graduated cylinder   • metric ruler
- straw   • water

Design a Plan

1. Practice making a sound by using a straw to blow across the mouth of a 1-L bottle. Then blow across the mouth of a 2-L bottle in the same way. Compare the pitches. Record your observations in your notebook.

2. Add 250 mL of water to both the 1-L bottle and the 2-L bottle. Blow across the mouth of each bottle and compare the pitches. Record your observations in your notebook.

3. Analyze your observations from Steps 1 and 2 to predict what may have affected the pitches. For example, measure the height of the air column, and calculate the volume of air in each bottle. (*Hint:* Subtract the volume of water in the bottle from the total volume of the bottle.)

4. Develop a hypothesis about what determines the pitch of the sound produced by blowing across the mouth of a bottle. Record your hypothesis in your notebook.

5. Design an experiment to test your hypothesis. Create a data table to record information about the variables. Write your plan. (*Hint:* You can change the height of the air column in a bottle by changing the amount of water in the bottle.)

6. After receiving your teacher's approval of your plan, conduct your experiment and record the results in your notebook.

Analyze and Conclude

1. **Observing** Describe the pitch of the sound produced by each bottle in Steps 1 and 2.

2. **Designing Experiments** Did your experiment support your hypothesis? Explain.

3. **Controlling Variables** Identify the manipulated and responding variables in your experiment.

4. **Inferring** If you had a 1-L bottle that contained 250 mL of water, what would you do to produce a higher-pitched sound?

5. **Drawing Conclusions** What is the relationship between the height of the air column and the pitch of the sound produced by blowing across the mouth of a bottle?

6. **Communicating** Based on your results, describe how you could use a set of bottles as a musical instrument.

More to Explore

Use a set of tuning forks or a pitch pipe to "tune" five bottles to match the notes C, D, E, F, and G. What can you conclude about the pitches of the five notes from the height of the air column in each bottle? Use the bottles to play the following notes: E D C D E E E D D D E G G E D C D E E E D D E D C.

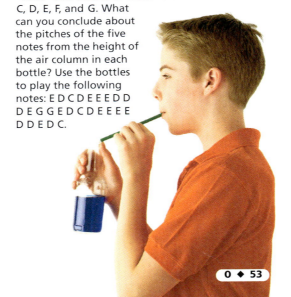

O ◆ 53

Lab zone **Design Your Own Lab**

Changing Pitch

Prepare for Inquiry

Skills Objectives

After this lab, students will be able to
- develop a hypothesis to explain how the level of water in a bottle will affect the pitch of sound
- design an experiment to test their hypothesis about water level and pitch
- control the variables in their experiment

Prep Time 10 minutes
Class Time 40 minutes

Advance Planning

Obtain a sufficient number of empty 1-L and 2-L soda bottles so that each student has a bottle of each size. Inexpensive pitch pipes can be obtained at most music stores.

Safety

⚠ Caution students to immediately wipe up any spilled water. Tell them not to share straws. Review the safety guidelines in Appendix A.

All in One Teaching Resources
- Lab Worksheet: *Changing Pitch*

Guide Inquiry

Invitation

Blow across the top of an empty bottle with a straw. Ask: **How could you change the pitch of the sound produced by the bottle?** (*Students may say by adding water to the bottle.*)

Introduce the Procedure

Use a pitch pipe to demonstrate tones with low, medium, and high pitches. Tell students they will try to produce different pitches by blowing across a bottle.

Expected Outcome

When the bottles are empty, the lowest pitch is produced and the 2-L bottle produces a lower pitch than the 1-L bottle. The pitch increases in each bottle as the water level rises.

Extend Inquiry

More to Explore Note C has the lowest pitch because it has the tallest air column, and pitch rises from notes C through F. The tune is "Mary Had a Little Lamb."

Analyze and Conclude

1. The 2-L bottle has a lower pitch than the 1-L bottle. Both bottles have a higher pitch after water is added.

2. Answers will vary but if students hypothesized that the height of the air column determines pitch, their answer will be yes, because pitch changed as the height of the air column changed.

3. The manipulated variable was height of air column; the responding variable was pitch.

4. Sample answer: Add more water.

5. As height of the air column increases, pitch decreases.

6. Sample answer: Add different amounts of water to several identical bottles to produce all the notes needed to play a song.

Objectives

After this lesson, students will be able to

O.2.4.1 Describe the function of each section of the ear.

O.2.4.2 Identify what causes hearing loss.

Target Reading Skill

Sequencing Explain that organizing information from beginning to end helps students understand a step-by-step process.

Answers

Sample Flowchart:

How You Hear Sound

- The outer ear funnels sound waves into the ear canal.
- Sound waves make the eardrum vibrate.
- Tiny bones in the middle ear transmit vibrations to the inner ear.
- Vibrations in the cochlea of the inner ear send messages to the brain.

All in One Teaching Resources

- Transparency O24

Preteach

Build Background Knowledge   L2

Channeling Sound to the Ears

Ask students what they could do to better hear a friend calling out across a soccer field. *(Sample answer: Turn one ear toward the friend, cup a hand behind their ear)* Explain that these actions help direct sound waves toward the ear. Tell students that in this section they will learn what happens to sound waves after they reach the ear.

Reading Preview

Key Concepts

- What is the function of each section of the ear?
- What causes hearing loss?

Key Terms

- ear canal
- eardrum
- cochlea

Target Reading Skill

Sequencing A sequence is the order in which the steps in a process occur. As you read, make a flowchart that shows how you hear sound. Put the steps of the process in separate boxes in the order in which they occur.

How You Hear Sound

> The outer ear funnels sound waves into the ear canal.
>
> ↓
>
> Sound waves make the eardrum vibrate.
>
> ↓

Lab zone Discover Activity

Where Is the Sound Coming From?

1. Ask your partner to sit on a chair, with eyes closed.
2. Clap your hands near your partner's left ear. Ask your partner what direction the sound came from. Record the answer.
3. Now clap near your partner's right ear. Again, ask your partner what direction the sound came from and record the answer. Continue clapping in different locations around your partner's head and face. How well did your partner identify the directions the sounds came from?
4. Switch places with your partner and repeat Steps 1–3.

Think It Over

Observing From which locations are claps easily identified? For which locations are claps impossible to identify? Is there a pattern? If so, suggest an explanation for the pattern.

The house is quiet. You are sound asleep. All of a sudden, your alarm clock goes off. Startled, you jump up out of bed. Your ears detected the sound waves produced by the alarm clock. But how exactly did your brain receive the information?

The Human Ear

The function of your ear is to gather sound waves and send, or transmit, information about sound to your brain. Your ear has three main sections: the outer ear, the middle ear, and the inner ear. Each section has a different function. **The outer ear funnels sound waves, the middle ear transmits the waves inward, and the inner ear converts sound waves into a form that travels to your brain.**

Outer Ear Look at Figure 17. The first section of your ear is the outer ear. The outermost part of your outer ear looks and acts like a funnel. It collects sound waves and directs them into a narrow region called the **ear canal.** Your ear canal is a few centimeters long and ends at the eardrum. The **eardrum** is a small, tightly stretched, drumlike membrane. The sound waves make your eardrum vibrate, just as a drum vibrates when you strike it.

Lab zone Discover Activity

Skills Focus Observing   L1

Time 10 minutes

Tips Have students carry out the activity in a quiet room. Caution students not to clap loudly near anyone's ear.

Expected Outcome Most students will correctly identify the horizontal position of the source, especially when it is near the left or right ear. It is more difficult to detect the vertical position of a sound, especially one directly in front of or behind the listener.

Think It Over The locations of claps at the left or right of the listener are easily identified. The locations of claps in front of or behind the listener are harder to identify. Sound waves traveling from the left or right arrive at each ear at slightly different times, allowing the listener to detect the location of the sound source.

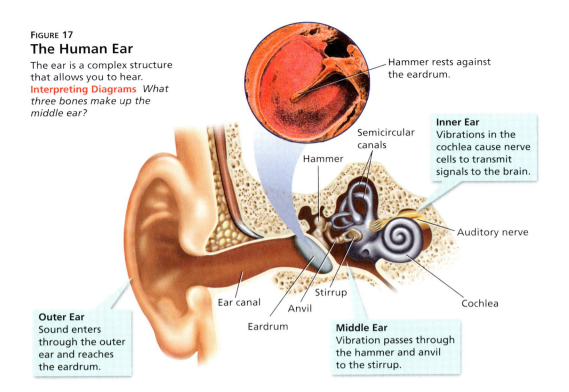

FIGURE 17
The Human Ear
The ear is a complex structure that allows you to hear.
Interpreting Diagrams *What three bones make up the middle ear?*

Hammer rests against the eardrum.

Semicircular canals

Hammer

Inner Ear
Vibrations in the cochlea cause nerve cells to transmit signals to the brain.

Auditory nerve

Cochlea

Stirrup

Anvil

Ear canal

Eardrum

Middle Ear
Vibration passes through the hammer and anvil to the stirrup.

Outer Ear
Sound enters through the outer ear and reaches the eardrum.

Middle Ear Behind the eardrum is the middle ear. The middle ear contains the three smallest bones in your body—the hammer, the anvil, and the stirrup. The hammer is attached to the eardrum, so when the eardrum vibrates, the hammer does too. The hammer then transmits vibrations first to the anvil and then to the stirrup.

Inner Ear A membrane separates the middle ear from the inner ear, the third section of the ear. When the stirrup vibrates against this membrane, the vibrations pass into the cochlea. The **cochlea** (KAHK lee uh) is a fluid-filled cavity shaped like a snail shell. The cochlea contains more than 10,000 tiny structures called hair cells. These hair cells have hairlike projections that float in the fluid of the cochlea. When vibrations move through the fluid, the hair cells move, causing messages to be sent to the brain through the auditory nerve. The brain processes these messages and tells you that you've heard sound.

 Reading Checkpoint What are the three main sections of the ear?

Lab zone Try This **Activity**

Listen to This

1. Tie two strings to the handle of a metal spoon. Each string should be about 40 cm long.
2. Hold the loose end of each string in each hand. Bump the spoon against a desk or other hard solid object. Listen to the sound.
3. Now wrap the ends of the string around your fingers. Put your index fingers against your ears and bump the spoon again. How is the sound different?

Inferring What can you infer about how sound travels to your ears?

Chapter 2 O ◆ 55

Lab zone Try This **Activity**

Skills Focus Inferring

Materials 2 strings about 40 cm long, metal spoon

Time 15 minutes

Tips Use heavy thread or string for best results. Caution students not to push their fingers into their ears.

L1

Expected Outcome The first sound is not as loud as the second sound. The expected inference is that sound waves travel better through string than through air.

Extend Allow students to test another medium, such as a wooden meter stick, for its ability to transmit sound waves.
learning modality: kinesthetic

Instruct

The Human Ear

Teach Key Concepts   **L2**
Structures of the Ear

Focus Introduce the sections of the ear by reading the boldface sentence on page 54.

Teach On the board, write *Outer Ear, Middle Ear,* and *Inner Ear* as table headings. Then, have students scan the text for structures of the ear and call them out. As students name a structure, ask: **Which section contains that structure?** Write each structure on the board under the correct heading.

Apply Have students copy the table, leaving room beside each structure to add its function as they read. **learning modality: visual**

Use Visuals: Figure 17   **L1**
The Path of Sound Waves

Focus Explain how Figure 17 shows the ear in cross section.

Teach Have students trace the path of sound waves through the ear. Note the order of structures through which the waves pass.

Apply After students have finished tracing the path of sound waves, check their comprehension by asking: **What is the first structure to vibrate in the middle ear when a sound wave passes through?** (*Hammer*) **learning modality: kinesthetic**

All in One Teaching Resources
• Transparency O25

Independent Practice   **L2**

All in One Teaching Resources
• Guided Reading and Study Worksheet: *How You Hear Sound*

O Student Edition on Audio CD

Monitor Progress _____   **L2**

Oral Presentation Call on students to name the structures of the ear. Call on other students to state their functions.

Answers
Figure 17 The hammer, anvil, and stirrup
 Reading Checkpoint Outer ear, middle ear, and inner ear

O ● 55

Hearing Loss

Teach Key Concepts
Causes of Hearing Loss

Focus State the causes of hearing loss.

Teach Ask: **Which causes might be prevented?** *(Injury, infection, and exposure to loud sounds)*

Apply Ask: **How can you reduce the risk of hearing loss?** *(Sample answer: Avoid exposure to loud sounds or wear hearing protectors.)*
learning modality: verbal

Monitor Progress ____ L2

Answers
Figure 18 A possible benefit is that a very small hearing aid is not noticeable. A possible drawback is that the controls are harder to manipulate.

> **Reading Checkpoint** A person may have difficulty hearing soft or high-pitch sounds.

Assess

Reviewing Key Concepts

1. a. Outer ear funnels sound waves; middle ear transmits waves inward; inner ear converts waves into a form that travels to the brain. **b.** The ear canal funnels sound waves toward the eardrum. **c.** Vibrations from the eardrum travel through the hammer, anvil, and stirrup to the inner ear.
2. a. Injury, infection, exposure to loud sounds, aging **b.** By damaging hair cells in the cochlea **c.** Yes, because they help prevent exposure to loud sounds and possible hearing loss

Reteach L1
Have students write the name of each structure of the ear on an index card. Then, ask students to shuffle the cards and arrange them in the order sound travels through the ear.

Performance Assessment L2
Writing Ask students to make pamphlets describing the causes of hearing loss.

All in One Teaching Resources
- Section Summary: *How You Hear Sound*
- Review and Reinforcement: *How You Hear Sound*
- Enrich: *How You Hear Sound*

FIGURE 18
A Modern Hearing Aid
Some hearing aids are about the size of a dime. **Inferring** *What are some benefits and drawbacks of tiny hearing aids?*

Hearing aid

Hearing Loss

When hearing loss occurs, a person may have difficulty hearing soft sounds or high-pitched sounds. **There are many causes of hearing loss, including injury, infection, exposure to loud sounds, and aging.**

Causes of Hearing Loss Hearing loss can occur suddenly if the eardrum is damaged or punctured. (Imagine trying to play a torn drum!) For this reason, it is dangerous to put objects into your ear, even to clean it. Infections also can damage the delicate inner ear, causing permanent hearing loss.

Extended exposure to loud sounds can damage hair cells in the ear. The damaged cells will no longer send signals to the brain. You can prevent this type of hearing loss by wearing hearing protection when you are around loud sounds.

The most common type of hearing loss occurs gradually. As a person gets older, some hair cells in the cochlea die and are not replaced. People with this kind of hearing loss often have difficulty hearing high-frequency sounds.

Hearing Aids For some types of hearing loss, hearing aids can restore some ability to hear. Hearing aids amplify sounds entering the ear. Some are so tiny that they can fit invisibly in the ear canal. Others can amplify specific frequencies that a person has lost the ability to hear.

> **Reading Checkpoint** What happens when a hearing loss occurs?

Section 4 Assessment

Target Reading Skill **Sequencing** Refer to your flowchart about hearing as you answer Question 1.

Reviewing Key Concepts
1. a. Identifying What is the function of each section of your ear?
  b. Interpreting Diagrams Look at Figure 17. What happens to a sound wave as it enters your ear canal?
  c. Relating Cause and Effect How are sound waves transmitted through the middle ear?
2. a. Listing What are four causes of hearing loss?
  b. Explaining How can loud sounds lead to hearing loss?

  c. Making Judgments Should people at a rock concert wear earplugs? Why or why not?

 At-Home Activity

Sound Survey Ask family members to survey the sounds they hear in a day. Ask them to rate the sounds as quiet, normal, loud, or painful. Then rate each sound as pleasant, neutral, or annoying. For each sound record the source, location, time of day, and time exposed to the sound. How are the ratings similar? How are they different?

 At-Home Activity

Sound Survey L3 Students may find that most family members generally agree on pleasant, neutral, and annoying sounds. However, there may be some differences in the ratings, especially between generations.

Chapter Project

Keep Students on Track At this point, students are expected to have constructed and tried out their musical instruments. They should now make any further adjustments necessary to allow them to alter loudness and pitch. Have students use a piano or pitch pipe to identify the different notes produced on their instruments. Encourage them to learn to play a simple song.

Design and Build Hearing Protectors

Problem

Can you design and build hearing protectors that block some sound from reaching your ears?

Design Skills

designing a solution, evaluating the design

Suggested Materials

- sound source (radio, tape player, or CD player)
- soundproofing materials
- tape measure
- scissors
- string
- pencil
- different types of headgear
- glue

Procedure ✂

PART 1 Research and Investigate

1. Copy the data table on a separate sheet of paper.
2. Select a soundproofing material.
3. Stand quietly at the back of the room. Your teacher will adjust the loudness of a sound source until you are just able to hear it. Ask your partner to measure and record your distance from the sound source. Record the measurement in your data table.
4. Cover both ears with the soundproofing material. **CAUTION:** *Do not insert any material into your ears.* Move slowly forward until you can just hear the sound source again. Stop. Then have your partner measure your distance from the sound source. Record the measurement in your data table.
5. Repeat Steps 2–4 using three other materials.

Data Table	
Soundproofing Material	Distance From Sound Source (m)
No material	
Material 1	
Material 2	
Material 3	
Material 4	

PART 2 Design and Build

6. Based on what you learned in Part 1, design and build hearing protectors. Your device should
   - keep you from hearing a pencil dropped on a table at a distance of 5 meters
   - fit comfortably on your head without needing to be held in place
   - be made of materials approved by your teacher
7. Sketch your design and list the materials you will use. After your teacher approves your design, build your hearing protectors.

Analyze and Conclude

1. **Designing a Solution** What did you learn about soundproofing materials in Part 1 that helped you design your device?
2. **Evaluating the Design** Test your hearing protectors. Did your device meet all of the goals stated in Step 6? Explain.
3. **Troubleshooting** As you designed, built, and tested your hearing protectors, what problems did you encounter? How did you solve them?

Communicate

A construction company is considering buying your hearing protectors. Write a summary of your test results to convince the company that the device meets the design goals stated in Step 6.

Chapter 2 O ◆ 57

Analyze and Conclude

1. Students may say they learned which material was best for soundproofing (most likely some type of foam).

2. Students might describe how well their protectors muffled sound and stayed in place.

3. Students may describe problems with their headgear staying in place or attaching soundproofing material to their headgear. Their solutions will vary from selecting all new materials to various modifications of their starting materials.

Extend Inquiry

Communicate Summaries should include quantitative data showing the effectiveness of the hearing protectors. They also might include a description of the protectors' comfort features, suggestions as to when they should be used, and the benefits of using them.

Design and Build Hearing Protectors

Prepare for Inquiry

Skills Objectives

After this lab, students will be able to
- design and build hearing protectors
- evaluate the design and redesign the hearing protectors, if necessary, for better performance

🕐 **Prep Time** 30 minutes
Class Time 40 minutes

Advance Planning

For health reasons, you should purchase new headgear for each student or have students provide their own.

Alternative Materials

Headgear might include headbands, helmets, and caps and other types of hats. Soundproofing materials might include quilted fabric, foam rubber, newspaper, Styrofoam®, fiberfill, and cardboard.

Safety

✂ Warn students to use scissors carefully. Tell them not to insert any materials into their ears. Review the safety guidelines in Appendix A.

All in One Teaching Resources
- Lab Worksheet: *Design and Build Hearing Protectors*

Guide Inquiry

Introduce the Procedure

Have students read through the procedure. Then, ask: **What will you measure when you test different materials?** (*The distance at which the sound first becomes audible*) **Why is it important to construct a device that is not held in place with the hands?** (*So people can have their hands free to do other tasks*)

Expected Outcome

Students are expected to create hearing protectors by attaching soundproofing material to headgear. The protectors must stay in place and keep students from hearing a pencil dropped on a table 5 m away. Students may need to redesign their device to meet these two criteria.

Science and Society

Keeping It Quiet...

Key Concept
Millions of people are exposed to noise pollution everyday, and many people suffer permanent hearing loss because of noise. Different approaches can help reduce exposure to noise and the risk of hearing loss.

Build Background Knowledge
Recalling Loud Noises
Ask: **What are some loud noises you have been exposed to in the past?** (*Sample answer: Sirens, lawn mowers, rock bands*) **How do loud noises make you feel?** (*Students may say that loud noises are annoying, stressful, or even painful. Some students may have experienced temporarily muffled hearing or ringing in their ears after being exposed to loud noises.*) Explain that continued exposure to loud noise can lead to permanent hearing loss.

Introduce the Debate
Point out that there are two general approaches to solving the noise-pollution problem. One approach places the responsibility mainly on communities and government; the other approach places the responsibility mainly on individuals. Communities and government can reduce noise levels by regulating the amount of noise that can be produced by machines, traffic, and other sources of loud noise. Communities and government can also educate consumers about protecting their hearing. Individuals can protect their own hearing by wearing hearing protectors and by avoiding loud noise.

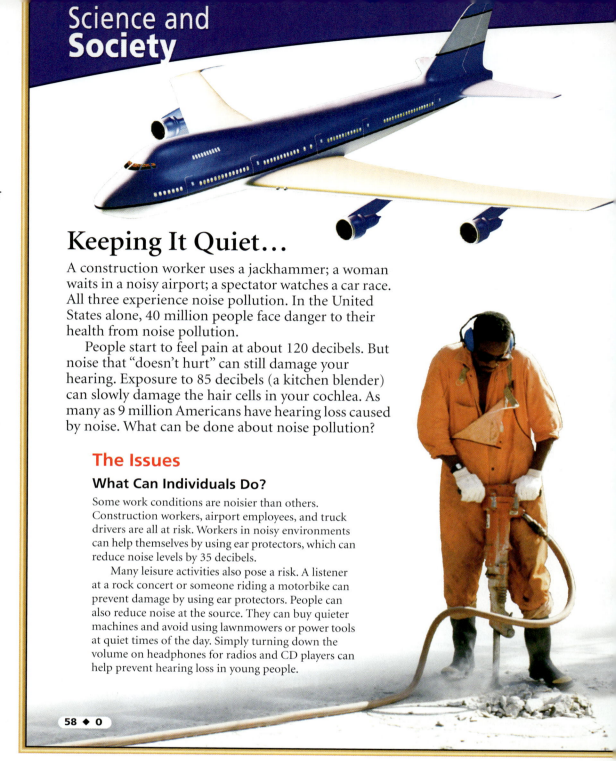

Science and Society

Keeping It Quiet...

A construction worker uses a jackhammer; a woman waits in a noisy airport; a spectator watches a car race. All three experience noise pollution. In the United States alone, 40 million people face danger to their health from noise pollution.

People start to feel pain at about 120 decibels. But noise that "doesn't hurt" can still damage your hearing. Exposure to 85 decibels (a kitchen blender) can slowly damage the hair cells in your cochlea. As many as 9 million Americans have hearing loss caused by noise. What can be done about noise pollution?

The Issues

What Can Individuals Do?
Some work conditions are noisier than others. Construction workers, airport employees, and truck drivers are all at risk. Workers in noisy environments can help themselves by using ear protectors, which can reduce noise levels by 35 decibels.

Many leisure activities also pose a risk. A listener at a rock concert or someone riding a motorbike can prevent damage by using ear protectors. People can also reduce noise at the source. They can buy quieter machines and avoid using lawnmowers or power tools at quiet times of the day. Simply turning down the volume on headphones for radios and CD players can help prevent hearing loss in young people.

Facilitate the Debate
Have students read the feature and answer the questions.

Guide the class in a discussion of the noise pollution problem by asking such questions as: **What are some common sources of loud noise? What can be done to reduce loud noise? What can be done to reduce exposure to loud noise? Whose responsibility is it to protect the hearing of individuals?**

Organize the class into two groups. Arbitrarily assign one group to argue that individuals should take responsibility for their own hearing. Assign the other group to argue that communities and governments should take responsibility for protecting people's hearing.

What Can Communities Do?

Transportation—planes, trains, trucks, and cars—is the largest source of noise pollution. About 15 million Americans live near airports or under airplane flight paths. Careful planning to locate airports away from dense populations can reduce noise. Cities can also prohibit late-night flights.

Many communities have laws against noise that exceeds a certain decibel level, but these laws are hard to enforce. In some cities, "noise police" can give fines to people who use noisy equipment.

What Can the Government Do?

A National Office of Noise Abatement and Control was set up in the 1970s. It required labels on power tools to tell how much noise they made. But in 1982, this office lost its funding. In 1997, lawmakers proposed The Quiet Communities Act to bring the office back and set limits to many types of noise. But critics say that national laws have little effect. They want the federal government to encourage—and pay for—research into making quieter vehicles and machines.

You Decide

1. Identify the Problem
In your own words, describe the issues of noise pollution.

2. Analyze the Options
List as many methods as you can for dealing with noise. How would each method reduce noise or protect people from noise?

3. Find a Solution
Choose one method for reducing noise in your community. Make a poster to convince people to support your proposal.

For: More on noise pollution
Visit: PHSchool.com
Web Code: cgh-5020

O ◆ 59

Background

Facts and Figures Highway noise is a problem for most communities, and different approaches have been taken to reduce the noise. For example, some communities prohibit large trucks from driving on residential streets. In many cities, heavily traveled highways are enclosed by walls made of concrete or wood that protect neighborhoods from the sound of traffic.

In Great Britain and France, new road surfaces are being developed to reduce traffic noise. The surfaces are a mixture of traditional paving materials and rubber granules made from recycled tires. The surfaces absorb sound and reduce traffic noise up to 70 percent. By recycling tires, the surfaces are also environmentally friendly.

Objectives

After this lesson, students will be able to

O.2.5.1 Explain why some animals use echolocation.

O.2.5.2 State the uses of ultrasound technologies.

Target Reading Skill

Comparing and Contrasting Explain that comparing and contrasting information shows how ideas, facts, and events are similar and different. The results of the comparison can have importance.

Answers

Sample compare/contrast table:

Echolocation — Ultrasound; Air, water; Navigate, find food

Sonar —Ultrasound; Water; Purposes; Find water depth, sunken objects, schools of fish

All in One Teaching Resources

• Transparency O26

Preteach

Build Background Knowledge   L2

Hearing Echoes

Ask: **What would happen if you yelled into the Grand Canyon toward the rock walls on the other side?** *(You would hear an echo.)* **What would cause this result?** *(Sample answer: Sound waves bouncing back from the rock wall of the canyon)* Tell students that in this section they will learn more about what happens when sound waves bounce back from surfaces.

Section 5
Using Sound

Reading Preview

Key Concepts
• Why do some animals use echolocation?
• What are ultrasound technologies used for?

Key Terms
• echolocation • sonar
• sonogram

Target Reading Skill
Comparing and Contrasting As you read, compare and contrast echolocation and sonar by completing a table like the one below.

Using Sound

Feature	Echolocation	Sonar
Type of wave	Ultrasound	
Medium(s)		Water
Purposes		

Lab zone Discover Activity

How Can You Use Time to Measure Distance?

1. Measure a distance 3 meters from a wall and mark the spot with a piece of masking tape.
2. Roll a soft ball in a straight line from that spot toward the wall. What happens to the ball?
3. Roll the ball again. Try to roll the ball at the same speed each time. Have a classmate use a stopwatch to record the time it takes for the ball to leave your hand, reflect off the wall, and then return to you.
4. Now move 6 meters away from the wall. Mark the spot with tape. Repeat Steps 2 and 3.
5. Compare the time for both distances.

Think It Over

Inferring What does the difference in time tell you about the distance the ball has traveled?

A dog trainer stands quietly, watching the dog a short distance away. To get the dog's attention, the trainer blows into a small whistle. You don't hear a thing. But the dog stops, cocks an ear, and then comes running toward the trainer. Dogs can hear ultrasound frequencies up to about 45,000 Hz, well above the upper limit for humans. Other animals, such as cats and mice, can also hear ultrasound frequencies.

Some types of animals not only hear ultrasound, but also produce ultrasound waves. They use ultrasound waves to "see in the dark."

◀ **Dog hearing an ultrasound whistle**

Lab zone Discover Activity

Skills Focus Inferring   L2

Materials meter stick, masking tape, soft ball, stopwatch

Time 10 minutes

Tips Test the ball before using it with students. A softer ball works better than a hard one. Explain how the activity models the reflection of sound.

Expected Outcome When the ball hits the wall, it bounces back. The ball takes longer to roll back to the student when it is 6 meters away from the wall than when it is 3 meters away.

Think It Over The more time it takes the ball to return to the student, the greater the distance the ball has traveled.

Echolocation

Imagine trying to walk around in a totally dark room. You would probably bump into objects every few steps. Unlike you, bats find it easy to move around in dark places. This is because they use echolocation. **Echolocation** (ek oh loh KAY shun) is the use of reflected sound waves to determine distances or to locate objects. **Some animals, including bats and dolphins, use echolocation to navigate and to find food.**

Bats Bats use ultrasound waves with frequencies up to 100,000 Hz to move around and hunt. As a bat flies, it sends out short pulses of ultrasound waves—as many as 200 pulses per second! The waves reflect off objects and return to the bat's ears. The time it takes for the sound waves to return tells the bat how far it is from obstacles or prey. The bat uses the reflected sound waves to build up a "picture" of what lies ahead.

Dolphins, Porpoises, and Whales Dolphins, porpoises, and some whales must often hunt in darkness. Like bats, these animals use echolocation. For example, dolphins send out ultrasound waves with frequencies up to 150,000 Hz. The sound waves travel through the water and bounce off fish or other prey, as shown in Figure 19. Dolphins sense the reflected sound waves through their jawbones. They use echolocation to hunt at night or in murky or deep water.

✓ **Reading Checkpoint** What animals use echolocation?

Sound

Video Preview
▶ Video Field Trip
Video Assessment

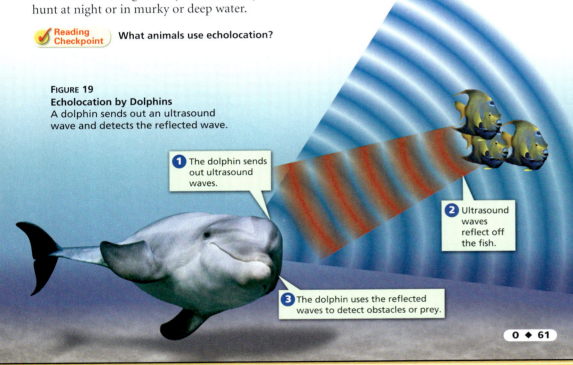

FIGURE 19
Echolocation by Dolphins
A dolphin sends out an ultrasound wave and detects the reflected wave.

1 The dolphin sends out ultrasound waves.

2 Ultrasound waves reflect off the fish.

3 The dolphin uses the reflected waves to detect obstacles or prey.

O ◆ 61

Ultrasound Technologies

Teach Key Concepts L2

Introducing Sonar

Focus Introduce sonar by comparing and contrasting it with radar, with which students may be more familiar.

Teach Explain that both sonar and radar use reflected waves to locate objects, but sonar uses sound waves, whereas radar uses radio waves.

Apply Ask: **How might this difference affect where the two methods are used?** *(Sample answer: Sound waves are mechanical and travel best in relatively dense mediums such as water. Radio waves are electromagnetic and can travel without a medium. Because of these differences, sonar can be used underwater and radar can be used in space.)* **learning modality: verbal**

Calculating Depth Using Sonar

Materials calculator

Time 5 minutes

Focus Tell students that sonar can be used to find water depth.

Teach Remind the class that the distance a wave travels is the product of time and speed. On the board, write $D = V \times T$. Tell students that D represents distance, V represents speed, and T represents time.

Apply Tell students that it takes 8.20 seconds for a sound wave to travel to the bottom of the ocean and back to the surface. Ask: **If the speed of sound in salt water is 1,530 m/s, how deep is the ocean at this point?**

$$V \times \underline{T} = \frac{1,530\, ms \times 8.20 s}{2} = (6,270 m)$$

If necessary, explain why it is necessary to divide the distance by 2. **learning modality: logical/mathematical**

For: More on sonar
Visit: PHSchool.com
Web Code: cgd-5025

Students can review sonar in an online interactivity.

Designing Experiments

1. Stand a square piece of cardboard on a table. Prop it up with a book.
2. Lay two cardboard tubes flat on the table. The tubes should be angled to make a V shape, with the point of the V near the cardboard square. Leave a gap of about 6 cm between the cardboard square and the ends of the tubes.
3. Place a ticking watch in one tube. Put your ear near the open end of the second tube. Cover your free ear with your hand. What do you hear?
4. Design an experiment to determine how well sound reflects off different materials.

For: More on sonar
Visit: PHSchool.com
Web Code: cgd-5025

Ultrasound Technologies

People cannot send out pulses of ultrasound to help them move around in the dark. But people sometimes need to explore places they cannot easily reach, such as deep underwater or inside the human body. **Ultrasound technologies such as sonar and ultrasound imaging are used to observe things that cannot be seen directly.**

Sonar A system that uses reflected sound waves to detect and locate objects underwater is called **sonar**. The word *sonar* comes from the initial letters of **so**und **n**avigation **a**nd **r**anging. *Navigation* means finding your way around on the ocean (or in the air), and *ranging* means finding the distance between objects. Today, sonar is used to determine the depth of water, to map the ocean floor, and to locate sunken ships, schools of fish, and other objects in the ocean.

A sonar device sends a burst of ultrasound waves that travel through the water. When the sound waves strike an object or the ocean floor, they reflect as shown in Figure 20. The sonar device detects the reflected waves.

The farther a sound wave travels before bouncing off an object, the longer it takes to return to the sonar device. A computer in the sonar device measures the time it takes for the sound waves to go out and return. Then, it multiplies this time by the speed of sound in water. The result is the total distance the sound waves traveled. The total distance is divided by two to find how far away the object is. You must divide by two because the sound waves travel out and back.

FIGURE 20
Using Sonar
A sonar device sends out ultrasound waves and then detects the reflected waves. **Interpreting Diagrams** *What happens to the reflected sound waves?*

Skills Activity

Skills Focus Designing experiments L2

Materials square piece of cardboard, 2 cardboard tubes, metric ruler, ticking watch

Time 15 minutes

Tip Make sure that students place the tubes at the same angle relative to the piece of cardboard.

Extend Students can describe how they would send sound waves toward the materials and list the materials they would use. Challenge students to predict how well the different materials will reflect sound. If students carry out the experiment, have them record their observations in a data table. **learning modality: kinesthetic**

Ultrasound Imaging Doctors use ultrasound imaging to look inside the human body. Ultrasound imaging devices send ultrasound waves into the body and detect the reflected sound waves. Different parts of the body, such as bones, muscles, the liver, or the heart, reflect sound differently. The device uses the reflected ultrasound waves to create a picture called a **sonogram**. A doctor can use sonograms to diagnose and treat many medical conditions.

Ultrasound imaging is used to examine developing babies before they are born. A technician or doctor holds a small probe on a pregnant woman's abdomen. The probe sends out very high frequency ultrasound waves (about 4 million Hz). By analyzing the reflected sound waves, the device builds up a sonogram. The sonogram can show the position of the baby. Sonograms can also show if more than one baby will be born. In addition to a still picture, ultrasound imaging can produce a video of a developing baby.

 **Reading Checkpoint** What is a sonogram?

◀ Sonogram

Section 5 Assessment

Target Reading Skill

Comparing and Contrasting Use your table about echolocation and sonar to help you answer the questions below.

Reviewing Key Concepts

1. a. **Defining** What is echolocation?
   b. **Summarizing** Why do bats and dolphins use echolocation?
   c. **Interpreting Diagrams** Look at Figure 19. Why would a dolphin need to continue sending out sound waves as it nears its prey?
2. a. **Reviewing** Why do people use ultrasound technologies?
   b. **Drawing Conclusions** A sonar device can show the size of a fish but not the type of fish. Explain why.
   c. **Comparing and Contrasting** How is sonar similar to ultrasound imaging used in medicine? How is it different?

Writing in Science

Advertisement Write a short advertisement for a depth finder used on fishing boats. Describe how the depth finder can determine the depth and direction of fish in the area. Include a diagram to show how the depth finder works.

Chapter 2 O ◆ 63

Interactive Textbook

- Complete student edition
- Section and chapter self-assessments
- Assessment reports for teachers

Help Students Read

Building Vocabulary

Word/Part Analysis Tell students that the word part *son-* means "sound." Words containing *son-* include *sonar, sonic, dissonance, resonance,* and *sonogram.* All of the words have something to do with sound. Challenge students to find and read the definition for each word and explain how each word is related to sound.

Word Origins Inform students that the term *acoustic* was coined in 1605. Based on the Greek word *akoustikos,* which means "of hearing," *acoustic* means "of, or relating to, hearing or sound." In 1683, the plural form of the word, *acoustics,* started being used to mean "the science of sound." Although the word *acoustics* is plural, it can be used as a singular noun. Ask: **Is it correct to say "Acoustics is a science" or "Acoustics are a science."?** *(Acoustics is a science.)*

Connecting Concepts

Concept Maps Help students develop one way to show how the information in this chapter is related. Sound travels as longitudinal waves that your ears and brain convert to a form you can hear. Sound waves combine to produce music, and reflected sound waves are used to locate objects and structures. Have students brainstorm to identify the key concepts, key terms, details, and examples, then write each one on a self-sticking note and attach it at random on chart paper or on the board.

Tell students that this concept map will be organized in a hierarchical order and to begin at the top with the key concepts. Ask students these questions to guide them to categorize the information on the self-sticking notes: **What are the properties of sound waves? What is music? How do you hear sound? How can sound waves be used?**

1 The Nature of Sound

Key Concepts

- Sound is a disturbance that travels through a medium as a longitudinal wave.
- Sound waves reflect off objects, diffract through narrow openings and around barriers, and interfere with each other.
- The speed of sound depends on the elasticity, density, and temperature of the medium the sound travels through.

Key Terms

echo
elasticity
density

2 Properties of Sound

Key Concepts

- The loudness of a sound depends on two factors: the amount of energy it takes to make the sound and the distance from the source of the sound.
- The pitch of a sound that you hear depends on the frequency of the sound wave.
- When a sound source moves, the frequency of the waves changes because the motion of the source adds to the motion of the waves.

Key Terms

loudness	ultrasound
intensity	infrasound
decibel (dB)	larynx
pitch	Doppler effect

64 ◆ O

3 Music

Key Concepts

- Sound quality results from the blending of a fundamental tone with its overtones. Resonance also plays a role in sound quality.
- There are three basic groups of musical instruments: stringed instruments, wind instruments, and percussion instruments.
- Acoustics is used in the design of concert halls to control reverberation and interference.

Key Terms

music
fundamental tone
overtone
acoustics
reverberation

4 How You Hear Sound

Key Concepts

- The outer ear funnels sound waves, the middle ear transmits the waves inward, and the inner ear converts sound waves into a form that travels to your brain.
- There are many causes of hearing loss, including injury, infection, exposure to loud sounds, and aging.

Key Terms

ear canal
eardrum
cochlea

5 Using Sound

Key Concepts

- Some animals, including bats and dolphins, use echolocation to navigate and to find food.
- Ultrasound technologies such as sonar and ultrasound imaging are used to observe things that cannot be seen directly.

Key Terms

echolocation
sonar
sonogram

Prompt students by using connecting words or phrases, such as "is produced by," "has properties of," "includes," and "can be used for," to indicate the basis for the organization of the map. The phrases should form a sentence between or among a set of concepts.

Answer

Accept logical presentations by students.

All in One Teaching Resources

- Key Terms Review: *Sound*
- Connecting Concepts: *Sound*

Review and Assessment

Organizing Information

Concept Mapping Copy the concept map about sound onto a separate sheet of paper. Then complete it and add a title. (For more on Concept Mapping, see the Skills Handbook.)

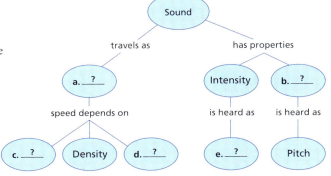

Reviewing Key Terms

Choose the letter of the best answer.

1. The ability of a medium to bounce back after being disturbed is called
   a. echolocation. **b.** elasticity.
   c. density. **d.** interference.

2. Which property of sound describes your perception of the energy of a sound?
   a. loudness
   b. intensity
   c. pitch
   d. wave speed

3. The lowest natural frequency of a sound is
   a. a standing wave.
   b. an overtone.
   c. an echo.
   d. the fundamental tone.

4. In the ear, a fluid-filled cavity that is shaped like a snail shell is the
   a. ear canal. **b.** eardrum.
   c. cochlea. **d.** larynx.

5. A system of using reflected sound waves to detect and locate objects underwater is called
   a. sonar. **b.** acoustics.
   c. echolocation. **d.** reverberation.

If the statement is true, write _true_. If it is false, change the underlined word or words to make the statement true.

6. <u>Intensity</u> is mass per unit volume.

7. <u>Loudness</u> is how the ear perceives frequency.

8. <u>Music</u> is a set of notes that are pleasing.

9. The <u>ear canal</u> is a small, drumlike membrane.

10. A <u>sonogram</u> is a picture made using reflected ultrasound waves.

Writing in Science

Firsthand Account Imagine that you are a dolphin researcher. Write a letter to a friend describing your latest research. Be sure to include information about how dolphins use their sonar.

Discovery CHANNEL SCHOOL
Sound
Video Preview
Video Field Trip
▶ Video Assessment

Chapter 2 O ◆ 65

Go Online
PHSchool.com
For: Take a practice test.
Visit: PHSchool.com
Web Code: cga-5020

Students can take a practice test online that is automatically scored.

 **Teaching Resources**
- Transparency O27
- Chapter Test
- Performance Assessment Teacher Notes
- Performance Assessment Student Worksheet
- Performance Assessment Scoring Rubric

 ExamView® Computer Test Bank CD-ROM

Review and Assessment

Concept Map

Sample title: Sound
a. Longitudinal waves
b. Frequency
c. Elasticity
d. Temperature
e. Loudness

Reviewing Key Terms

1. b 2. a 3. d 4. c 5. a
6. Density
7. Pitch
8. true
9. eardrum
10. true

Writing in Science

Writing Mode Description
Scoring Rubric
4 Exceeds criteria; includes a vivid firsthand account that accurately describes how a dolphin uses echolocation to navigate and find food
3 Meets criteria
2 Description is brief and/or includes some errors
1 Description is incomplete and/or contains serious errors

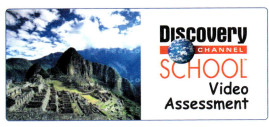

Discovery CHANNEL SCHOOL
Video Assessment

Sound

Show the Video Assessment to review chapter content and as a prompt for the writing assignment. Discussion questions: **What are some similarities between the echolocation systems used by dolphins and bats?** *(Both use echolocation to navigate and find food, and both are very precise.)* **In what ways might humans benefit from research into animal echolocation?** *(Scientists might be able to improve how ultrasound is used to help humans navigate the seas, diagnose medical conditions, and even help blind people navigate around objects.)*

Checking Concepts

11. Sound is a wave. The vibrating air particles next to the gong transmit energy to particles farther away. This process continues to carry the energy of the sound wave to your ear but does not transfer the particles themselves to your ear.

12. Loudness of a sound depends on both intensity and distance. A whisper has low intensity, but if the distance is small enough it may be louder than a more intense sound source that is farther away.

13. Because sound waves diffract, or bend, around corners

14. Because of the Doppler effect, the pitch of the horn will be higher when the car approaches you and lower after the car has passed by.

15. The two instruments have different sound qualities. For the same note, they have the same fundamental tone but different overtones. The difference in overtones causes the difference in sound quality.

16. Reverberation allows you to continue to hear a sound after the sound source stops. Reverberation is caused by sound waves reflecting back and forth.

17. Loud noises can damage hair cells in the cochlea. This causes hearing loss because the damaged hair cells can no longer send messages to the brain.

18. Ultrasound is used in medicine to diagnose and treat many medical conditions and to examine developing babies for problems before they are born.

Thinking Critically

19. Both waves are longitudinal waves, but sound waves can be heard, whereas waves in the spring toy can be seen.

20. You see the lightning first because light travels much faster than sound.

21. Because sound moves more slowly in rubber, rubber would reduce the transmission of sound waves most effectively.

22. A guitar and harp are stringed instruments, a tuba and clarinet are wind instruments, and a bell and drum are percussion instruments.

Checking Concepts

11. When a gong vibrates, the air particles next to the gong do not reach your ears, yet you hear the sound of the gong. Explain.

12. Explain when a whisper would sound louder than a shout.

13. Why do you hear friends talking in the hallway even though you cannot see them around a corner?

14. As a car drives past you, the driver keeps a hand pressing on the horn. Describe what you hear as the car approaches and after it has passed by.

15. The same note is played on a flute and a cello. Why is there a difference in the sound?

16. How can a sound continue to be heard after a sound source stops making the sound?

17. How can loud noises damage your hearing?

18. How are ultrasound waves used in medicine?

Thinking Critically

19. **Comparing and Contrasting** How do sound waves behave like waves in a spring toy? How are they different?

20. **Inferring** Thunder and lightning happen at the same time. Explain why you see the lightning before you hear the thunder.

21. **Predicting** Look at the data table below. Which substance would you select to reduce the transmission of sound waves? Explain your answer.

Substance	Speed (m/s)
Rubber	60
Plastic	1,800
Gold	3,240
Brick	3,650
Steel	5,200

22. **Classifying** Classify the following instruments into three groups: a guitar, a tuba, a bell, a clarinet, a drum, and a harp.

Applying Skills

Use the data in the table below to answer Questions 23–25.

The table shows the range of frequencies produced and heard by various animals.

Animal	Highest Frequency Heard (Hz)	Highest Frequency Produced (Hz)
Human	20,000	1,100
Dog	50,000	1,800
Cat	65,000	1,500
Bat	120,000	120,000
Porpoise	150,000	120,000

23. **Interpreting Data** Can you hear the ultrasound waves that a bat uses for echolocation? Why or why not?

24. **Graphing** Draw a bar graph to compare the highest frequencies heard and the highest frequencies produced by the animals.

25. **Calculating** If the speed of sound in air is 343 m/s, what is the shortest wavelength of sound that humans can hear? (*Hint:* Wavelength = Speed ÷ Frequency)

Lab zone — Chapter Project

Performance Assessment Present your musical instrument to your class. Explain how it was built and how you solved any design problems. Then demonstrate how you can change the pitch or loudness of your instrument. Brainstorm with the class methods for improving the design of the instrument. How is your instrument similar to or different from instruments your classmates built?

Lab zone — Chapter Project L3

Performance Assessment Give students a chance to demonstrate their instruments and explain the design process, including how their instruments were built and any modifications they made. Have students demonstrate how they can vary loudness and change pitch. Ask them to them to play a simple tune. Encourage students to reflect on the development process they went through to produce their instruments. Have them identify problem areas and anything they might have done differently to improve their projects.

Standardized Test Prep

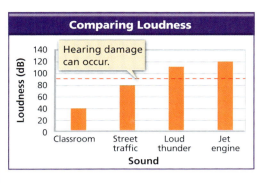

Comparing Loudness

Hearing damage can occur.

Loudness (dB) vs. Sound (Classroom, Street traffic, Loud thunder, Jet engine)

Choose the letter of the best answer.

1. Bats and dolphins use echolocation to determine distances and find prey. What characteristic of sound waves is most important for echolocation?
 A Sound waves reflect when they hit a surface.
 B Sound waves spread out from a source.
 C Sound waves diffract around a corner.
 D Sound waves interfere when they overlap.

2. A scientist is doing research with 110-dB sound waves. What piece of safety equipment must she wear in the lab?
 F goggles
 G gloves
 H lab apron
 J hearing protectors

3. Use the graph above to determine how much more intense the sound of a jet engine is than the sound of loud thunder.
 A ten times more intense
 B two times more intense
 C four times more intense
 D Both sounds are about the same intensity.

4. An experiment was conducted in which two containers held solids A and B at the same temperature. The speed of a sound wave traveling through solid A was greater than its speed through solid B. What can you conclude from this experiment?
 F Solid A is denser than solid B.
 G Solid A is less dense than solid B.
 H Solid A is more elastic than solid B.
 J Solid A is less dense than solid B or solid A is more elastic than solid B.

5. After a new concert hall is built, it is found that the acoustics are poor because of reverberation. How can the acoustics be improved?
 A Add metal seats to the hall.
 B Remove the drapes covering the windows.
 C Cover the wooden floor with carpeting.
 D Install a wooden backdrop behind the stage.

Constructed Response

6. You drop a book onto the floor in the bedroom of your apartment. Your neighbor downstairs hears the sound. Describe how the sound travels to your neighbor's ears. What mediums do the sound waves have to travel through?

Applying Skills

23. No, because ultrasound waves have frequencies higher than the human ear can detect

24. Graphs should have the names of the animals on the x-axis and the frequencies on the y-axis. There will be two bars for each animal, one for the highest frequency heard and one for the highest frequency produced. The two bars should be distinguished by shading or color, and there should be a key identifying what the bars represent.

25. The shortest wavelength heard by humans is 0.0172 m (1.72 cm). This is found by dividing the speed of sound (343 m/s) by the highest frequency heard by humans (20,000 Hz).

Standardized Test Prep

1. A   2. J   3. A   4. J   5. C

6. When you drop a book on the floor, the material that makes up the floor vibrates. The vibrations create sound waves that travel through the floor to your neighbor's ceiling in the apartment below. After the sound waves pass through the ceiling, they travel through the air to reach your neighbor's ears.

Chapter at a Glance

Chapter at a Glance (left vertical tab)

Chapter Project *You're on the Air*

Technology   **Local Standards**

All in One Teaching Resources
- Chapter Project Teacher Notes, pp. 176–177
- Chapter Project Student Overview, pp. 178–179
- Chapter Project Student Worksheets 1–2, pp. 180–181
- Chapter Project Scoring Rubric, p. 182

Video Preview

Section 1
The Nature of Electromagnetic Waves
2 periods
1 block
- **O.3.1.1** State what an electromagnetic wave consists of.
- **O.3.1.2** Identify models that explain the behavior of electromagnetic waves.

Section 2
Waves of the Electromagnetic Spectrum
5 periods
2 1/2 blocks
- **O.3.2.1** Explain how electromagnetic waves are alike and how they are different.
- **O.3.2.2** Name the waves that make up the electromagnetic spectrum.

Section 3
Producing Visible Light
3 periods
1 1/2 blocks
- **O.3.3.1** Describe the different types of light bulbs.

Section 4
Wireless Communication
5 periods
2 1/2 blocks
- **O.3.4.1** Explain how radio waves transmit information.
- **O.3.4.2** Describe how cellular phones work.
- **O.3.4.3** Explain how communications satellites relay information.

Video Field Trip

Review and Assessment

All in One Teaching Resources
- Key Terms Review, p. 216
- Transparency O38
- Performance Assessment Teacher Notes, p. 223
- Performance Assessment Scoring Rubric, p. 224
- Performance Assessment Student Worksheet, p. 225
- Chapter Test, pp. 226–229

Video Assessment

Test Preparation

Test Preparation Blackline Masters

Chapter Activities Planner

 **LAB ZONE Easy Planner CD-ROM**

Student Edition	Inquiry	Time	Materials	Skills	Resources
Chapter Project, p. 69	Open-Ended	Ongoing (2–3 weeks)	**All in One** Teaching Resources See p. 176	Posing questions, interpreting data, creating data tables	**Lab zone Easy Planner** **All in One** Teaching Resources Support pp. 176–177
Section 1					
Discover Activity, p. 70	Guided	10 minutes	4 large index cards, hole punch, metric ruler, binder clips or modeling clay, string, flashlight	Inferring	**Lab zone Easy Planner**
Try This Activity, p. 73	Directed	10 minutes	2 plastic cups, water, pan or sink, slide projector, slide, flashlight	Drawing conclusions	**Lab zone Easy Planner**
At-Home Activity, p. 73	Guided	Home		Observing	**Lab zone Easy Planner**
Section 2					
Discover Activity, p. 74	Guided	15 minutes	Cardboard box, white paper, prism, colored pencils	Forming operational definitions	**Lab zone Easy Planner**
Try This Activity, p. 76	Directed	15 minutes	Glass beaker, 25 mL of water, thermometer, microwave oven, 25 mL of corn oil, 25 mL of sugar	Drawing conclusions	**Lab zone Easy Planner**
Section 3					
Discover Activity, p. 84	Guided	10 minutes	Clear (uncoated) incandescent light bulb, fluorescent light bulb, goggles	Posing questions	**Lab zone Easy Planner**
Skills Activity, p. 85	Directed	15 minutes	Spectroscope, ordinary light bulb, fluorescent light bulb, colored pencils	Observing	**Lab zone Easy Planner**
At-Home Activity, p. 87	Guided	Home		Observing	**Lab zone Easy Planner**
Consumer Lab, pp. 88–89	Guided	40 minutes	A variety of incandescent light bulbs that can fit in the same lamp or socket, medium-sized cardboard box, light socket or lamp (without shade), meter stick, wax paper, scissors, plain paper, tape	Inferring, interpreting data, drawing conclusions	**Lab zone Easy Planner Lab Activity Video** **All in One** Teaching Resources Consumer Lab: *Comparing Light Bulbs*, pp. 204–205
Section 4					
Discover Activity, p. 90	Guided	10 minutes	Tracing paper, flat piece of stretchable latex about 20 cm square (from a balloon or glove)	Making models	**Lab zone Easy Planner**
Skills Lab, pp. 97–99	Guided	60 minutes	Cardboard tube (paper towel roll), 3 pieces of enameled or insulated wire (1 about 30 m long and 2 about 30 cm long), wirestrippers or sandpaper, 2 alligator clips, scissors, aluminum foil, 2 pieces of cardboard (sizes can range from 12.5 cm × 20 cm to 30 cm × 48 cm), masking tape, crystal diode, earphone, 2 pieces of insulated copper antenna wire (1 about 30 m long and 1 about 0.5 m long)	Observing, drawing conclusions, making models	**Lab zone Easy Planner Lab Activity Video** **All in One** Teaching Resources Skills Lab: *Build a Crystal Radio*, pp. 213–215

Section 1 The Nature of Electromagnetic Waves

 2 periods, 1 block

Objectives

O.3.1.1 State what an electromagnetic wave consists of.

O.3.1.2 Identify models that explain the behavior of electromagnetic waves.

Local Standards

Key Terms

• electromagnetic wave • electromagnetic radiation • polarized light
• photoelectric effect • photon

Preteach

Build Background Knowledge

Using what they already know about radio signals, students infer how far radio waves can travel.

 **Discover Activity** *How Does a Beam of Light Travel?* **L1**

Targeted Print and Technology Resources

All in One Teaching Resources

L2 Reading Strategy Transparency O28: *Outlining*

⊙ **Presentation-Pro CD-ROM**

Instruct

What Is an Electromagnetic Wave? Use Figure 1 to show students that electromagnetic waves are transverse waves.

Models of Electromagnetic Waves Use questioning to help students distinguish between the wave behavior and the particle behavior of electromagnetic waves.

Targeted Print and Technology Resources

All in One Teaching Resources

L2 Guided Reading, pp. 185–186
L2 Transparency O29

www.SciLinks.org Web Code: scn-1531

⊙ **Student Edition on Audio CD**

Assess

Section Assessment Questions

Have students use their completed outlines to answer the questions.

Reteach

Students fill in missing key terms in sentences in which the terms are defined.

Targeted Print and Technology Resources

All in One Teaching Resources

• Section Summary, p. 184
L1 Review and Reinforce, p. 187
L3 Enrich, p. 188

Section 2 Waves of the Electromagnetic Spectrum

 5 periods, 2 1/2 blocks

ABILITY LEVELS
L1 Basic to Average
L2 For All Students
L3 Average to Advanced

Objectives

O.3.2.1 Explain how electromagnetic waves are alike and how they are different.

O.3.2.2 Name the waves that make up the electromagnetic spectrum.

Local Standards

Key Terms

• electromagnetic spectrum • radio wave • microwave • radar • infrared ray
• thermogram • visible light • ultraviolet ray • X-ray • gamma ray

Preteach

Build Background Knowledge

Students recall what they already know about X-rays.

 **Discover Activity** *What Is White Light?* **L1**

Targeted Print and Technology Resources

 Teaching Resources

L2 Reading Strategy Transparency O30: *Previewing Visuals*

 Presentation-Pro CD-ROM

Instruct

What Is the Electromagnetic Spectrum? Relate the speed, wavelength, and frequency of electromagnetic waves.

Radio Waves Introduce radio waves by asking students to infer the waves' energy from their frequency.

Infrared Rays Help students identify the properties of infrared rays.

Visible Light Use Figure 3 and Figure 6 to guide students in understanding how visible light relates to other electromagnetic waves and how white light can be separated into colored light.

Ultraviolet Rays Guide students in recalling what they already know about ultraviolet rays.

X-Rays Introduce X-rays by discussing X-ray images, which will be familiar to most students.

Gamma Rays Guide students in using what they already know about the rest of the electromagnetic spectrum to predict properties of gamma rays.

Targeted Print and Technology Resources

Teaching Resources

L2 Guided Reading, pp. 191–194
L2 Transparencies O31, O32, O33

PHSchool.com Web Code: cgp-5032

PHSchool.com Web Code: cgh-5030

Student Edition on Audio CD

Assess

Section Assessment Questions

Have students use their completed graphic organizers to answer the questions.

Reteach

Students name the types of electromagnetic waves in order from lowest to highest frequencies and identify a property, use, or effect of each type of wave.

Targeted Print and Technology Resources

Teaching Resources

• Section Summary, p. 190
L1 Review and Reinforce, p. 195
L3 Enrich, p. 196

Section 3 **Producing Visible Light**

 3 periods, 1 1/2 blocks

ABILITY LEVELS
L1 Basic to Average
L2 For All Students
L3 Average to Advanced

Objectives

O.3.3.1 Describe the different types of light bulbs.

Local Standards

Key Terms

- illuminated • luminous • spectroscope • incandescent light
- tungsten-halogen bulb • fluorescent light • vapor light • neon light

---

Preteach

Build Background Knowledge

Students use their prior knowledge of ordinary light bulbs to infer properties of light sources.

 **Discover Activity** *How Do Light Bulbs Differ?* **L1**

Targeted Print and Technology Resources

  Teaching Resources

L2 Reading Strategy Transparency
O34: *Comparing and Contrasting*

○ **Presentation-Pro CD-ROM**

Instruct

Incandescent Lights Draw a Venn diagram on the board comparing and contrasting ordinary light bulbs and tungsten-halogen light bulbs.

Other Light Sources Distinguish between incandescent lights and other light sources, including neon and sodium vapor lights.

 **Consumer Lab** *Comparing Light Bulbs* **L2**

Targeted Print and Technology Resources

Section Assessment

Teaching Resources

L2 Guided Reading, pp. 199–201
L2 Transparency O35
L2 Consumer Lab: *Comparing Light Bulbs,* pp. 204–205

▭ **Lab Activity Video/DVD**
Consumer Lab: *Comparing Light Bulbs*

PHSchool.com Web Code: cgd-5033

○ **Student Edition on Audio CD**

Assess

Questions

⊙ Have students use their completed compare/contrast tables to answer the questions.

Reteach

Students state facts about each of the five types of light bulbs described in the section.

Targeted Print and Technology Resources

Teaching Resources

- Section Summary, p. 198
L1 Review and Reinforce, p. 202
L3 Enrich, p. 203

Section 4 Wireless Communication

 5 periods, 2 1/2 blocks

ABILITY LEVELS
L1 Basic to Average
L2 For All Students
L3 Average to Advanced

Objectives

O.3.4.1 Explain how radio waves transmit information.
O.3.4.2 Describe how cellular phones work.
O.3.4.3 Explain how communications satellites relay information.

Local Standards

Key Terms

• amplitude modulation • frequency modulation

Preteach

Build Background Knowledge

Students recall certain television broadcasts they have seen and infer that the signals were transmitted by satellite.

 **Discover Activity** *How Can Radio Waves Change?* **L1**

Targeted Print and Technology Resources

 Teaching Resources

L2 Reading Strategy Transparency O36: *Identifying Main Ideas*

 Presentation-Pro CD-ROM

Instruct

Radio and Television Use Figure 13 to explain how AM and FM radio waves differ.

Cellular Phones Help students recall what they already know about microwaves and apply it to cellular phone technology.

Communications Satellites Use a familiar sports analogy to introduce communications satellites.

 **Skills Lab** *Build a Crystal Radio* **L2**

Targeted Print and Technology Resources

 Teaching Resources

L2 Guided Reading, pp. 208–210
L2 Transparency O37
L2 Skills Lab: *Build a Crystal Radio*, pp. 213–215

Lab Activity Video/DVD
Skills Lab: *Build a Crystal Radio*

www.SciLinks.org Web Code: scn-1534

Video Field Trip

Student Edition on Audio CD

Assess

Section Assessment Questions

Have students use their completed graphic organizers to answer the questions.

Reteach

Students identify the different uses of radio waves in wireless communication and state details about each use.

Targeted Print and Technology Resources

Teaching Resources

• Section Summary, p. 207
L1 Review and Reinforce, p. 211
L3 Enrich, p. 212

Chapter 3 **Content Refresher**

Section 1 The Nature of Electromagnetic Waves

Light as Waves and Particles Physicists generally agree that electromagnetic waves sometimes act like waves and sometimes act like discrete particles of energy. However, the dual nature of electromagnetic waves was not appreciated when the waves were discovered in the 1860s. Electromagnetic waves were discovered by the British physicist James Clerk Maxwell, who also discovered that electromagnetic waves travel at the speed of light and that light consists of electromagnetic waves. Since then, the wave nature of light has been widely accepted.

Around 1900, the German physicist Max Planck introduced the idea that light sometimes acts like particles instead of waves. Planck used the word *photon* to describe particles of light. The idea of photons was soon adopted by German-American physicist Albert Einstein, who was studying a phenomenon called the photoelectric effect. The photoelectric effect occurs when light shines on a metal surface and causes the surface to give off electrons. Einstein argued that the photoelectric effect could happen only if light struck the metal as particles and not as waves. Einstein reasoned that waves would cause each surface electron to gain more and more energy. In fact, each electron gains the same amount of energy for any given electromagnetic wave. Einstein observed that even increasing the energy of a wave does not cause individual electrons to gain more energy. Instead, it causes more electrons to gain the same amount of energy. Based on his observations, Einstein theorized that light strikes a metal surface as particles of energy and that each electron absorbs the energy of one particle of light.

Today, physicists classify photons as elementary particles, or particles that cannot be divided into smaller units. Photons have no mass or electrical charge. Without mass, they can travel at the speed of light. Photons also have energy and momentum. The pressure an object exerts when it strikes a surface depends on its momentum. Because of their momentum, photons affect other particles when they collide with them.

Section 2 Waves of the Electromagnetic Spectrum

Infrared Rays and Ultraviolet Rays The frequencies and wavelengths of the electromagnetic spectrum are given in the diagram. The text devotes a whole section or chapter to some frequencies of electromagnetic waves, including radio waves and visible light. Background is provided here on two other frequencies of electromagnetic waves: infrared rays and ultraviolet rays. Both types of rays travel at the speed of light, but they have different wavelengths and frequencies as the diagram shows.

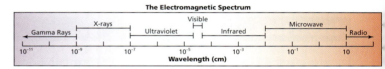

The Electromagnetic Spectrum

Infrared rays fall between microwaves and visible light in frequency and wavelength. They have a number of uses, including infrared photography, which is important in medicine, industry, and agriculture. An infrared camera has an opaque filter that prevents visible light from entering but lets infrared rays pass through. Infrared is also used in special goggles that allow "night vision." In night-vision goggles, beams of infrared rays bounce off objects, and the returning rays are detected and converted to images. Infrared rays are also used by astronomers. One use in astronomy is observing stars that give off infrared radiation.

Ultraviolet rays fall between visible light and X-rays in frequency and wavelength. Ultraviolet rays are often separated into three groups based on their wavelength: UV-A, UV-B, and UV-C. UV-A rays have the longest wavelengths, and UV-C rays have the shortest wavelengths. UV-A rays are the least harmful because they have the lowest frequencies and least energy. UV-B rays can cause sunburn and, over long periods of exposure, skin cancer. UV-C rays are the most harmful. They are strong enough to kill microorganisms.

Address Misconceptions

Students may think that microwaves travel faster than other radio waves because they have higher frequencies. For a strategy for overcoming this misconception, see **Address Misconceptions** in Section 2, *Waves of the Electromagnetic Spectrum*.

Section 3 Producing Visible Light

Types of Light Sources Until recently, there have been two general ways to produce visible light using electricity: incandescent light bulbs and electric-discharge lights. In an incandescent light bulb, a filament of fine tungsten wire is heated above 525°C, which causes it to glow and produce light. Tungsten is used because it has a high melting point (about 3400°C). An incandescent bulb cannot contain any oxygen, because the heated filament would quickly burn up, so an inert gas, such as argon or krypton, is usually used in the bulb. The gas also helps prevent the filament from evaporating. A small amount of nitrogen is generally added to the bulb as well. Some incandescent light bulbs contain halogen gas instead of argon or krypton and nitrogen. Under very high temperatures, halogen helps reduce evaporation of the filament even more. Halogen lights have a bulb made of quartz instead of glass, which allows them to withstand the high temperatures required. However, their high temperatures also make halogen lights more dangerous to use.

Electric-discharge lights produce light by passing an electric current through vapors or gases, which causes an electric discharge. One type of electric-discharge light is neon light. A neon light bulb is basically a glass tube filled with neon gas. The neon gas produces red light when current passes through it. Other gases are sometimes used to produce other colors of light. For example, argon can be used to produce blue light. Another type of electric-discharge light is fluorescent light. A fluorescent light bulb is a glass tube containing mercury vapor. The tube is coated with a powdered substance called phosphor. Phosphor gives off visible light when it is excited. This occurs when current passes through the mercury vapor and ultraviolet light is produced. Some fluorescent lights produce visible light that is closer in quality to daylight than other types of lights. Fluorescent lights also are highly efficient: a 40-watt fluorescent tube can produce as much light as a 150-watt incandescent bulb.

A relatively new development in light sources is the use of electroluminescence. This technology is used in panel lighting. In this type of light, particles of phosphor are embedded in a thin layer of a nonconducting material such as plastic. When current is passed through the embedded phosphor, it becomes excited and produces light. Because the light is scattered through the plastic, it casts a pearly glow. Luminescent panels are used in the dials of clocks and radios and in interior decorating.

Section 4 Wireless Communication

Global Positioning System One important and relatively new use of wireless communication is the Global Positioning System, or GPS. It consists of 24 orbiting satellites and several stations on the ground that monitor the satellites. GPS was developed by the U.S. Department of Defense. Beginning in the early 1970s, communications satellites were launched by Delta rockets from Cape Canaveral into circular orbits about 20,000 km above Earth's surface. Each satellite circles the globe twice a day.

The other component of the GPS system is the large number of users who receive the GPS signals to determine their location. A hand-held receiver, like the one in the sketch, uses the difference in time between the broadcast of a signal from a satellite and the signal's reception by the receiver to determine the receiver's distance from the satellite. With information from four satellites, a receiver can calculate its exact location in time and space, including latitude, longitude, and altitude. Some receivers even display maps showing the receiver's location.

GPS Satellite System

Interactive Textbook
- Complete student edition
- Video and audio
- Simulations and activities
- Section and chapter activities

Interactive Textbook

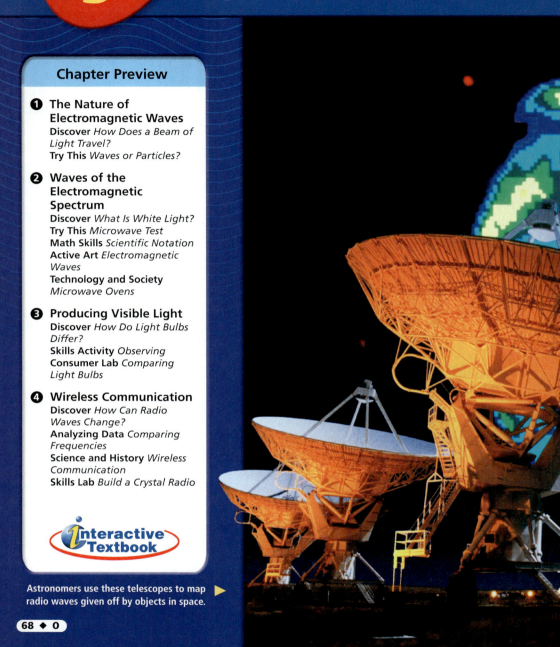

Astronomers use these telescopes to map radio waves given off by objects in space. ▶

Lab zone • Chapter Project L3

Objectives

This Chapter Project will give students a chance to learn about how people use different wireless communication devices. After completing this Chapter Project, students will be able to
- design and implement a survey to collect relevant data
- compile and analyze the data gathered in the survey
- create tables and graphs to communicate the results of the data analysis

Skills Focus

Posing questions, interpreting data, creating data tables

Project Time Line 2–3 weeks

All in One Teaching Resources
- Chapter Project Teacher Notes
- Chapter Project Worksheet 1
- Chapter Project Worksheet 2
- Chapter Project Scoring Rubric

Developing a Plan

Allow students two or three days to brainstorm and design their surveys. At the end of the first week, they should have composed and tested their surveys and distributed them to other students, family members, and neighbors. During the second week, students can collect the completed surveys and analyze the data. By the end of the second week or during the third week, students can create data tables and graphs and present their findings to the class.

Possible Materials

Suggested materials for this project include copy paper, a computer spreadsheet program, graph paper, poster board, and colored markers. Encourage students to suggest and use other relevant materials for their presentations.

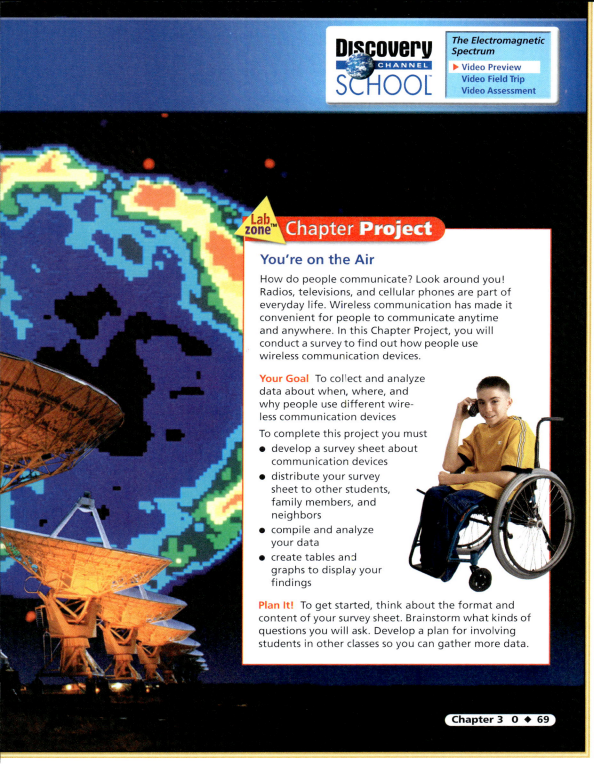

Discovery CHANNEL SCHOOL
Video Preview

The Electromagnetic Spectrum

Show the Video Preview to introduce satellite communication as an example of wireless communication that students will focus on in the Chapter Project. Discussion question: **What types of electromagnetic energy are used for communication to and from satellite systems?** *(Radio signals)*

Lab zone™ Chapter **Project**

You're on the Air

How do people communicate? Look around you! Radios, televisions, and cellular phones are part of everyday life. Wireless communication has made it convenient for people to communicate anytime and anywhere. In this Chapter Project, you will conduct a survey to find out how people use wireless communication devices.

Your Goal To collect and analyze data about when, where, and why people use different wireless communication devices

To complete this project you must
- develop a survey sheet about communication devices
- distribute your survey sheet to other students, family members, and neighbors
- compile and analyze your data
- create tables and graphs to display your findings

Plan It! To get started, think about the format and content of your survey sheet. Brainstorm what kinds of questions you will ask. Develop a plan for involving students in other classes so you can gather more data.

Chapter 3 O ◆ 69

Launching the Project

Stimulate a class brainstorming session by asking students how they communicate with people who do not live in the same city or local area. Then, ask: **Is it possible to communicate with anyone at any time in any place?** *(Most students will say that they can use a telephone or the Internet to communicate with anyone else who has a telephone or Internet connection.)* Mention specific types of wireless communication devices to the class, such as pagers, cellular phones, and communication satellites. Challenge students to explain how they think the devices work and how popular or useful they are.

Have students read the Chapter Project overview. Divide the class into small groups, and tell members of each group to brainstorm a list of questions they might use in their surveys. Students may complete the Chapter Project in these small groups or individually.

Performance Assessment

The Chapter Project Scoring Rubric will help you evaluate how well students complete the Chapter Project. You may want to share the scoring rubric with your students so they will know what is expected. Students will be assessed on
- how well designed and relevant their survey questions are
- how well they organize and analyze their data
- the clarity of their tables and graphs
- the thoroughness and organization of their presentations

Students can keep their tables and graphs in their portfolios.

Portfolio

Objectives

After this lesson, students will be able to

O.3.1.1 State what an electromagnetic wave consists of.

O.3.1.2 Identify models that explain the behavior of electromagnetic waves.

Target Reading Skill 🎯

Outlining Explain that using an outline format helps students organize information by main topic, subtopic, and details.

Answers

Nature of Electromagnetic Waves
I. What is an electromagnetic wave?
  A. Producing electromagnetic waves
  B. Energy
  C. Speed
II. Models of electromagnetic waves
  A. Wave model of light
  B. Particle model of light

All in One Teaching Resources

• Transparency O28

Preteach

Build Background Knowledge   L2

Radio Signals

Guide students in using what they already know about radio signals to infer how far radio waves can travel. Ask: **How far from home can you travel before you can no longer hear local radio stations?** (*Sample answer: Radio signals usually can be received many miles, and sometimes hundreds of miles, from their source.*) Tell students that radio signals are a type of wave, called *electromagnetic wave*, which they will read about in this section.

Section
1
The Nature of Electromagnetic Waves

Reading Preview

Key Concepts
• What does an electromagnetic wave consist of?
• What models explain the behavior of electromagnetic waves?

Key Terms
• electromagnetic wave
• electromagnetic radiation
• polarized light
• photoelectric effect
• photon

🎯 Target Reading Skill

Outlining An outline shows the relationship between major ideas and supporting ideas. As you read, make an outline about electromagnetic waves. Use the red headings for the main topics and the blue headings for the subtopics.

The Nature of Electromagnetic Waves
I. What is an electromagnetic wave?
A. Producing electromagnetic waves
B.
C.
II. Models of electromagnetic waves
A.
B.

Electromagnetic waves ▶

Lab zone Discover Activity

How Does a Beam of Light Travel?

1. Punch a hole (about 0.5 cm in diameter) through four large index cards.
2. Use binder clips or modeling clay to stand each card upright so that the long side of the index card is on the tabletop. Space the cards about 10 cm apart, as shown in the photo. To line the holes up in a straight line, run a piece of string through them and pull it tight.
3. Place a flashlight in front of the card nearest you. Shut off all light except the flashlight. What do you see on the wall?
4. Move one of the cards sideways about 3 cm and repeat Step 3. Now what do you see on the wall?

Think It Over
Inferring Explain what happened in Step 4. What does this activity tell you about the path of light?

Have you ever been caught in a rain shower? You run for cover until it passes, so you don't get wet. Believe it or not, you are being "showered" all the time, not by rain but by waves. You cannot see, feel, or hear most of these waves. But as you read this, you are surrounded by radio waves, infrared rays, visible light, ultraviolet rays, and maybe even tiny amounts of X-rays and gamma rays. They are all electromagnetic waves.

Lab zone Discover Activity

Skills Focus Inferring

Materials 4 large index cards, hole punch, metric ruler, binder clips or modeling clay, string, flashlight

Time 10 minutes

Tip Use a small pocket flashlight or penlight for best results.

L1 **Expected Outcome** When the cards are positioned so that all the holes line up, the light from the flashlight is visible on the wall. When one card is moved out of alignment, the light is no longer visible.

Think It Over Moving the card in Step 4 blocked the path of the light. Students might infer that light travels in a straight line and cannot pass through a card.

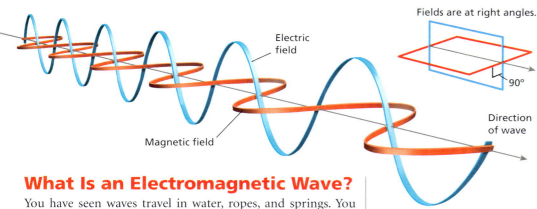

Fields are at right angles.

Electric field

Magnetic field

Direction of wave

90°

What Is an Electromagnetic Wave?

You have seen waves travel in water, ropes, and springs. You have heard sound waves that travel through air and water. All these waves have two things in common—they transfer energy and they also require a medium through which to travel. But electromagnetic waves can transfer energy without a medium. An **electromagnetic wave** is a transverse wave that transfers electrical and magnetic energy. **An electromagnetic wave consists of vibrating electric and magnetic fields that move through space at the speed of light.**

Producing Electromagnetic Waves Light and all other electromagnetic waves are produced by charged particles. Every charged particle has an electric field surrounding it. The electric field produces electric forces that can push or pull on other charged particles.

When a charged particle moves, it produces a magnetic field. A magnetic field exerts magnetic forces that can act on certain materials. If you place a paper clip near a magnet, for example, the paper clip moves toward the magnet because of the magnetic field surrounding the magnet.

When a charged particle changes its motion, its magnetic field changes. The changing magnetic field causes the electric field to change. When one field vibrates, so does the other. In this way, the two fields constantly cause each other to change. The result is an electromagnetic wave, as shown in Figure 1. Notice that the two fields vibrate at right angles to each other.

Energy The energy that is transfered through space by electromagnetic waves is called **electromagnetic radiation.** Electromagnetic waves do not require a medium, so they can transfer energy through a vacuum, or empty space. This is why you can see the sun and stars—their light reaches Earth through the vacuum of space.

FIGURE 1
Electromagnetic Wave
In an electromagnetic wave, electric and magnetic fields vibrate at right angles to each other. **Classifying** *What type of wave is an electromagnetic wave?*

Go Online
SCi **LINKS** NSTA

For: Links on the nature of waves
Visit: www.SciLinks.org
Web Code: scn-1531

What Is an Electromagnetic Wave?

Teach Key Concepts L2
Electromagnetic Waves as Transverse Waves

Focus Read the boldface statement describing an electromagnetic wave.

Teach Call students' attention to Figure 1. Point out how the electric and magnetic fields in the figure are at right angles to one another. Ask: **What does the long arrow in the figure represent?** (*The direction of the wave*) **In what direction does the wave travel relative to the vibrations of the electric and magnetic fields?** (*The wave's direction is perpendicular to the vibrations of the fields.*)

Apply Have students answer the caption question. **learning modality: visual**

All in One Teaching Resources
• Transparency O29

Go Online
SCi **LINKS** NSTA

For: Links on the nature of waves
Visit: www.SciLinks.org
Web Code: scn-1531

Download a worksheet that will guide students' review of Internet resources on the nature of waves.

Independent Practice L2

All in One Teaching Resources
• Guided Reading and Study Worksheet: *The Nature of Electromagnetic Waves*

⊙ Student Edition on Audio CD

Monitor Progress _____ L2

Drawing Ask students to draw a diagram showing how the electric and magnetic fields vibrate in an electromagnetic wave.

Answer
Figure 1 A transverse wave

⌐ Differentiated Instruction ⌐

English Learners/Beginning L1
Vocabulary: Word Analysis Write the word *electromagnetic*, and draw a line to separate the word into its two parts. Tell students that *electro-* means "electric." Relate *electric* and *magnetic* to familiar objects. Explain that both electric and magnetic energy are carried by electromagnetic waves. **learning modality: verbal**

English Learners/Intermediate L2
Comprehension: Ask Questions Check their comprehension by asking: **What is an electromagnetic wave?** (*A transverse wave that consists of vibrating electric and magnetic fields that move through space at the speed of light*) **What is electromagnetic radiation?** (*The energy that is transferred through space by electromagnetic waves*) **learning modality: verbal**

Models of Electromagnetic Waves

Teach Key Concepts
Modeling Wave and Particle Behaviors

Focus Help students distinguish between the wave behavior and the particle behavior of electromagnetic waves.

Teach Explain that an electromagnetic wave vibrates back and forth like a transverse mechanical wave when it travels through space. However, when an electromagnetic wave strikes some substances, it acts like a stream of tiny particles of energy. Ask: **How could you model the wave behavior of an electromagnetic wave?** (*Sample answer: By making waves in a rope*) **How could you model the particle behavior of an electromagnetic wave?** (*Sample answer: By striking a surface with tiny particles, such as grains of sand*)

Apply Ask: **Which model helps explain how light can knock electrons out of some substances when it strikes them?** (*Particle model*) **learning modality: verbal**

Lab zone **Build Inquiry** L2

Observing How Filters Polarize Light

Materials flashlight, 2 polarizing light filters

Time 10 minutes

Focus Tell students that a polarizing filter transmits only light waves that are vibrating in a certain direction.

Teach Have students shine the flashlight through one of the polarizing filters. Ask: **Why does the light appear dimmer through the filter?** (*Only some of the light is transmitted.*) Have students experiment with placement of the second filter behind the first until they find an arrangement that blocks all the light. Ask: **Why are two filters needed to block all the light?** (*Sample answer: The first filter blocks all the light waves except those vibrating in one direction. The second filter is needed to block the remaining waves.*)

Apply Ask students to draw diagrams to show how light waves are affected by one polarizing filter alone and then by two polarizing filters together. **learning modality: kinesthetic**

Speed All electromagnetic waves travel at the same speed in a vacuum—about 300,000 kilometers per second. This speed is called the speed of light. At this speed, light from the sun takes about 8 minutes to travel the 150 million kilometers to Earth. When light waves travel through a medium such as air, they travel more slowly. But the speed of light waves in air is still about a million times faster than the speed of sound waves in air.

> **Reading Checkpoint** What is the speed of light in a vacuum?

Models of Electromagnetic Waves

Many properties of electromagnetic waves can be explained by a wave model. However, some properties are best explained by a particle model. As you have learned, light is an electromagnetic wave. Both a wave model and a particle model are needed to explain all of the properties of light.

Wave Model of Light The lenses of many sunglasses, like the ones shown in Figure 2, are polarizing filters. Light acts as a wave when it passes through a polarizing filter. Ordinary light has waves that vibrate in all directions—up and down, left and right, and at all other angles. A polarizing filter acts as though it has tiny slits that are aligned in one direction.

Only some light waves pass through a polarizing filter. The light that passes through vibrates in only one direction and is called **polarized light.** No light passes through two polarizing filters that are placed at right angles to each other.

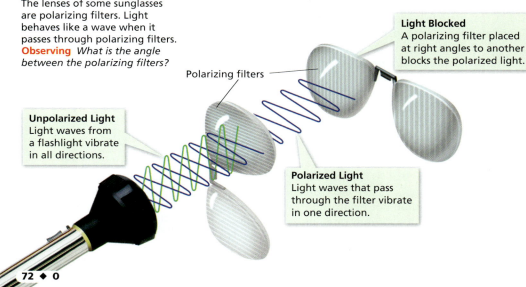

FIGURE 2
Light as a Wave
The lenses of some sunglasses are polarizing filters. Light behaves like a wave when it passes through polarizing filters.
Observing What is the angle between the polarizing filters?

Polarizing filters

Unpolarized Light
Light waves from a flashlight vibrate in all directions.

Light Blocked
A polarizing filter placed at right angles to another blocks the polarized light.

Polarized Light
Light waves that pass through the filter vibrate in one direction.

72 ◆ O

Lab zone **Try This Activity**

Skills Focus Drawing conclusions L2

Materials 2 plastic cups, water, pan or sink, slide projector, slide, flashlight

Time 10 minutes

Expected Outcome The streams of water collide and splash into the sink, whereas the beams of light pass through each other without affecting the projected picture. This activity supports the wave model of light, because the water streams, which consist of particles, do not pass through each other without interference as light does.

Extend Ask: **How could a stream of water be used as a model for the particle behavior of light?** (*Sample answer: A stream of water strikes a surface as particles, the way light strikes some surfaces.*) **learning modality: kinesthetic**

To help you understand the wave model of light, think of waves of light as being like transverse waves on a rope. If you shake a rope through a fence with vertical slats, only waves that vibrate up and down will pass through. If you shake the rope side to side, the waves will be blocked. A polarizing filter acts like the slats in a fence. It allows only waves that vibrate in one direction to pass through.

Particle Model of Light Sometimes light behaves like a stream of particles. When a beam of light shines on some substances, it causes tiny particles called electrons to move. The movement of electrons causes an electric current to flow. Sometimes light can even cause an electron to move so much that it is knocked out of the substance. This is called the **photoelectric effect.** The photoelectric effect can be explained only by thinking of light as a stream of tiny packets, or particles, of energy. Each packet of light energy is called a **photon.** Albert Einstein first explained the science behind the photoelectric effect in 1905.

It may be difficult for you to picture light as being particles and waves at the same time. But both models are necessary to explain all the properties of light.

 Reading Checkpoint What is a photon?

Try This Activity

Waves or Particles?

1. Fill two plastic cups with water. Slowly pour the water from both cups into a sink so the streams of water cross. How do the two streams interfere with each other?
2. Darken a room. Use a slide projector to project a slide on a wall. Shine a flashlight beam across the projector's beam. What is the effect on the projected picture?

Drawing Conclusions Compare the interference of light beams with the interference of water streams. Does this activity support a wave model or a particle model of light? Explain.

Section 1 Assessment

Target Reading Skill Outlining Use the information in your outline about electromagnetic waves to help you answer the questions below.

Reviewing Key Concepts

1. **a. Defining** What is an electromagnetic wave?
   b. Explaining How do electromagnetic waves travel?
   c. Comparing and Contrasting What is an electric field? What is a magnetic field?
2. **a. Reviewing** What two models explain the properties of electromagnetic waves?
   b. Describing Use one of the models of light to describe what happens when light passes through a polarizing filter.

   c. Relating Cause and Effect Use one of the models of light to explain what causes the photoelectric effect.

At-Home Activity

Polarized Sunglasses On a sunny day, go outside with your family members and compare your sunglasses. Do any have polarizing lenses? If so, which ones? Try rotating sunglasses as you look through them at surfaces that create glare, such as water or glass. Which sunglasses are best designed to reduce glare? **CAUTION:** *Do not look directly at the sun.*

Chapter 3 O ◆ 73

Monitor Progress [L2]

Answers
Figure 2 The angle is 90°.

 Reading Checkpoint 300,000 km/s

 Reading Checkpoint A tiny packet of light energy

Assess

Reviewing Key Concepts

1. a. A transverse wave that transfers electrical and magnetic energy **b.** As vibrations in electric and magnetic fields that move through space at the speed of light **c.** An electric field surrounds every charged particle and produces electric forces that can push or pull on other charged particles. A magnetic field is produced when a charged particle moves, and it exerts magnetic forces that can act on certain materials.
2. a. The wave model and the particle model of light **b.** When light strikes a polarizing filter, only some waves pass through. These waves vibrate in only one direction and are called polarized light. **c.** When light acts like a stream of tiny particles of energy, called photons, the photons can cause electrons to be knocked out of some substances. This is the photoelectric effect.

Reteach [L1]

Read aloud sentences with a key term, substituting the word "*blank*" for the term. Ask students for the term.

Performance Assessment [L2]

Writing Have students write a paragraph describing how electromagnetic waves act like waves and how they act like particles.

At-Home Activity

Polarized Sunglasses [L1] Students will observe that polarizing lenses are better than regular sunglasses at reducing the glare from surfaces such as water or glass. When two polarized lenses overlap and one lens is rotated 90° relative to the other lens, no light shines through.

All in One Teaching Resources

- Section Summary: *The Nature of Electromagnetic Waves*
- Review and Reinforcement: *The Nature of Electromagnetic Waves*
- Enrich: *The Nature of Electromagnetic Waves*

Objectives

After this lesson, students will be able to

O.3.2.1 Explain how electromagnetic waves are alike and how they are different.

O.3.2.2 Describe the waves that make up the electromagnetic spectrum.

Target Reading Skill

Previewing Visuals Explain that looking at the visuals before they read helps students activate prior knowledge and predict what they are about to read.

Answers

The Electromagnetic spectrum

Which electromagnetic waves have the shortest wavelength? *Gamma rays have the shortest wavelength.*

Which electromagnetic waves have the lowest frequency? *Radio waves have the lowest frequency.*

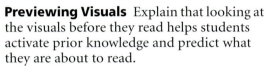 **Teaching Resources**

• Transparency O30

Preteach

Build Background Knowledge   L2

X-Rays

Guide students in recalling what they already know about X-rays. Ask: **What can you see in an X-ray image?** *(Sample answer: Bones inside the body or teeth inside the jaw)* **What can X-rays pass through?** *(Sample answer: Clothing, skin, muscles)* Explain that X-rays are a type of electromagnetic wave. Tell students they will learn about X-rays and other types of electromagnetic waves in this section.

Reading Preview

Key Concepts

• How are electromagnetic waves alike, and how are they different?

• What waves make up the electromagnetic spectrum?

Key Terms

• electromagnetic spectrum
• radio waves   • microwaves
• radar   • infrared rays
• thermogram   • visible light
• ultraviolet rays   • X-rays
• gamma rays

Target Reading Skill

Previewing Visuals Before you read, preview Figure 3. Then write two questions that you have about the diagram in a graphic organizer like the one below. As you read, answer your questions.

The Electromagnetic Spectrum

Q. Which electromagnetic waves have the shortest wavelength?
A.
Q.

Discover Activity

What Is White Light?

1. Line a cardboard box with white paper. Hold a small triangular prism up to direct sunlight. **CAUTION:** *Do not look directly at the sun.*

2. Rotate the prism until the light coming out of the prism appears on the inside of the box as a wide band of colors. Describe the colors and their order.

3. Using colored pencils, draw a picture of what you see inside the box.

Think It Over

Forming Operational Definitions The term *spectrum* describes a range. How is this term related to what you just observed?

Can you imagine trying to take a photo with a radio? How about trying to tune in a radio station on your flashlight or heat your food with X-rays? Light, radio waves, and X-rays are all electromagnetic waves. But each has properties that make it more useful for some purposes and less useful for others. What makes light different from radio waves and X-rays?

Radio waves

Microwaves

Long wavelength
Low frequency

Discover Activity

Skills Focus Forming operational definitions   L1

Materials cardboard box, white paper, prism, colored pencils

Time 15 minutes

Tips Caution students not to look directly at the sun. Student may need some guidance positioning the prism so that the band of colors is visible.

Expected Outcome The prism will form a rainbow inside the box, including the colors red, orange, yellow, green, blue, and violet. Each color will blend into the next.

Think It Over The band of colors shows the range of colors that makes up white light.

What Is the Electromagnetic Spectrum?

All electromagnetic waves travel at the same speed in a vacuum, but they have different wavelengths and different frequencies. Radiation in the wavelengths that your eyes can see is called visible light. But only a small portion of electromagnetic radiation is visible light. The rest of the wavelengths are invisible. Your radio detects radio waves, which have much longer wavelengths than visible light. X-rays, on the other hand, are waves with much shorter wavelengths than visible light.

Recall how speed, wavelength, and frequency are related:

Speed = Wavelength × Frequency

Because the speed of all electromagnetic waves is the same, as the wavelength decreases, the frequency increases. Waves with the longest wavelengths have the lowest frequencies. Waves with the shortest wavelengths have the highest frequencies. The amount of energy carried by an electromagnetic wave increases with frequency. The higher the frequency of a wave, the higher its energy.

The **electromagnetic spectrum** is the complete range of electromagnetic waves placed in order of increasing frequency. The full spectrum is shown in Figure 3. **The electromagnetic spectrum is made up of radio waves, infrared rays, visible light, ultraviolet rays, X-rays, and gamma rays.**

✓ **Reading Checkpoint** What is the electromagnetic spectrum?

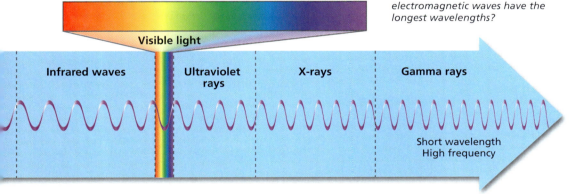

FIGURE 3

The Electromagnetic Spectrum

The electromagnetic spectrum shows the range of different electromagnetic waves in order of increasing frequency and decreasing wavelength.

Interpreting Diagrams Which electromagnetic waves have the longest wavelengths?

Red   Orange   Yellow   Green   Blue   Violet

Visible light

Infrared waves   **Ultraviolet rays**   **X-rays**   **Gamma rays**

Short wavelength
High frequency

Chapter 3 O ◆ 75

Radio Waves

Teach Key Concepts

Introducing Radio Waves

Focus Introduce radio waves as the type of electromagnetic waves that have the longest wavelengths and lowest frequencies.

Teach Remind students that the frequency of electromagnetic waves determines how much energy they have. Ask: **Are radio waves low-energy or high-energy electromagnetic waves?** *(Low energy)*

Apply Ask: **What are some uses of radio waves?** *(Sample answer: To broadcast radio programs)* Mention uses of microwaves and radar if students do not. **learning modality: verbal**

 Address Misconceptions

The Speed of Microwaves

Focus Students may think that microwaves travel faster than other radio waves because they have higher frequencies.

Teach State that microwaves, like other radio waves and electromagnetic waves in general, travel at the speed of light, or at about 300,000 km/s. Therefore, all radio waves, including microwaves, take the same amount of time to travel a given distance, regardless of their frequency of vibrations.

Apply Remind students that wave speed is a product of wavelength and frequency. Ask: **How do the wavelengths of microwaves compare with the wavelengths of other radio waves?** *(Microwaves have the shortest wavelengths.)* **learning modality: logical/mathematical**

 Try This Activity

Microwave Test

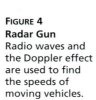

In this activity, you will compare how water, corn oil, and sugar absorb microwaves.

1. Add 25 mL of water to a glass beaker. Record the temperature of the water.
2. Microwave the beaker for 10 seconds and record the water temperature again.
3. Repeat Steps 1 and 2 two more times, using 25 mL of corn oil and 25 mL of sugar.

Drawing Conclusions
Compare the temperature change of the three materials. Which material absorbed the most energy from the microwaves?

FIGURE 4
Radar Gun
Radio waves and the Doppler effect are used to find the speeds of moving vehicles.

76 ◆ O

Radio Waves

Radio waves are the electromagnetic waves with the longest wavelengths and lowest frequencies. They include broadcast waves (for radio and television) and microwaves.

Broadcast Waves Radio waves with longer wavelengths are used in broadcasting. They carry signals for both radio and television programs. A broadcast station sends out radio waves at certain frequencies. Your radio or TV antenna picks up the waves and converts the radio signal into an electrical signal. Inside your radio, the electrical signal is converted to sound. Inside your TV, the signal is converted to sound and pictures.

Microwaves The radio waves with the shortest wavelengths and the highest frequencies are **microwaves.** When you think of microwaves, you probably think of microwave ovens that cook and heat your food. But microwaves have many uses, including cellular phone communication and radar.

Radar stands for **ra**dio **d**etection **a**nd **r**anging. **Radar** is a system that uses reflected radio waves to detect objects and measure their distance and speed. To measure distance, a radar device sends out radio waves that reflect off an object. The time it takes for the reflected waves to return is used to calculate the object's distance. To measure speed, a radar device uses the Doppler effect, which you learned about in Chapter 2. For example, a police radar gun like the one in Figure 4 sends out radio waves that reflect off a car. Because the car is moving, the frequency of the reflected waves is different from the frequency of the original waves. The difference in frequency is used to calculate the car's speed.

 What does *radar* stand for?

 Try This Activity

Skills Focus Drawing conclusions

Materials glass beaker; 25 mL each of water, corn oil, and sugar; thermometer; microwave oven

Time 15 minutes

Tips Clean and dry the beaker after each test. Caution students to wear goggles and heat-resistant gloves, and to be careful handling glassware.

Expected Outcome The water will have the greatest increase in temperature, followed by the corn oil, and then the sugar. Students are expected to conclude that the water absorbed the most energy.

Extend Ask students to predict how much energy some other substances might absorb from microwaves. Let them test their predictions. **learning modality: kinesthetic**

Infrared Rays

If you turn on a burner on an electric stove, you can feel it warm up before the heating element starts to glow. The invisible heat you feel is infrared radiation, or infrared rays. **Infrared rays** are electromagnetic waves with wavelengths shorter than those of radio waves.

Heat Lamps Infrared rays have a higher frequency than radio waves, so they have more energy than radio waves. Because you can feel the energy of infrared rays as heat, these rays are often called heat rays. Heat lamps have bulbs that give off mostly infrared rays and very little visible light. These lamps are used to keep food warm at a cafeteria counter. Some people use heat lamps to warm up their bathrooms quickly.

Infrared Cameras Most objects give off some infrared rays. Warmer objects give off infrared waves with more energy and higher frequencies than cooler objects. An infrared camera takes pictures using infrared rays instead of light. These pictures are called thermograms. A **thermogram** is an image that shows regions of different temperatures in different colors. Figure 5 shows a thermogram of a house. You can use an infrared camera to see objects in the dark. Firefighters use infrared cameras to locate fire victims inside a dark or smoky building. Satellites in space use infrared cameras to study the growth of plants and the motions of clouds.

 Reading Checkpoint What is recorded by an infrared camera?

FIGURE 5
Infrared Images
An infrared camera produced this image, called a thermogram. Regions of different temperatures appear in different colors.
Interpreting Photographs Which areas of the house are warmest (color-coded white)? Which are coolest (color-coded blue)?

Teach Key Concepts `L2`
Properties of Infrared Rays

Focus Remind students that infrared rays are next to radio waves in the electromagnetic spectrum.

Teach Ask: **Which have higher frequencies, radio waves or infrared waves?** *(Infrared)* **Which have more energy?** *(Infrared)* Tell students that infrared rays are often called heat rays because you can feel their energy as heat.

Apply Ask: **Why does sunlight feel warm on your skin?** *(Sample answer: Because it contains infrared waves)* **learning modality: verbal**

Observing Infrared Rays

Materials warm tap water, hot tap water, 2 plastic foam cups, thermometer, metric ruler

Time 5 minutes

Focus State that most objects give off some infrared rays.

Teach Have students fill one cup with warm tap water and the other cup with hot tap water. Then, have students measure the greatest distance at which they can feel heat from each cup. Ask: **Which cup's heat can you feel a greater distance?** *(The cup containing hot water)*

Apply Ask: **What can you conclude about the temperature of objects and the infrared rays they emit?** *(Sample answer: The higher the temperature of an object, the stronger the infrared rays it gives off.)* **learning modality: kinesthetic**

Monitor Progress `L2`

Oral Presentation Call on students to state how radio and infrared waves are used.

Answers
Figure 5 The windows and edges of the roof appear to be the warmest areas, and the wooden frame appears to be the coolest area.

 Radio detection and ranging

 Infrared rays, which are used to make a thermogram

Differentiated Instruction

Less Proficient Readers `L1`
Taking Notes on Electromagnetic Waves Suggest to students that they write the name of each type of electromagnetic wave on one side of an index card. On the other side of the cards, they can list important details about the types of electromagnetic waves as they read about them in this section. **learning modality: verbal**

Gifted and Talented `L3`
Researching Uses Infrared Waves Ask interested students to learn more about a use of infrared cameras and thermograms that is mentioned in the text. For example, students might research how these tools are used by biologists to study plant growth from space. Urge students to share what they learn in an oral report. **learning modality: verbal**

Visible Light

Teach Key Concepts
Wavelengths and Frequencies of Visible Light

Focus Have students shut their eyes tightly for a few seconds before opening them again. Then, tell students that the difference between what they see with their eyes shut and their eyes open is due to visible light.

Teach Refer students to Figure 3 at the beginning of this section, and have them identify the place of visible light in the electromagnetic spectrum. Ask: **Which type of electromagnetic waves have a shorter wavelength and higher frequency, visible light or infrared rays?** (*Visible light*) **Within the range of visible light, which color of light has the shortest wavelength and highest frequency?** (*Violet*) Now, refer students to Figure 6. Ask: **What color does visible light appear when all its wavelengths are combined?** (*White*) **How can visible light of different wavelengths be separated to produce light of different colors?** (*By passing white light through a prism*)

Apply Ask: **How does a prism separate white light into its separate colors?** (*By bending, or refracting, light of different wavelengths by different amounts*) **learning modality: visual**

Ultraviolet Rays

Teach Key Concepts
Recalling Knowledge About Ultraviolet Rays

Focus Guide students in recalling what they already know about ultraviolet rays.

Teach Explain that ultraviolet rays are often called UV rays. Then, ask: **What are some products that have phrases such as "UV protection" or "UV block" on their labels?** (*Sample answer: Sunblock, skin lotion, makeup, some types of clothing, sunglasses*) **Why do people need to be protected from ultraviolet rays?** (*Sample answer: Because they can cause skin cancer*)

Apply Ask: **Do ultraviolet rays have more or less energy than visible light?** (*More energy*) **How do you know?** (*Because they have higher frequencies*) **learning modality: verbal**

FIGURE 6
Refraction in a Prism
When white light passes through a prism, refraction causes the light to separate into its wavelengths.
Observing *Which color of light is refracted the least?*

Scientific Notation
Frequencies of waves often are written in scientific notation. A number in scientific notation consists of a number between 1 and 10 that is multiplied by a power of 10. To write 150,000 Hz in scientific notation, move the decimal point left to make a number between 1 and 10:

150,000 Hz

In this case, the number is 1.5. The power of 10 is the number of spaces you moved the decimal point. In this case, it moved 5 places, so

$$150{,}000 \text{ Hz} = 1.5 \times 10^5 \text{ Hz}$$

Practice Problem A radio wave has a frequency of 5,000,000 Hz. Write this number in scientific notation.

Math Skill Scientific notation
Answer 5.0×10^6 Hz

Visible Light

Electromagnetic waves that you can see are called **visible light.** They make up only a small part of the electromagnetic spectrum. Visible light waves have shorter wavelengths and higher frequencies than infrared rays. Visible light waves with the longest wavelengths appear red in color. As the wavelengths decrease, you can see other colors of light. The shortest wavelengths of visible light appear violet in color.

Visible light that appears white is actually a mixture of many colors. White light from the sun can be separated by a prism into the colors of the visible spectrum—red, orange, yellow, green, blue, and violet. Recall that when waves enter a new medium, the waves bend, or refract. The prism refracts different wavelengths of visible light by different amounts and thereby separates the colors. Red light waves refract the least. Violet light waves refract the most.

Ultraviolet Rays

Electromagnetic waves with wavelengths just shorter than those of visible light are called **ultraviolet rays.** Ultraviolet rays have higher frequencies than visible light, so they carry more energy. The energy of ultraviolet rays is great enough to damage or kill living cells. In fact, ultraviolet lamps are often used to kill bacteria on hospital equipment.

Small doses of ultraviolet rays are useful. For example, ultraviolet rays cause skin cells to produce vitamin D, which is needed for healthy bones and teeth. However, too much exposure to ultraviolet rays is dangerous. Ultraviolet rays can burn your skin, cause skin cancer, and damage your eyes. If you apply sunblock and wear sunglasses that block ultraviolet rays, you can limit the damage caused by ultraviolet rays.

Reading Checkpoint How can ultraviolet rays be useful?

X-Rays

X-rays are electromagnetic waves with wavelengths just shorter than those of ultraviolet rays. Their frequencies are just a little higher than ultraviolet rays. Because of their high frequencies, X-rays carry more energy than ultraviolet rays and can penetrate most matter. But dense matter, such as bone or lead, absorbs X-rays and does not allow them to pass through. Therefore, X-rays are used to make images of bones inside the body or of teeth, as shown in Figure 7. X-rays pass through skin and soft tissues, causing the photographic film in the X-ray machine to darken when it is developed. The bones, which absorb X-rays, appear as the lighter areas on the film.

Too much exposure to X-rays can cause cancer. If you've ever had a dental X-ray, you'll remember that the dentist gave you a lead apron to wear during the procedure. The lead absorbs X-rays and prevents them from reaching your body.

X-rays are sometimes used in industry and engineering. For example, to find out if a steel or concrete structure has tiny cracks, engineers can take an X-ray image of the structure. X-rays will pass through tiny cracks that are invisible to the human eye. Dark areas on the X-ray film show the cracks. This technology is often used to check the quality of joints in oil and gas pipelines.

Reading Checkpoint What kind of matter blocks X-rays?

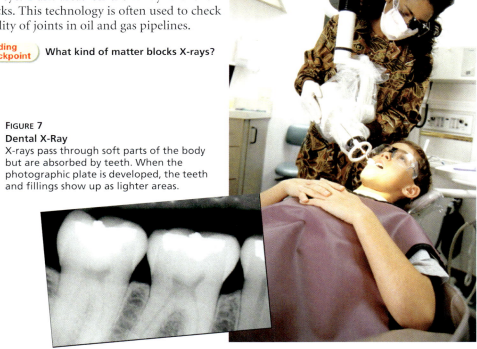

FIGURE 7
Dental X-Ray
X-rays pass through soft parts of the body but are absorbed by teeth. When the photographic plate is developed, the teeth and fillings show up as lighter areas.

X-Rays

Teach Key Concepts L2
Observing X-Ray Images

Focus Discuss X-ray images, which will be familiar to most students.

Teach Ask: **What type of matter appears white in the X-ray in Figure 7?** *(Bones)* Explain that bones appear white because they absorb X-rays. Ask: **What tissues did the X-rays pass through to make this image?** *(Skin, muscle, blood)*

Apply Ask: **Why would a break in a bone appear as a dark line on the bone in an X-ray image?** *(Because X-rays pass through the crack in the bone instead of being absorbed)* **learning modality: visual**

L2

Modeling X-rays and Other Electromagnetic Waves

Materials phone book, cardboard, tissue paper, cotton ball, dull pencil, push pin

Time 15 minutes

Focus Students will model how electromagnetic waves penetrate matter.

Teach Have students make a stack with the phone book on the bottom and the paper on top. The other materials represent types of electromagnetic waves. Have students press each material into the top of the stack and observe how it affects the layers. Then, ask: **In its energy and ability to penetrate matter, which object best represents X-rays?** *(The pin)* **Which type of electromagnetic waves might the dull pencil and cotton ball represent?** *(Sample answer: ultraviolet rays, and infrared rays, respectively)*

Apply Ask: **If the paper and cardboard represent skin and muscle, what might the book represent?** *(Bones or teeth)* **learning modality: kinesthetic**

Monitor Progress L2

Oral Presentation Ask students to identify uses of ultraviolet rays and X-rays.

Answers
Figure 6 Red light is refracted the least.

 They can kill bacteria and help skin produce vitamin D.

Reading Checkpoint Dense matter, such as bone or lead

Differentiated Instruction

English Learners/Beginning Comprehension: Modified Cloze L1
Distribute a simplified version of the first paragraph about X-rays. Leave some of the important terms blank. Provide students with a list of the answers, and have them fill in each blank with one of the words on the list. Show how to fill in the blanks with a model sentence. **learning modality: visual**

English Learners/Intermediate Vocabulary: Writing L2
Have students use the names of the different electromagnetic waves in sentences. Tell them to find and read the sentence in which each name appears in boldface and also a few of the sentences around it. Then, they can write an original sentence containing the word. Show them how, using radio waves as an example. **learning modality: verbal**

Help Students Read

Relating Text and Figures Have students read the captions and study the drawings in Figure 8, which summarizes how the different types of electromagnetic waves affect people's lives. Then, ask students questions about each type of wave and its stated use or effect that require them to integrate information from the text. For example, ask: **Would you expect a television station to broadcast low-frequency or high-frequency electromagnetic waves?** *(Low frequency)* **Which of the two types of electromagnetic waves that can be used to cook food has shorter wavelengths?** *(Infrared rays)* **Why are ultraviolet rays more dangerous than visible light?** *(Ultraviolet rays have higher frequencies and therefore more energy than visible light, so they are more penetrating.)* If students are unable to answer any of the questions, have them reread the relevant parts of the section to find the answers.

Go Online
active art

For: Electromagnetic Waves activity
Visit: PHSchool.com
Web Code: cgp-5032

Students can interact with the art of electromagnetic waves online.

All in One Teaching Resources

• Transparency O32

Gamma Rays

Teach Key Concepts

Predicting Properties of Gamma Rays

Focus Guide students in using what they already know about the rest of the electromagnetic spectrum to predict properties of gamma rays.

Teach State that gamma rays are the electromagnetic waves with the highest frequencies. Ask: **How do the wavelengths of gamma rays compare with those of other electromagnetic waves?** *(Gamma rays have the shortest wavelengths.)* **How much energy do gamma rays have compared with other types of electromagnetic waves?** *(More than any other type)* **What types of matter do you think gamma rays might be able to penetrate?** *(Sample answer: Bones, teeth, or lead)* Confirm that gamma rays can penetrate most types of matter.

FIGURE 8
Electromagnetic Waves

Electromagnetic waves are all around you—in your home, your neighborhood, and your town.

Radio waves carry information and entertainment through radio and television.

Microwaves are used to transmit cellular phone messages and to cook food.

Infrared rays provide the energy that makes your morning toast.

Go Online
active art

For: Electromagnetic Waves activity
Visit: PHSchool.com
Web Code: cgp-5032

Gamma Rays

Gamma rays are the electromagnetic waves with the shortest wavelengths and highest frequencies. Because they have the greatest amount of energy, gamma rays are the most penetrating of all the electromagnetic waves.

Some radioactive substances and certain nuclear reactions produce gamma rays. Because of their great penetrating ability, gamma rays have some medical uses. For example, gamma rays can be used to kill cancer cells inside the body. To examine the body's internal structures, a patient can be injected with a fluid that emits gamma rays. Then a gamma-ray detector can form an image of the inside of the body.

Some objects in space give off bursts of gamma rays. The gamma rays are blocked by Earth's atmosphere, so gamma-ray telescopes that detect them must orbit above Earth's atmosphere. Astronomers think that explosions of stars in distant galaxies are one way of producing these gamma rays.

 Reading Checkpoint How are gamma rays produced?

Apply Point out that gamma rays can be used to kill cancer cells and create images of the inside of the body. **learning modality: verbal**

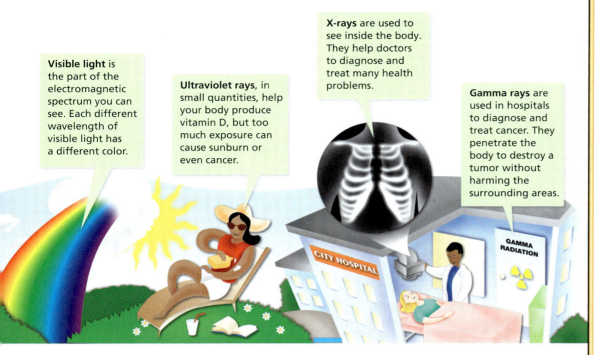

Visible light is the part of the electromagnetic spectrum you can see. Each different wavelength of visible light has a different color.

Ultraviolet rays, in small quantities, help your body produce vitamin D, but too much exposure can cause sunburn or even cancer.

X-rays are used to see inside the body. They help doctors to diagnose and treat many health problems.

Gamma rays are used in hospitals to diagnose and treat cancer. They penetrate the body to destroy a tumor without harming the surrounding areas.

CITY HOSPITAL

GAMMA RADIATION

Section 2 Assessment

Target Reading Skill Previewing Visuals Refer to your questions and answers about Figure 3 to help you answer Question 2 below.

Reviewing Key Concepts

1. a. Reviewing What is the mathematical relationship among wavelength, frequency, and speed?
  b. Summarizing In what way are all electromagnetic waves the same? In what ways are they different?
  c. Making Generalizations As the wavelengths of electromagnetic waves decrease, what happens to their frequencies? To their energies?
2. a. Listing List the waves in the electromagnetic spectrum in order from lowest frequency to highest frequency.
  b. Explaining Why are some electromagnetic waves harmful to you but others are not?

  c. Classifying List one or more types of electromagnetic waves that are useful for each of these purposes: cooking food, communication, seeing inside the body, curing diseases, reading a book, warming your hands.

Math ▶ **Practice**

Scientific Notation

3. An FM radio station broadcasts at a frequency of 9×10^5 Hz. Write the frequency as a number without an exponent.

4. Red light has a frequency of 4×10^{14} Hz. Express the frequency without using an exponent.

Chapter 3 O ◆ 81

 **Chapter Project**

Keep Students on Track By now, students should have completed their list of survey questions. Advise students to limit their number of survey questions. When students distribute their surveys, they should tell respondents when to return the completed surveys.

Monitor Progress ____ L2

Answer

✓ **Reading Checkpoint** Gamma rays are produced by some radioactive substances and certain nuclear reactions. Some objects in space give off gamma rays.

Assess

Reviewing Key Concepts

1. a. Speed = Wavelength × Frequency
b. All electromagnetic waves travel at the same speed in a vacuum, but they have different wavelengths and frequencies.
c. As wavelengths decrease, frequencies and energies increase.
2. a. Radio waves, infrared rays, visible light, ultraviolet rays, X-rays, gamma rays
b. High-frequency waves (ultraviolet rays, X-rays, and gamma rays) can penetrate matter and cause damage because they have high energy. Low-frequency waves (radio waves, infrared rays, and visible light) have less energy and are less likely to cause harm.
c. Cooking food: microwaves and infrared rays; communication: radio waves and microwaves; seeing inside the body: X-rays and gamma rays; curing diseases: gamma rays; reading a book: visible light; warming your hands, infrared rays

Reteach L1

Call on students to name the types of electromagnetic waves in order from lowest to highest frequencies. Call on other students to state a property, use, or effect of each type of wave. Correct any errors.

Performance Assessment L2

Skills Check Ask students to make a table comparing and contrasting the different types of electromagnetic waves. Students can keep their tables in their portfolios.

Portfolio

All in One Teaching Resources

- Section Summary: *Waves of the Electromagnetic Spectrum*
- Review and Reinforcement: *Waves of the Electromagnetic Spectrum*
- Enrich: *Waves of the Electromagnetic Spectrum*

Microwave Ovens

Key Concept
Using microwave ovens has made preparing food faster and easier than using conventional ovens. However, microwave ovens also have drawbacks that require users to follows safety guidelines.

Build Background Knowledge
Advantages of Microwave Ovens
Guide students in recognizing the convenience of using microwave ovens. Ask: **What foods do you heat or cook in a microwave oven?** (Sample answers: Popcorn, soup, frozen pizzas and dinners, frozen pancakes and pastries, leftovers) **How would you heat or cook these foods if you did not have a microwave oven?** (Sample answers: These foods can be cooked using conventional ovens, stovetops, or other cooking methods.) **Which method of heating and cooking food is generally faster and easier?** (Sample answer: Microwave ovens generally make heating and cooking food faster and easier.)

Introduce the Debate
Have students read about the drawbacks of microwave ovens in the feature. Explain that microwaves, like other radio waves, cannot be seen, heard, or felt. Ask: **Why do these properties of microwaves make them even more dangerous?** (Sample answer: Because you cannot tell if you are being exposed to microwaves) **Do you think the advantages of microwaves outweigh the drawbacks?** (Students may say yes or no.)

Microwave Ovens

In 1946, as Dr. Percy Spencer worked on a radar device that produced microwaves, a candy bar melted in his pocket. Curious, he put some popcorn kernels near the device—they popped within minutes. Then, he put an egg near the device. It cooked so fast that it exploded. Dr. Spencer had discovered a new way of cooking food quickly. The microwave-oven industry was born.

Cooking With Microwaves

How do microwave ovens cook food? The answer lies in the way microwaves are reflected, transmitted, and absorbed when they strike different types of materials, such as food, metal, and plastic. In a microwave oven, microwaves reflect off the inner metal walls, bouncing around in the cooking chamber. They mostly pass right through food-wrapping materials such as plastic, glass, and paper. But foods absorb microwaves. Within seconds, the energy from the absorbed microwaves causes water and fat particles in the foods to start vibrating rapidly. These vibrations produce the heat that cooks the food.

Faster Cooking, But Is It Safe?

Using microwave ovens has made preparing food faster and easier than using conventional ovens. But, using microwave ovens has drawbacks. Overheating liquids in a microwave oven can cause the liquids to boil over or can cause serious burns. Also, microwave ovens can cook foods unevenly. This can result in foods being undercooked. Health risks can result from not cooking some foods, such as meats and poultry, thoroughly.

Making Microwave Popcorn

1. Popcorn kernels are enclosed in a paper bag that microwaves pass through.

   Microwave

2. Microwaves strike water particles in the kernels, causing them to vibrate rapidly and produce heat.

3. The heat turns the water to steam, causing the kernels to explode.

   Water particle

Facilitate the Debate
- Ask students to read the rest of the feature and answer the first Weigh the Impact question.
- As a homework or computer lab assignment, direct students to do the research in question 2 on microwave technology guidelines and user safety measures.
- After students have completed their research, divide the class into two groups.

Assign one group to argue that microwave ovens are easy and safe for anyone to use. Assign the other group to argue that microwave ovens are potentially dangerous and should be used only if proper safety measures are followed.

- Give members of each groups a chance to discuss the issue and make a list of points to support their side of the argument. Each group should then elect one student to express the group's views in the debate.

How a Microwave Oven Works

A microwave oven produces microwaves and scatters them throughout the oven to reach the food to be cooked.

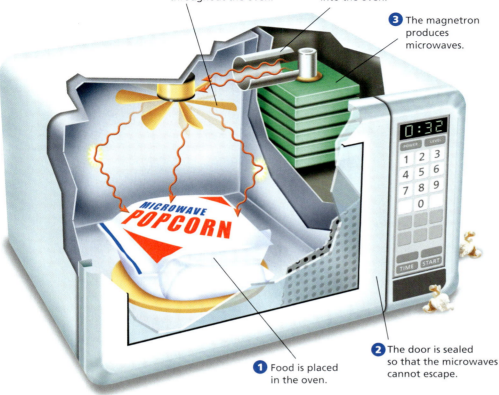

5 A rotating paddle scatters the microwaves throughout the oven.

4 The microwaves travel through a tube into the oven.

3 The magnetron produces microwaves.

2 The door is sealed so that the microwaves cannot escape.

1 Food is placed in the oven.

Weigh the Impact

1. Identify the Need
What advantages do microwave ovens have over conventional ovens?

2. Research
The U.S. Food and Drug Administration (FDA) regulates safety issues for microwave ovens. Research microwave ovens on the Internet to find FDA guidelines about this technology. What safety measures does the FDA recommend?

3. Write
Based on your research, create a poster showing how to use microwave ovens safely. With your teacher's permission, display your poster in the school cafeteria.

For: More on microwave ovens
Visit: PHSchool.com
Web Code: cgh-5030

Background

Facts and Figures In a microwave oven, an electronic device, called a magnetron, produces an oscillating beam of microwaves that changes direction millions of times per second. These oscillations cause water molecules in food to vibrate. The vibrations produce heat, which cooks the food.

High densities of microwave radiation can cause serious health problems.

Microwave ovens use low levels of microwaves, but leakage of microwaves may be dangerous for people nearby if they are exposed over a long period. Although it is not yet known if long-term exposure to low levels of microwaves is dangerous, the U.S. government limits exposure to microwaves in general to 10 milliwatts/cm^2 and places stricter limits on microwave ovens.

Weigh the Impact

1. Microwave ovens heat or cook food in much less time than conventional ovens. Using microwave ovens makes preparing food faster and easier than using conventional ovens.

2. The FDA limits the amount of microwaves that can leak from an oven in its lifetime to 5 milliwatts/cm^2 (at a distance of 5 cm). This is well below the level of microwave exposure known to be dangerous.

3. Posters should incorporate FDA safety tips for consumers, which include: follow the manufacturer's instruction manual for recommended operating procedures and safety precautions for your oven model; do not operate a microwave oven if the door does not close firmly or is damaged; never operate a microwave oven if you think it might continue to operate with the door open; do not stand directly against a microwave oven for long periods of time while it is operating; do not heat water or liquids in the microwave oven for excessive amounts of time. Posters should be illustrated and easy to read from a distance. Students might organize the safety recommendations under headings, such as: Where Should I Stand When Using a Microwave Oven? When Is a Microwave Oven Not Safe to Use?

All in One Teaching Resources
• Transparency O33

Go Online
PHSchool.com

For: More on microwave ovens
Visit: PHSchool.com
Web Code: cgh-5030

Students can research microwave ovens online.

Extend

Tell students that some microwaves have a rotating plate where the food is placed. Ask: **How does constantly rotating the food in a microwave oven help overcome one of its drawbacks?** *(Sample answer: Microwave ovens can cook foods unevenly. Rotating the food helps to cook it more evenly.)*

Objectives

After this lesson, students will be able to
O.3.3.1 Describe the different types of light bulbs.

Target Reading Skill

Comparing and Contrasting Explain that comparing and contrasting information shows how ideas, facts, and events are similar and different. The results of the comparison can have importance.

Answers

Ordinary light bulb: bulb made of glass, gets hot, has a tungsten filament and nitrogen gas and argon gas inside, is not efficient; *Tungsten-halogen bulb*: bulb made of quartz, gets very hot, has a tungsten filament and a halogen gas inside, is more efficient than an ordinary light bulb; *Fluorescent light*: bulb made of glass, stays cool, has a gas and a powder coating inside, is very efficient; *Vapor light*: has neon or argon gas and solid sodium or mercury inside, is very efficient; *Neon light*: bulb made of glass, has neon gas inside

All in One Teaching Resources

• Transparency O34

Preteach

Build Background Knowledge   L2

Properties of Ordinary Light Bulbs
Use students' prior knowledge to introduce properties of light sources. Ask: **If a 100-watt light bulb that has been on for a while suddenly burned out, would you immediately unscrew it?** *(No; you would wait for it to cool down.)* **Do all light bulbs get hot?** *(Sample answer: Fluorescent lights do not.)* Tell students they will learn about five types of light bulbs in this section.

Reading Preview

Key Concept
• What are the different types of light bulbs?

Key Terms
• illuminated
• luminous
• spectroscope
• incandescent light
• tungsten-halogen bulb
• fluorescent light
• vapor light
• neon light

Target Reading Skill

Comparing and Contrasting
Compare and contrast the five types of light bulbs by completing a table like the one below.

Light Bulbs

Feature	Ordinary Light Bulb	Tungsten-Halogen
Bulb material	Glass	
Hot/Cool		

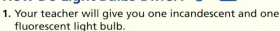

Discover Activity

How Do Light Bulbs Differ?

1. Your teacher will give you one incandescent and one fluorescent light bulb.
2. Examine the bulbs. Record your observations and describe any differences. Draw each type of bulb.
3. How do you think each bulb produces light?

Think It Over
Posing Questions Make a list of five questions you could ask to help you understand how each bulb works.

Look around you. Most of the objects you see are visible because they reflect light from some kind of light source. An object is **illuminated** if you see it by reflected light. The page you are reading, your desk, and the moon are examples of illuminated objects. An object is **luminous** if it gives off its own light. A light bulb, a burning log, and the sun all are examples of luminous objects.

Different types of light bulbs may be used to illuminate the spaces around you. **Common types of light bulbs include incandescent, tungsten-halogen, fluorescent, vapor, and neon lights.** Some light bulbs produce a continuous spectrum of all of the wavelengths of visible light. Others produce only a few wavelengths. You can use an instrument called a **spectroscope** to view the different colors of light produced by a light bulb.

Incandescent Lights

Have you heard the phrase "red hot"? When a glassblower heats glass, it glows and gives off red light. At a higher temperature, it gives off white light and the glass is said to be "white hot." An **incandescent light** (in kun DES unt) is a light bulb that glows when a filament inside it gets white hot. Thomas Edison, the American inventor, patented the first practical incandescent light bulb in 1879.

◀ Glassblower working with heated glass

Discover Activity

Skills Focus Posing questions   L1

Materials clear (uncoated) incandescent light bulb, fluorescent light bulb, goggles

Time 10 minutes

Tips Students must avoid breaking the glass bulbs, and advise you immediately if a bulb breaks. Wear gloves and follow appropriate procedures for cleaning up broken glass.

Expected Outcome Students might describe differences in the shape or size of the bulbs or might know that an ordinary light bulb produces light when the wire inside it glows.

Think It Over Questions will vary. Sample question: What substance gives off the light?

FIGURE 9
Incandescent Lights

A filament glows when electric current passes through it. **Comparing and Contrasting** *How are ordinary light bulbs like tungsten-halogen bulbs? How are they different?*

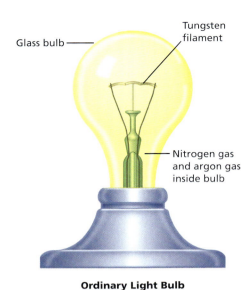

Glass bulb

Tungsten filament

Nitrogen gas and argon gas inside bulb

Ordinary Light Bulb

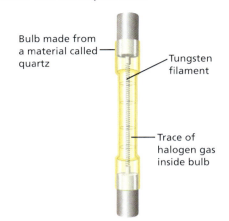

Bulb made from a material called quartz

Tungsten filament

Trace of halogen gas inside bulb

Tungsten-Halogen Bulb

Ordinary Light Bulbs Look closely at the ordinary light bulb shown in Figure 9. Notice the thin wire called the filament. It is made of a metal called tungsten. When an electric current passes through the filament, it quickly heats up and becomes hot, giving off white light. The filament is enclosed in an airtight glass bulb. Most ordinary light bulbs contain small amounts of nitrogen and argon gases.

Ordinary light bulbs are not efficient. Less than 10 percent of their energy is given off as light. Most of their energy is given off as infrared rays. That's why they get so hot.

Tungsten-Halogen Bulbs A bulb that has a tungsten filament and contains a halogen gas such as iodine or bromine is called a **tungsten-halogen bulb.** The filament of this bulb gets much hotter than in an ordinary light bulb, so the bulb looks whiter.

Tungsten-halogen bulbs are more efficient than ordinary bulbs because they give off more light and use less electrical energy. But they also give off more heat. Because tungsten-halogen bulbs get so hot, they must be kept away from materials that could catch fire.

 Reading Checkpoint What gases are used in tungsten-halogen bulbs?

Lab zone Skills Activity

Observing

Use a spectroscope to view light from two sources. **CAUTION:** *Do not view the sun with the spectroscope.*

1. Look through the spectroscope at an ordinary light bulb. Use colored pencils to draw and label what you see.

2. Now, look at a fluorescent light through the spectroscope. Again, draw and label what you see.

How are the colors you see the same? How are they different?

Chapter 3 O ◆ 85

Lab zone Skills Activity

Skills Focus Observing **L3**

Materials spectroscope, ordinary light bulb, fluorescent light bulb, colored pencils

Time 15 minutes

Tips Before the activity, explain how fluorescent lights produce light. Demonstrate the spectroscope.

Expected Outcome The incandescent spectrum will be continuous; the fluorescent spectrum will have distinct colored lines.

Extend Explain that the bands of color are not the same because the two types of light bulbs give off light of different wavelengths. Encourage interested students to examine other types of lights. **learning modality: kinesthetic**

Incandescent Lights

Teach Key Concepts **L2**

Comparing and Contrasting Types of Incandescent Lights

Focus State that an incandescent light is a light bulb that glows when a thin wire inside it, called a filament, becomes so hot that it glows white.

Teach Tell students that there are two common types of incandescent light bulbs: ordinary light bulbs and tungsten-halogen light bulbs. Draw a Venn diagram on the board to compare and contrast the two types of incandescent light bulbs. For example, both have a tungsten filament and produce white light; but ordinary bulbs are made of glass and have low efficiency, whereas tungsten-halogen bulbs are made of quartz and have medium efficiency.

Apply Tell students that tungsten-halogen lights become even hotter than ordinary light bulbs. Ask: **How might that be a drawback or limitation of tungsten-halogen lights?** (*Sample answer: It might limit where they can be safely used, because they must be kept away from materials that could catch fire.*) **learning modality: verbal**

 **Teaching Resources**

• Transparency O35

Independent Practice **L2**

All in One Teaching Resources

• Guided Reading and Study Worksheet: *Producing Visible Light*

🔘 **Student Edition on Audio CD**

Monitor Progress _____ **L2**

Writing Have students write a paragraph explaining how electric current produces light in ordinary light bulbs and in tungsten-halogen light bulbs.

Answers

Figure 9 Both have a tungsten filament inside a bulb that contains gases. The bulbs differ in shape, the material they are made of, and the gases they contain.

 Reading Checkpoint A halogen gas, such as iodine or bromine

Other Light Sources

Introducing Other Light Sources

Focus Introduce the three other light sources covered in this section: fluorescent lights, vapor lights, and neon lights.

Teach State that a basic difference between incandescent light bulbs and these other types of light bulbs is the part of the bulb that gives off light. Remind students that a metal wire inside incandescent light bulbs gives off light. Explain that in the other three types of light bulbs, either a powder coating the inside of the bulb or gas inside the bulb gives off light. Ask: **What type of gas do you think gives off light in a neon light?** *(Neon)* **In a sodium vapor light?** *(Sodium)*

Apply Ask: **How might this difference between incandescent and other types of light sources affect their performance?** *(Students might predict that the other types of lights are cooler or more efficient or that they produce light of different colors.)* **learning modality: verbal**

Integrating Life Science L2

Inform students that some organisms can produce light and "glow in the dark." State that the ability of an organism to produce light is called *bioluminescence.* Write the word on the board so students can see how it is spelled. Explain that the light is produced when a chemical reaction takes place. The reaction involves phosphorus, which is also contained in the head of matches. State that bioluminescence may be used by an organism to attract prey or to attract a mate. Then, ask: **What are some examples of organisms that are bioluminescent?** *(Sample answer: Fireflies, some species of fish)* Mention that certain species of bacteria and algae are also bioluminescent. Point out that most bioluminescent organisms are active after dark, in deep water, or in other environments where there is very little light. **learning modality: verbal**

FIGURE 10
Fluorescent Light
A fluorescent light is cool because very little energy is given off as infrared rays. **Inferring** *Why is a fluorescent light efficient?*

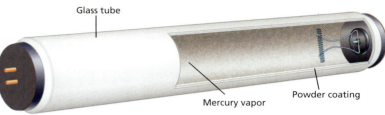

Glass tube

Mercury vapor

Powder coating

Other Light Sources

Incandescent light bulbs are not the only light bulbs you see around you. Some spaces are lit by fluorescent lights. Streets and parking lots may be lit with vapor lights. Neon lights are often used to attract attention to stores and theaters.

Fluorescent Lights Have you ever noticed long, narrow glass tubes that illuminate schools and stores? These are fluorescent light bulbs. A **fluorescent light** (floo RES unt) is a bulb that contains a gas and is coated on the inside with a powder. When an electric current passes through the bulb, it causes the gas inside to give off ultraviolet rays. When the ultraviolet rays hit the powder in the tube, the powder gives off visible light.

Fluorescent lights give off most of their energy as visible light and only a little energy as infrared rays. Therefore, fluorescent lights do not get as hot as incandescent light bulbs. They also usually last longer than incandescent lights and use less electrical energy for the same brightness. So, fluorescent lights are very efficient.

Vapor Lights A bulb that contains neon or argon gas and a small amount of solid sodium or mercury is a **vapor light.** When an electric current passes through the gas, the gas heats up. The hot gas then heats the sodium or mercury. The heating causes the sodium or mercury to change from a solid into a gas. In a sodium vapor light, the particles of sodium gas glow to give off a yellowish light. A mercury vapor light produces a bluish light.

Both sodium and mercury vapor lights are used for street lighting and parking lots. They require very little electrical energy to give off a great deal of light, so they are quite efficient.

FIGURE 11
Sodium Vapor Lights
Sodium vapor lights give off a yellowish light.

Differentiated Instruction

Less Proficient Readers L1
Comparing and Contrasting Guide students in making a graphic organizer, such as a Venn diagram, to compare and contrast fluorescent lights, vapor lights, and neon lights. Suggest that students compare and contrast how these lights produce visible light and how efficient they are. **learning modality: visual**

Special Needs L1
Observing Different Light Sources Point out different types of light bulbs in the school. There might be fluorescent lights in the classroom, neon lights in the cafeteria, and vapor lights in the parking lot. Suggest that students note the size and shape of the bulbs, the color of light they produce, and how bright they are. **learning modality: visual**

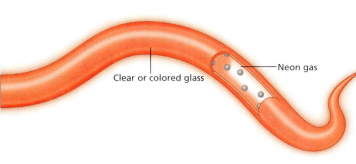
Clear or colored glass — Neon gas

FIGURE 12
Neon Lights
The color of a neon light depends in part on which gas or gases are in the tube.

Neon Lights A **neon light** is a sealed glass tube that contains neon gas. When an electric current passes through the neon, particles of the gas absorb energy. However, the gas particles cannot hold the energy for very long. The energy is released in the form of light. This process is called electric discharge through gases.

A true neon light gives off red light, as shown in Figure 12. But often, lights that contain different gases or a mixture of gases are also called neon lights. Different gases produce different colors of light. For example, both argon gas and mercury vapor produce greenish-blue light. Helium gives pink light. Krypton gives a pale violet light. Sometimes colored glass tubes are used to produce other colors. Neon lights are commonly used for bright, flashy signs.

 Reading Checkpoint What color of light does a neon light give off?

Section 3 Assessment

 Target Reading Skill Comparing and Contrasting Use the information in your table about light bulbs to help you answer Question 1 below.

Reviewing Key Concepts
1. a. **Listing** What are five common types of light bulbs?
   b. **Explaining** How do incandescent light bulbs work?
   c. **Inferring** Lamps that use ordinary light bulbs often have cloth or paper shades. But tungsten-halogen lamps usually have metal shades. Explain.
   d. **Making Generalizations** What gives off light in incandescent light bulbs? What gives off light in other types of light bulbs?

Lab zone At-Home Activity

Buying Light Bulbs Invite family members to visit a hardware store. Ask a salesperson to describe the different kinds of light bulbs available. Read the information about each bulb on the packages. Look for the cost and the expected life of the bulbs. How does this information help you and your family to choose bulbs for different purposes?

Lab zone At-Home Activity

Buying Light Bulbs **L2** Encourage students to describe to their family how the different types of light bulbs work. Ask students to state the criteria they used to choose the most economical bulb.

Comparing Light Bulbs

Prepare for Inquiry

Key Concept
Different types of light bulbs can be used to provide light for different purposes.

Skills Objective
After this lab, students will be able to
- infer which light bulb gives the most illumination based on their observations
- interpret their data to identify factors that affect a light bulb's illumination
- draw conclusions about whether the most expensive light bulb is best

 Prep Time 15 minutes
Class Time 40 minutes

Advance Planning
Purchase a variety of incandescent light bulbs that fit the same socket. You might include "soft white" bulbs, clear glass bulbs, standard-life bulbs, long-life bulbs, and, within each type, bulbs with different power, such as 40-watt, 60-watt, and 75-watt bulbs. Provide each student team with a light socket and a cardboard box about the size of the box in the picture. Make sure the other materials are on hand.

Safety
 Remind students that light bulbs must be allowed to cool for several minutes before they are unscrewed. Make sure students unplug the lamps or sockets before they change bulbs. Advise students to tell you immediately about any broken bulbs. Review the safety guidelines in Appendix A.

All in One Teaching Resources
- Lab Worksheet: *Comparing Light Bulbs*

Guide Inquiry

Invitation
Show students several light bulbs and their packages. Explain what the wattage rating and life expectancy rating mean. Ask: **What types of light bulbs do you use at home?** *(Students are likely to identify one or more types from those on display.)* Urge students to think about where and when they use the different types of light bulbs.

 **Lab zone** Consumer **Lab**

Comparing Light Bulbs

Problem
Which types of light bulbs provide the best illumination?

Skills Focus
inferring, interpreting data, drawing conclusions

Materials
- a variety of incandescent light bulbs that can fit in the same lamp or socket
- medium-sized cardboard box
- light socket or lamp (without shade)
- meter stick
- wax paper
- scissors
- plain paper
- tape

Procedure

1. Following the instructions below, construct your own light box. The box allows you to test the illumination that is provided by each light bulb.

2. Make a data table like the one shown to record your data.

3. With a partner, examine the different bulbs. What is the power (watts), light output (lumens), and life (hours) for each bulb? Predict which light bulb will be the brightest. Explain your choice.

4. How will you test your prediction? What kinds of incandescent light bulbs will you use? What variables will you keep constant? What variables will you change?

5. Review your plan. Will your procedure help you find an answer to the problem?

6. Ask your teacher to check your procedure.

7. Before you repeat the steps for a second light bulb, look back at your procedure. How could you improve the accuracy of your results?

8. Test the illumination of the rest of your light bulbs.

How to Build and Use a Light Box

A Use a medium-sized cardboard box, such as the kind of box copy paper comes in. If the box has flaps, cut them off.

B Carefully cut a viewing hole (about 2 cm x 4 cm) in the bottom of the box. This will be on top when the box is used. This is hole A.

C Punch another hole (about 1 cm x 1 cm) on one side of the box. This is hole B. It will allow light from the bulb to enter the box.

D To decrease the amount of light that can enter, cover hole B with two layers of wax paper.

E Put one of your light bulbs in the lamp and place it at the side of the box, about 1 m from hole B

F Have your partner write a secret letter on a piece of plain paper. Put the paper on the table. Place the light box over the paper with the viewing hole facing up.

G Now look through hole A. Turn the lamp on and move the light toward the box until you can read the secret letter. Measure the distance between the light bulb and hole B.

Introduce the Procedure
Have students read through the procedure. Suggest that each team limit its comparison to light bulbs that differ in just one variable. For example, a team might compare regular-life and long-life light bulbs of the same power, such as 40 watts. Another team might compare 40-watt and 75-watt light bulbs of the same type, such as clear glass.

Troubleshooting the Experiment
- The same student should do all the viewing for each team to reduce observer error.
- Remind students to wait for their eyes to adjust to the light before making observations and to avoid looking directly at the light.

Data Table

Bulb Number	Brand Name	Power (watts)	Light Output (lumens)	Life (h)	Cost (dollars)	Distance From Bulb to Light Box (cm)

Analyze and Conclude

1. **Observing** How does the distance between the bulb and hole B affect how easily you can read the secret letter?

2. **Inferring** Based on your observations, what can you infer about the illumination provided by each bulb? Which bulb gave the most illumination?

3. **Interpreting Data** How did your results compare with your prediction? What did you learn that you did not know when you made your prediction?

4. **Interpreting Data** What factors affect the illumination given by a light bulb?

5. **Drawing Conclusions** Based on your results, do you think that the most expensive bulb is the best?

6. **Communicating** Using what you have learned, write an advertisement for the best light bulb. Explain why it is the best.

Design an Experiment

A lighting company claims that one of their 11-watt fluorescent bulbs gives off as much light as a 75-watt ordinary light bulb. Design an experiment to test this claim. *Obtain your teacher's permission before carrying out your investigation.*

Expected Outcome

Students should use their data to draw a conclusion about which type of light bulb provides the best illumination. Results will vary depending on the light bulbs students compared.

Analyze and Conclude

1. The closer the bulb is to hole B, the easier it is to read the secret letter.

2. Answers will vary depending on the light bulbs students compared. The bulb with the greatest distance measurement produces the greatest illumination.

3. Answers will vary depending on students' predictions. Students may learn that bulbs with higher wattages generally produce greater illumination. Students may also find that, at the same wattage, different bulbs may vary in the amount of illumination they produce. For example, long-life bulbs emit a little less light than normal-life bulbs of the same wattage.

4. Factors include wattage, life expectancy, and whether it is incandescent or fluorescent.

5. Answers may vary depending on the light bulbs compared. Students might conclude that the most expensive light bulb is best if it has the greatest light output or longest life.

6. Advertisements should describe how the chosen light bulb surpasses the other light bulbs tested.

Extend Inquiry

Design an Experiment Students might use the same experimental design as in this lab and compare an 11-watt fluorescent light bulb with a 75-watt ordinary light bulb. Give interested students a chance to carry out the investigation.

Sample Data Table

Bulb#	Brand Name	Power (watts)	Light Output (lumens)	Life (hrs)	Cost ($)	Distance from bulb to Light Box (cm)
1	A, soft-white	75	1,170	750	1.89	43
2	B, long-life	75	1,125	1,125	2.59	42
3	C, discount	75	1,170	1,000	.99	39
4	D, soft-white	60	860	1,000	1.68	30
5	E, fluorescent	15	860	10,000	4.05	53

Wireless Communication

Objectives

After this lesson, students will be able to

O.3.4.1 Explain how radio waves transmit information.

O.3.4.2 Describe how cellular phones work.

O.3.4.3 Explain how communications satellites relay information.

Target Reading Skill

Identifying Main Ideas Explain that using prior knowledge helps students connect what they already know to what they are about to read.

Answers

Possible answers:

What You Know

1. Cellular phones don't use wires.
2. Radio and television signals travel through the air.

What You Learned

1. The signals for radio and television programs are carried by radio waves.
2. The signals can be transmitted by changing either the amplitude or the frequency of the radio waves.
3. Cellular phones transmit and receive signals using microwaves.

All in One Teaching Resources

• Transparency O36

Preteach

Build Background Knowledge L2

Live Satellite Broadcasts

Encourage students to recall live television broadcasts they have seen in which the signal originated on the other side of Earth, for example, in Australia. Ask: **How did the signal travel to the United States from there?** (*Sample answer: It was transmitted by a satellite.*) Tell students that in this section they will learn how these and other messages are transmitted using radio waves.

Wireless Communication

Reading Preview

Key Concepts
• How do radio waves transmit information?
• How do cellular phones work?
• How do communications satellites relay information?

Key Terms
• amplitude modulation
• frequency modulation

Target Reading Skill

Using Prior Knowledge Your prior knowledge is what you know before you read about a topic. Before you read, write what you know about wireless communication in a graphic organizer. As you read, continue to write in what you learn.

FIGURE 13
Miniature Television
Radio waves transmit the signals for this small portable television.

90 ◆ 0

Lab zone Discover Activity

How Can Radio Waves Change?

1. Trace the wave diagram onto a piece of tracing paper. Then transfer the tracing onto a flat piece of latex from a balloon or a glove.
2. Stretch the latex horizontally. How is the stretched wave different from the wave on the tracing paper?
3. Now stretch the latex vertically. How is this wave different from the wave on the tracing paper? How is it different from the wave in Step 2?

Think It Over
Making Models Which stretch changes the wave's amplitude? The wave's frequency?

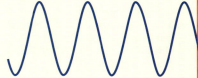

You race home from school and switch on the TV to catch the final innings of your favorite team's big game. In an instant, you see and hear the game just as if you were sitting in the stands.

Today you can communicate with people far away in just seconds. You can watch a live television broadcast of a soccer game from Europe or listen to a radio report from Africa. How do these radio and television programs reach you?

Radio and Television

Radio waves carry, or transmit, signals for both radio and television programs. The radio waves are produced by charged particles moving back and forth inside transmission antennas. **Transmission antennas send out, or broadcast, radio waves in all directions. Radio waves carry information from the antenna of a broadcasting station to the receiving antenna of your radio or television.** There are two methods of transmitting the signals—amplitude modulation and frequency modulation. Radio stations broadcast using either method. Television stations use both methods—amplitude modulation for pictures and frequency modulation for sound.

Lab zone Discover Activity

Skills Focus Making models

Materials tracing paper, flat piece of stretchable latex about 20 cm square

Time 10 minutes

Tips Review the wave concepts of *amplitude, wavelength,* and *frequency.*

Expected Outcome The wave on the stretched latex in Step 2 is wider and

L1

spread farther apart. The wave on the stretched latex in Step 3 is taller and narrower.

Think It Over The vertical stretch (Step 3) changes the wave's amplitude. The horizontal stretch (Step 2) changes the wave's frequency.

Amplitude Modulation AM stands for amplitude modulation. **Amplitude modulation** is a method of transmitting signals by changing the amplitude of a wave. The information that will become sound, such as speech and music, is coded in changes, or modulations, of a wave's amplitude. The frequency of the wave remains constant, as shown in Figure 14. At a radio broadcasting station, sound is converted into electronic signals. The electronic signals are then converted into a pattern of changes in the amplitude of a radio wave. Your radio receives the wave and converts it back into sound.

AM radio waves have relatively long wavelengths and are easily reflected by Earth's ionosphere. The ionosphere is a region of charged particles high in the atmosphere. The reflected waves bounce back to Earth's surface. Therefore, AM radio stations can broadcast over long distances.

Frequency Modulation FM stands for frequency modulation. **Frequency modulation** is a method of transmitting signals by changing the frequency of a wave. FM signals travel as changes, or modulations, in the frequency of the wave. The amplitude of the wave remains constant.

FM waves have higher frequencies and more energy than AM waves. As shown in Figure 14, they pass through the ionosphere instead of being reflected back to Earth. Thus, FM waves do not travel as far as AM waves. So, if you go on a long car trip with an FM radio station tuned in, you may quickly lose reception of the station. But FM waves are usually received clearly and produce better sound quality than AM waves.

FIGURE 14
AM and FM Radio Waves
In AM transmissions, the amplitude of a radio wave is changed. In FM transmissions, the frequency is changed.
Interpreting Diagrams *What property is constant in the AM wave? In the FM wave?*

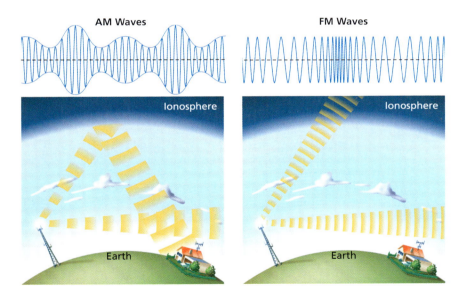

AM Waves

FM Waves

Ionosphere

Ionosphere

Earth

Earth

O ◆ 91

Radio and Television

Teach Key Concepts L2
Introducing AM and FM Radio Waves

Focus Tell students that there are two ways of sending signals with radio waves: amplitude modulation and frequency modulation.

Teach State that modulation means "change." Ask: **What do you think amplitude modulation means?** *(Change in amplitude)* **What do you think frequency modulation means?** *(Change in frequency)* Have students look at Figure 13 and read the caption. Point out how amplitude changes in the AM wave and how wavelength changes in the FM wave.

Apply Ask: **If the wavelength of FM waves changes, what happens to their frequency?** *(It also changes, but in the opposite direction.)* **Why?** *(Because the product of wavelength and frequency is the speed of light, which is constant for electromagnetic waves in a given medium)* **learning modality: logical/mathematical**

All in One Teaching Resources
• Transparency O37

Independent Practice L2

All in One Teaching Resources
• Guided Reading and Study Worksheet: *Wireless Communication*

⊙ **Student Edition on Audio CD**

Differentiated Instruction

English Learners/Beginning L1
Comprehension: Ask Questions
Distribute a rewritten, simplified version of the paragraph under the *Radio and Television* heading. Ask straightforward questions that can be answered directly from the rewritten text. For example, ask: **What are two methods of transmitting signals in radio and television broadcasts?** **learning modality: verbal**

English Learners/Intermediate L2
Comprehension: Ask Questions Have students read the simplified paragraph and the actual text paragraph. Ask if they find anything confusing in the text paragraph, and try to clarify it for them. Finally, check comprehension by asking questions based on the actual text. For example, ask: **What happens to radio waves that reach your radio or television?** **learning modality: verbal**

Monitor Progress L2

Skills Check Have students create a Venn diagram comparing and contrasting AM and FM radio waves. Students can keep their Venn diagrams in their portfolios.

Portfolio

Answer
Figure 13 In the AM wave, frequency is constant. In the FM wave, amplitude is constant.

Math Skill Interpreting data

Focus State that different types of radio and television broadcasts are restricted to using radio waves of a certain range of frequencies.

Teach Point out the units used to measure wave frequency. Make sure students know that kHz represents kilohertz, or 1,000 hertz, and that MHz represents megahertz, or 1,000,000 hertz. Ask: **Which frequency is greater, 54MHz or 1,605 kHz?** (*54 MHz*)

Answers

1. Kilohertz (kHz) and megahertz (MHz)
2. UHF television uses the highest-frequency radio waves, and AM radio broadcast uses the lowest-frequency radio waves.
3. UHF television uses waves with the highest frequency and therefore the shortest wavelength.
4. You cannot tell from this data if it is a television or radio program, because VHF television and FM radio both broadcast radio waves with a frequency of 100 MHz.

Help Students Read   `L1`

Visualizing Refer to the Content Refresher in this chapter, which provides guidelines for using the Visualizing strategy.

Suggest that students visualize the radio spectrum as a band of increasing wave frequencies, like the electromagnetic spectrum band diagrammed in Figure 3 of Section 2, *Waves of the Electromagnetic Spectrum*. Help students visualize the order of waves in such a radio band diagram by asking: **Which type of radio waves would you place at the low-frequency/long-wavelength end of the diagram?** (*AM radio waves*). **Which type of radio waves would you place at the high-frequency/short-wavelength end of the diagram?** (*UHF television*) **Which type of radio waves would follow AM radio in the diagram?** (*VHF television*) You might want to have students actually draw and label such a radio band diagram to help in their visualizing.

Comparing Frequencies

The table shows the ranges of radio broadcast frequencies used for AM radio, UHF television, FM radio, and VHF television.

1. **Interpreting Data** In the table, what units of measurement are used for frequency?
2. **Interpreting Data** Which type of broadcast shown in the table uses the highest-frequency radio waves? Which uses the lowest-frequency waves?
3. **Calculating** Which type of broadcast uses waves with the shortest wavelength?
4. **Inferring** A broadcast uses a frequency of 100 MHz. Can you tell from this data if it is a television or a radio program? Explain.

Broadcast Frequencies	
Type of Broadcast	**Frequency Range**
AM radio broadcast	535 kHz to 1,605 kHz
VHF television	54 MHz to 216 MHz
FM radio broadcast	88 MHz to 108 MHz
UHF television	470 MHz to 806 MHz

The Radio Spectrum In addition to radio and television broadcasts, radio waves are used for many types of communication. For example, taxi drivers, firefighters, and police officers all use radio waves to do their jobs. The Federal Communications Commission, or FCC, assigns different radio frequencies for different uses. Radio stations are allowed to use one part of the radio spectrum. Television stations use other parts. Taxi and police radios are also each assigned a set of frequencies. Because the signals all have different assigned frequencies, they travel without interfering.

You probably have seen these assigned frequencies when you tune a radio. AM radio stations use frequencies measured in kilohertz (kHz), while FM radio stations use frequencies measured in megahertz (MHz). Recall that a hertz is one cycle per second. If something vibrates 1,000 times a second, it has a frequency of 1,000 Hz, or 1 kilohertz (kHz). (The prefix *kilo-* means "one thousand.") If something vibrates 1,000,000 times a second, it has a frequency of 1,000,000 Hz, or 1 megahertz (MHz). (The prefix *mega-* means "one million.")

AM radio stations range from 535 kHz to 1,605 kHz. FM radio stations range between 88 MHz and 108 MHz. A television station uses one of two sets of frequencies: Very High Frequency (VHF) or Ultra High Frequency (UHF). VHF stations range from 54 MHz to 216 MHz, corresponding to Channels 2 through 13 on your television set. UHF channels range from 470 MHz to 806 MHz, corresponding to Channels 14 through 69.

 Reading Checkpoint What does the term *kilohertz* stand for?

Discovery CHANNEL SCHOOL

The Electromagnetic Spectrum

Video Preview
▶ Video Field Trip
Video Assessment

Discovery CHANNEL SCHOOL
Video Field Trip

The Electromagnetic Spectrum

Show the Video Field Trip to let students see how electromagnetic waves are used to help find ships or people lost at sea. Discussion question: **What characteristic of radio waves makes them an important part of search-and-rescue operations?** (*Some radio waves can travel from Earth into space and back again.*)

Cellular Phones

Cellular telephones have become very common, but they only work if they are in or near a cellular system. The cellular system, which is shown in Figure 15, works by dividing regions into many small cells, or geographical areas. Each cell has one or more towers that relay signals to a central hub.

Cellular phones transmit and receive signals using high-frequency microwaves. When you place a call on a cellular phone, the phone sends out microwaves. The microwaves are tagged with a number unique to your phone. A tower picks up the microwaves and transfers the signal to a hub. In turn, the hub channels and transmits the signal to a receiver. The receiver may be another tower or another hub, depending on the distance between the two phones. That tower or hub transmits the signal to the receiving cellular phone. The receiving phone rings when it picks up the microwave signal from a tower or hub. The whole exchange seems to be instantaneous.

In addition to making phone calls, you can also use some cellular phones to page someone, to send text messages, or to get information from the Internet. Some modern cellular phones can even be used as digital cameras.

 Reading Checkpoint What are three ways to communicate with a cellular phone?

FIGURE 15
Cellular Phone System
In the cellular phone system, cellular phones transmit and receive radio waves that travel to the nearest tower.
Predicting What happens if a cellular phone is far away from a tower?

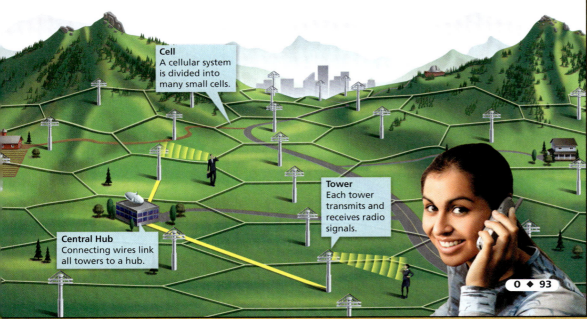

Cell
A cellular system is divided into many small cells.

Tower
Each tower transmits and receives radio signals.

Central Hub
Connecting wires link all towers to a hub.

Differentiated Instruction

Less Proficient Readers L1
Using Prior Knowledge of Cellular Phone Towers Challenge students to locate two or more adjacent cellular phone towers in the area. Ask: **How far apart are the towers?** *(The towers are likely to be a few miles apart.)* **Why are cellular phone towers so close together?** *(Because cellular phones transmit weak signals)* **learning modality: visual**

Gifted and Talented L3
Cellular Phone Frequencies Challenge interested students to find the range of frequencies used by cellular phone systems. Urge them to report back to the class with the frequencies and compare them with the frequencies used for radio and television transmissions. **learning modality: logical/mathematical**

Cellular Phones

Teach Key Concepts   L2
Cellular Phones and Microwaves

Focus State that cellular phones send and receive radio signals over short distances.

Teach Tell students that the radio waves used for cellular phones are microwaves. Ask: **Where are microwaves in the electromagnetic spectrum?** *(At the upper end of radio waves, just below infrared rays)* **How much energy do microwaves have, compared with other radio waves?** *(More energy, because of their higher frequencies)*

Apply Ask: **If microwaves are high-energy radio waves, why can cellular phone signals travel only short distances?** *(Sample answer: Because cellular phones are small, low-power units)* **learning modality: verbal**

Lab zone **Build Inquiry**   L2

Modeling Cellular Phone Transmission

Materials small ball

Time 5 minutes

Focus Tell students they will model how a cellular phone system works.

Teach Organize students into small groups, or "cells." Give the first group the ball, and tell them it represents a message. Then, have groups pass the ball from one to another. Ask: **How is the model like an actual cellular phone system, and how is it different?** *(Sample answer: The message was transmitted from cell to cell, but much more slowly.)*

Apply Ask: **How fast are messages transmitted in a cellular phone system?** *(At the speed of light)* **learning modality: kinesthetic**

Monitor Progress   L2

Writing Ask students to write a paragraph describing how microwaves are transmitted by a cellular phone system.

Answers
Figure 15 It will not be able to transmit and receive radio waves.

 Reading Checkpoint 1,000 hertz

 Reading Checkpoint Regular calls, paging, and short text messages and video.

Communications Satellites

Teach Key Concepts L2
Bouncing Radio Waves

Focus Use a familiar sports analogy to introduce communications satellites.

Teach Call on a student to describe how to make a basket in basketball by bouncing the ball off the backboard. Explain that a communications satellite is somewhat like the backboard. Radio waves cannot be sent great distances directly over Earth's surface because the surface is curved. Instead, the waves are bounced off a satellite, which returns them to Earth on the other side of the horizon.

Apply Ask: **Why might more than one satellite be needed for this purpose?** *(Sample answer: One satellite might not be able to bounce the radio waves far enough.)*
learning modality: verbal

Modeling a Communications Satellite L1

Materials globe, marble

Time 5 minutes

Focus Use a globe and a marble to model how a communications satellite is positioned to reflect radio waves over Earth's surface.

Teach In the feature, have students find the altitude at which communications satellites orbit Earth. *(About 35,000 km)* Tell students that Earth's diameter is a little less than 13,000 km. Then, ask: **About how far above the globe would a communications satellite be?** *(A little less than three times the globe's diameter.)* Holding the marble at the correct height, point out the area of Earth's surface that the satellite could "see."

Apply Ask: **How would you use communications satellites to transmit radio waves from one side of Earth to the other?** *(Sample answer: By using more than one)* **learning modality: logical/mathematical**

Go Online
SciLINKS NSTA

For: Links on using waves to communicate
Visit: www.SciLinks.org
Web Code: scn-1534

Download a worksheet that will guide students' review of Internet resources on using waves to communicate.

Go Online
SciLINKS NSTA

For: Links on using waves to communicate
Visit: www.SciLinks.org
Web Code: scn-1534

Communications Satellites

Satellites orbiting Earth are used to send information around the world. Communications satellites work like the receivers and transmitters of a cellular phone system. **Communications satellites receive radio, television, and telephone signals and relay the signals back to receivers on Earth.** Because a satellite can "see" only part of Earth at any given time, more than one satellite is needed for any given purpose.

Satellite Phone Systems Several companies have developed satellite phone systems. The radio waves from one phone are sent up to a communications satellite. The satellite transmits the waves back to the receiving phone on Earth. With this kind of phone, you can call anywhere in the world, but the cost is greater than using a cellular phone.

Science and **History**

Wireless Communication
Since the late 1800s, many developments in communication have turned our world into a global village.

1888 Electromagnetic Waves
German scientist Heinrich Hertz proved that radio waves exist. Hertz demonstrated that the waves could be reflected, refracted, diffracted, and polarized just like light waves.

1895 First Wireless Transmission
Italian engineer and inventor Guglielmo Marconi successfully used radio waves to send a coded wireless signal a distance of more than 2 km.

1901 First Transatlantic Signals
On December 12, the first transatlantic radio signal was sent from Poldhu Cove, Cornwall, England, to Signal Hill, Newfoundland. The coded radio waves traveled more than 3,000 km through the air.

1923 Ship-to-Ship Communication
For the first time, people on one ship could talk to people on another. The signals were sent as electromagnetic waves, received by an antenna, and converted into sound.

1880	1900	1920

94 ◆ O

Background

Facts and Figures Before the first working cellular phone network was implemented in Japan in 1979, another wireless phone technology, the mobile telephone, was developed and used in the United States. The first mobile phones were introduced in the U. S. in 1946. To place a call, the caller would scan the dial for an unused channel and call the operator, who would then dial the number. The phones worked like a CB radio or two-way radio set: the caller had to hold down a button to talk, so only one person at a time could talk. In 1964, an improved mobile telephone service was introduced. These phones dialed automatically and allowed callers to talk without pushing a button. However, only a limited number of channels was available. The first cellular phone system in the U. S. was installed in 1983.

Television Satellites Both television networks and cable companies use communications satellites. First, the television signals are changed into AM and FM waves. These radio waves are sent up to satellites. Then the signals are relayed to local stations around the world.

Some people have their own antennas to receive signals for television programs directly from satellites. Many of the antennas are dish-shaped, so they are known as satellite dishes. Older satellite dishes were very large, more than 2 meters in diameter. But newer dishes are much smaller because the signals from satellites have become more powerful.

Television signals from satellites often are scrambled to make sure that only people who pay for the programs can use the signal. Customers need a decoding box to unscramble the signals.

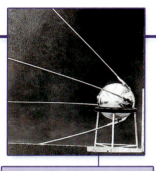

Writing in Science

Research and Write Use library or Internet resources to find out more about Guglielmo Marconi. Imagine that you were hired as his assistant. Write a short letter to a friend that describes your new job.

1957 *Sputnik I*
On October 4, the Soviet Union became the first country to successfully launch an artificial satellite into orbit. This development led to a new era in communications. Since then, more than 5,000 artificial satellites have been placed in orbit.

1963 Geosynchronous Orbit
Communications satellites are launched into orbits at altitudes of about 35,000 km. At this altitude, a satellite orbits Earth at the same rate as Earth rotates.

1979 Cellular Phone Network
In Japan, the world's first cellular phone network allowed people to make wireless phone calls. Today, cellular phone towers like the one above are common.

1960   1980   2000

Chapter 3 O ◆ 95

Monitor Progress _____ L2

Answers

 Reading Checkpoint   Global Positioning System

Assess

Reviewing Key Concepts

1. a. Radio waves **b.** A radio station converts sound into electronic signals that are then converted into a pattern of changes in the amplitude of a radio wave. A transmitting antenna broadcasts the radio wave. Your radio receives it and converts it back into sound. **c.** In AM waves, signals are coded as changes in wave amplitude; in FM, signals are coded as changes in wave frequency. AM waves have constant frequency; FM waves have constant amplitude. AM waves reflect off the ionosphere, so they can be received at a greater distance than FM waves, which penetrate the ionosphere. FM waves are received more clearly and produce better sound quality. Both AM and FM waves are radio waves that carry a coded signal from a broadcasting station to a receiver.
2. a. Microwave signals are transmitted by a cellular phone and received by a tower that relays the signals to a hub. **b.** The signal is passed via connecting wires to the hub. The hub sends the signal to another tower, which transmits it. The signal can then be received by another cellular phone user. **c.** The phones might interfere with each other.
3. a. Phone-system satellites, television satellites, and GPS satellites **b.** Communications satellites receive radio, television, and telephone signals and relay the signals back to receivers on Earth. **c.** Your altitude

Reteach   L1

Call on students to identify the different uses of radio waves in wireless communication.

Performance Assessment   L2

Drawing Have students draw a diagram to show how communications satellites receive and transmit radio waves.

All in One Teaching Resources

- Section Summary: *Wireless Communication*
- Review and Reinforcement: *Wireless Communication*
- Enrich: *Wireless Communication*

FIGURE 16
Global Positioning System
In the Global Positioning System (GPS), signals from four satellites are used to pinpoint a location on Earth.

Global Positioning System The Global Positioning System (GPS) is a system of navigation originally designed for the military. Now many other people use the system. GPS uses a network of satellites that broadcast radio signals to Earth. These signals carry information that tells you your exact location on Earth's surface, or even in the air. Anybody with a GPS receiver can pick up these signals.

Figure 16 shows how the signals from four GPS satellites are used to determine your position. The signals from three satellites tell you where you are on Earth's surface. The signal from the fourth satellite tells you how far above Earth's surface you are.

Today, GPS receivers are found in airplanes, boats, and cars. In a car, you can type your destination into a computer. The computer uses GPS data to map out your route. A computerized voice might even tell you when to turn right or left.

 Reading Checkpoint   **What does GPS stand for?**

Section 4 Assessment

⟳ **Target Reading Skill** **Using Prior Knowledge** Review your graphic organizer and revise it based on what you just learned in this section.

Reviewing Key Concepts

1. a. Identifying What type of wave carries signals for radio and television programs?
  b. Sequencing Describe the events that bring an AM broadcast into your home.
  c. Comparing and Contrasting How are AM waves different from FM waves? How are they the same?
2. a. Summarizing How does a cellular telephone work?
  b. Interpreting Diagrams A cellular phone transmits a signal to a receiving tower in Figure 15. How is the signal passed on to another cellular phone user?
  c. Relating Cause and Effect Your cellular phone transmits a signal at a specific frequency. What will happen if a cellular phone next to you also uses this frequency?

3. a. Listing What are three kinds of communications satellites?
  b. Reviewing How do communications satellites work?
  c. Predicting If your GPS device received signals from only three satellites, what information about your location would you be missing?

Writing in Science

Cause and Effect Paragraph Just before going to sleep one night, you search for an AM station on your radio. To your surprise, you pick up a station coming from a city 1,000 kilometers away. Your older brother tells you it is because of Earth's ionosphere. Write a paragraph explaining your brother's statement. Be sure to describe how the ionosphere affects AM radio transmissions.

96 ◆ O

Lab zone Chapter Project

Keep Students on Track At this point, students can collect their surveys and analyze the data. Allow them to use a computer spreadsheet program for this purpose, if one is available. Review graphing skills with the class, and suggest that students also write one or two paragraphs explaining their findings. This will help them organize their findings and conclusions before presenting them.

Writing in Science

Writing Mode Exposition: cause and effect
Scoring Rubric
4 Exceeds criteria; includes concise, accurate explanation with precise description
3 Meets criteria
2 Includes explanation and description but contains errors
1 Includes only general statements and errors

Build a Crystal Radio

Problem

Can you build a device that can collect and convert radio signals?

Skills Focus

observing, drawing conclusions, making models

Materials

- cardboard tube (paper towel roll)
- 3 pieces of enameled or insulated wire, 1 about 30 m long, and 2 about 30 cm long
- wirestrippers or sandpaper
- 2 alligator clips
- scissors
- aluminum foil
- 2 pieces of cardboard (sizes can range from 12.5 cm × 20 cm to 30 cm × 48 cm)
- masking tape
- crystal diode
- earphone
- 2 pieces of insulated copper antenna wire, 1 about 30 m long, and 1 about 0.5 m long

Procedure ✂

PART 1 **Wind the Radio Coil**

(*Hint*: All ends of the insulated wires need to be stripped to bare metal. If the wire is enameled, you need to sandpaper the ends.)

1. Carefully punch two holes approximately 2.5 cm apart in each end of a cardboard tube. The holes should be just large enough to thread the insulated wire through.

2. Feed one end of the 30-m piece of insulated wire through one set of holes. Leave a 50-cm lead at that end. Attach alligator clip #1 to this lead. See Figure 1.

▲ **Figure 1** Winding the Coil

3. Wind the wire tightly around the cardboard tube. Make sure the coils are close together but do not overlap one another.

4. Wrap the wire until you come to the end of the tube. Feed the end of the wire through the other set of holes, leaving a 50-cm lead as before. Attach alligator clip #2 to this lead. See Figure 2.

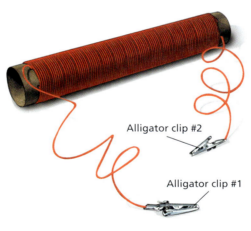

Alligator clip #2

Alligator clip #1

▲ **Figure 2** The Finished Coil

Guide Inquiry

Invitation

Ask: **How does a radio work?** (*Sample answer: A radio receives radio waves and converts the waves into sound.*) Explain that radio waves are received by the radio's antenna. Then, the waves are converted into electronic signals. Finally, the electronic signals are converted into sound by the speaker. Remind students how sound waves travel through the air, into the ear, and finally as signals to the brain. Then, ask: **How many different radio stations can you receive with a radio at home?** (*Sample answer: Dozens of radio stations*) **How many radio stations do you predict you will be able to receive with your crystal radio?** (*Sample answer: Few if any stations*)

Build a Crystal Radio

Prepare for Inquiry

Key Concept

Students will build crystal radios to receive radio signals and convert the signals into sound.

Skills Objective

After this lab, students will be able to

- observe how many stations their radios can receive and where the stations are located
- draw conclusions about how adjusting the tuning plates affects the reception of radio signals
- make models to determine how they can improve the antennas of their radios

🕐 **Prep Time** 30 minutes

Class Time 60 minutes

Advance Planning

Purchase earphones, crystal diodes, wires, and alligator clips from an electronics supply company. Collect enough cardboard and cardboard tubes for each group, or have students bring them from home. To save time and reduce risk of injury, you may want to strip the ends of the wires yourself. Test the diodes and earphones with an ammeter or multimeter to make sure they work. You may want to set up a demonstration radio ahead of time for students to use as a model as they construct their own radios.

Alternative Materials

You may mount the circuit on a board and use screws instead of clips to make connections.

Safety

✂ Caution students to handle the diodes carefully because they can break easily. Tell students not to connect their radios to electrical outlets or electrical appliances. Students should wear safety goggles when using the wire stripper. Advise them that wire strippers are sharp and to use care when stripping the wire. Review the safety guidelines in Appendix A.

All in One Teaching Resources

- Lab Worksheet: *Build a Crystal Radio*

Introduce the Procedure

Have students read through the procedure. Review the steps in the construction process to make sure students understand them. Refer to the apparatus diagrams and explain the purpose of each component. Ask students if they have any questions before they begin. Clear up any questions they may have.

Troubleshooting the Experiment

• Students should test the diode and earphone to make sure they work before connecting them.

• Tell students that the diode arrow must point toward the earphone for the radio to work.

• For Part 4, students can use themselves as the ground by holding the loose end of the shorter antenna wire instead of connecting it to the water pipe or faucet. The longer antenna wire should be extended and lie flat.

Expected Outcome

Students should be able to pick up the signals of some radio stations with the crystal radios they construct.

PART 2   Make the Tuning Plates

5. Without wrinkling the aluminum foil, cover one side of each piece of cardboard with the foil. Trim off any excess foil and tape the foil in place.

6. Hold the pieces of cardboard together with the foil facing inward. Tape along one edge to make a hinge. It is important for the foil pieces to be close together but not touching. See Figure 3.

▼ **Figure 3** Taping the Tuning Plates

7. Make a small hole through the cardboard and foil near a corner of one side. Feed one of the short pieces of insulated wire through the hole and tape it onto the foil as shown. Tape the other short piece of insulated wire to the corner of the other side. See Figure 4.

▼ **Figure 4** Connecting the Tuning Plates

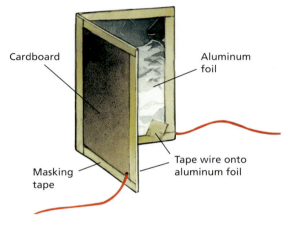

Cardboard

Aluminum foil

Masking tape

Tape wire onto aluminum foil

8. Connect one end of the wire from the foil to alligator clip #1. Connect the other wire from the foil to alligator clip #2.

PART 3   Prepare the Earphone

9. Handle the diode carefully. Connect one wire from the diode to alligator clip #1. The arrow on the diode should point to the earphone. Tape the other end of the diode wire to one of the earphone wires.

10. Connect the other wire from the earphone to alligator clip #2. See Figure 5.

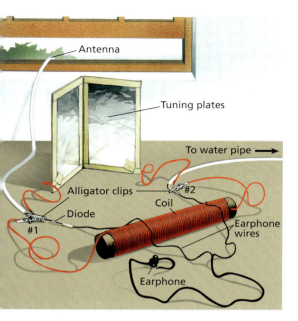

Antenna

Tuning plates

To water pipe →

Alligator clips

#2

Coil

Diode

#1

Earphone wires

Earphone

▲ **Figure 5** The Completed Radio

PART 4 Hook Up the Antenna

11. String the long piece of antenna wire along the floor to an outside window. Connect the other end of the wire to alligator clip #1.

12. Connect one end of the shorter piece of antenna wire to a cold-water pipe or faucet. Connect the other end to alligator clip #2. See Figure 5.

13. Put on the earphone and try to locate a station by squeezing the tuning plates slowly until you hear a signal. Some stations will come in when the plates are close together. Other stations will come in when the plates are opened far apart.

Analyze and Conclude

1. **Observing** How many stations can you pick up? Where are these stations located, and which station has the strongest signal? Keep a log of the stations your receive.

2. **Forming Operational Definitions** In your own words, give a definition of "signal strength." How did you compare the signal strengths of different radio stations?

3. **Drawing Conclusions** How does adjusting the tuning plates affect reception of the radio signals?

4. **Making Models** You can improve reception by having a good antenna. How can you improve your antenna?

5. **Communicating** Write a paragraph describing the various parts of the radio and how they are linked together.

Design an Experiment

Use a radio to test signal reception at various times of the day. Do you receive more stations at night or in the morning? Does weather affect reception? *Obtain your teacher's permission before carrying out your investigation.*

Analyze and Conclude

1. Answers will vary. Students' logs should describe the position of the tuning plates and the antenna for each station they receive. They should also record observations about the strength of the signal and the amount of static.

2. Students might define signal strength as the amount of energy with which a signal arrives at the radio, which affects how clearly and loudly the station is heard. Students might have compared signal strengths of different stations by rating the amount of static interference on a scale of 1 to 5 or by rating the loudness on a similar scale, with 1 corresponding to the softest station received and 5 to the loudest.

3. Adjusting the tuning plates allows the radio to receive signals of different frequencies from different stations because different stations transmit signals at different frequencies.

4. Students' responses should use examples from their observations to support their opinions. Students might suggest they could improve their antenna and improve reception by using a different type of wire or by changing the length or thickness of the wire.

5. Students' paragraphs should include the main parts of the radio: the radio coil, the tuning plates, the earphone, and the antenna. One end of the coil, one wire from the earphone, and one side of the tuning plates are connected to the antenna. The other wires from the coil, tuning plates, and earphone are connected to the grounding wire that goes to the water pipe.

Extend Inquiry

Design an Experiment Students are likely to receive more stations at night than in the morning. To test whether weather affects reception, students might propose comparing their radio's reception on sunny days with its reception on cloudy days. Give students a chance to test their predictions.

Interactive Textbook

- Complete student edition
- Section and chapter self-assessments
- Assessment reports for teachers

Help Students Read

Building Vocabulary

Word/Part Analysis It is important that students remember the order of electromagnetic waves by frequency because of the relationship between frequency and energy. Help students remember how infrared rays and ultraviolet rays are ordered relative to visible light. Write *infrared* and *ultraviolet* on the board, and divide each word into its two parts. Have students find the meanings of *infra-* ("below") and *ultra-* ("beyond"). Then, ask: **How would you define infrared?** *(Below red)* **Ultraviolet?** *(Beyond violet)* Remind students that red light has the lowest frequency of visible light and violet the highest. Ask: **Do ultraviolet rays have lower or higher frequencies than infrared rays?** *(Higher)*

Words in Context Explain that the acronyms AM and FM can be used in two contexts: they can refer to a method of modifying radio waves to send signals, or they can refer to two types of radio stations, each with a different range of assigned wave frequencies.

Connecting Concepts

Concept Maps Help students develop one way to show how the information in this chapter is related. Waves of the electromagnetic spectrum, which range from low-frequency radio waves to high-frequency gamma rays, transmit electric and magnetic energy. Visible light can be produced by many types of light bulbs. Radio waves are used in many types of wireless communications, including radio, television, cellular phone, and satellite communications. Have students brainstorm to identify the key concepts, key terms, details, and examples. Then, write each one on a self-stick note and attach it at random on chart paper or on the board.

1 The Nature of Electromagnetic Waves

Key Concepts

- An electromagnetic wave consists of vibrating electric and magnetic fields that move through space at the speed of light.
- Many properties of electromagnetic waves can be explained by a wave model. However, some properties are best explained by a particle model.

Key Terms

electromagnetic wave
electromagnetic radiation
polarized light
photoelectric effect
photon

2 Waves of the Electromagnetic Spectrum

Key Concepts

- All electromagnetic waves travel at the same speed in a vacuum, but they have different wavelengths and different frequencies.
- The electromagnetic spectrum is made up of radio waves, infrared rays, visible light, ultraviolet rays, X-rays, and gamma rays.

Key Terms

electromagnetic
 spectrum
radio waves
microwaves
radar
infrared rays

thermogram
visible light
ultraviolet rays
X-rays
gamma rays

100 ◆ O

3 Producing Visible Light

Key Concept

- Common types of light bulbs include incandescent, tungsten-halogen, fluorescent, vapor, and neon lights.

Key Terms

illuminated
luminous
spectroscope
incandescent light
tungsten-halogen bulb
fluorescent light
vapor light
neon light

4 Wireless Communication

Key Concepts

- Transmission antennas send out, or broadcast, radio waves in all directions. Radio waves carry information from the antenna of a broadcasting station to the receiving antenna of your radio or television.
- Cellular phones transmit and receive signals using high-frequency microwaves.
- Communications satellites receive radio, television, and telephone signals, and relay the signals back to receivers on Earth.

Key Terms

amplitude modulation
frequency modulation

Tell students that this concept map will be organized in hierarchical order and to begin at the top with the key concepts. Ask students these questions to guide them to categorize the information on the self-stick notes: **How do electromagnetic waves transmit energy? What waves make up the electromagnetic spectrum? How do light bulbs produce visible light? What types of communications use radio waves?** Prompt students by using connecting words, such

as "consists of," "are characterized by," and "are used for," to indicate the basis for the organization of the map. The phrases should form a sentence between or among a set of concepts.

Answer Accept logical presentations.

All in One Teaching Resources

- Key Terms Review: *The Electromagnetic Spectrum*
- Connecting Concepts: *The Electromagnetic Spectrum*

Review and Assessment

Go Online
PHSchool.com
For: Self-Assessment
Visit: PHSchool.com
Web Code: cga-5030

Organizing Information

Concept Mapping Copy the concept map about electromagnetic waves onto a separate sheet of paper. Then complete it and add a title. (For more on Concept Mapping, see the Skills Handbook.)

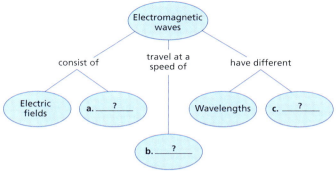

Reviewing Key Terms

Choose the letter of the best answer.

1. Electromagnetic waves are transverse waves that transfer
   a. sound energy.
   b. photons.
   c. electrical and magnetic energy.
   d. the particles of a medium.

2. Light that vibrates in only one direction is called
   a. luminous.
   b. illuminated.
   c. visible light.
   d. polarized light.

3. The electromagnetic waves with the longest wavelengths and lowest frequencies ares
   a. radio waves.
   b. infrared rays.
   c. X-rays.
   d. gamma rays.

4. Radar is a system that uses reflected radio waves to
   a. detect objects and measure their speed.
   b. kill bacteria.
   c. carry AM signals.
   d. cook food.

5. A light bulb that glows when a filament inside it gets hot is a(n)
   a. vapor light.
   b. fluorescent light.
   c. incandescent light.
   d. neon light.

If the statement is true, write *true*. If it is false, change the underlined word or words to make the statement true.

6. In the photoelectric effect, light strikes a material and causes electrons to be ejected.

7. Electromagnetic waves that you can see are called infrared rays.

8. An illuminated object gives off its own light.

9. A(n) incandescent light contains a gas and is coated on the inside with a powder.

10. In frequency modulation, the amplitude of a wave is changed.

Writing in Science

Letter Write a letter to a friend about the rescue of a ship's crew at sea. Include details about the ship's emergency radio and the role of satellites.

Discovery CHANNEL SCHOOL

The Electromagnetic Spectrum
Video Preview
Video Field Trip
► Video Assessment

Go Online
PHSchool.com
For: Self-Assessment
Visit: PHSchool.com
Web Code: cga-5030

Students can take a practice test online that is automatically scored.

All in One Teaching Resources
- Transparency O38
- Chapter Test
- Performance Assessment Teacher Notes
- Performance Assessment Student worksheet
- Performance Assessment Scoring Rubric

ExamView® Computer Test Bank CD-ROM

Review and Assessment

Organizing Information
a. Magnetic fields b. Light c. Frequencies

Reviewing Key Terms
1. c 2. d 3. a 4. a 5. c
6. true
7. visible light
8. luminous
9. fluorescent light
10. amplitude modulation

Writing in Science

Writing Mode Description

Scoring Rubric

4 Exceeds criteria; includes a vivid, journalistic description with many accurate details about the radio and the role of satellites

3 Meets criteria

2 Includes a description and some details but contains errors

1 Includes only a general description and/or contains serious errors

Discovery CHANNEL SCHOOL
Video Assessment

The Electromagnetic Spectrum

Show the Video Assessment to review chapter content and as a prompt for the writing assignment. Ask: **How are EPIRB radio signals able to reach satellites orbiting in the vacuum of space?** (*Radio waves have the longest wavelengths of electromagnetic waves, and they can pass through clouds to reach satellites high above any cloud cover. EPIRB radio signals can travel from Earth into space and back again.*) **What is the purpose of geostationary satellites for search-and-rescue missions?** (*They provide advance warning by detecting the geographical region of emergency beacons and sending out alerts.*) **What is the purpose of other orbiting satellites in these missions?** (*They use the Doppler effect to pinpoint the exact location of emergency beacons.*)

Checking Concepts

11. Sample answers: Because sunlight travels to Earth through the vacuum of space; because radio waves travel back and forth between Earth and satellites in space

12. The overlapping area looks dark because no light passes through the second filter. The first polarizing filter produces polarized light that vibrates in only one direction. The second filter does not allow this polarized light to pass through because it is placed at a 90° angle to the first filter.

13. Infrared rays have higher frequencies, and therefore more energy, than radio waves.

14. Red light has the longest wavelength, and violet light has the shortest wavelength.

15. Ultraviolet rays in sunlight can burn your skin, cause skin cancer, and damage your eyes. Damage can be limited by using sunscreen on your skin and wearing sunglasses that block ultraviolet rays.

16. Fluorescent light bulbs give off very little energy as infrared rays.

17. A fluorescent light is most efficient; an ordinary light bulb is least efficient.

18. Wave A is an AM wave (only its amplitude varies), and Wave B is an FM wave (only its frequency varies).

19. A network of GPS satellites broadcasts radio signals to Earth. A GPS receiver picks up signals from four GPS satellites. The information in the signals is used to determine position, including altitude above Earth's surface.

Math Practice

20. 1,900,000,000 Hz

Review and Assessment

Checking Concepts

11. How do you know that electromagnetic waves can travel through a vacuum?

12. Two polarizing filters overlap at right angles. Why does the area of overlap look dark?

13. Explain why the energy of infrared rays is greater than the energy of radio waves.

14. Which color of light has the longest wavelength? The shortest wavelength?

15. What damage is caused by ultraviolet rays in sunlight? How can this damage be limited?

16. Which light bulbs give off very little energy as infrared rays?

17. Which of these is most efficient: an ordinary light bulb, a tungsten-halogen bulb, or a fluorescent light? Which is least efficient?

18. Which wave shown below is an AM wave? Which is an FM wave? Explain your answers.

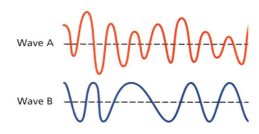

19. Explain how the Global Positioning System works.

Math Practice

20. **Scientific Notation** A cellular phone uses a frequency of 1.9×10^9 Hz. Write this frequency as a number without an exponent.

Thinking Critically

21. **Relating Cause and Effect** Gamma rays can cause more harm than X-rays. Explain why.

22. **Classifying** List examples of five luminous objects and five illuminated objects.

23. **Problem Solving** To build an incubator for young chicks, you need a source of heat. What type of light bulb could you use? Explain.

24. **Comparing and Contrasting** Make a table to compare the different types of wireless communication. Include headings such as type of information transmitted, frequencies, and one-way or two-way communication.

Applying Skills

Use the table below to answer Questions 25–27.

The table gives data about four radio stations.

Radio Station Frequencies

Station Name	Frequency
KLIZ	580 kHz
KMOM	103.7 MHz
WDAD	1030 kHz
WJFO	89.7 MHz

25. **Interpreting Data** Which radio station broadcasts at the longest wavelength? The shortest wavelength?

26. **Classifying** Which radio stations are AM? Which are FM?

27. **Predicting** You are going on a car trip across the United States. Which station would you expect to receive for the greater distance: KLIZ or KMOM?

Lab zone Chapter **Project**

Performance Assessment Decide how to present to your class the results of your survey about wireless communication. You might make a poster to display tables and graphs. Or you could make a computer presentation. Prepare summary statements for each table and graph. Then make your presentation to the class.

Lab zone Chapter **Project** L3

Performance Assessment Students may present their findings using posters, overhead transparencies, or a computer presentation program. In addition to presenting tables and graphs, students are expected to explain their findings and conclusions in writing. Presentations should address such questions as: **Which type of wireless communications device was used the most? Which type was used the least? What features made one type of device more popular than others? Were there any differences in types of devices used by different age groups?** Students' presentations should also include a description of how the data were collected and analyzed.

Standardized Test Prep

Choose the letter of the best answer.

1. The moon does not give off its own light. You can infer that the moon
   A is luminous.
   B has no atmosphere.
   C is illuminated.
   D is incandescent.

2. Ultraviolet rays from the sun are able to reach Earth's surface because
   F they require air to travel through.
   G they have more energy than infrared rays.
   H they can travel through empty space.
   J they can penetrate through clouds.

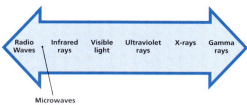

Microwaves

Use the diagram to answer Questions 3 and 4.

3. The amount of energy carried by an electromagnetic wave increases with frequency. Which of the following groups of waves is listed correctly in order of increasing energy?
   A X-rays, visible light, radio waves
   B radio waves, visible light, X-rays
   C infrared rays, visible light, radio waves
   D visible light, gamma rays, X-rays

4. Microwaves are a type of
   F radio wave.
   G X-ray.
   H visible light.
   J ultraviolet ray.

5. An experiment is set up to determine the efficiency of a 60-W light bulb. The light output is measured as 6 watts. The power used is assumed to be 60 watts. The experimenter calculates the efficiency using this equation:

$$\text{Efficiency} = \frac{\text{Measured light output (watts)}}{\text{Measured power used (watts)}}$$

Why is this experiment flawed?
   A The efficiency cannot be measured.
   B The efficiency of the light bulb can only be compared to a second light bulb.
   C The light output needs to be measured more precisely.
   D The actual power used was not measured.

Constructed Response

6. Explain how a spectrum is formed when white light passes through a prism. In your answer, explain what white light is composed of.

Thinking Critically

21. Gamma rays have higher frequencies, and therefore more energy, than X-rays. Gamma rays can cause more harm because they are the most penetrating of the electromagnetic waves. They give up more energy when they are absorbed.

22. Examples of luminous objects include a burning match, light bulb, computer screen, stars, and the sun. Examples of illuminated objects include a chair, person, computer keyboard, Earth, and the moon.

23. You could use an ordinary light bulb, because it is the only type of light bulb that produces mainly heat.

24. Tables should include the types of information transmitted, frequencies of the waves used, and whether the communication is one-way or two-way. For example, AM radio stations broadcast sound using low-frequency radio waves in one-way communication; communications satellites transmit sound, video, and data, using high-frequency radio waves in two-way communication.

Applying Skills

25. KLIZ broadcasts at the longest wavelength, and KMOM broadcasts at the shortest wavelength.

26. KLIZ and WDAD are AM radio stations. KMOM and WJFO are FM radio stations.

27. You would expect to receive KLIZ a greater distance, because it is an AM radio station and AM waves are reflected back to Earth by the ionosphere. This allows AM station to be received wherever the reflected waves reach.

Standardized Test Prep

1. C   **2.** H   **3.** B   **4.** F   **5.** D
6. White light contains all the colors of visible light. Each color of light has a different wavelength, which causes it to slow and bend by a different amount when it passes through a prism. These differences in bending cause the white light to be separated into a spectrum of colors of light.

Chapter at a Glance

 Chapter Project *Design and Build an Optical Instrument*

Technology

Local Standards

All in One Teaching Resources
- Chapter Project Teacher Notes, pp. 240–241
- Chapter Project Student Introduction, pp. 242–243
- Chapter Project Student Worksheets 1–2, pp. 244–245
- Chapter Project Scoring Rubric, p. 246

Video Preview

Section 1 Light and Color

3 periods
1 1/2 blocks

O.4.1.1 State what happens to the light that strikes an object.

O.4.1.2 Describe what determines the color of an opaque, transparent, or translucent object.

O.4.1.3 Explain how mixing pigments is different from mixing colors of light.

Section 2 Reflection and Mirrors

3 periods
1 1/2 blocks

O.4.2.1 Identify the kinds of reflection.

O.4.2.2 Describe the types of images produced by plane, concave, and convex mirrors.

Section 3 Refraction and Lenses

3 periods
1 1/2 blocks

O.4.3.1 Explain why light rays bend when they enter a medium at an angle.

O.4.3.2 Identify what determines the types of images formed by convex and concave lenses.

Section 4 Seeing Light

2 periods
1 block

O.4.4.1 Explain how one sees objects.

O.4.4.2 Identify the types of lenses that are used to correct vision problems.

Section 5 Using Light

4 periods
2 blocks

O.4.5.1 Describe how lenses are used in telescopes, microscopes, and cameras.

O.4.5.2 Identify what makes up laser light, and state how laser light is used.

O.4.5.3 Explain why optical fibers can carry laser beams a long distance.

Video Field Trip

Review and Assessment

Test Preparation

All in One Teaching Resources
- Key Terms Review, p. 288
- Transparency O55
- Performance Assessment Teacher Notes, p. 295
- Performance Assessment Scoring Rubric, p. 296
- Performance Assessment Student Worksheet, p. 297
- Chapter Test, pp. 298–301

Video Assessment

Test Preparation Blackline Masters

Chapter Activities Planner

For more activities

LAB ZONE Easy Planner CD-ROM

Student Edition	Inquiry	Time	Materials	Skills	Resources
Chapter Project, p. 105	Open-Ended	Ongoing (3 weeks)	**All in One** Teaching Resources See p. 240	Posing questions, designing experiments, controlling variables, communicating	**Lab zone Easy Planner** **All in One** Teaching Resources Support pp. 240–241
Section 1					
Discover Activity, p. 106	Directed	15 minutes	White cardboard, metric ruler, scissors, markers (red, green, and blue), 1 m of string	Observing	**Lab zone Easy Planner**
Skills Activity, p. 109	Directed	10 minutes	American flag, light source, red and yellow filters	Developing hypotheses	**Lab zone Easy Planner**
At-Home Activity, p. 111	Guided	Home		Observing, communicating	**Lab zone Easy Planner**
Skills Lab, p. 112	Guided	40 minutes	Shoe box, scissors, flashlight, removable tape, red object (such as a ripe tomato), yellow object (such as a ripe lemon), blue object (such as blue construction paper), enough red, green, and blue cellophane to cover the top of the shoe box	Observing, inferring, predicting	**Lab zone Easy Planner Lab Activity Video** **All in One** Teaching Resources Skills Lab: *Changing Colors,* pp. 254–255
Section 2					
Discover Activity, p. 113	Directed	10 minutes	2 plane mirrors, tape	Observing	**Lab zone Easy Planner**
Skills Activity, p. 114	Directed	10 minutes	Flashlight, metal can, white paper cup	Observing	**Lab zone Easy Planner**
Section 3					
Discover Activity, p. 119	Guided	10 minutes	Hand lens, white paper	Observing	**Lab zone Easy Planner**
At-Home Activity, p. 123	Guided	Home		Communicating	**Lab zone Easy Planner**
Skills Lab, p. 124	Guided	40 minutes	Tape, convex lens, cardboard stand, blank sheet of paper, light bulb and socket, clay (for holding the lens), battery and wires, meter stick, centimeter ruler	Controlling variables, interpreting data	**Lab zone Easy Planner Lab Activity Video** **All in One** Teaching Resources Skills Lab: *Looking at Images,* pp. 270–272
Section 4					
Discover Activity, p. 125	Guided	10 minutes	White paper, pencil	Posing questions	**Lab zone Easy Planner**
Try This Activity, p. 126	Directed	5 minutes	White paper	Observing	**Lab zone Easy Planner**
At-Home Activity, p. 128	Guided	Home		Observing, inferring	**Lab zone Easy Planner**
Section 5					
Discover Activity, p. 129	Guided	15 minutes	Paper cup, pin, wax paper, rubber band	Classifying	**Lab zone Easy Planner**
Try This Activity, p. 130	Guided	10 minutes	2 hand lenses of different strengths	Classifying	**Lab zone Easy Planner**

Section 1 Light and Color

 *3 periods, 1 1/2 blocks*

Objectives

O.4.1.1 State what happens to the light that strikes an object.

O.4.1.2 Describe what determines the color of an opaque, transparent, or translucent object.

O.4.1.3 Explain how mixing pigments is different from mixing colors of light.

Local Standards

Key Terms

• transparent material • translucent material • opaque material • primary colors
• secondary color • complementary colors • pigment

Preteach

Build Background Knowledge

Students predict how colors of light combine, based on their prior knowledge of colors.

 **Discover Activity** *How Do Colors Mix?* **L2**

Targeted Print and Technology Resources

All in One Teaching Resources

L2 Reading Strategy: *Using Prior Knowledge*

Presentation-Pro CD-ROM

Instruct

When Light Strikes an Object Compare and contrast transparent, translucent, and opaque materials, and ask students to identify materials of each type.

The Color of Objects Explain how the color of an object depends on its material, and have students explain the colors of specific objects made of different materials.

Combining Colors List the primary and secondary colors of light and of pigments, and explain how they are related.

 **Skills Lab** Changing Colors **L2**

Targeted Print and Technology Resources

All in One Teaching Resources

L2 Guided Reading, pp. 249–251
L2 Transparencies O39, O40, O41
L2 Skills Lab: *Changing Colors*, pp. 254–255

Lab Activity Video/DVD
Skills Lab: *Changing Colors*

www.SciLinks.org Web Code: scn-1543

Student Edition on Audio CD

Assess

Section Assessment Questions

Have students use their completed statements about what they learned to answer the questions.

Reteach

Students identify the key terms from their definitions.

Targeted Print and Technology Resources

All in One Teaching Resources

• Section Summary, p. 248
L1 Review and Reinforce, p. 252
L3 Enrich, p. 253

Section 2 Reflection and Mirrors

 3 periods, 1 1/2 blocks

ABILITY LEVELS
L1 Basic to Average
L2 For All Students
L3 Average to Advanced

Objectives

O.4.2.1 Identify the kinds of reflection.

O.4.2.2 Describe the types of images produced by plane, concave, and convex mirrors.

Local Standards

Key Terms

• ray • regular reflection • diffuse reflection • plane mirror • image • virtual image • concave mirror • optical axis • focal point • real image • convex mirror

Preteach

Build Background Knowledge

Students focus on mirrors and reflection by explaining how mirrors are used in a vehicle.

 **Discover Activity** *How Does Your Reflection Wink?* **L1**

Targeted Print and Technology Resources

 Teaching Resources

L2 Reading Strategy Transparency O42: *Comparing and Contrasting*

 Presentation-Pro CD-ROM

Instruct

Reflection of Light Rays Make a Venn diagram comparing and contrasting regular and diffuse reflection.

Plane Mirrors Familiarize students with plane mirrors and virtual images by helping them recall how images appear in plane mirrors.

Concave Mirrors Use Figure 9 or a similar sketch to show students how light is reflected from a concave surface.

Convex Mirrors Use Figure 12 to explain how a convex mirror produces a virtual image.

Targeted Print and Technology Resources

Teaching Resources

L2 Guided Reading, pp. 258–260
L2 Transparencies O43, O44, O45, O46

PHSchool.com Web Code: cgp-5042

Student Edition on Audio CD

Assess

Section Assesment Questions

Have students use their completed Venn diagrams to answer Question 2.

Reteach

Students identify which type of mirror produced a real image and which types produced a virtual image.

Targeted Print and Technology Resources

Teaching Resources

• Section Summary, p. 257
L1 Review and Reinforce, p. 261
L3 Enrich, p. 262

Section 3 Refraction and Lenses

 3 periods, 1 1/2 blocks

ABILITY LEVELS
L1 Basic to Average
L2 For All Students
L3 Average to Advanced

Objectives

O.4.3.1 Explain why light rays bend when they enter a medium at an angle.

O.4.3.2 Identify what determines the types of images formed by convex and concave lenses.

Local Standards

Key Terms

• index of refraction • mirage • lens • convex lens • concave lens

Preteach

Build Background Knowledge

Help students recall how a hand lens makes objects appear.

 **Discover Activity** *How Can You Make an Image Appear?* **L1**

Targeted Print and Technology Resources

All in One Teaching Resources

L2 Reading Strategy Transparency O47: *Asking Questions*

⊙ **Presentation-Pro CD-ROM**

Instruct

Refraction of Light Review refraction of waves to help students understand how light is refracted when it enters a new medium.

Lenses Guide students in using what they learned about mirrors to predict how lenses might form images.

 Skills Lab *Looking at Images* **L2**

Targeted Print and Technology Resources

All in One Teaching Resources

L2 Guided Reading, pp. 265–267
L2 Transparencies O48, O49
L2 Skills Lab: *Looking at Images*, pp. 270–272

📼 **Lab Activity Video/DVD**
Consumer Lab: *Looking at Images*

www.SciLinks.com Web Code: scn-1133

⊙ **Student Edition on Audio CD**

Assess

Section Assesment Questions

 Have students use their completed questions and answers to answer the questions.

Reteach

Targeted Print and Technology Resources

Students identify missing terms in key concept sentences.

All in One Teaching Resources

• Section Summary, p. 264
L1 Review and Reinforce, p. 268
L3 Enrich, p. 269

Section 4  Seeing Light

🕐 *2 periods, 1 block*

Objectives

O.4.4.1 Explain how one sees objects.
O.4.4.2 Identify the types of lenses that are used to correct vision problems.

Local Standards

Key Terms

• cornea • pupil • iris • retina • rods • cones • optic nerve • nearsighted • farsighted

---

Preteach

Build Background Knowledge

Students observe how their eyes automatically focus on a moving object.

 **Discover Activity** *Can You See Everything With One Eye?* **L1**

Targeted Print and Technology Resources

 **Teaching Resources**

L2 Reading Strategy Transparency O50: *Sequencing*

💿 **Presentation-Pro CD-ROM**

Instruct

The Human Eye Describe the role of the eye in vision, and have students predict the role of the brain in vision.

Correcting Vision Use Figure 21 to help students identify similarities and differences between nearsightedness and farsightedness.

Targeted Print and Technology Resources

 Teaching Resources

L2 Guided Reading, pp. 275–277
L2 Transparencies O51, O52

PHSchool.com Web Code: cgd-5044

💿 **Student Edition on Audio CD**

Assess

Section Assessment Questions

🔁 Have students use their completed flowcharts to answer Question 1.

Reteach

Students name structures of the eye and identify their functions.

Targeted Print and Technology Resources

 Teaching Resources

• Section Summary, p. 274
L1 Review and Reinforce, p. 278
L3 Enrich, p. 279

Section 5 **Using Light**

 4 periods, 2 blocks

Objectives

O.4.5.1 Describe how lenses are used in telescopes, microscopes, and cameras.

O.4.5.2 Identify what makes up laser light, and state how laser light is used.

O.4.5.3 Explain why optical fibers can carry laser beams a long distance.

Local Standards

Key Terms

• telescope • refracting telescope • objective • eyepiece • reflecting telescope
• microscope • camera • laser • hologram • optical fiber • total internal reflection

Preteach

Build Background Knowledge

Students recall how binoculars produce enlarged images of objects.

 **Discover Activity** *How Does a Pinhole Viewer Work?* **L2**

Targeted Print and Technology Resources

All in One Teaching Resources

L2   Reading Strategy: *Building Vocabulary*

 Presentation-Pro CD-ROM

Instruct

Optical Instruments Introduce the three common types of optical instruments, and have students identify their uses.

Lasers Define laser light, and explain how the term *laser* was coined to help students understand why laser light is so intense.

Uses of Lasers Review uses of lasers, and have students identify ways in which they regularly use lasers.

Optical Fibers Compare and contrast optical fibers with electrical wires, with which students are already familiar.

Targeted Print and Technology Resources

All in One Teaching Resources

L2   Guided Reading, pp. 282–285
L2   Transparency O53, O54

www.SciLinks.org Web Code: scn-1545

Video Field Trip

 Student Edition on Audio CD

Assess

Section Assessment Questions

 Have students use their completed definitions to answer the questions.

Reteach

Students explain how each key term in the section is related to light.

Targeted Print and Technology Resources

All in One Teaching Resources

• Section Summary, p. 281
L1   Review and Reinforce, p. 286
L3   Enrich, p. 287

Chapter 4 Content Refresher

Section 1 Light and Color

Models of Color The colors of light are represented by the Additive Color (RGB) Model. The model is called additive because the primary colors of red, green, and blue are "added" to get white. This model applies to the colors seen in televisions and computer monitors. Even our eyes respond to color according to the RGB model. The cones in our retinas perceive all the colors of the spectrum by sensing light of only these three primary colors.

The Subtractive Color (CMY) Model is used for pigments, especially the inks used in printing. The model is called subtractive because the primary colors of cyan, magenta, and yellow must be "subtracted" from white to produce other colors. Adding the three primary pigments produces more of a dark gray than pure black, so black ink is used as well in printing. This is why color printing is often referred to as four-color printing. This model is also the basis of color wheels, with which you or your students may be familiar. A color wheel is a circle that is divided into wedges of different colors. It describes relationships among pigment colors and is commonly used by artists and designers to help them mix pigments and choose color combinations. Color wheels are typically based on red, yellow, and blue as the primary colors, with orange, violet, and green as the secondary colors.

Address Misconceptions

Students may confuse the primary and secondary colors of pigments with the primary and secondary colors of light. For a strategy for overcoming this misconception, see **Address Misconceptions** in Section 1, *Light and Color.*

Help Students Read

DRTA

Finding the Answer to a Key Question

Strategy Guide students in looking for the most important information when they read about a topic, such as the color of transparent and translucent objects in Section 1, *Light and Color.*

Example
1. Before students read about the topic, challenge them to answer a significant question about it. Turning a heading, subheading, key term definition, or boldface sentence into a question usually produces an important question about the topic.
2. Ask students to read the section in the text pertaining to the topic and look for the answer to the question. If the answer is a boldface sentence or sentence with a boldface term, it will be easy to find.
3. After students have found the answer, give them a chance to demonstrate their comprehension of the topic. Ask them a question that requires them to use the information they found.

See Section 1, *Light and Color,* for a script using the DRTA strategy with students.

Section 2 **Reflection and Mirrors**

Types of Mirrors The concave and convex mirrors students will read about in Section 2, *Reflection and Mirrors*, can be any conic section, including spherical or paraboloidal sections. The diagram shows how a concave spherical mirror is part of the inside surface of sphere. The center of the imaginary sphere, of which the mirror is a part, is called the center of curvature. The midpoint of the curved surface of the mirror is called the vertex. Drawing a straight line between the center of curvature and the vertex produces the optical axis. All rays of light parallel to the optical axis that strike the mirror are reflected to the focal point, which is halfway between the vertex and the center of curvature. The focal length is the distance from the focal point to the surface of the mirror.

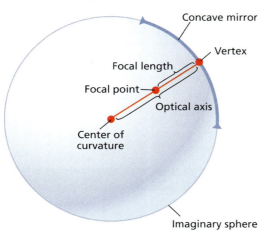

Spherical Mirror

The only difference between the concave spherical mirror shown in the diagram and a convex spherical mirror is the side of the spherical surface that reflects light. For a convex mirror, it is the convex outer surface of the sphere that reflects light. Spherical mirrors work well only when the object is near the optical axis. Otherwise, the image is not well focused. Parabolic mirrors, in contrast, work well no matter where the object is located and always produce a clear image.

A two-way mirror is a special type of plane, or flat, mirror. From one side, a two-way mirror appears to be a window. From the other side, it appears to be a mirror. Two-way mirrors are typically used in police work and psychological testing, so people in one room can be observed by people in an adjacent room without knowing they are being watched. To understand how two-way mirrors work, think about how a brightly lit room looks from outside on a dark night. You can see clearly through the windows and observe what is going on inside the room. Now, consider how a dark room looks from outside on a bright day. The windows act like mirrors, and you can see very little inside the room. A two-way mirror works the same way, but instead of transparent glass, it is made of glass with about half as much reflective coating as a regular mirror. The coating helps the mirror work like a mirror from one side and still transmit enough light to work like a window from the other side.

Section 3 **Refraction and Lenses**

Snell's Law A Dutch mathematician named Willebrord Snell determined how a light ray bends when it passes into a new medium at an angle other than 90°. The amount and direction that the light ray bends depend on the angle of incidence and the index of refraction for both mediums. The relationship is given by the equation:

$$n_1 \sin\theta_1 = n_2 \sin\theta_2$$

where n_1 is the index of refraction of medium 1, n_2 the index of refraction of medium 2, θ_1 the angle of incidence of medium 1, and θ_2 the angle of refraction of medium 2. Both θ_1 and θ_2 are measured relative to the normal, which is a line perpendicular to the surface at the point of incidence, as shown in the diagram.

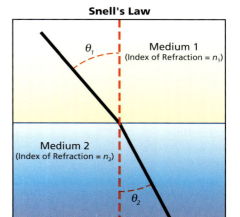

Snell's Law

From Snell's law we know that, if a ray strikes a new medium at an angle and the new medium has a higher index of refraction, the ray will bend toward the normal. If the new medium has a lower index of refraction, the ray will bend away from the normal. In the diagram, n_2 must be greater than n_1, because the ray bends toward the normal as it moves from medium 1 to medium 2.

Address Misconceptions

Students may think that mirages are imaginary and not realize that they are images of real objects. For a strategy for overcoming this misconception, see **Address Misconceptions** in Section 3, *Refraction and Lenses*.

Section 4 Seeing Light

Layers of the Eye and Errors of Refraction The human eye rests in a protective bony socket at the front of the skull. The thick wall of the eyeball consists of three layers: the sclera, the choroid, and the retina. The sclera is the outermost layer of eye tissue. The visible part of the sclera is seen as the white of the eye. In the center of the visible sclera is the cornea. This is a slightly raised transparent membrane that acts as the window of the eye. A delicate membrane called the conjunctiva covers the visible part of the sclera.

The choroid layer of the eye lies underneath the sclera. It is composed of dense pigment and blood vessels. Near the center of the visible eye, the choroid layer forms the ciliary body, which contains the ciliary muscles that control the shape of the lens. The pigmentation of the choroid layer is only visible in the iris, because the iris is the only part of the choroid layer that is not covered by the sclera.

The retina is the third and innermost layer of tissue in the eye. It consists of a network of nerve cells and fibers that spread out from the optic nerve at the rear of the eyeball. Unlike the outer two layers of the eye, the retina does not extend to the front of the eyeball. The space between the retina and the front of the eye is filled with the jellylike vitreous humor.

Many people have eye disorders generally termed errors of refraction. In addition to nearsightedness and farsightedness, which are described in the text, another common error of refraction is astigmatism. This disorder is caused by nonuniform curvature in either the cornea or the lens. As a result, light rays do not produce a single focal point on the retina. Instead, some rays focus on the retina and other rays focus in front of it or behind it. People with astigmatism may also be nearsighted or farsighted. Lenses can correct astigmatism, as they can the other two errors of refraction.

Address Misconceptions

Students may think that people who are colorblind cannot see any colors at all. For a strategy for overcoming this misconception, see **Address Misconceptions** in Section 4, *Seeing Light*.

Section 5 Using Light

Lasers and Optic Fibers Lasers have many applications in scientific research, military technology, medicine, and communication. They can produce an extremely narrow beam of intense energy that can be controlled to perform delicate tasks. For example, laser light can be used to drill holes in diamonds, make microelectronic components, and help doctors perform surgery without damaging surrounding tissues. Lasers are also used in space for communications between satellites, because laser light can carry a great deal of information and travel long distances without the signal weakening.

Laser beams are usually sent through optical fibers. As shown in the figure, optical fibers are made up of three layers. The inner layer, or core, is a cylinder made of glass and/or polymer with a high index of refraction. The core is surrounded by a layer called the *cladding*, which is also made of glass and/or polymer but with a lower index of refraction. The cladding protects the core from scratches. It also reflects all the light traveling through the core, as long as the light strikes the core/cladding boundary at an angle greater than the critical angle. To ensure that the core has a higher refractive index than the cladding, a small amount of an impurity, called a *dopant*, is added to the glass or polymer of the core. The dopant slows the speed at which light travels through the core without absorbing any of the light. The outer layer of an optical fiber is called the *jacket*. It is usually made of polyurethane or PVC. Its function is to protect the fiber from damage.

Optical Fiber

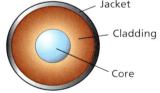

Cross-sectional View

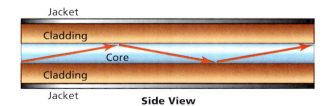

Side View

interactive Textbook
- Complete student edition
- Video and audio
- Simulations and activities
- Section and chapter activities

Chapter 4

Light

Chapter Preview

1 Light and Color
Discover *How Do Colors Mix?*
Skills Activity *Developing Hypotheses*
At-Home Activity *Color Mix*
Skills Lab *Changing Colors*

2 Reflection and Mirrors
Discover *How Does Your Reflection Wink?*
Skills Activity *Observing*
Active Art *Images in Mirrors*

3 Refraction and Lenses
Discover *How Can You Make an Image Appear?*
Analyzing Data *Bending Light*
Active Art *Images in Lenses*
At-Home Activity *Bent Pencil*
Skills Lab *Looking at Images*

4 Seeing Light
Discover *Can You See Everything With One Eye?*
Try This *True Colors*
At-Home Activity *Optical Illusion*

5 Using Light
Discover *How Does a Pinhole Viewer Work?*
Try This *What a View!*
Tech & Design in History *Instruments That Use Light*

interactive Textbook

These windows reflect light, but they also let light pass straight through. ▶

Lab zone · Chapter Project L3

Objectives
This Chapter Project will give students a chance to apply what they learn about light to design and build an optical instrument. After completing this Chapter Project, students will be able to

- pose questions about how reflection and refraction of light affect images
- design experiments with reflection and refraction to find answers to their questions
- control variables, such as distance between lenses, that they can apply to the design and construction of an optical instrument
- communicate about the design and use of their optical instrument

Skills Focus
Posing questions, designing experiments, controlling variables, communicating

Project Time Line 3 weeks

 **Teaching Resources**
- Chapter Project Teacher Notes
- Chapter Project Worksheet 1
- Chapter Project Worksheet 2
- Chapter Project Scoring Rubric

Developing a Plan
During the first week, have students experiment with reflection and refraction. During the second week, have them apply what they learn from their experiments to design an optical instrument with a specific use, such as seeing around opaque materials or magnifying very small or distant objects. Give students time and materials to construct their instruments. Also allow time for students to test their instruments and modify them if necessary. In the third week, students can demonstrate the design and use of their optical instruments.

Possible Materials
Provide a wide variety of materials from which students can choose. Miscellaneous items they will need include tape, clay, light filters (such as colored cellophane), cardboard tubes and boxes, flashlights, protractors, rulers, and meter sticks. Some optical components will be required and can be purchased from a scientific supply house. These include: concave and convex lenses, and plane, concave, and convex mirrors. An optical bench kit is useful but optional.

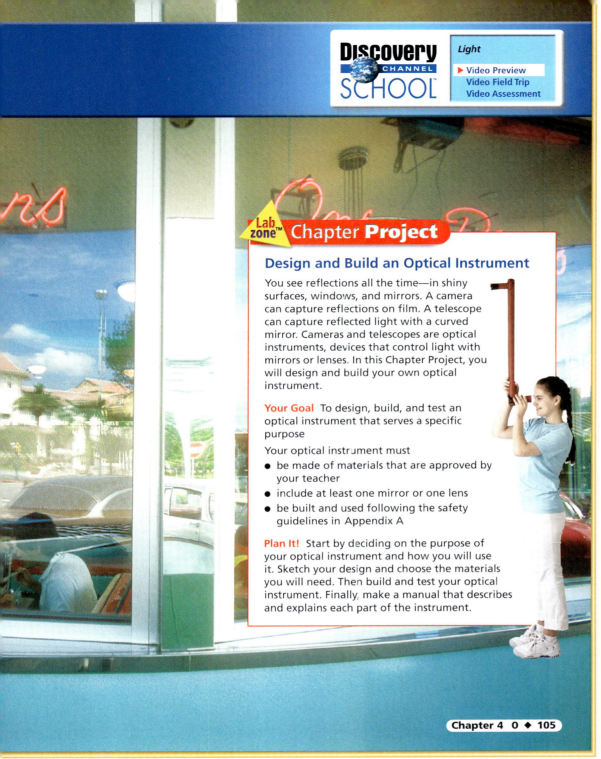

Lab zone™ Chapter **Project**

Design and Build an Optical Instrument

You see reflections all the time—in shiny surfaces, windows, and mirrors. A camera can capture reflections on film. A telescope can capture reflected light with a curved mirror. Cameras and telescopes are optical instruments, devices that control light with mirrors or lenses. In this Chapter Project, you will design and build your own optical instrument.

Your Goal To design, build, and test an optical instrument that serves a specific purpose

Your optical instrument must

- be made of materials that are approved by your teacher
- include at least one mirror or one lens
- be built and used following the safety guidelines in Appendix A

Plan It! Start by deciding on the purpose of your optical instrument and how you will use it. Sketch your design and choose the materials you will need. Then build and test your optical instrument. Finally, make a manual that describes and explains each part of the instrument.

Chapter 4 O ◆ 105

DISCOVERY CHANNEL SCHOOL
Video Preview

Light

Show the Video Preview to introduce the chapter and provide an overview of chapter content. Discussion question: **What discoveries about the moon and Jupiter did Galileo make with the help of the telescope?** *(Sample answer: Galileo discovered that the moon is not smooth, but has mountains and craters. He also was the first to see the four largest moons that orbit Jupiter.)*

Performance Assessment

The Chapter Project Scoring Rubric will help you evaluate how well students complete the Chapter Project. You may want to share the scoring rubric with your students so they will know what is expected. Students will be assessed on

- How much they learn about reflection and refraction from their experiments
- How well they control variables and apply what they learn to the design of their optical instruments
- How well their optical instruments perform the function for which they were designed
- The thoroughness and organization of their presentations

  Students can keep the designs and descriptions of their optical instruments in their portfolios.

Portfolio

Launching the Project

Construct and set up a telescope, microscope, and/or periscope. To construct a telescope or microscope, tape a convex lens to each end of a cardboard tube. For a telescope, the distance between the lenses must be equal to the sum of the focal lengths of the lenses. For a microscope, the distance between the lenses must be greater than the sum of the focal lengths of the lenses. To construct a periscope, tape two plane mirrors inside a cardboard tube with two windows cut in the side at either end. (The angle of the mirrors must allow light entering the tube through one window to exit through the other.) Alternatively, you can show students actual examples of optical instruments such as these. Invite students to examine and look through the instruments. Then, have students read the description of the project in their text. Stress that the optical instruments they design should have a particular function, such as magnifying distant objects like a telescope or seeing around corners like a periscope.

Objectives

After this lesson, students will be able to

O.4.1.1 State what happens to the light that strikes an object.

O.4.1.2 Describe what determines the color of an opaque, transparent, or translucent object.

O.4.1.3 Explain how mixing pigments is different from mixing colors of light.

Target Reading Skill

Building Vocabulary Explain that knowing the definition of key-concept words helps students understand what they read.

Answers

As students read each passage that contains a Key Term, remind them to write a sentence in their own words about the term. Encourage students to write one or two descriptive phrases to help them remember the Key Term. Invite students to share their sentences and phrases.

Preteach

Build Background Knowledge `L2`

Introducing Color

Ask: **What color would you get if you combined blue and yellow paint?** *(Most students will say green.)* Then ask: **What color would you get if you combined blue and yellow light?** *(Students may say green.)* Reply that the correct answer is white. Tell students that, in this section, they will learn why blue and yellow light combine to make white light.

Section 1
Light and Color

Reading Preview

Key Concepts
• What happens to the light that strikes an object?
• What determines the color of an opaque, transparent, or translucent object?
• How is mixing pigments different from mixing colors of light?

Key Terms
• transparent material
• translucent material
• opaque material
• primary colors
• secondary color
• complementary colors
• pigment

Target Reading Skill

Building Vocabulary Using a word in a sentence helps you think about how to best explain the word. As you read, carefully note the definition of each Key Term. Also note other details in the paragraph that contains the definition. Use all this information to write a sentence using the Key Term.

Flowers in sunlight ▼

106 ♦ O

Lab zone Discover Activity

How Do Colors Mix?

1. Cut a disk with a diameter of 10 cm out of white cardboard. Divide the disk into three equal-sized segments. Color one segment red, the next green, and the third blue.
2. Carefully punch two holes, 2 cm apart, on opposite sides of the center of the disk.
3. Thread a 1-m long string through the holes. Tie the ends of the string together to make a loop that passes through both holes.
4. With equal lengths of string on each side of the disk, tape the string in place. Turn the disk to wind up the string. Predict what color(s) you will see if the disk spins fast.
5. Spin the disk by pulling the loops to unwind the string.

Think It Over

Observing What color do you see as the wheel spins fast? Was your prediction correct?

It was hard work, but you are finally finished. You stand back to admire your work. Color is everywhere! The bright green grass rolls right up to the flower garden you just weeded. In the bright sunlight, you see patches of yellow daffodils, purple hyacinths, and red tulips. The sun's light allows you to see each color. But sunlight is white light. What makes each flower appear to be a different color?

Lab zone Discover Activity

Skills Focus Observing   `L2`

Materials white cardboard, metric ruler, scissors, markers (red, green, and blue), 1 m of string

Time 15 minutes

Tips Students can punch holes in the disk with the tip of a ballpoint pen. Taping the disk to the strings helps the disk to stay perpendicular to the strings. Demonstrate how to make the disk spin if students are having difficulty.

Expected Outcome When the disk spins rapidly, it appears almost white.

Think It Over The disk looks grayish white when it spins fast. Some students may have predicted this outcome.

When Light Strikes an Object

To understand why objects have different colors, you need to know how light can interact with an object. **When light strikes an object, the light can be reflected, transmitted, or absorbed.** Think about a pair of sunglasses. If you hold the sunglasses in your hand, you can see light that reflects off the lenses. If you put the sunglasses on, you see light that is transmitted by the lenses. The lenses also absorb some light. That is why objects appear darker when seen through the lenses.

Lenses, like all objects, are made of one or more materials. Most materials can be classified as transparent, translucent, or opaque based on what happens to light that strikes the material.

Transparent Materials A **transparent material** transmits most of the light that strikes it. The light passes right through without being scattered. This allows you to see clearly what is on the other side. Clear glass, water, and air all are transparent materials. In Figure 1, you can clearly see the straw through the glass on the left.

Translucent Materials A **translucent material** (trans LOO sunt) scatters light as it passes through. You can usually see something behind a translucent object, but the details are blurred. Wax paper and a frosted glass like the middle glass in Figure 1 are translucent materials.

Opaque Materials An **opaque material** (oh PAYK) reflects or absorbs all of the light that strikes it. You cannot see through opaque materials because light cannot pass through them. Wood, metal, and tightly woven fabric all are opaque materials. You cannot see the straw through the white glass in Figure 1 because the glass is opaque.

 Reading Checkpoint What happens when light strikes an opaque material?

FIGURE 1
Types of Materials
Different types of materials reflect, transmit, and absorb different amounts of light.
Comparing and Contrasting
How does a straw seen through transparent glass compare with a straw seen through translucent glass?

Transparent   Translucent   Opaque

O ◆ 107

When Light Strikes an Object

Teach Key Concepts   L2
Transparent, Translucent, and Opaque Materials

Focus Tell students that most materials are transparent, translucent, or opaque.

Teach Write the three terms on the board. Explain that materials of the three types differ in how much light they reflect, scatter, and transmit. State that transparent materials transmit most of the light without scattering it; translucent materials transmit most of the light but scatter it; opaque materials either reflect or absorb all the light, so no light is transmitted. Ask: **What are some materials of each type in the classroom?** (*Sample answer: Wood for opaque material, glass for transparent material, thin paper for translucent material*)

Apply Ask: **Which type of material is water?** (*Transparent*) **learning modality: verbal**

Independent Practice   L2

All in One Teaching Resources
- Guided Reading and Study Worksheet: *Light and Color*

⊙ Student Edition on Audio CD

Monitor Progress   L2

Skills Check Have students make a table comparing and contrasting materials that are transparent, translucent, and opaque.

Answers
Figure 1 A straw can be seen clearly through transparent glass. Through translucent glass, it can be seen only as a shape without details.

 Reading Checkpoint It is reflected or absorbed.

Differentiated Instruction

English Learners/Beginning   L1
Comprehension: Key Concepts Work with students to make a Venn diagram comparing and contrasting materials that are transparent and translucent. (*Sample answer: Both types of materials let light pass through, but only transparent materials let you clearly see objects through them.*)
learning modality: visual

English Learners/Intermediate   L2
Vocabulary: Word Analysis Help students remember the difference between the similar-looking words, *transparent* and *translucent*. Write both words on the board and divide each word into its prefix and root. Explain that *trans-* means "through," *-parent* means "to show," and *-lucent* means "to shine." Challenge students to define each word by combining the meanings of the prefix and root. **learning modality: verbal**

The Color of Objects

Teach Key Concepts

Explaining an Object's Color

Focus Ask students to find objects of different colors in the classroom.

Teach Tell students that the color of an object depends on the material it is made of. State that objects made of opaque materials are the same color as the light they reflect, whereas objects made of transparent or translucent materials are the same color as the light they transmit. Ask: **If a red object transmits red light, what type of material is it made of?** *(Transparent or translucent)*

Apply Ask: **Why is a blueberry blue?** *(It reflects blue light.)* **Why is blue glass blue?** *(The blue glass transmits only blue light.)*
learning modality: logical/mathematical

 **Teaching Resources**

Transparency O39

Go Online
SciLINKS

For: Links on colors
Visit: www.SciLinks.org
Web Code: scn-1543

Download a worksheet that will guide students' review of internet resources on colors.

Lab zone **Teacher Demo**
L1

Light Reflected by Opaque Materials

Materials white light source, blue filter, green filter, red paper triangle, sheet of white paper

Time 10 minutes

Focus Say that the color of light shining on an opaque object affects the object's color.

Teach Place the red triangle on the sheet of white paper. Without letting students see the triangle in white light, have them view it in blue light and then in green light. (The triangle appears black in both cases.) Ask: **What color will the triangle appear in white light?** *(Students should predict a color other than blue or green.)* Show students the triangle in white light.

Apply Ask: **How can you explain your observations?** *(Sample answer: The red triangle reflects red light, but absorbs blue light and green light.)* **learning modality: logical/mathematical**

FIGURE 2
Colored Light

The color an apple appears to be depends on the color of the light that strikes it.
Applying Concepts *What color of light is reflected by a red apple?*

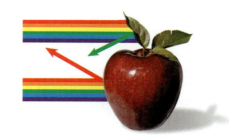

In red light, the apple appears red because it reflects the red light. But the leaves look black.

In green light, the apple appears black because no red light strikes it. But the leaves look green.

In blue light, both the apple and the leaves appear black.

The Color of Objects

If you know how light interacts with objects, you can explain why objects such as flowers have different colors. The color of any object depends on the material the object is made of and the color of light striking the object.

Color of Opaque Objects The color of an opaque object depends on the wavelengths of light that the object reflects. Every opaque object absorbs some wavelengths of light and reflects others. **The color of an opaque object is the color of the light it reflects.** For example, look at the apple shown at the top of Figure 2. The apple appears red because it reflects red wavelengths of light. The apple absorbs the other colors of light. The leaf looks green because it reflects green light and absorbs the other colors.

Objects can appear to change color if you view them in a different color of light. In red light, the apple appears red because there is red light for it to reflect. But the leaf appears black because there is no green light to reflect. In green light, the leaf looks green but the apple looks black. And in blue light, both the apple and the leaf look black.

Go Online
SciLINKS

For: Links on colors
Visit: www.SciLinks.org
Web Code: scn-1543

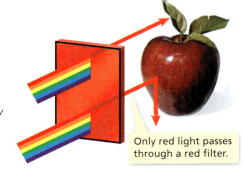

FIGURE 3
Color Filters

When you look at an apple through different filters, the color of the apple depends on the color of the filter. **Interpreting Photographs** *Why do both the apple and the leaves appear black through the blue filter?*

Only red light passes through a red filter.

The red filter transmits red light, so the apple looks red. But the leaf looks black.

The green filter transmits green light, so the leaf looks green. But the apple looks black.

The blue filter transmits blue light. Both the apple and the leaf look black.

Color of Transparent and Translucent Objects Materials that are transparent or translucent allow only certain colors of light to pass through them. They reflect or absorb the other colors. **The color of a transparent or translucent object is the color of the light it transmits.** For example, when white light shines through a transparent blue glass, the glass appears blue because it transmits blue light.

Transparent or translucent materials are used to make color filters. For example, a piece of glass or plastic that allows only red light to pass through is a red color filter. When you look at an object through a color filter, the color of the object may appear different than when you see the object in white light, as shown in Figure 3.

The lenses in sunglasses often are color filters. For example, lenses that are tinted yellow are yellow filters. Lenses that are tinted green are green filters. When you put on these tinted sunglasses, some objects appear to change color. The color you see depends on the color of the filter and on the color that the object appears in white light.

Reading Checkpoint What is a color filter?

Lab zone Skills **Activity**

Developing Hypotheses

1. Predict what colors you will see if you view a red, white, and blue flag through a red filter. Write a hypothesis of what the outcome will be. Write your hypothesis as an "If … then …" statement.
2. View an American flag using a red filter. What do you see? Is your hypothesis confirmed?
3. Repeat Steps 1 and 2 using a yellow filter.

Chapter 4 O ◆ 109

Lab zone Skills **Activity**

Skills Focus Developing hypotheses **L2**

Materials American flag, light source, red and yellow filters

Time 10 minutes

Tip If the room is darkened, the affects of the filters will be more obvious.

Expected Outcome With a red filter, both red and white stripes appear red, and the white stars appear to be red on a black background. With a yellow filter, the white stripes and stars appear yellow, the red stripes appear orange, and the blue areas appear black.

Help Students Read **L1**

DRTA Refer to the DRT guidelines in this chapter's Content Refresher.

Before students read this page, ask: **What determines the color of a transparent or translucent object?** *(Students may say the color of light the object reflects.)* Tell students to scan the text under the heading *Color of Transparent and Translucent Objects* for the answer. Ask: **Which sentence contains the answer?** *(The boldface sentence)* Check students' comprehension by asking: **What color of light is transmitted by blue glass?** *(Blue light)* **What colors of light are absorbed by blue glass?** *(All except blue)*

 **Teaching Resources**

- Transparency O40

Lab zone Teacher **Demo** **L1**

Color of Transmitted Light

Materials differently-colored transparent or translucent materials such as glass, plastic, paper, and fabric; flashlight

Time 15 minutes

Focus Remind students that colored transparent and translucent materials transmit light of only certain colors.

Teach In a darkened room, shine a flashlight on a white screen or wall. Then, shine the flashlight on the white surface through each of the colored materials. In each case, ask: **How does the light appear?** *(It is the same color as the material it shines through.)*

Apply Ask: **What conclusion can you draw about the color of light transmitted by transparent and translucent materials?** *(Sample answer: It is the same as the color of the material.)* **learning modality: visual**

Monitor Progress _____ **L2**

Writing Have students write a paragraph explaining why green apples and green traffic lights appear green.

Answers

Figure 2 A red apple reflects red light.
Figure 3 Only blue light is transmitted.

Reading Checkpoint A color filter is a piece of glass or plastic that allows light of only a certain color to pass through.

Combining Colors

Teach Key Concepts L2

Primary and Secondary Colors

Focus Remind students that colors can combine to form different colors.

Teach On the board, write the headings *Primary Colors of Light* and *Secondary Colors of Light*. Under *Primary Colors of Light*, list red, green, and blue. State that white light consists of equal amounts of light of the three primary colors and that the primary colors combine in different ways to make all other colors of light. Under *Secondary Colors of Light*, list magenta, cyan, and yellow. State that secondary colors result from combining equal amounts of two primary colors. Call students' attention to Figure 4. Then, ask: **Which two primary colors of light combine to produce magenta light?** (*Red and blue*) Repeat this procedure for pigment colors, listing the primary and secondary pigment colors under the correct headings. Then, have students look at Figure 6. Ask: **Which two primary colors of pigments combine to produce green pigment?** (*Cyan and yellow*)

Apply Ask: **Can you produce white light by combining magenta light and green light? Why or why not?** (*Yes, because magenta light contains red and blue light, and combining red, blue, and green light produces white light*) **learning modality: visual**

🚩 Address Misconceptions L1

Primary Colors of Light vs. Pigments

Students may not understand why they cannot combine red and green ink, paint, or dye to produce yellow, as shown in Figure 4. Help students overcome this misconception by having them color a square with a red marker and then with a green marker. When they are finished, ask: **What happens when you combine red and green markers?** (*The square appears black.*) Explain that Figure 4 applies only to light and that the colors in markers are pigments. Have students look at Figure 6, which applies to pigments. Point out that red and green are secondary colors in pigments and that they combine to produce black. **learning modality: kinesthetic**

All in One Teaching Resources

- Transparency O41

Combining Colors

Color is used in painting, photography, theater lighting, and printing. People who work with color must learn how to produce a wide range of colors using just a few basic colors. Three colors that can combine to make any other color are called **primary colors.** Two primary colors combine in equal amounts to produce a **secondary color.**

Mixing Colors of Light The primary colors of light are red, green, and blue. **When combined in equal amounts, the three primary colors of light produce white light.** If they are combined in different amounts, the primary colors can produce other colors. For example, red and green combine to form yellow light. Yellow is a secondary color of light because two primary colors produce it. The secondary colors of light are yellow (red + green), cyan (green + blue), and magenta (red + blue). Figure 4 shows the primary and secondary colors of light.

A primary and a secondary color can combine to make white light. Any two colors that combine to form white light are called **complementary colors.** Yellow and blue are complementary colors, as are cyan and red, and magenta and green.

A color television produces many colors using only the primary colors of light—red, green, and blue. Figure 5 shows a magnified view of a color television screen. The picture in the screen is made up of little groups of red, green, and blue light. By varying the brightness of each colored bar, the television can produce thousands of different colors.

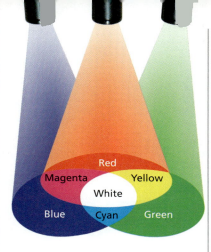

FIGURE 4
Primary Colors of Light
The primary colors of light combine in equal amounts to form white light.

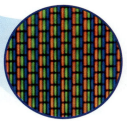

FIGURE 5
Colors in Television
A television produces many colors using only the primary colors of light.
Predicting *For a yellow area on a television screen, what color would you expect the bars to be?*

Equal amounts of red, green, and blue appear white from a distance.

Differentiated Instruction

Less Proficient Readers L1
Listing Important Points About Light and Color Have students listen to this section of the chapter on the **Student Edition on Audio CD**. Tell them to write down important points as they listen. After students have finished, have them compare their list of points with the text and correct any errors or omissions. **learning modality: verbal**

Special Needs L2
Combining Colors of Pigment Have students make a colored diagram similar to Figure 6 by combining primary pigment colors using markers. Tell students to draw three overlapping circles (like the circles in the figure) and to color each circle with one of the primary pigment colors. Have students identify and label the secondary pigment colors that appear in the areas where the circles overlap. **learning modality: kinesthetic**

Mixing Pigments How does a printer produce the many shades of colors you see in this textbook? Inks, paints, and dyes contain **pigments,** or colored substances that are used to color other materials. Pigments absorb some colors and reflect others. The color you see is the result of the colors that particular pigment reflects.

Mixing colors of pigments is different from mixing colors of light. **As pigments are added together, fewer colors of light are reflected and more are absorbed.** The more pigments that are combined, the darker the mixture looks.

Cyan, yellow, and magenta are the primary colors of pigments. These colors combine in equal amounts to produce black. By combining pigments in varying amounts, you can produce many other colors. If you combine two primary colors of pigments, you get a secondary color, as shown in Figure 6. The secondary colors of pigments are red, green, and blue.

Look at the pictures in this book with a magnifying glass. You can see tiny dots of different colors of ink. The colors used are cyan, yellow, and magenta. Black ink is also used, so the printing process is called four-color printing.

 **What are pigments?**

FIGURE 6
Primary Colors of Pigments
The primary colors of pigments combine in equal amounts to form black.

Section 1 Assessment

Target Reading Skill Building Vocabulary Use your definitions to help answer the questions.

Reviewing Key Concepts

1. a. Identifying What three things may happen to the light that strikes an object?
  b. Applying Concepts What happens to light that strikes the following materials: clear plastic, aluminum foil, and tissue paper?
  c. Problem Solving Room-darkening window shades are used to keep sunlight out of a theater. What type of material should the shades be made of? Explain.

2. a. Reviewing What determines the color of an opaque object? Of a transparent or translucent object?
  b. Drawing Conclusions An actor's red shirt and blue pants both appear black. What color is the stage light shining on the actor?

3. a. Describing What are the primary colors of light? The primary colors of pigments?
  b. Comparing and Contrasting How does the result of mixing the primary colors of pigments compare to the result of mixing the primary colors of light?
  c. Interpreting Diagrams In Figure 6, which pairs of colors combine to make black?

Lab zone At-Home **Activity**

Color Mix See how many different shades of green you can make by mixing blue and yellow paint in different proportions. On white paper, paint a "spectrum" from yellow to green to blue. Show the results to your family. Then explain how magazine photos reproduce thousands of colors.

Lab zone At-Home **Activity**

Color Mix L2 Suggest that students start with a small amount of yellow paint and gradually add very small quantities of blue, until the mixture contains mostly blue paint. Remind students to paint a stripe of each color on white paper to create a "spectrum" of colors from yellow through green to blue.

Lab zone Chapter **Project**

Keep Students on Track Check that students have decided on the purpose of their optical instrument. Tell them to draw and label a sketch of the optical instrument they would like to build. Urge them to consider how light will enter the instrument and be affected by lenses or mirrors. Encourage students to try out different mirrors and lenses as they plan their designs.

Monitor Progress ____ L2

Answers
Figure 5 For a yellow area on a television screen, you would expect to see red- and green-colored bars.

✓ Reading Checkpoint Pigments are colored substances that are used to color other materials.

Assess

Reviewing Key Concepts

1. a. The light may be reflected, transmitted, or absorbed. **b.** Light that strikes clear plastic is mostly transmitted and partly reflected. Light that strikes aluminum foil is mostly reflected and partly absorbed. Light that strikes tissue paper is partly transmitted, reflected, and absorbed. **c.** The shades should be made of an opaque material, which does not transmit light.
2. a. The color of an opaque object is determined by the color of light it reflects. The color of a transparent or translucent object is determined by the color of light it transmits. **b.** The stage light does not contain red or blue light, because no red or blue light is reflected, so the stage light must be green.
3. a. The primary colors of light are red, blue, and green. The primary colors of pigments are cyan, yellow, and magenta. **b.** Mixing the primary colors of pigments in equal amounts produces black pigment. Mixing the primary colors of light in equal amounts produces white light. **c.** Pairs of pigment colors that add to make black: green and magenta, red and cyan, and yellow and blue

Reteach L1
Read the definitions of the key terms, and call on students to identify the terms from their definitions.

Performance Assessment L2
Skills Check Have students create a graphic organizer comparing and contrasting colors of light with colors of pigments.

All in One Teaching Resources
- Section Summary: *Light and Color*
- Review and Reinforcement: *Light and Color*
- Enrich: *Light and Color*

Changing Colors

Prepare for Inquiry

Skills Objective
After this lab, students will be able to
- observe how color filters affect white light
- infer what color(s) of light different filters allow through
- predict how colored objects appear through different filters

 Prep Time 15 minutes
Class Time 40 minutes

Advance Planning
Gather colored objects, cellophane, flashlights, and shoe boxes.

Safety
Caution students to take care when using the scissors.

All in One Teaching Resources
- Lab Worksheet: *Changing Colors*

Guide Inquiry

Introduce the Procedure
Tell students that they will observe objects in light of just one color at a time.

Troubleshooting the Experiment
Pair any students who are colorblind with those who are not.

Expected Outcome
Colored objects are their usual colors when viewed through a filter of the same color; they are another color when viewed through filters of other colors. White objects viewed through colored filters are the color of the filter.

Analyze and Conclude
1. A red filter absorbs green and blue light, but allows red light to pass through. The red object appeared red, because the light it reflected passed through the filter. The blue object appeared black, because the light it reflected was absorbed by the filter. The yellow object appeared red or orange, depending on the filter.

2. A blue filter absorbs red and green light and transmits blue light. The yellow and green objects appeared black, because the light they reflect was absorbed by the filter. The blue object appeared blue.

3. Red—red; green—green; blue—blue

Changing Colors

Problem
How do color filters affect the appearance of objects in white light?

Skills Focus
observing, inferring, predicting

Materials
- shoe box
- scissors
- flashlight
- removable tape
- red object
  (such as a ripe tomato)
- yellow object
  (such as a ripe lemon)
- blue object
  (such as blue construction paper)
- red, green, and blue cellophane, enough to cover the top of the shoe box

Procedure
1. Carefully cut a large rectangular hole in the lid of the shoe box.
2. Carefully cut a small, round hole in the center of one of the ends of the shoe box.
3. Tape the red cellophane under the lid of the shoe box, covering the hole in the lid.
4. Place the objects in the box and put the lid on.
5. In a darkened room, shine the flashlight into the shoe box through the side hole. Note the apparent color of each object in the box.
6. Repeat Steps 3–5 using the other colors of cellophane.

Analyze and Conclude
1. **Observing** What did you see when you looked through the red cellophane? Explain why each object appeared as it did.
2. **Observing** What did you see when you looked through the blue cellophane? Explain.
3. **Inferring** What color(s) of light does each piece of cellophane allow through?
4. **Predicting** Predict what you would see under each piece of cellophane if you put a white object in the box. Test your prediction.
5. **Predicting** What do you think would happen if you viewed a red object through yellow cellophane? Draw a diagram to support your prediction. Then test you prediction.
6. **Communicating** Summarize your conclusions by drawing diagrams to show how each color filter affects white light. Write captions to explain your diagrams.

Design an Experiment
Do color filters work like pigments or like colors of light? Design an experiment to find out what happens if you shine a light through both a red and a green filter. *Obtain your teacher's permission before carrying out your investigation.*

---

4. Students may predict that a white object will appear the same color as the cellophane.

5. Students may predict that the red object will appear black. Their diagrams might show that light reflected by the red object is absorbed by the yellow cellophane. By viewing a red object through yellow cellophane, they will see that the red object appears orange.

6. Students' diagrams are expected to show that each colored filter transmits light of its own color.

Extend Inquiry

Design an Experiment Experiments should test whether overlapping red and green filters produce yellow or black. The filters are, in fact, more like pigments, because overlapping red and green filters produce gray or black.

Reading Preview

Key Concepts
- What are the kinds of reflection?
- What types of images are produced by plane, concave, and convex mirrors?

Key Terms
- ray • regular reflection
- diffuse reflection
- plane mirror • image
- virtual image
- concave mirror • optical axis
- focal point • real image
- convex mirror

Target Reading Skill
Comparing and Contrasting As you read, compare and contrast concave and convex mirrors in a Venn diagram like the one below. Write the similarities in the space where the circles overlap and the differences on the left and right sides.

Concave Mirrors   Convex Mirrors

Real images | Virtual images

Lab zone Discover **Activity**

How Does Your Reflection Wink?

1. Look at your face in a mirror. Wink your right eye. Which eye does your reflection wink?
2. Tape two mirrors together so that they open and close like a book. Open them so they form a 90-degree angle with each other. **CAUTION:** *Be careful of any sharp edges.*
3. Looking into both mirrors at once, wink at your reflection again. Which eye does your reflection wink now?

Think It Over
Observing How does your reflection wink at you? How does the second reflection compare with the first reflection?

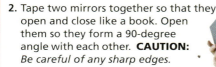

You laugh as you and a friend move toward the curved mirror. First your reflections look tall and skinny. Then they become short and wide. At one point, your reflections disappear even though you are still in front of the mirror. Imagine what it would be like if this happened every time you tried to comb your hair in front of a mirror!

Funhouse mirror ▶

Chapter 4 O ◆ 113

Section
2
Reflection and Mirrors

Objectives
After this lesson, students will be able to
O.4.2.1 Identify the kinds of reflection.
O.4.2.2 Describe the types of images produced by plane, concave, and convex mirrors.

Target Reading Skill

Comparing and Contrasting Explain that comparing and contrasting information shows how ideas, facts, and events are similar and different. The results of the comparison can have importance.

Answers
Sample Venn diagram:
Concave Mirror
Real images
Enlarged images
Curves inward
Convex Mirror
Curves outward
Similarities
Virtual images
Reduced images

All in One Teaching Resources
- Transparency O42

Preteach

Build Background Knowledge   L2

Focusing on Reflection
Ask: **How do the mirrors on the inside and outside of vehicles help drivers?** *(Sample answer: Allow drivers to see what is behind them)* Explain that mirrors work by reflecting light. Tell students that in this section they will learn more about reflection of light and about other types of mirrors.

Lab zone Discover **Activity**

Skills Focus Observing   L1

Materials 2 plane mirrors, tape

Time 10 minutes

Tips Use hand mirrors or cosmetic mirrors. Tape any sharp edges and caution students not to touch them.

Expected Outcome When the student looks into one mirror and winks the right eye, the left eye of the reflection winks. When the student looks into two mirrors at right angles and winks the right eye, the right eye of the reflection winks.

Think It Over The reflection winks the opposite eye. The second reflection is a reflection of the first image, so it winks the same eye as the student.

Instruct

Reflection of Light Rays

Teach Key Concepts **L2**
Types of Reflection

Focus Tell students there are two types of reflection: regular and diffuse.

Teach Make a Venn diagram on the board comparing and contrasting regular and diffuse reflection. *(Both involve the reflection of light rays from a surface, and in both the rays obey the law of reflection. However, regular reflection occurs with a smooth surface and creates a sharp image, whereas diffuse reflection occurs with a bumpy surface and creates a fuzzy image or no image at all.)*

Apply Ask: **Why do we see most objects by diffuse reflection?** *(Sample answer: Because most objects have relatively rough surfaces that reflect parallel rays at different angles)*
learning modality: visual

Use Visuals: Figure 7 **L2**
Comparing Angles of Incidence and Reflection

Focus Remind students that the angle of incidence and the angle of reflection of light are always equal.

Teach For the diagram of regular reflection, have students identify the angles of incidence and the angles of reflection. Ask: **Why are there several different angles of reflected light rays shown in the diagram on the left and just one angle in the diagram on the right?** *(In the left diagram, the surface is rough, so light rays strike the surface at different angles, so rays are reflected at different angles. In the right diagram, the surface is smooth, so all light rays strike the surface at the same angle and are reflected at the same angle.)*

Apply Ask: **What determines whether the reflection from the surface of the water is regular or diffuse?** *(Whether the water is smooth or choppy)* **learning modality: logical/mathematical**

Independent Practice **L2**

All in One Teaching Resources

- Guided Reading and Study Worksheet: *Reflection and Mirrors*
- Transparency O43

🔘 **Student Edition on Audio CD**

114 ● O

Lab zone Skills Activity

Observing

In a dark room, hold a flashlight next to a table. **CAUTION:** *Do not look directly into the flashlight.* Point its beam straight up so no light shines on the tabletop. Then hold a metal can upright 5 cm above the flashlight. Tilt the can so its flat bottom reflects light onto the table. Try this again using a white paper cup. How does the light reflected by the can compare with the light reflected by the cup?

FIGURE 7
Diffuse and Regular Reflection
The type of reflection that occurs at a surface depends on whether the surface is rough or smooth.

Reflection of Light Rays

The reflection you see in a mirror depends on how the surface reflects light. To show how light reflects, you can represent light waves as straight lines called **rays.** Recall from Chapter 1 that light rays obey the law of reflection—the angle of reflection equals the angle of incidence.

Figure 7 shows two kinds of reflection. In the choppy water, you do not see a clear reflection of the person in the boat. But in the smooth water, you see a sharp reflection. **The two ways in which a surface can reflect light are regular reflection and diffuse reflection.**

Regular Reflection When parallel rays of light hit a smooth surface, **regular reflection** occurs. All of the light rays are reflected at the same angle because of the smooth surface. So, you see a sharp reflection.

Diffuse Reflection When parallel rays of light hit a bumpy or uneven surface, **diffuse reflection** occurs. Each light ray obeys the law of reflection but hits the surface at a different angle because the surface is uneven. Therefore, each ray reflects at a different angle, and you don't see a clear reflection.

 Reading Checkpoint What kind of surface results in diffuse reflection?

Diffuse Reflection
When parallel light rays strike a rough surface, the rays are reflected at different angles.

Regular Reflection
When parallel light rays strike a smooth surface, all of the rays are reflected at the same angle.

114 ◆ O

Lab zone Skills Activity

Skills Focus Observing **L2**
Materials flashlight, metal can, white paper cup

Time 10 minutes

Tips Make sure students keep the light and reflective material in the same positions when they compare the can and the cup. You may want to do this activity as a demonstration.

Expected Outcome The reflection from the can is a brighter, narrower beam or spot of light. The reflection from the paper cup is weak and diffuse.

Extend Ask: **Why is the light reflected by the cup not as bright as the light reflected by the can?** *(The surface of the cup is not as smooth as the surface of the can, so it scatters light.)* **learning modality: kinesthetic**

FIGURE 8

Image in a Plane Mirror
A plane mirror forms a virtual image. The reflected light rays appear to come from behind the mirror, where the image forms.
Observing *Is the raised hand in the image a left hand or a right hand?*

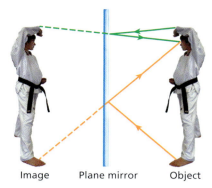

Image   Plane mirror   Object

Plane Mirrors

Did you look into a mirror this morning to comb your hair or brush your teeth? If you did, you probably used a plane mirror. A **plane mirror** is a flat sheet of glass that has a smooth, silver-colored coating on one side. Often the coating is on the back of the mirror to protect it from damage. When light strikes a mirror, the coating reflects the light. Because the coating is smooth, regular reflection occurs and a clear image forms. An **image** is a copy of an object formed by reflected or refracted rays of light.

What Kind of Image Forms The image you see in a plane mirror is a **virtual image**—an upright image that forms where light seems to come from. "Virtual" describes something that does not really exist. Your image appears to be behind the mirror, but you can't reach behind the mirror and touch it.

A plane mirror produces a virtual image that is upright and the same size as the object. But the image is not quite the same as the object. The left and right of the image are reversed. For example, when you look in a mirror, your right hand appears to be a left hand in the image.

How Images Form Figure 8 shows how a plane mirror forms an image. Some light rays from the karate student strike the mirror and reflect toward his eye. Even though the rays are reflected, the student's brain treats them as if they had come from behind the mirror. The dashed lines show where the light rays appear to come from. Because the light appears to come from behind the mirror, this is where the student's image appears to be located.

 Reading Checkpoint   Where does an image in a plane mirror appear to be located?

Differentiated Instruction

Special Needs L1
Observing Virtual Images Help students understand how an object's virtual image differs from the object. Have pairs of students play a game in one student pretends to be the object and the other student pretends to be the image. Tell them to face each other and move their arms and legs in unison to show how the image reverses left and right relative to the object. **learning modality: kinesthetic**

Gifted and Talented L3
Diagramming Virtual Images Challenge students to draw a diagram including an object, plane mirror, image, and light rays to show why a virtual image reverses left and right. Give them an opportunity to explain their diagrams to the class. **learning modality: visual**

Plane Mirrors

Teach Key Concepts L2
Plane Mirrors and Virtual Images

Focus Familiarize students with plane mirrors and virtual images.

Teach Define plane mirrors, and say they are the mirrors students use everyday when they brush their teeth or comb their hair. Define virtual images as the images that form in plane mirrors. Ask: **When you see your virtual image in a plane mirror, how is it similar to the real you?** *(Sample answer: The image has the same details and color, is the same size, and is upright.)* **How is your virtual image different?** *(Some students may correctly say the left and right of the image are reversed.)*

Apply Ask: **Why does a virtual image appear to be located behind a plane mirror?** *(The reflected light appears to come from the image, making the image appear to be as far behind the mirror as the object is in front of the mirror.)* **learning modality: verbal**

All in One Teaching Resources

• Transparency O44

Monitor Progress L2

Drawing Have students draw a diagram showing how a plane mirror forms a virtual image.

Students can keep their drawings in their portfolios.   **Portfolio**

Answers
Figure 8 The raised hand in the image is a left hand (left and right are reversed).

Reading Checkpoint A bumpy or uneven surface results in diffuse reflection.

Reading Checkpoint An image in a plane mirror appears to be located behind the mirror.

Concave Mirrors

Teach Key Concepts L2

Introducing Concave Mirrors

Focus Describe how a concave mirror is curved like the inside of a bowl.

Teach Use Figure 9 or a similar sketch on an overhead projector to show students how light is reflected from a concave surface. Point to the angles of incidence and angles of reflection of the rays in Figure 9 or your sketch. Then, ask: **Why are parallel rays no longer parallel after they are reflected by the concave surface of the mirror?** *(Because the rays strike the curved surface at different angles, causing them to be reflected at different angles as well.)*

Apply Ask: **When rays parallel to the optical axis strike a concave mirror, where do all the reflected rays meet?** *(At the focal point)* **learning modality: visual**

Teacher Demo L1

Modeling Reflection From a Concave Mirror

Materials large round bowl, modeling clay, water-filled squirt toy, paper towels

Time 10 minutes

Focus Tell students you will use the bowl to represent a concave mirror and a stream of water from the toy to represent a ray of light.

Teach Use modeling clay to hold the bowl vertically (on its side) on a table top. As students observe, spray a horizontal stream of water directly at the center of the bottom of the bowl. Ask: **What happens to the stream of water?** *(It bounces off the bottom of the bowl toward the center.)* Then, spray streams of water toward other locations inside the bowl. Ask: **What keeps happening to the streams of water?** *(As long as the spray is parallel to the bowl's "optical axis," the water bounces back toward the center of the bow, but in front of the bowl.)*

Apply Ask: **What happens to light rays when they strike the concave surface of a mirror?** *(Sample answer: They bounce back toward the mirror's focal point.)* **learning modality: visual**

FIGURE 9
Focal Point of a Concave Mirror
A concave mirror reflects rays of light parallel to the optical axis back through the focal point.

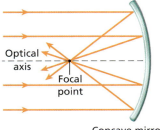

Concave mirror

Concave Mirrors

A mirror with a surface that curves inward like the inside of a bowl is a **concave mirror.** Figure 9 shows how a concave mirror can reflect parallel rays of light so that they meet at a point. Notice that the rays of light shown are parallel to the optical axis. The **optical axis** is an imaginary line that divides a mirror in half, much like the Equator that divides Earth into northern and southern halves. The point at which rays parallel to the optical axis meet is called the **focal point.** The location of the focal point depends on the shape of the mirror. The more curved the mirror is, the closer the focal point is to the mirror.

Representing How Images Form Ray diagrams are used to show where a focused image forms in a concave mirror. A ray diagram shows rays of light coming from points on the object. Two rays coming from one point on the object meet or appear to meet at the corresponding point on the image. Figure 10 shows how a ray diagram is drawn.

FIGURE 10
Drawing a Ray Diagram

Ray diagrams show where an image forms and the size of the image. The steps below show how to draw a ray diagram.

1 Draw a red ray from a point on the object (point **A**) to the mirror. Make this ray parallel to the optical axis. Then draw the reflected ray, which passes through the focal point.

2 Draw the green ray from the same point on the object to the mirror. Draw this ray as if it comes from the focal point. Then draw the reflected ray, which is parallel to the optical axis.

3 Draw dashed lines behind the mirror to show where the reflected rays appear to come from. The corresponding point on the image is located where the dashed lines cross.

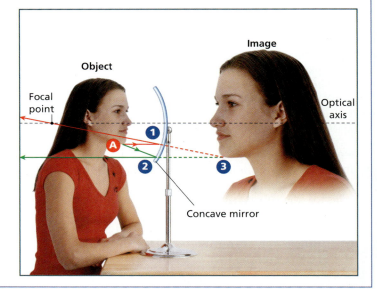

FIGURE 11
Images in Concave Mirrors
The type of image formed depends on the location of the object.
Interpreting Diagrams *When light rays actually meet, what kind of image is formed?*

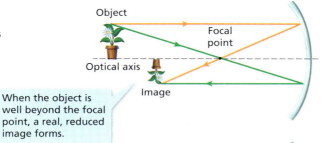

When the object is well beyond the focal point, a real, reduced image forms.

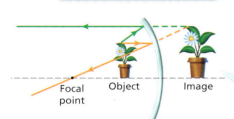

When the object is beyond the focal point but near it, a real, enlarged image forms.

When the object is closer than the focal point, a virtual, enlarged image forms.

Determining the Type of Image The type of image that is formed by a concave mirror depends on the location of the object. **Concave mirrors can form either virtual images or real images.** If the object is farther away from the mirror than the focal point, the reflected rays form a real image as shown in Figure 11. A **real image** forms when rays actually meet. Real images are upside down. A real image may be larger or smaller than the object.

If the object is between the mirror and the focal point, the reflected rays form a virtual image. The image appears to be behind the mirror and is upright. Virtual images formed by a concave mirror are always larger than the object. Concave mirrors produce the magnified images you see in a makeup mirror.

If an object is placed at the focal point, no image forms. But if a light source is placed at the focal point, the mirror can project parallel rays of light. A car headlight, for example, has a light bulb at the focal point of a concave mirror. Light hits the mirror, forming a beam of light that shines on the road ahead.

✓ **Reading Checkpoint** What is a real image?

Go Online
active art

For: Mirrors activity
Visit: PHSchool.com
Web Code: cgp-5042

Chapter 4 O ◆ 117

Lab zone **Build Inquiry** L2

Finding the Focal Point of a Concave Mirror

Materials concave mirror, white paper, flashlight

Time 15 minutes

Focus Challenge small groups of students to produce real images of the flashlight bulb on the paper to determine where the focal point of a mirror is.

Teach Have students look at the positions of the objects, mirrors, and images in Figure 11 to determine where to place the flashlight, mirror, and paper. Suggest that one student hold the mirror, another the white paper, and a third the flashlight.

Apply Ask: **Where is the focal point?** *(The location of the flashlight beyond which the image becomes inverted and real)* **learning modality: kinesthetic**

All in One Teaching Resources
• Transparency O45

Go Online
active art

For: Mirror activity
Visit: PhSchool.com
Web Code: cgp-5042

Students can interact with ray diagrams of mirrors online.

Differentiated Instruction

Less Proficient Readers L1
Comparing and Contrasting Images
Pair less proficient readers with more proficient readers. Have each pair make a table comparing and contrasting the real and virtual images produced by a concave mirror. Tables should compare and contrast how the images form and how they appear. **learning modality: visual**

Gifted and Talented L3
Diagramming Reflected Rays
Challenge students to draw diagrams showing how the shiny concave surface behind the bulb of a flashlight reflects light. *(Diagrams should show rays of light from the bulb, which is placed at the focal point, striking the concave surface at different angles and being reflected in rays parallel to the optical axis.)* **learning modality: logical/mathematical**

Monitor Progress _____ L2

Writing Have students explain the difference between a real and a virtual image.

Answers
Figure 11 A real image forms.

✓ **Reading Checkpoint** An upside-down image that forms when rays of light actually meet

O ● 117

Convex Mirrors

Teach Key Concepts `L2`
Reflection From Convex Mirrors

Focus Call students' attention to Figure 12.

Teach Ask: **Why does a convex mirror never produce a real image?** (*Because rays reflected from any point on the object never meet*)

Apply Ask: **What are examples of convex mirrors you use?** (*Sample answer: Rearview mirrors of vehicles*) **learning modality: visual**

 Teaching Resources
• Transparency O46

Monitor Progress `L2`
Answers

Figure 12 The rays spread out as they move away from the mirror.

 Passenger-side mirrors in cars

Assess

Reviewing Key Concepts

1. a. Regular and diffuse **b.** In both, the angle of reflection equals the angle of incidence. In regular reflection, parallel rays strike and are reflected from a smooth surface at the same angle; in diffuse reflection, parallel rays strike and are reflected from a bumpy surface at different angles. **c.** The shiny spoon produces a regular reflection and the tarnished spoon a diffuse reflection.
2. a. Copy of an object formed by reflected or refracted rays of light **b.** All three types form virtual images. Concave mirrors also form real images. **c.** In both types, the size of the image depends on the distance of the object from the mirror. A concave mirror produces images that are real or virtual, reduced or enlarged, and upright or upside-down. A convex mirror produces only upright, reduced, virtual images.

Reteach `L1`
Describe a real and a virtual image, and have students identify which types of mirrors can produce each image.

Performance Assessment `L2`
Ask students to draw diagrams showing how concave and convex mirrors form virtual images.

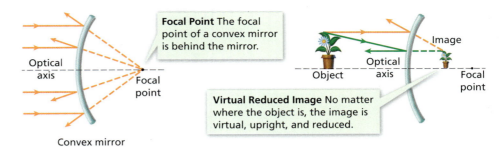

Focal Point The focal point of a convex mirror is behind the mirror.

Optical axis — Focal point — Convex mirror

Virtual Reduced Image No matter where the object is, the image is virtual, upright, and reduced.

Object — Optical axis — Image — Focal point

FIGURE 12
Convex Mirrors
Light rays parallel to the optical axis reflect as if they came from the focal point behind the mirror. The image formed by a convex mirror is always virtual.
Making Generalizations *Describe the directions of the parallel rays reflected by a convex mirror.*

Convex Mirrors

A mirror with a surface that curves outward is called a **convex mirror.** Figure 12 shows how convex mirrors reflect parallel rays of light. The rays spread out but appear to come from a focal point behind the mirror. The focal point of a convex mirror is the point from which the rays appear to come. **Because the rays never meet, images formed by convex mirrors are always virtual and smaller than the object.**

Perhaps you have seen this warning on a car mirror: "Objects in mirror are closer than they appear." Convex mirrors are used in cars as passenger-side mirrors. The advantage of a convex mirror is that it allows you to see a larger area than you can with a plane mirror. The disadvantage is that the image is reduced in size, so it appears to be farther away than it actually is.

Reading Checkpoint Where are convex mirrors typically used?

Section 2 Assessment

🎯 Target Reading Skill
Comparing and Contrasting Use your Venn diagram about mirrors to help you answer Question 2 below.

Reviewing Key Concepts
1. a. Reviewing What are two kinds of reflection?
   b. Explaining Explain how both kinds of reflection obey the law of reflection.
   c. Inferring Why is an image clear in a shiny spoon but fuzzy in a tarnished spoon?
2. a. Defining What is an image?
   b. Classifying Which mirrors can form real images? Which can form virtual images?
   c. Comparing and Contrasting How are images in concave mirrors like images in convex mirrors? How are they different?

Writing in Science
Dialogue At a funhouse mirror, your younger brother notices he can make his image disappear as he walks toward the mirror. He asks you to explain, but your answer leads to more questions. Write the dialogue that might take place between you and your brother.

118 ◆ O

All in One Teaching Resources
• Section Summary: *Reflection and Mirrors*
• Review and Reinforcement: *Reflection and Mirrors*
• Enrich: *Reflection and Mirrors*

Writing in Science

Writing Mode Dialogue
Scoring Rubric
4 Exceeds criteria
3 Meets criteria
2 Includes a dialogue but makes errors and/or does not provide enough detail
1 Includes no dialogue and/or fails to explain reflection from a concave mirror

Section 3
Refraction and Lenses

Section 3
Refraction and Lenses

Reading Preview

Key Concepts
- Why do light rays bend when they enter a medium at an angle?
- What determines the types of images formed by convex and concave lenses?

Key Terms
- index of refraction
- mirage
- lens
- convex lens
- concave lens

Target Reading Skill
Asking Questions Before you read, preview the red headings. In a graphic organizer like the one below, ask a *what, when, where* or *how* question for each heading. As you read, write the answers to your questions.

Refraction and Lenses

Question	Answer
When does refraction occur?	Refraction occurs . . .

Lab zone — Discover **Activity**

How Can You Make an Image Appear?
1. Stand about 2 meters from a window. Hold a hand lens up to your eye and look through it. What do you see? **CAUTION:** *Do not look at the sun.*
2. Move the lens farther away from your eye. What changes do you notice?
3. Now hold the lens between the window and a sheet of paper, but very close to the paper. Slowly move the lens away from the paper and toward the window. Keep watching the paper. What do you see? What happens as you move the lens?

Think It Over
Observing How is an image formed on a sheet of paper? Describe the image. Is it real or virtual? How do you know?

A fish tank can play tricks on you. If you look through the side of a fish tank, a fish seems closer than if you look over the top. If you look through the corner, you may see the same fish twice. You see one image of the fish through the front of the tank and another through the side. The two images appear in different places! How can this happen?

FIGURE 13
Optical Illusion in a Fish Tank
There is only one fish in this tank, but refraction makes it look as though there are two.

Chapter 4 O ◆ 119

Lab zone — Discover **Activity**

Skills Focus Observing

Materials hand lens, white paper

Time 10 minutes

Tips You may substitute an overhead fluorescent light for the sunlit scene viewed through a window. Caution students never to look directly at the sun, even on a cloudy day. This activity works best in a darkened room.

L1 **Expected Outcome** Students should see an image of the window on the paper, including the scenery seen through the window. They should observe that the scenery is upside-down.

Think It Over The image is formed as the rays of light pass through the lens and onto the paper. The image is real. It is inverted and has been projected onto the paper.

Objectives
After this lesson, students will be able to
O.4.3.1 Explain why light rays bend when they enter a medium at an angle.
O.4.3.2 Identify what determines the types of images formed by convex and concave lenses.

Target Reading Skill

Asking Questions Explain that changing a heading into a question helps students anticipate the ideas, facts, and events they are about to read.

Answers
Sample graphic organizer:

Refraction and Lenses

Questions
1. When does refraction occur?
2. What are the types of lenses?

Answers
1. When light rays enter a medium at an angle
2. Concave and convex lenses

All in One Teaching Resources
- Transparency O47

Preteach

Build Background Knowledge **L2**
Introducing Lenses
Show students a hand lens, and have them recall a time when the used a hand lens to observe something small in detail. Ask: **How do objects appear through a hand lens?** (*Bigger than they really are*) Point out the convex surfaces of the lens. Tell students they will learn in this section how a hand lens magnifies objects and how other types of lenses change light.

Instruct

Refraction of Light

Teach Key Skills   L2
Bending Light Rays

Focus Review refraction of waves.

Teach Tell students that light waves, like other waves, change in speed and bend as they enter a new medium at an angle. Say that some mediums slow and bend light more than others. Ask: **Do you think light waves travel more slowly through water or air?** *(Students might answer correctly that light waves travel more slowly through water.)*

Apply Ask: **What happens when light travels from water into air?** *(Sample answer: Light waves speed up and bend opposite to the way they would when traveling from air into water.)* **learning modality: verbal**

Math   Analyzing Data

Math Skill Making and interpreting graphs

Focus Have students read about the index of refraction in the feature.

Teach Call students' attention to the table. Explain that the lower the number for the index of refraction, the faster light travels through the medium and the less it bends when it enters the medium. Ask: **When light moves from air into a new medium, which medium in the table bends light least?** *(Water)*

Answers

1. Diamond causes the greatest change in the direction of a light ray traveling from air.
2. According to the graph, most solids bend light more than liquids (quartz is an exception).
3. You would not expect light to bend if it entered corn oil at an angle after traveling through glycerol, because corn oil and glycerol have the same value for the index of refraction.

Independent Practice   L2

All in One Teaching Resources

- Guided Reading and Study Worksheet: *Refraction and Lenses*

💿 **Student Edition on Audio CD**

Math   Analyzing Data

Bending Light

The index of refraction of a medium is a measure of how much light bends as it travels from air into the medium. The table shows the index of refraction of some common mediums.

1. **Interpreting Data** Which medium causes the greatest change in the direction of a light ray?

2. **Interpreting Data** According to the table, which tends to bend light more: solids or liquids?

3. **Predicting** Would you expect light to bend if it entered corn oil at an angle after traveling through glycerol? Explain.

Index of Refraction	
Medium	**Index of Refraction**
Air (gas)	1.00
Water (liquid)	1.33
Ethyl alcohol (liquid)	1.36
Quartz (solid)	1.46
Corn oil (liquid)	1.47
Glycerol (liquid)	1.47
Glass, crown (solid)	1.52
Sodium chloride (solid)	1.54
Zircon (solid)	1.92
Diamond (solid)	2.42

FIGURE 14
Refraction of Light
As light passes from a less dense medium into a more dense medium, it slows down and is refracted.

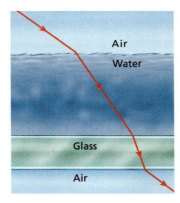

120 ◆ 0

Refraction of Light

Refraction can cause you to see something that may not actually be there. As you look at a fish in a tank, the light coming from the fish to your eye bends as it passes through three different mediums. The mediums are water, the glass of the tank, and air. As the light passes from one medium to the next, it refracts. **When light rays enter a medium at an angle, the change in speed causes the rays to bend, or change direction.**

Refraction in Different Mediums Some mediums cause light to bend more than others, as shown in Figure 14. When light passes from air into water, the light slows down. Light slows down even more when it passes from water into glass. When light passes from glass back into air, the light speeds up. Light travels fastest in air, a little slower in water, and slower still in glass. Notice that the ray that leaves the glass is traveling in the same direction as it was before it entered the water.

Glass causes light to bend more than either air or water. Another way to say this is that glass has a higher index of refraction than either air or water. A material's **index of refraction** is a measure of how much a ray of light bends when it enters that material. The higher the index of refraction of a medium, the more it bends light. The index of refraction of water is 1.33, and the index of refraction of glass is about 1.5. So light is bent more by glass than by water.

Prisms and Rainbows Recall that when white light enters a prism, each wavelength is refracted by a different amount. The longer the wavelength, the less the wave is bent by a prism. Red, with the longest wavelength, is refracted the least. Violet, with the shortest wavelength, is refracted the most. This difference in refraction causes white light to spread out into the colors of the spectrum—red, orange, yellow, green, blue, and violet.

The same process occurs in water droplets suspended in the air. When white light from the sun shines through the droplets, a rainbow may appear. The water droplets act like tiny prisms, refracting and reflecting the light and separating the colors.

Mirages You're traveling in a car on a hot day, and you notice that the road ahead looks wet. Yet when you get there, the road is dry. Did the puddles dry up? No, the puddles were never there! You saw a **mirage** (mih RAHJ)—an image of a distant object caused by refraction of light. The puddles on the road are light rays from the sky that are refracted to your eyes.

Figure 16 shows a mirage. Notice the shiny white areas on the road behind the white car. The air just above the road is hotter than the air higher up. Light travels faster in hot air. So, light rays from the white car that travel toward the road are bent upward by the hot air. Your brain assumes that the rays traveled in a straight line. So the rays look as if they have reflected off a smooth surface. What you see is a mirage.

✓ **Reading Checkpoint** What causes a mirage?

FIGURE 15
Rainbows
A rainbow forms when sunlight is refracted and reflected by tiny water droplets. **Observing** *What is the order of colors in a rainbow?*

FIGURE 16
Mirages
The puddles and white reflections on the road are mirages. Light refracts as it goes from hot air to cool air. The refracted light appears to come from the ground.

Mirage

O ◆ 121

Lenses

Teach Key Concepts [L2]

Lenses and Refraction of Light

Focus Review what students know about convex and concave mirrors and reflection of light. Then, have them use their prior knowledge to predict how convex and concave lenses might form images.

Teach Ask: **What do you think a convex lens looks like? A concave lens?** *(A convex lens is curved outward. A concave lens is curved inward.)*

Apply Ask: **How do you think the curved surface of a lens affects the transmission of light?** *(Sample answer: It causes light to bend at angles. It creates real or virtual images that may be bigger or smaller than the object.)*
learning modality: verbal

Use Visuals: Figure 18 [L1]

Images in Convex Lenses

Focus Have students read the Figure 18 caption.

Teach Ask: **How do the two parts of the figure differ?** *(In the top part of the figure, the object is farther from the lens than the focal point; the image is real, larger than the object, and upside down. In the bottom part of the figure, the object is located between the focal point and lens; the image is virtual, larger than the object, and upright.)*

Apply Ask: **What causes the differences in the images?** *(The different positions of the object)* **Which diagram shows how the hand lens forms an image of the ladybug? How do you know?** *(The bottom diagram, because the image is a virtual image)* **learning modality: visual**

All in One Teaching Resources

• Transparency O48

FIGURE 17
Convex and Concave Lenses
A convex lens can focus parallel rays at a focal point. A concave lens causes parallel rays to spread apart.

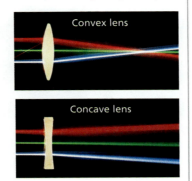

Convex lens

Concave lens

Lenses

Anytime you look through binoculars, a camera, or eyeglasses, you are using lenses to bend light. A **lens** is a curved piece of glass or other transparent material that is used to refract light. A lens forms an image by refracting light rays that pass through it. Like mirrors, lenses can have different shapes. The type of image formed by a lens depends on the shape of the lens and the position of the object.

Convex Lenses A **convex lens** is thicker in the center than at the edges. As light rays parallel to the optical axis pass through a convex lens, they are bent toward the center of the lens. The rays meet at the focal point of the lens and continue to travel beyond. The more curved the lens, the more it refracts light. A convex lens acts somewhat like a concave mirror, because it focuses rays of light.

An object's position relative to the focal point determines whether a convex lens forms a real image or a virtual image. Figure 18 shows that if the object is farther away than the focal point, the refracted rays form a real image on the other side of the lens. If the object is between the lens and the focal point, a virtual image forms on the same side of the lens as the object.

FIGURE 18
Images in Convex Lenses
The type of image formed by a convex lens depends on the object's position.

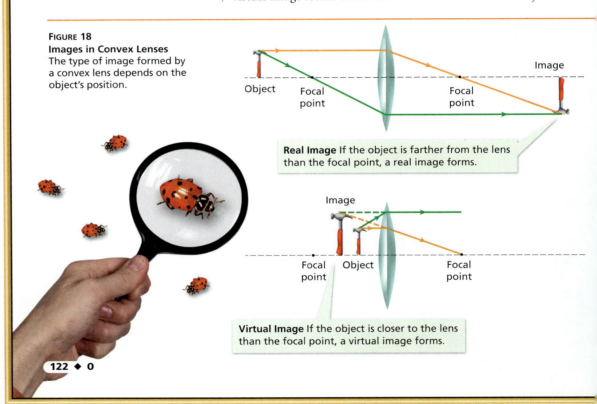

Real Image If the object is farther from the lens than the focal point, a real image forms.

Virtual Image If the object is closer to the lens than the focal point, a virtual image forms.

122 ◆ O

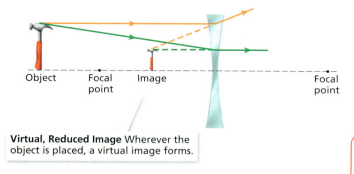

Object Focal point Image Focal point

Virtual, Reduced Image Wherever the object is placed, a virtual image forms.

FIGURE 19
Images in Concave Lenses
A concave lens produces virtual images that are upright and smaller than the object.
Interpreting Diagrams *Why can a concave lens only form a virtual image?*

Go Online
active art

For: Lenses activity
Visit: PHSchool.com
Web Code: cgp-5042

Concave Lenses A **concave lens** is thinner in the center than at the edges. When light rays traveling parallel to the optical axis pass through a concave lens, they bend away from the optical axis and never meet. **A concave lens can produce only virtual images because parallel light rays passing through the lens never meet.**

Figure 19 shows how an image forms in a concave lens. The virtual image is located where the light rays appear to come from. The image is always upright and smaller than the object.

 Reading Checkpoint What is the shape of a concave lens?

Section 3 Assessment

Target Reading Skill **Asking Questions** Use the answers to the questions you wrote about the headings to help you answer the questions below.

Reviewing Key Concepts
1. **a. Identifying** What is a material's index of refraction?
   b. Relating Cause and Effect What causes light rays to bend when they enter a new medium at an angle?
   c. Predicting If a glass prism were placed in a medium such as water, would it separate white light into different colors? Explain.
2. **a. Defining** What is a lens?
   b. Comparing and Contrasting Describe the shapes of a concave lens and a convex lens.

c. Interpreting Diagrams Use Figure 18 to explain how you can tell whether a convex lens will form a real or virtual image.

Lab zone **At-Home Activity**

Bent Pencil Here's how you can bend a pencil without touching it. Put a pencil in a glass of water so that it is half in and half out of the water. Have your family members look at the pencil from the side. Using your understanding of refraction, explain to your family why the pencil appears as it does.

Chapter 4 O ◆ 123

Go Online
active art

For: Lens activity
Visit: PHSchool.com
Web Code: cgp-5042

Students can interact with the ray diagrams of lenses online.

Monitor Progress L2

Answers
Figure 19 Because parallel light rays passing through the lens never meet

 Reading Checkpoint A concave lens is thinner in the center than at the edges.

Assess

Reviewing Key Concepts
1. **a.** A measure of how much a ray of light bends when it enters that material **b.** One side of the light rays changes speed before the other side. **c.** Yes, because the index of refraction of glass is different than that of water.
2. **a.** A curved piece of glass or other transparent material that is used to refract light **b.** A concave lens is thicker in the middle; a convex lens is thicker at the edges. **c.** If the object is farther from the lens than the focal point, a real image will form. If the object is closer to the lens than the focal point, a virtual image will form.

Reteach L1
Read aloud the boldface sentences, leaving out one or more important terms in each sentence. Ask students to identify the missing terms.

Performance Assessment L2
Oral Presentation Call on students to define refraction, index of refraction, and mirage. Call on other students to explain how the three terms are related.

Lab zone **At-Home Activity**

Bent Pencil L1 Students are expected to explain to their families that the pencil appears to bend because light from the pencil bends when it travels between the air and water. They also might say that the brain assumes light travels in a straight line from the image to the eye, so the pencil is perceived as bent.

Lab zone **Chapter Project**

Keep Students on Track Make sure students have begun to build their optical instruments. Answer any questions and address any design difficulties they may have. If students are having trouble because their designs are too elaborate, guide them in simplifying their designs.

Looking at Images

Prepare for Inquiry
L2

Skills Objective
After this lab, students will be able to
- control variables by keeping some variables constant and manipulating others
- interpret data by correlating the size of an image with experimental conditions

 Prep Time 15 minutes

Time 40 minutes

Advance Planning
Obtain enough convex lenses and light sockets with bulbs and batteries for each group of students. Buy or make cardboard stands.

Safety
 Review the safety guidelines in Appendix A.

All in One Teaching Resources
- Lab Worksheet: *Looking at Images*

Guide Inquiry

Invitation
Tell students that convex lenses are used in telescopes and microscopes. Ask: **What do you think convex lenses do?** (*Magnify images of very small or distant objects*)

Introduce the Procedure
Tell students they will use a convex lens to investigate images in this lab.

Troubleshooting the Experiment
- If necessary, demonstrate how to determine the focal length of the lens.
- Lenses with very short focal lengths will not produce clear images at large distances.

Expected Outcome
When the light bulb is much farther from the lens than the focal point, the image is real and smaller than the object. The closer to the focal point the bulb is, the larger the real image becomes.

Analyze and Conclude
1. Students kept constant the focal length and the position of the lens. They manipulated position of the bulb and the cardboard. Responding variables were size and location of image.

Looking at Images

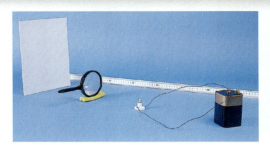

Problem
How does the distance between an object and a convex lens affect the image formed?

Skills Focus
controlling variables, interpreting data

Materials
- tape
- convex lens
- cardboard stand
- blank sheet of paper
- light bulb and socket
- clay, for holding the lens
- battery and wires
- meter stick
- centimeter ruler

Procedure
1. Tape the paper onto the cardboard stand.
2. Place a lit bulb more than 2 m from the paper. Use the lens to focus light from the bulb onto the paper. Measure the distance from the lens to the paper. This is the approximate focal length of the lens you are using.
3. Copy the data table into your notebook.
4. Now place the bulb more than twice the focal length away from the lens. Adjust the cardboard until the image is focused. Record the size of the image on the paper and note the orientation of the image. Record the distance from the bulb to the lens and from the lens to the cardboard.
5. Now, move the bulb so that it is just over one focal length away from the lens. Record the position and size of the image.

Analyze and Conclude
1. **Controlling Variables** Make a list of the variables in this experiment. Which variables did you keep constant? Which was the manipulated variable? Which were the responding variables?
2. **Observing** What happened to the position of the image as the bulb moved toward the lens?
3. **Interpreting Data** Was the image formed by the convex lens always enlarged? If not, under what conditions was the image reduced?
4. **Predicting** What would happen if you look through the lens at the bulb when it is closer to the lens than the focal point? Explain your prediction.
5. **Communicating** Write a paragraph explaining how the distance between an object and a convex lens affects the image formed. Use ray diagrams to help you summarize your results.

Design an Experiment
Design an experiment to study images formed by convex lenses with different thicknesses. How does the lens thickness affect the position and size of the images? *Obtain your teacher's permission before carrying out your investigation.*

Data Table			
Focal Length of Lens: _____ cm		Height of Bulb: _____ cm	
Distance From Bulb to Lens (cm)	Distance From Lens to Cardboard (cm)	Image Orientation (upright or upside down)	Image Size (height in cm)

---

2. As the bulb moved toward the lens, the image moved farther from the lens.

3. No; the image was reduced when the object was farther from the lens than twice the focal length.

4. Students might predict that no image would be projected onto the paper, because the image is virtual when the object is in this position.

5. Students are expected to draw diagrams showing how rays from a bulb are refracted through a convex lens when the object is placed at different distances from the lens. They can use them to explain their results.

Extend Inquiry

Design an Experiment Students' experiments should repeat the procedure in this lab using convex lenses of varying thicknesses.

Seeing Light

Reading Preview

Key Concepts
• How do you see objects?
• What types of lenses are used to correct vision problems?

Key Terms
• cornea • pupil • iris • retina
• rods • cones • optic nerve
• nearsighted • farsighted

Target Reading Skill
Sequencing A sequence is the order in which the steps in a process occur. As you read, make a flow-chart that shows how you see objects. Put the steps of the process in separate boxes in the flowchart in the order in which they occur.

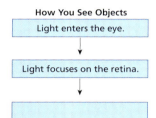

How You See Objects

| Light enters the eye. |
| Light focuses on the retina. |

Lab zone · Discover Activity

Can You See Everything With One Eye?

1. Write an X and an O on a sheet of paper. The O should be about 5 cm to the right of the X.
2. Hold the sheet of paper at arm's length.
3. Close or cover your left eye. Stare at the X with your right eye.
4. Slowly move the paper toward your face while staring at the X. What do you notice?
5. Repeat the activity, keeping both eyes open. What difference do you notice?

Think It Over
Posing Questions Write two questions about vision that you could investigate using the X and the O.

The pitcher goes into her windup, keeping her eye on the strike zone. The batter watches the pitcher release the ball and then swings. Crack! She drops the bat and sprints toward first base. From your seat, you watch the ball travel toward the outfield. Will it be a base hit? The left fielder watches the ball speed toward her. It's over her head for a double!

Players and spectators alike followed the first rule of baseball: Keep your eye on the ball. As the ball moves near and far, your eyes must adjust continuously to keep it in focus. Fortunately, this change in focus happens automatically.

Keep your eye on the ball! ▶

Chapter 4 O ◆ 125

Section 4

Seeing Light

Objectives
After this lesson, students will be able to
O.4.4.1 Explain how one sees objects.
O.4.4.2 Identify the types of lenses that are used to correct vision problems.

Target Reading Skill
Sequencing Explain that organizing information from beginning to end helps students understand a step-by-step process.

Answers
Sample flowchart:
How You See Objects
Light enters the eye.
Light focuses on the retina.
An image forms.
Rods and cones send signals to the brain.

All in One Teaching Resources
• Transparency O50

Preteach

Build Background Knowledge   L2
Observing the Eye's Ability to Focus
Have students hold an index finger close to their face and focus their eyes on the tip of the finger. Point out how focusing on their finger makes the background unfocused. Then, tell students to move their finger slowly away from their face as they continue to focus on the tip. Point out how background starts to come into focus as their finger gets farther away. Tell students that the ability of the eye to focus automatically on moving objects at different distances is one of the functions of the eye they will learn about in this section.

Lab zone · Discover Activity

Skills Focus Posing questions
Materials white paper, pencil
Time 10 minutes
Tip Suggest that students repeat the activity to be certain of their result.

L1 **Expected Outcome** As students move the paper closer to their eyes, the O disappears. This does not occur when the activity is done with both eyes open.

Think It Over Sample questions: At what distance does the letter O disappear? If I repeat the activity but stare at the O instead of the X, will the X disappear?

Instruct

The Human Eye

Teach Key Concepts L2
Role of the Eyes and Brain in Vision

Focus State that the eyes are the organs that focus and sense light but that vision also depends on the brain.

Teach Explain that the eyes receive light, form images, and convert the images to signals that are sent along the optic nerve to the brain. The images that form in the eyes are upside down.

Apply Ask: **What do you think causes us to see upright images?** (*Sample answer: The brain interprets the signals from the eyes as upright images.*) **learning modality: logical/ mathematical**

⚑ Address Misconceptions L2
Colorblindness

Students may think that people who are colorblind see no color at all but only shades of gray. Correct this misconception by saying that, due to a defect in the cones of their eyes, most colorblind people can see one or two of the primary colors of light but not all three primary colors. For example, a colorblind person might be able to see the blue and green primary colors but not red. Ask: **How would red objects appear to this person? Why?** (*Black or gray, because no red light is perceived*) **learning modality: verbal**

For: More on eyesight
Visit: PHSchool.com
Web Code: cgd-5044

Students can investigate eyesight in an online interactivity.

Independent Practice L2

 **Teaching Resources**

• Guided Reading and Study Worksheet: *Seeing Light*

💿 **Student Edition on Audio CD**

Lab zone Try This Activity

True Colors

When you stare too long at a color, the cones in your eyes get tired.

1. Stare at the bottom right star of the flag for at least 60 seconds. Do not move your eyes or blink during that time.

2. Now stare at a sheet of blank white paper.

Observing What do you see when you look at the white paper? How are the colors you see related to the colors in the original art?

For: More on eyesight
Visit: PHSchool.com
Web Code: cgd-5044

126 ◆ O

The Human Eye

Your eyes allow you to sense light. The eye is a complex structure with many parts, as you can see in Figure 20. Each part plays a role in vision. **You see objects when a process occurs that involves both your eyes and your brain.**

Light Enters the Eye Light enters the eye through the transparent front surface called the **cornea** (KAWR nee uh). The cornea protects the eye. It also acts as a lens to help focus light rays.

After passing through the cornea, light enters the pupil, the part of the eye that looks black. The **pupil** is an opening through which light enters the inside of the eye. In dim light, the pupil becomes larger to allow in more light. In bright light, the pupil becomes smaller to allow in less light. The **iris** is a ring of muscle that contracts and expands to change the size of the pupil. The iris gives the eye its color. In most people the iris is brown; in others it is blue, green, or hazel.

An Image Forms After entering the pupil, the light passes through the lens. The lens is a convex lens that refracts light to form an image on the lining of your eyeball. Muscles, called ciliary muscles, hold the lens in place behind the pupil. When you focus on a distant object, the ciliary muscles relax, and the lens becomes longer and thinner. When you focus on a nearby object, the muscles contract, and the lens becomes shorter and fatter.

When the cornea and the lens refract light, an upside-down image is formed on the retina. The **retina** is a layer of cells that lines the inside of the eyeball. (Cells are the tiny structures that make up living things.)

The retina is made up of tiny, light-sensitive cells called rods and cones. **Rods** are cells that contain a pigment that responds to small amounts of light. The rods allow you to see in dim light. **Cones** are cells that respond to color. They may detect red light, green light, or blue light. Cones respond best in bright light. Both rods and cones help change images on the retina into signals that then travel to the brain.

A Signal Goes to the Brain The rods and cones send signals to the brain along a short, thick nerve called the **optic nerve.** The optic nerve begins at the blind spot, an area of the retina so called because it has no rods or cones. Your brain interprets the signals as an upright image. It also combines the images from each of your eyes into a single three-dimensional image.

 Reading Checkpoint Where does an image form in the eye?

Lab zone Try This Activity

Skills Focus Observing

Materials white paper

Time 5 minutes

Tip Set a timer for 60 seconds, and tell students when to start staring at the star on the flag and when to look at the white paper.

L2

Expected Outcome Students will see an image of a red, white, and blue flag on the white paper. These are the complementary colors of the flag in the original art.

Extend Ask: **What colors would you see if you stared at a red, white, and blue flag?** (*The colors of the flag in the original art*) Let students test their predictions. **learning modality: visual**

FIGURE 20
The Human Eye

The eye is a complex structure with many parts that allow you to see.

Relating Cause and Effect *What is the main function of each part of the eye?*

Ciliary muscles

Retina

Cornea

Lens

Iris

Blood vessels

Pupil

Optic nerve

Pupil and Iris
The iris controls the size of the pupil, which determines how much light enters the eye.

Pupil

Iris

Dim Light The iris contracts, making the pupil large.

Bright Light The iris expands, making the pupil small.

Lens and Ciliary Muscles
The ciliary muscles change the shape of the lens.

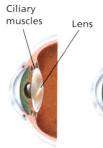

Ciliary muscles

Lens

Seeing Far Away The ciliary muscles relax, making the lens thin.

Seeing Close Up The ciliary muscles contract, making the lens thick.

Retina
The retina has two kinds of cells that detect light. The rods respond to dim light. The cones respond to red, green, and blue light.

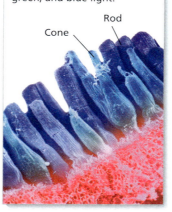

Rod

Cone

Chapter 4 O ◆ 127

Differentiated Instruction

Less Proficient Readers **L1**
Organizing Information on the Eye
Make a table titled *Structures of the Eye*, with the headings *Structure, Location, Function*. Give students copies of the table, and have them complete it as they read about the eye. Tell them to use Figure 20 to locate the structures and the text to find out their functions. Suggest that they save their tables for study guides. **learning modality: visual**

Special Needs **L1**
Observing a Model of the Eye Some students may have difficulty understanding the anatomy of the eye from the two-dimensional diagram in Figure 20. Give them a chance to use an enlarged three-dimensional model of the eye to trace the path of light as they read about the eye in the text. **learning modality: kinesthetic**

 **Teaching Resources**
• Transparency O51

Lab zone **Build Inquiry** **L2**

Observing the Functions of Rods and Cones

Materials objects of different colors

Time 10 minutes

Focus State that rods and cones are cells in the retina that respond to light. Add that rods are especially sensitive to dim light and cones to colored light.

Teach Darken the room. When students' eyes have adjusted to the dark, show them the colored objects. Ask: **What color do the objects appear to be?** (*Different shades of gray or black*) Turn on the lights, and show students the objects again. Ask: **What color do the objects appear to be now?** (*Their actual colors*)

Apply Ask: **Which type of cells, rods or cones, helped you see in the dark room?** (*Rods*) **In the bright room?** (*Cones*) **Why did the objects appear gray or black in the dark and colored in the light?** (*Sample answer: Rods are sensitive to dim light but not to color, whereas cones are sensitive to color but not to dim light.*) **learning modality: visual**

Monitor Progress _____ **L2**

Oral Presentation Read the function of each structure of the eye, and call on students to identify the structures based on their functions.

Answers
Figure 20 Cornea protects eye and helps focus light; pupil allows light to enter eye; iris controls size of pupil; lens focuses light on retina; ciliary muscles change shape of lens to help focus light; retina receives image and contains cells that sense light; rods respond to dim light; cones respond to color; optic nerve carries signals from rods and cones to brain.

 Reading Checkpoint An image forms on the retina.

Correcting Vision

Teach Key Concepts `L2`

Comparing and Contrasting Vision Problems

Focus Have students read the caption of Figure 21.

Teach Tell students to compare the drawings for nearsightedness with the drawings for farsightedness. Ask: **How does a nearsighted eye differ from a farsighted eye?** *(A nearsighted eye is too long, so the image forms in front of the retina; a farsighted eye is too short, so the image forms behind the retina.)*

Apply Ask: **How are nearsightedness and farsightedness corrected?** *(Nearsightedness is corrected with concave lenses, farsightedness with convex lenses.)* **learning modality: visual**

All in One Teaching Resources

• Transparency O52

Assess

Reviewing Key Concepts

1. a. Eyes and brain **b.** Light rays passing through the cornea and lens are refracted to form an image on the retina. **c.** Rods and cones in the retina detect the image and convert it into signals that then travel to the brain.
2. a. Concave lenses help correct nearsightedness; convex lenses help correct farsightedness. **b.** The eyeball is too long, which causes images of distant objects to be blurred. **c.** In a nearsighted person's eye, an image forms in front of the retina. In a farsighted person's eye, an image forms on the retina but is out of focus.

Reteach `L1`

Show students Transparency O51. As you point to each structure, ask students to identify its function.

Performance Assessment `L2`

Drawing Have students draw a diagram showing how lenses correct farsightedness.

All in One Teaching Resources

• Section Summary: *Seeing Light*
• Review and Reinforcement: *Seeing Light*
• Enrich: *Seeing Light*

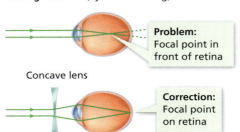

Nearsightedness (eyeball too long)

Concave lens

Problem: Focal point in front of retina

Correction: Focal point on retina

Farsightedness (eyeball too short)

Convex lens

Problem: Focal point behind retina

Correction: Focal point on retina

FIGURE 21
Vision Correction
Nearsightedness and farsightedness are caused when the eyeball is too long or too short. Both can be corrected with lenses.

Correcting Vision

If the eyeball is slightly too long or too short, the image on the retina is out of focus. Fortunately, wearing glasses or contact lenses can correct this type of vision problem. **Concave lenses are used to correct nearsightedness. Convex lenses are used to correct farsightedness.**

A **nearsighted** person can see nearby things clearly, but objects at a distance are blurred. The eyeball is too long, so the lens focuses the image in front of the retina. To correct this, a concave lens in front of the eye spreads out light rays before they enter the eye. As a result, the image forms on the retina.

A **farsighted** person can see distant objects clearly, but nearby objects appear blurry. The eyeball is too short, so the image that falls on the retina is out of focus. A convex lens corrects this by bending light rays toward each other before they enter the eye. An image then focuses on the retina.

Section 4 Assessment

🎯 **Target Reading Skill** **Sequencing** Refer to your flowchart about how you see as you answer Question 1.

Reviewing Key Concepts

1. a. Identifying Which parts of your body are involved in seeing objects?
   b. Explaining How is an image formed on the retina?
   c. Sequencing What happens to light after it strikes the retina?
2. a. Reviewing What types of lenses help correct vision problems?
   b. Describing Describe a nearsighted person's eye.

c. Comparing and Contrasting With uncorrected vision, where does an image form in a nearsighted person's eye? In a farsighted person's eye?

Lab zone At-Home **Activity**

Optical Illusion Look through a cardboard tube with your right eye. Hold your left hand against the far end of the tube with the palm facing you. Keeping both eyes open, look at a distant object. Draw what you see. What do you think causes this illusion?

Lab zone At-Home **Activity**

Optical Illusion `L2` Students see an image of their left hand with a hole in it, which is a combination of images from both eyes.

Reading Preview

Key Concepts
- How are lenses used in telescopes, microscopes, and cameras?
- What makes up laser light, and how is it used?
- Why can optical fibers carry laser beams a long distance?

Key Terms
- telescope
- refracting telescope
- objective
- eyepiece
- reflecting telescope
- microscope
- camera
- laser
- hologram
- optical fiber
- total internal reflection

Target Reading Skill
Building Vocabulary A definition states the meaning of a word or a phrase by telling about its most important feature or function. Carefully read the definition of each Key Term and also read the neighboring sentences. Then write a definition of each Key Term in your own words.

Lab zone Discover Activity

How Does a Pinhole Viewer Work? ✂

1. Carefully use a pin to make a tiny hole in the center of the bottom of a paper cup.
2. Place a piece of wax paper over the open end of the cup. Hold the paper in place with a rubber band.
3. Turn off the room lights. Point the end of the cup with the hole in it at a bright window. **CAUTION:** *Do not look directly at the sun.*
4. Look at the image on the wax paper.

Think It Over

Classifying Describe the image you see. Is it upside down or right-side up? Is it smaller or larger than the actual object? What type of image is it?

Have you ever seen photos of the moons of Jupiter? Have you ever thought it would be exciting to fly close to the rings of Saturn? You know that traveling in space has been done for only a few decades. But you might be surprised to know that the moons of Jupiter and the rings of Saturn had not been seen before the year 1600. It was only about 1607 that a new invention, the telescope, made those objects visible to people.

Since the 1600s, astronomers have built more powerful telescopes that allow them to see objects in space that are very far from Earth. For example, the star-forming nebula, or cloud of gas and dust in space, shown below is located trillions of kilometers from Earth. It took about 3 million years for light from this nebula to travel to Earth.

◀ Nebula image from the Hubble Space Telescope

O ◆ 129

Lab zone Discover Activity

Skills Focus Classifying L2

Materials paper cup, pin, wax paper, rubber band

Time 15 minutes

Tips You may wish to make the holes in the cups prior to the activity. Make sure students do not crumple the cup with the rubber band. Instead of a bright window in a darkened room, you may use a burning candle or light bulb to form the image.

Expected Outcome Students will see an image of the window, light bulb, or candle on the wax paper.

Think It Over The image is upside down, smaller than the actual object, and real.

Section
5
Using Light

Objectives
After completing this lesson, students will be able to

O.4.5.1 Describe how lenses are used in telescopes, microscopes, and cameras.

O.4.5.2 Identify what makes up laser light, and state how laser light is used.

O.4.5.3 Explain why optical fibers can carry laser beams a long distance.

Target Reading Skill

Building Vocabulary Explain that knowing the definitions of key terms helps students understand what they read.

Answers
Sample definitions:
Telescope: device that uses lenses or mirrors to collect and focus light from distant objects; **Refracting telescope**: telescope that uses convex lenses to focus light; **Objective**: large lens in a telescope or microscope that gathers and focuses light; **Eyepiece**: lens near the eye in a telescope or microscope that magnifies the image; **Reflecting telescope**: telescope that uses a concave mirror to gather light; **Microscope**: instrument that forms enlarged images of tiny objects using lenses; **Camera**: device that uses lenses to focus light on film to record an image; **Laser**: device that produces an intense beam of coherent light; **Hologram**: three-dimensional photograph created by a laser; **Optical fiber**: strand of glass or plastic that can carry light long distances; **Total internal reflection**: complete reflection of light by the inside surface of a medium

Preteach

Build Background Knowledge L2

Recalling How Binoculars Enlarge Objects
Most students will have experience with binoculars. Ask: **How do binoculars change what you see?** *(Sample answer: They make distant objects look bigger.)* Explain that binoculars have lenses that focus light, as do other devices they will read about.

Optical Instruments

Teach Key Concepts `L2`

Types of Optical Instruments

Focus Introduce the three common types of optical, or light-using, instruments: telescopes, microscopes, and cameras.

Teach Ask: **What are some uses of these optical instruments?** (*Sample answer: Telescopes make stars and planets look larger. Microscopes make tiny objects such as cells look larger and more detailed. Cameras record images on film.*) Explain that all three instruments work by gathering and focusing light using concave mirrors and/or concave or convex lenses. Briefly review how concave mirrors and convex lenses focus light rays.

Apply Tell students that a camera contains a convex lens that focuses images on film. Ask: **Are the images on film real or virtual? Why?** (*Real, because the images can be projected, are inverted, and are on the opposite side of the lens from the object being photographed*) **learning modality: verbal**

Use Visuals: Figure 22 `L2`

Refracting and Reflecting Telescopes

Focus Call students' attention to the figure. Point out the refracting telescope on the left and the reflecting telescope on the right.

Teach Review or ask students to define the terms *reflect* and *refract*. Then, ask: **Would you expect a reflecting telescope to use mirrors or lenses to gather light?** (*Mirrors*) **A refracting telescope?** (*Lenses*) In the figure, have students compare and contrast the two types of telescopes and note whether they contain mirrors and/or lenses.

Apply Ask: **What is the function of the lens in a reflecting telescope?** (*To focus the image from the mirrors*) **learning modality: visual**

All in One Teaching Resources

• Transparency O53

Independent Practice `L2`

All in One Teaching Resources

• Guided Reading and Study Worksheet: *Using Light*

🔘 **Student Edition on Audio CD**

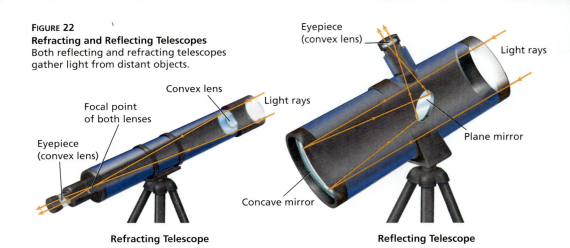

FIGURE 22
Refracting and Reflecting Telescopes
Both reflecting and refracting telescopes gather light from distant objects.

Refracting Telescope

Reflecting Telescope

Optical Instruments

A telescope helps you see objects that are far away. But another type of optical instrument, a microscope, helps you see objects that are nearby. Three common types of optical instruments are telescopes, microscopes, and cameras.

Telescopes Distant objects are difficult to see because light from them has spread out by the time it reaches your eyes. Your eyes are too small to gather much light. A **telescope** forms enlarged images of distant objects. **Telescopes use lenses or mirrors to collect and focus light from distant objects.** The most common use of telescopes is to study objects in space.

Figure 22 shows the two main types of telescopes: refracting telescopes and reflecting telescopes. A **refracting telescope** consists of two convex lenses, one at each end of a tube. The larger lens is called the objective. The **objective** gathers the light coming from an object and focuses the rays to form a real image. The lens close to your eye is called the eyepiece. The **eyepiece** magnifies the image so you can see it clearly. The image seen through the refracting telescope in Figure 22 is upside down.

A **reflecting telescope** uses a large concave mirror to gather light. The mirror collects light from distant objects and focuses the rays to form a real image. A small mirror inside the telescope reflects the image to the eyepiece. The images you see through a reflecting telescope are upside down, just like the images seen through a refracting telescope.

Lab zone Try This Activity

What a View!

You can use two hand lenses of different strengths to form an image.

1. Hold the stronger lens close to your eye.
2. Hold the other lens at arm's length.
3. Use your lens combination to view a distant object. **CAUTION:** *Do not look at the sun.* Adjust the distance of the farther lens until the image is clear.

Classifying What type of image do you see? What type of telescope is similar to this lens combination?

130 ◆ O

Lab zone Try This Activity

Skills Focus Classifying `L2`

Materials 2 hand lenses of different strengths

Time 10 minutes

Tips To determine which lens is stronger, students can look at a book or other object through the two hand lenses. Or, you may wish to use a burning candle or a flashlight bulb to help students form an image. Caution students not to look directly at the sun.

Expected Outcome The image is real, inverted, and smaller than the object. This combination of lenses is similar to a refracting telescope. **learning modality: kinesthetic**

Microscopes To look at small, nearby objects, you would use a microscope. A **microscope** is an optical instrument that forms enlarged images of tiny objects. **A microscope uses a combination of lenses to produce and magnify an image.** For example, the microscope shown in Figure 23 uses two convex lenses to magnify an object, or specimen. The specimen is placed near the objective. The objective forms a real, enlarged image of the specimen. Then the eyepiece enlarges the image even more.

Cameras A **camera** uses one or more lenses to focus light, and film to record an image. Figure 24 shows the structure of a camera. Light from an object travels to the camera and passes through the lens. **The lens of the camera focuses light to form a real, upside-down image on film in the back of the camera.** In many cameras, the lens automatically moves closer to or away from the film until the image is focused.

To take a photo, you press a button that briefly opens the shutter, a screen in front of the film. Opening the shutter allows light passing through the lens to hit the film. The diaphragm is a device with a hole that can be made smaller or larger. Changing the size of the hole controls how much light hits the film. This is similar to the way the pupil of your eye changes size.

 Reading Checkpoint What part of a camera controls the amount of light that enters the camera?

FIGURE 24
Camera
A camera uses a lens to project an image onto film. *Interpreting Diagrams* *What happens to each light ray as it passes through the lens?*

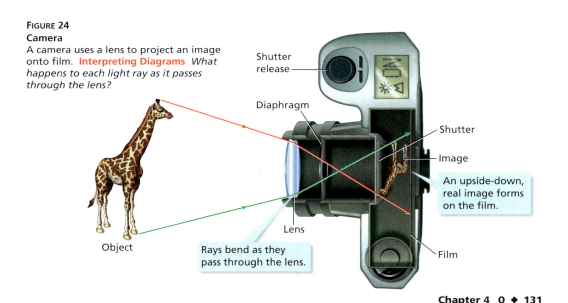

Shutter release

Diaphragm

Shutter

Image

An upside-down, real image forms on the film.

Lens

Film

Object

Rays bend as they pass through the lens.

FIGURE 23
Microscope
This microscope uses a combination of lenses to form enlarged images of tiny objects.

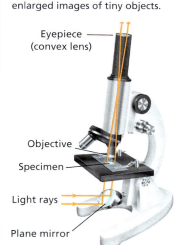

Eyepiece (convex lens)

Objective

Specimen

Light rays

Plane mirror

Chapter 4 O ◆ 131

Lasers

Teach Key Concepts L2

Introducing Laser Light

Focus Urge students to recall laser light swords and similar uses of laser light in movies and video games. Say that laser light is in fact used to cut human tissue in surgery and metals in industry.

Teach Define laser light. Explain how the word *laser* comes from the phrase *light amplification by stimulated emission of radiation.* Ask: **What do you think** *amplification* **means?** *(Sample answer: Strengthening)*

Apply Ask: **Why do you think laser light is so intense that it can cut tissues and metals?** *(Sample answer: Laser light has been strengthened.)* Have students read in the text about producing laser light to see how it is strengthened. **learning modality: verbal**

 Teacher **Demo**

Demonstrating Laser Light L2

Materials laser pointer, flashlight

Time 10 minutes

Focus After students have read the material on lasers, show them a laser pointer.

Teach Ask: **What will happen inside the pointer when I turn it on?** *(Sample answer: Electricity will cause the material inside to release photons.)* **How long will it take for the laser beam to emerge from the pointer?** *(From the description in the text, students may think it will take at least a few seconds.)* Turn on the laser pointer to test their predictions. *(The beam will emerge immediately.)* Shine the laser light on a spot across the room. Point out the color of the beam and how the beam does not spread out, even across long distances. Shine the flashlight across the room as well, and compare its beam, which is white, with the laser beam.

Apply Ask: **What might a laser light be better suited for than a flashlight?** *(Sample answer: Sending signals across long distances, focusing light energy on a small area)*
learning modality: visual

FIGURE 25
Coherent and Incoherent Light
White light is made up of many different wavelengths. Laser light waves all have the same wavelength.

Flashlight   **Laser**

Lasers

When you turn on a flashlight, the light spreads out as it travels. Ordinary light is made up of different colors and wavelengths. Laser light is different from ordinary light. **Laser light consists of light waves that all have the same wavelength, or color. The waves are coherent, or in step.** All of the crests of the waves align with one another, as shown in Figure 25.

What Is a Laser? A **laser** is a device that produces a narrow beam of coherent light. The word *laser* comes from a phrase that describes how it works: **l**ight **a**mplification by **s**timulated **e**mission of **r**adiation. *Light amplification* means that the light is strengthened. *Stimulated emission* means that the atoms emit light when exposed to electromagnetic radiation.

Producing Laser Light A helium-neon laser is shown in Figure 26. The laser tube contains a mixture of helium and neon gases. An electric current causes this gas mixture to emit photons. Recall from Chapter 3 that a photon is a packet of light energy. The mirrors at both ends of the tube reflect the photons back and forth. As a photon travels back and forth, it may bump into a neon particle. This causes the neon particle to emit a photon with the same energy as the one that caused the collision. Then the two photons travel together in step with one another. This process continues until there is a stream of in-step photons traveling up and down the tube. Some of the light "leaks" through the partially reflecting mirror. This light is the laser beam.

 What is a laser?

FIGURE 26
Helium-Neon Laser
Photons travel in step up and down the laser tube. The light that comes out of the tube is laser light.

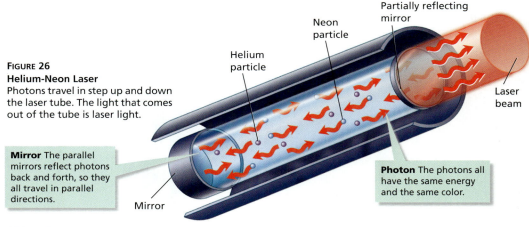

Mirror The parallel mirrors reflect photons back and forth, so they all travel in parallel directions.

Mirror

Helium particle

Neon particle

Partially reflecting mirror

Laser beam

Photon The photons all have the same energy and the same color.

Uses of Lasers

Lasers have many practical uses. Many stores use lasers to scan bar codes. The store's computer then displays the price of the item. Lasers are used in industry to cut through metal. Engineers use laser beams to make sure that surfaces are level and bridges or tunnels are properly aligned. **In addition to their use by stores, industry, and engineers, lasers are used to read information on compact discs, create holograms, and perform surgery.**

Go Online
SciLINKS NSTA

For: Links on lasers
Visit: www.SciLinks.org
Web Code: scn-1545

FIGURE 27
Using Lasers
Lasers are found at home, in stores, and in industry. **Applying Concepts** *How could you use a laser as a level to hang a picture?*

Scientists use laser scan microscopes to study cells.

▲ Lasers are used for precision cutting in industry.

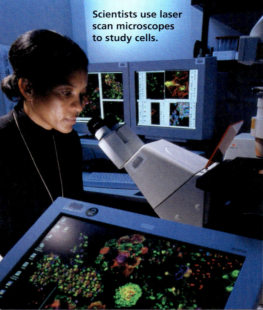

▼ Bar codes are scanned with lasers.

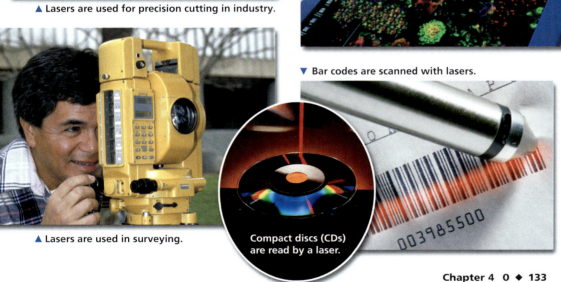
▲ Lasers are used in surveying.

Compact discs (CDs) are read by a laser.

003985500

Chapter 4 O ◆ 133

Uses of Lasers

Teach Key Concepts L2
Using Lasers

Focus State that lasers have many uses.

Teach Ask: **What are some ways that you regularly use lasers?** *(Sample answer: Playing compact discs, scanning barcodes)*

Apply Have students keep track of how many times a day they use lasers and report back to the class. **learning modality: verbal**

Lab zone **Build Inquiry** L2

Barcode Scanners

Materials several barcodes from product packages

Time 10 minutes

Focus Show students the barcodes.

Teach Explain that the black lines absorb the laser light, the white spaces reflect it, and the scanner recognizes the pattern of reflected light. Remind students that laser light consists of light of just one wavelength.

Apply Ask: **Why is laser light more useful for barcode scanners than white light?** *(White light includes light of many different wavelengths. If a scanner was set to pick up many different wavelengths, it might be affected by other light sources, such as the overhead lights.)* **learning modality: logical/mathematical**

Go Online
SciLINKS NSTA

For: Links on lasers
Visit: www.SciLinks.org
Web Code: scn-1545

Download a worksheet that will guide students' review of Internet resources on lasers.

Differentiated Instruction

Less Proficient Readers L1
Building Vocabulary List the following words on the board: *light, amplification, stimulated, emission, radiation*. Explain how the words are related to the term *laser*. Have students find a definition for each word in a dictionary and then rewrite the definition in their own words. Finally, have students use their definitions to define the term *laser* in their own words. **learning modality: verbal**

Gifted and Talented L3
Communicating Information Ask students to research and prepare an oral report on the uses of lasers in industry, construction, or engineering. Give students an opportunity to present their reports to the class. **learning modality: verbal**

Monitor Progress L2

Oral Presentation Call on students at random to state the uses of lasers.

Answers
Figure 25 Because a laser beam is coherent light, the beam of light forms a straight line.

Reading Checkpoint Device that produces a narrow beam of coherent light.

O ● 133

Discovery CHANNEL SCHOOL
Video Field Trip

Light

Show the Video Field Trip to let students experience how telescopes collect light to form images of distant objects. Discussion question: **What are the main differences between reflecting and refracting telescopes?** *(Sample answer: Reflecting telescopes have one or more mirrors that reflect light while refracting telescopes usually have two glass lenses. Reflecting telescopes can be much larger than refracting telescopes, because they use mirrors which do not weigh as much as similar-sized glass lenses.)*

Help Students Read　L1

Sequencing Have students read about compact discs on this page. Then, guide them in making two flowcharts, one showing how a compact disc is made and the other showing how a compact disc is read. *(Steps in making a compact disc include: Data are converted to electrical signals; the signals control a laser beam; the laser beam cuts a pattern of pits in a blank disc. Steps in reading a compact disc include: A laser beam shines on the surface of a disc; the laser beam is reflected; the reflection patterns are converted into electrical signals; the signals are converted into sound or data.)*

Lab zone Teacher **Demo**

Observing Holograms　L1

Materials examples of holograms from books, magazines, and other products

Time 10 minutes

Focus Show the class examples of holograms.

Teach Tell students that most holograms they see are reflection holograms, because they can be viewed in ordinary white light. Ask: **How can you alter the way a hologram looks?** *(Sample answer: By tilting it or viewing it from an angle)*

Apply Ask: **Why do think holograms appear to move when you look at them from different angles?** *(Sample answer: Light strikes the uneven surface at different angles.)*

learning modality: visual

Discovery CHANNEL SCHOOL

Light
Video Preview
▶ Video Field Trip
Video Assessment

Compact Discs Lasers can be used to store and read information. A compact disc is produced by converting data into electrical signals. The electrical signals are used to control a laser beam, which cuts a pattern of pits on a blank disc. When you play a compact disc or read one with a computer, a laser beam shines on the surface and is reflected. The reflection patterns vary because of the pits. The compact disc player or disc drive changes these patterns into electrical signals. The signals are then converted into sound or computer data.

Holography Check out your local video store or newsstand. Some videos and magazines have pictures that appear to move as you walk by. These pictures are called holograms. A **hologram** is a three-dimensional photograph created by using the light from a laser. The process of making these photographs is called holography.

• Tech & Design in History •

Instruments That Use Light
The development of technologies that use light has changed the way we look at the world and beyond. It has allowed major scientific discoveries.

1595 Microscope
The first useful microscope is thought to have been constructed in the Netherlands by Zacharias Jansen or his father, Hans. The Jansen microscope could magnify images up to nine times the size of the object. By the mid-1600s, microscopes looked like the one shown here.

1286 Spectacles
Italian craftsmen made small disks of glass that could be framed and worn in front of the eyes. Early spectacles consisted of convex lenses. They were used as reading glasses.

1608 Telescope
The first telescope was made of two convex lenses. From this simple invention the Italian scientist Galileo developed his more powerful telescopes shown here.

| 1300 | 1400 | 1500 | 1600 |

134 ◆ O

Background

History of Science In 1953, an American scientist named Charles Townes and two colleagues produced the first device to amplify microwave radiation. They called it a *masar*, which stood for "microwave amplification by stimulated emission of radiation." In 1958, Townes and another American scientist, A.L. Schawlow, showed that it was possible to make a similar device that used light. The first successful laser was operated in 1960 by Theodore Maiman, an American physicist who had heard of Townes and Schawlow's maser. In 1964, Townes and two Russian physicists (who had proposed related ideas independently) were awarded the Nobel Prize in Physics for their work in developing lasers.

Laser Surgery A beam of laser light can be powerful enough to replace a sharp knife. For example, doctors may use lasers instead of scalpels to cut into a person's body. As the laser cuts, it seals the blood vessels. This reduces the amount of blood a patient loses. Wounds from laser surgery usually heal faster than wounds from surgery done with a scalpel.

A common use of laser surgery is to correct vision by reshaping the cornea of the eye. Doctors can also use lasers to repair detached retinas. If the retina falls away from the inside of the eye, the rods and cones can no longer send signals to the brain. This can lead to total or partial blindness. The doctor can use a laser to "weld" or burn the retina back onto the eyeball. Lasers can also be used to destroy or remove skin blemishes and cancerous growths.

 Reading Checkpoint What are three types of surgery done with lasers?

Writing in Science

Research and Write Find out more about early photography. Then imagine you are a newspaper reporter in 1855 asked to interview a photographer. Write a newspaper article about the photographic processes and the possible uses it might have in the future.

1826 Camera
The earliest camera, the pinhole camera, was adapted to form and record permanent images by Joseph Nicéphore Niépce and Louis-Jacques-Mandé Daguerre of France. This is one of Niépce's earliest photographic images.

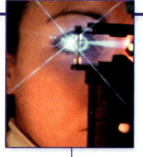

1960 Laser
The first laser, built by American Theodore Maiman, used a rod of ruby to produce light. Since then, lasers have been used in numerous ways, including in engineering, medicine, and communications.

1990 Hubble Space Telescope
This large reflecting telescope was launched by the crew of the space shuttle *Discovery*. It can detect infrared, visible, and ultraviolet rays in space and send pictures back to Earth.

1700	1800	1900	2000

Chapter 4 0 ◆ 135

Focus Point out that the timeline covers a period of 700 years, from A.D. 1300 to A.D. 2000.

Teach Tell students that only some of the important developments in the history of instruments that use light are included in the time line because of the long time span covered. Many other discoveries were made during this time period. For example, cameras developed from the earliest, pinhole cameras to the complex digital cameras of today. Have students read about the earliest camera. Then, ask: **For how many years have cameras been undergoing improvements, from the earliest camera to the present?** *(About 180 years)* Also, tell students that some optical instruments were advanced by developments in other areas. Ask: **Based on information in the time line, how was the Hubble Space Telescope advanced by developments in another area of technology?** *(Launching the telescope depended on the development of the space shuttle.)* **learning modality: verbal**

Writing in Science

Writing Mode Research

Scoring Rubric
4 Exceeds criteria; contains an abundance of historical information and information on the photographic process and/or is written in an engaging style
3 Meets criteria
2 Meets some but not all criteria
1 Has little historical information or information on the photographic process and/or is poorly written

Background

Integrating Science Photorefractive keratectomy, or PRK, is a type of laser surgery used to correct nearsightedness. PRK can be carried out in the office of a specially trained ophthalmologist. The surgery involves a computer-guided laser that makes extremely precise alterations to the shape of the cornea. The newly shaped cornea changes the refraction of light entering the eye so it focuses on the retina. Many formerly nearsighted individuals have obtained perfect or near-perfect vision with the surgery. However, there may be complications, including hazing or scarring of the cornea, over- or under-correction of the refraction error, or infection. The surgery is still too new for its long-term effects to be known.

Monitor Progress L2

Oral Presentation Call on students to describe several different uses of lasers.

Answer

Reading Checkpoint Three types of surgery done with lasers are reshaping the cornea of the eye to correct vision, repairing detached retinas, and destroying or removing skin blemishes and cancerous growths.

Optical Fibers

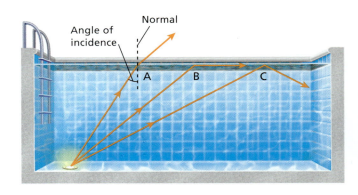

FIGURE 28
Total Internal Reflection
The floodlight in the swimming pool gives off light rays that travel to the surface. If the angle of incidence is great enough, a light ray is completely reflected back into the water.

Optical Fibers

Laser beams, like radio waves, can carry signals from one place to another. But, laser beams are not usually sent through the air. Instead, they are sent through optical fibers. **Optical fibers** are long, thin strands of glass or plastic that can carry light for long distances without allowing the light to escape.

Optical fibers can carry a laser beam for long distances because the beam stays totally inside the fiber as it travels. Figure 28 shows how light rays can stay inside a medium and not pass through the surface to the outside. The angle of incidence determines whether or not light passes through the surface.

When ray A strikes the water's surface, some light is reflected, but most passes through and is bent. As the angle of incidence gets larger, the light is bent more and more. Ray B is bent so much that it travels parallel to the surface. If the angle of incidence is great enough, no light passes through the surface. Then all of the light is reflected back into the water, as shown by ray C. This complete reflection of light by the inside surface of a medium is called **total internal reflection.**

Figure 29 shows how total internal reflection allows light to travel a long distance in an optical fiber. Each time the light ray strikes the side of the optical fiber, the angle of incidence is large. Because the angle is large, the light ray is always completely reflected. So, no light can escape through the sides of the optical fiber.

Because the angle of incidence is large, all of the laser light reflects each time it strikes the edge of the optical fiber.

FIGURE 29
Optical Fibers
Light travels long distances through optical fibers. **Drawing Conclusions** *Why doesn't light exit through the sides of the optical fiber?*

136 ◆ O

Medicine Optical fibers are commonly used in medical instruments. Doctors can insert a thin optical fiber inside various parts of the body, such as the heart or the stomach. The optical fiber can be attached to a microscope or a camera. In this way, doctors can examine internal organs without having to perform major surgery.

Doctors often use optical fibers to repair damage to joints. In knee surgery, for example, doctors make small cuts to insert optical fibers and tiny surgical tools. Because the surgery does less damage to the knee, the recovery is easier.

Communications To send signals through optical fibers, the electrical signals that start out over copper wires are changed into pulses of light by tiny lasers. Then the signals can travel over long distances in the optical fiber. Optical fibers have led to great improvements in telephone service, computer networks, and cable television systems. Signals sent over optical fibers are usually faster and clearer than those sent over copper wire. One tiny optical fiber can carry thousands of phone conversations at the same time. Optical fibers are so much thinner than copper wire that many more fibers can be bundled together in the same space.

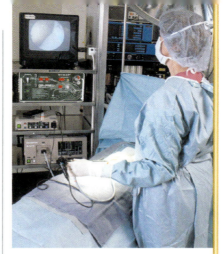

FIGURE 30
Optical-Fiber Surgery
Using optical fibers, surgeons can avoid damaging nearby healthy parts of the body.

 Reading Checkpoint How do optical fibers carry signals?

Target Reading Skill **Building Vocabulary** Use your definitions to help you answer the questions below.

Reviewing Key Concepts

1. a. Reviewing How are lenses used in telescopes, microscopes, and cameras?
 b. Comparing and Contrasting Compare and contrast how images form in a refracting telescope, a reflecting telescope, and a microscope.
 c. Classifying A pair of binoculars has two lenses in each tube. Which type of optical instrument are the binoculars most similar to?
2. a. Identifying What is laser light?
 b. Summarizing How can laser light be used?
 c. Sequencing How does a laser produce laser light?

3. a. Defining What are optical fibers?
 b. Describing What are three uses of optical fibers?
 c. Relating Cause and Effect Why can optical fibers carry laser beams long distances?

Writing in Science

Advertisement A company has asked you to write an advertisement for its new, easy-to-use camera. In the ad, the company wants you to describe the camera's features so that buyers will understand how the camera works. Be sure to mention the shutter, lens, and diaphragm.

Chapter 4 O ◆ 137

Keep Students on Track As students test their optical instruments, guide them in identifying problems and making any necessary changes. Check that their instruments do what they are supposed to do, that adjustments can be made to change the focus, and that any moving parts move smoothly and easily. Advise students to keep a record of any changes they make and refer to it when they prepare their presentation.

Writing in Science

Writing Mode Persuasion
Scoring Rubric
4 Exceeds criteria; includes a clear, concise explanation that correctly uses all three terms
3 Meets criteria
2 Includes an explanation that contains some errors and/or incorrectly uses some of the terms
1 Includes a general description only and/or fails to use or incorrectly uses at least two of the terms

Answers
Figure 29 Because the angle of incidence is large enough at each reflection for all the light to be reflected back into the fiber

Reading Checkpoint Electrical signals are changed into pulses of laser light, and optical fibers carry the light long distances.

Assess

Reviewing Key Concepts

1. a. Telescopes use lenses or mirrors to collect and focus light from distant objects; microscopes use lenses to produce and magnify images of nearby objects; cameras use lenses to focus light and form images on film. **b.** All three produce inverted images and use an eyepiece. A refracting telescope uses a second lens to gather light, and a reflecting telescope uses mirrors. Both types of telescopes focus on large distant objects, whereas a microscope focuses on tiny nearby objects. **c.** Refracting telescope
2. a. Coherent light waves that all have the same wavelength, or color **b.** To scan barcodes, cut through metal, ensure surfaces are level, read compact discs, and perform surgery **c.** Electric current causes gases in the laser tube to emit photons. Mirrors reflect the photons back and forth. The photons bump neon particles and cause them to emit more photons, which are in-step with the others. Some of the in-step photons "leak out" of the tube to form the laser beam.
3. a. Long, thin strands of glass or plastic that can carry light for long distances without allowing the light to escape **b.** Examine internal organs, perform surgery, transmit signals **c.** Because total internal reflection keeps the beams inside the fibers.

Reteach **L1**
Call on students to explain how each key term in the section is related to light.

Performance Assessment **L2**
Writing Have students explain how one of the optical instruments in the section uses light.

All in One Teaching Resources
• Section Summary: *Using Light*
• Review and Reinforcement: *Using Light*
• Enrich: *Using Light*

Interactive Textbook

- Complete student edition
- Section and chapter self-assessment
- Assessment reports for teachers

Help Students Read

Building Vocabulary

Word/Part Analysis Help students understand key terms containing the word part *fract-*. Tell them that *fract-* comes from a Latin verb meaning "to break." Explain that when refraction occurs, a straight ray of light "breaks," or bends. Ask: **In addition to refraction, which key terms contain *fract-*?** (*Diffraction, refracting telescope, index of refraction*) Challenge students to relate each of these key terms to the meaning of *fract-*.

Paraphrasing Have students rewrite, in their own words, the paragraph in Section 5, under the heading *Producing Laser Light*, that describes how laser light is produced. Tell them to try to make the paragraph shorter and more concise by expressing the main ideas in simpler terms and by deleting some of the details.

Connecting Concepts

Concept Maps Help students develop one way to show how the information in this chapter is related. Light gives objects their color; can be reflected by mirrors and refracted by lenses to create images; is perceived by the eye; and is used in instruments such as telescopes, microscopes, and lasers. Have students brainstorm to identify the key concepts, key terms, details, and examples. Then, write each one on a self-sticking note and attach it at random on chart paper or on the board.

Tell students that this concept map will be organized in hierarchical order and to begin at the top with the key concepts. Ask students these questions to guide them to categorize the information on the self-sticking notes: **How is light related to the color of objects? How do mirrors and lenses produce images? What is the role of the eye in vision? What are optical instruments,**

and how do they use light? Prompt students to use connecting words or phrases, such as "cause," "can be," "are characterized by," and "include," to indicate the basis for the connections in the map. The phrases should form a sentence between or among a set of concepts.

① Light and Color

Key Concepts

- When light strikes an object, the light can be reflected, transmitted, or absorbed.
- An opaque object is the color of the light it reflects. A transparent or translucent object is the color of the light it transmits.
- When combined in equal amounts, the three primary colors of light produce white light. As pigments are added together, fewer colors of light are reflected and more are absorbed.

Key Terms

transparent material	secondary color
translucent material	complementary colors
opaque material	pigment
primary colors	

② Reflection and Mirrors

Key Concepts

- There are two types of reflection—regular reflection and diffuse reflection.
- A plane mirror produces a virtual image that is upright and the same size as the object.
- Concave mirrors form virtual or real images. Convex mirrors form only virtual images.

Key Terms

ray	concave mirror
regular reflection	optical axis
diffuse reflection	focal point
plane mirror	real image
image	convex mirror
virtual image	

③ Refraction and Lenses

Key Concepts

- A convex lens can form virtual images or real images. A concave lens can produce only virtual images.

Key Terms

index of refraction	convex lens
mirage	concave lens
lens	

138 ◆ O

④ Seeing Light

Key Concepts

- You see objects when a process occurs that involves both your eyes and your brain.
- Convex lenses are used to correct near-sightedness. Concave lenses are used to correct farsightedness.

Key Terms

cornea	retina	optic nerve
pupil	rods	nearsighted
iris	cones	farsighted

⑤ Using Light

Key Concepts

- Telescopes use lenses or mirrors to collect and focus light from distant objects. A microscope uses a combination of lenses to produce and magnify an image. The lens of a camera focuses light to form a real, upside-down image on film in the back of the camera.
- Laser light consists of light waves that all have the same wavelength, or color. The waves are coherent, or in step.
- In addition to their use by stores, industry, and engineers, lasers are used to read information on compact discs, create holograms, and perform surgery.
- Optical fibers can carry a laser beam for long distances because the beam stays totally inside the fiber as it travels.

Key Terms

telescope	camera
refracting telescope	laser
objective	hologram
eyepiece	optical fiber
reflecting telescope	total internal reflection
microscope	

Answer Accept logical presentations by students.

![All in One] **Teaching Resources**

- Key Terms Review: *Light*
- Connecting Concepts: *Light*

Review and Assessment

Organizing Information

Comparing and Contrasting
Copy the graphic organizer about mirrors and lenses onto a separate sheet of paper. Then complete it and add a title. (For more on Comparing and Contrasting, see the Skills Handbook.)

Mirrors and Lenses

Type of Mirror	Effect on Light Rays	Type of Image
Plane	Regular reflection	a. ___?___
b. ___?___	c. ___?___	Real or virtual
Convex	Spread out	d. ___?___

Type of Lens	Effect on Light Rays	Type of Image
Convex	e. ___?___	f. ___?___
g. ___?___	h. ___?___	Virtual

Reviewing Key Terms

Choose the letter of the best answer.

1. A material that reflects or absorbs all of the light that strikes it is a(n)
   a. translucent material.
   b. opaque material.
   c. transparent material.
   d. polarizing filter.

2. When light bounces off an uneven surface, the result is called
   a. regular reflection.
   b. refraction.
   c. diffuse reflection.
   d. internal reflection.

3. A curved piece of glass or other transparent material that is used to refract light is a
   a. prism.   b. lens.
   c. mirage.   d. mirror.

4. A ring of muscle that changes the size of the eye's pupil is the
   a. retina.
   b. cornea.
   c. iris.
   d. ciliary muscle.

5. A device that produces coherent light is a(n)
   a. telescope.
   b. microscope.
   c. laser.
   d. optical fiber.

If the statement is true, write _true_. If it is false, change the underlined word or words to make the statement true.

6. <u>Primary colors</u> combine to make any color.

7. Lines that represent light waves are called <u>rays</u>.

8. An upright image that forms where light seems to come from is a <u>virtual</u> image.

9. For a <u>nearsighted</u> person, nearby objects appear blurry.

10. <u>Holograms</u> are long, thin strands of glass or plastic that can carry light for long distances.

Writing in Science

Persuasive Letter Write a short letter to your representative in Congress asking him or her to continue supporting telescopes in space. Include at least two advantages of space telescopes in your letter.

	Light
	Video Preview
	Video Field Trip
	▶ Video Assessment

Chapter 4 O ◆ 139

Review and Assessment

Organizing Information
a. Virtual
b. Concave
c. Converge or meet
d. Virtual
e. Converge, or meet
f. Real or virtual
g. Concave
h. Spread out

Reviewing Key Terms
1. b 2. c 3. b 4. c 5. c
6. True
7. True
8. True
9. farsighted
10. Optical fibers

Writing in Science

Writing Mode Persuasion

Scoring Rubric
4 Exceeds criteria
3 Meets criteria
2 Includes a weak argument and/or gives only one advantage of space telescopes
1 Fails to make an argument and/or give advantages of space telescopes

Video Assessment

Light

Show the Video Assessment to review chapter content. Discussion question: **What phenomena on Earth affect the images produced by conventional telescopes?** (*Water vapor, dust, heat, and other things in Earth's atmosphere can all distort light that reaches telescopes on Earth. Light pollution on Earth can also reduce clarity of a telescope image.*) **Why can the Hubble Space Telescope produce sharper images than earthbound telescopes?** (*Because it orbits 600 km above Earth's surface, it can provide images that are free from atmospheric distortion.*)

Go Online
PHSchool.com
For: Take a practice test
Visit: PHSchool.com
Web Code: cga-5040

Students can take a practice test online that is automatically scored.

All in One Teaching Resources
- Transparency O55
- Chapter Test
- Performance Assessment Teacher Notes
- Performance Assessment Student Worksheet
- Performance Assessment Scoring Rubric

 ExamView® Computer Test Bank CD-ROM

Checking Concepts

11. Transparent materials, such as clear glass, transmit light. Translucent materials, such as frosted glass, transmit and scatter light. Opaque materials, such as wood, reflect and/or absorb light but do not transmit light.

12. Rose petals reflect red light and absorb light of all other colors. The leaves reflect green light and absorb light of all other colors.

13. Complementary colors of light can be combined to form white light.

14. Students' diagrams should correctly identify the type of mirror and the location of the focal point and optical axis. The optical axis should divide the mirror into a top and bottom half. The focal point should be on the optical axis. It is in front of a concave mirror and behind a convex mirror.

15. Real images are upside-down images that form where rays of light meet. They are produced by concave mirrors when the object is beyond the focal point. Virtual images are upright images that form where rays of light appear to meet. They are produced by plane mirrors, convex mirrors, and concave mirrors (in the latter, only when the object is closer than the focal point).

16. The index of refraction is higher in materials in which light travels more slowly.

17. As light rays move through hot air, they are bent upward and appear as though they are coming from the surface of the road.

18. The cornea and lens help focus light. The rods and cones in the retina send signals to the brain along the optic nerve.

19. The ciliary muscles relax or contract to change the shape of the lens. The lens is made thicker to focus on near objects, and it is made thinner to focus on distant objects.

20. Light rays are totally reflected off the internal surface of a medium if the angle of incidence is great enough.

Checking Concepts

11. Describe transparent, translucent, and opaque materials. Give an example of each.

12. Why do you see the petals of a rose as red and the leaves as green?

13. What colors can be formed by combining complementary colors?

14. Sketch the optical axis and focal point(s) of a concave mirror and a convex mirror.

15. Describe real and virtual images. How can each type of image be formed by mirrors?

16. How is the index of refraction of a substance related to the speed of light in the substance?

17. Explain why you see a mirage on a hot road.

18. Which parts of the eye help to focus light? Which part carries a signal to the brain?

19. Explain how your eyes are able to clearly see both near and distant objects.

20. How does total internal reflection depend on the angle of incidence of light rays?

Thinking Critically

21. Classifying Do the colors shown below represent pigments or colors of light? Explain.

22. Applying Concepts Can a plane mirror produce a real image? Explain.

23. Comparing and Contrasting How are convex and concave mirrors alike? How are they different?

24. Inferring You shine a light through a convex lens so it forms a spot on an index card. Where should the lens and card be located to make the spot as small as possible?

25. Relating Cause and Effect Explain why your eyes can only see shades of gray in dim light.

26. Problem Solving A telescope produces an upside-down image. How could you modify the telescope so the image is upright?

27. Comparing and Contrasting How is a microscope similar to a convex lens used as a magnifying lens? How is it different?

28. Making Generalizations Why is laser light never white?

Applying Skills

Use the diagram to answer Questions 29–31.

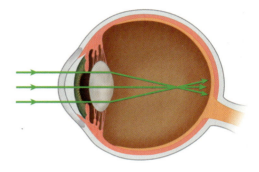

29. Classifying Which type of vision problem does this eye have?

30. Problem Solving What type of lens can correct this vision problem?

31. Communicating Copy the diagram above on a separate sheet of paper. Add a correcting lens to your diagram and show how the lens makes the three rays focus on the retina.

Lab zone Chapter **Project**

Performance Assessment Demonstrate your optical instrument to your class. Explain how your instrument works and how it can be used. Use diagrams that show how the mirrors or lenses in your instrument reflect or refract light.

Lab zone Chapter **Project**

Performance Assessment
Give students an opportunity to demonstrate their optical instruments to the class. Have them explain how their instruments work. Tell them to use diagrams to show how light is reflected and refracted by mirrors and lenses in their instruments.

Ask students to identify ways their instruments could be used. They might compare their instruments to those they have read about in the text. Urge them to explain their design process and to identify ways they improved their instruments or ways it might be improved.

Standardized Test Prep

Choose the letter of the best answer.

1. The index of refraction for water is 1.33 and for glass is 1.5. When light moves from glass into water, the speed of light
   A increases.
   B decreases.
   C remains the same.
   D depends on the angle of incidence.

2. A convex lens can produce a real or a virtual image. Which type of mirror is most similar to a convex lens?
   F plane mirror
   G convex mirror
   H concave mirror
   J none of the above

Periscope

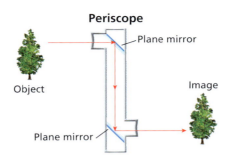

Use the diagram above and your knowledge of science to answer Question 3.

3. If you want to build a periscope, what measurement is most important?
   A the angle between the two mirrors
   B the distance between the mirrors
   C the width of the mirrors
   D the width of the tube

4. A friend hypothesizes that a periscope produces an upright image that reverses left and right. How could you test this hypothesis?
   F Test A: Draw a ray diagram to determine the type of image that is produced.
   G Test B: Look at your friend through the periscope to see if her image is upright.
   H Test C: Look at your friend through the periscope and ask her to move her right hand. Observe which hand (left or right) is moving in the image.
   J Conduct both Test B and Test C.

5. You view an American flag through sunglasses that are tinted green. What colors do you see?
   A green
   B black
   C green and black
   D red and blue

Constructed Response

6. How is a camera like a human eye? Give the function of each part of a camera and identify the part of the eye that has the same function. Use the following terms in your answer: *lens, diaphragm, film, cornea, pupil,* and *retina*.

Thinking Critically
21. The colors represent colors of light, because red and green light combine to form yellow light.

22. No; the image is always virtual, because a plane mirror cannot focus light rays.

23. Both types of mirrors have shiny surfaces, an optical axis, and a focal point; both can produce virtual images. Concave mirrors can produce real images as well, but convex mirrors cannot. Concave mirrors are curved inward, whereas convex mirrors are curved outward.

24. The lens and card should be located as far from the light as possible.

25. Rods, which allow you to see in dim light, are not sensitive to color. Cones, which are sensitive to color, are not effective in dim light.

26. You could add another convex lens to invert the image again.

27. Both can form enlarged images and are focused by moving a lens. However, magnification can be changed in a microscope by changing objectives. Microscopes also can have much higher magnification.

28. Laser light is never white because it consists of light of just one wavelength, whereas white light consists of light of many different wavelengths.

Applying Skills
29. Nearsightedness

30. Concave lens

31. Students' diagrams should show how a concave lens spreads out the rays of light before they pass into the eye. The light passing through the lens of the eye should focus on the retina.

Standardized Test Prep

1. A **2.** H **3.** A **4.** J **5.** C
6. Light enters the camera through the lens, which focuses light like the cornea and lens of the eye. The camera's diaphragm, like the eye's pupil, can change in size to control the amount of light that enters. An image forms on the film at the back of a camera, similar to the way an image forms on the retina at the back of the eye.

Interdisciplinary Exploration

The Magic of the Movies

This interdisciplinary feature presents the central theme of motion pictures by connecting four different disciplines: language arts, science, mathematics, and social studies. The four explorations are designed to capture students' interest and help them see how the content they are studying in science relates to other school subjects and to real-world events. Share the unit with others for a team-teaching experience.

All in One Teaching Resources

- Interdisciplinary Exploration: *Language Arts*
- Interdisciplinary Exploration: *Science*
- Interdisciplinary Exploration: *Mathematics*
- Interdisciplinary Exploration: *Social Studies*

Build Background Knowledge

How Movie Cameras Work

Help students recall what they learned about cameras in the chapter on Light by asking questions such as: **What is the purpose of the lens in a movie camera?** (*The lens forms an image on film by refracting light.*) **What does the shutter in a movie camera do?** (*It allows light to expose the film for a brief amount of time.*) State that most movies are filmed at a rate of 24 exposures per second. Ask: **What does that tell you about the shutter?** (*The shutter opens to expose 24 frames of film every second.*)

Introduce the Exploration

Ask: **In what ways do movie makers need to be aware of sound and light?** (*Accept all reasonable answers. Sample answers: Actors must speak loudly and clearly enough for the sound waves to be recorded. Sound engineers must make sure that unwanted background sounds are not recorded and that background sounds added later match the actions the audience sees. Light engineers have to provide light that allows the scene to be visible but also fits the place and time in which the action takes place. Makeup artists must know how bright lights make actors appear on film.*)

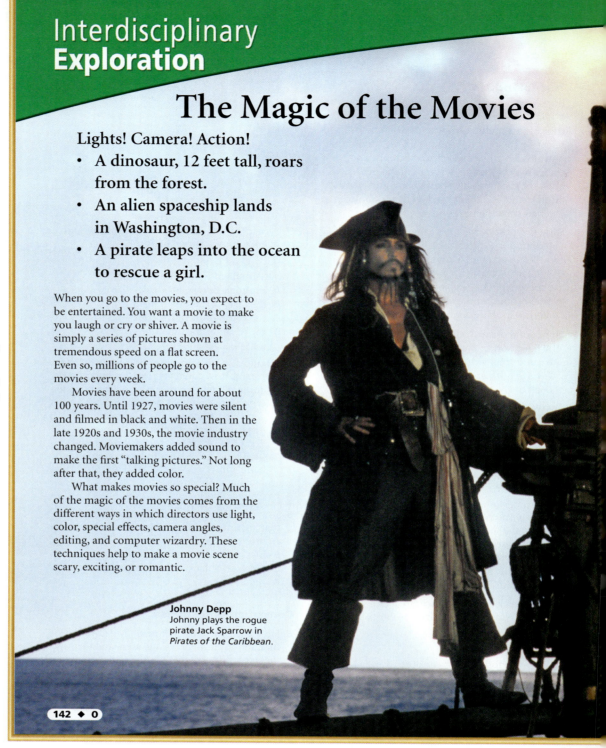

Interdisciplinary Exploration

The Magic of the Movies

Lights! Camera! Action!

- A dinosaur, 12 feet tall, roars from the forest.
- An alien spaceship lands in Washington, D.C.
- A pirate leaps into the ocean to rescue a girl.

When you go to the movies, you expect to be entertained. You want a movie to make you laugh or cry or shiver. A movie is simply a series of pictures shown at tremendous speed on a flat screen. Even so, millions of people go to the movies every week.

Movies have been around for about 100 years. Until 1927, movies were silent and filmed in black and white. Then in the late 1920s and 1930s, the movie industry changed. Moviemakers added sound to make the first "talking pictures." Not long after that, they added color.

What makes movies so special? Much of the magic of the movies comes from the different ways in which directors use light, color, special effects, camera angles, editing, and computer wizardry. These techniques help to make a movie scene scary, exciting, or romantic.

Johnny Depp
Johnny plays the rogue pirate Jack Sparrow in *Pirates of the Caribbean*.

Language Arts

On Board the *Black Pearl*
Here camera operators film Orlando Bloom, playing the part of Will Turner.

Choosing a Point of View

A screenwriter writes the script, or story, for a movie from one or more distinct points of view. For example, when a movie tells a story from the point of view of one main character, the audience shares that character's thoughts and feelings.

Often, the point of view shifts from one character to another in a film. In the movie *Pirates of the Caribbean: The Curse of the Black Pearl*, for instance, the story is told by alternating the point of view of three characters. They are Elizabeth Swann, the governor's daughter; Will Turner, the blacksmith; and Jack Sparrow, the pirate.

When Elizabeth is kidnapped by pirates of the ship named the *Black Pearl*, Jack leads Will on a treacherous journey to rescue her. Each of these three main characters encounters different challenges and obstacles. The "camera" follows the progress of one character for a few minutes, then shifts to follow another. Alternating these three points of view allows the audience to understand the very different experiences of each character.

The director and the film editor decide what the audience will see in each frame of the movie and which point of view will be portrayed. In choosing the point of view, the director plans the actions and conversations that will make viewers like or admire certain characters and not like others. The director and film editor skillfully weave the plot through the point of view.

Language Arts Activity

Think of a story or book you have read that you would like to see as a movie. In one or two paragraphs, write a summary of the movie plot. Then choose the point of view you will use in the movie. Explain why you chose that point of view.

O ◆ 143

Background

Facts and Figures Making a movie requires the skills of many different people. The producer of a movie finds investors to pay for the movie's production. The producer also arranges for the movie to be distributed when it is finished.

The screenwriter describes in a script what the audience will see and hear. If the movie is based on a book, the screenwriter may or may not be the author of the book. During

production, the director and other personnel may make changes in the script.

The director visualizes how best to make the movie and guides the team to create a product that matches the director's vision of the finished work. Assistant directors arrange for the cast, set, and props to be in place at the right time according to the shooting schedule. Casting directors select and hire actors for the different roles.

Language Arts

Explore Language Arts Concepts

Compare and Contrast Ask students to think of a movie they have seen that is based on a book they have read. (Examples might include movies based on the novels of Stephen King or Michael Crichton.) Ask **How does the movie differ from the book?** *(Sample answers: The movie deletes scenes or characters that are in the book. The movie seems more real or believable than the book.)* **Which tells a story better, a movie or a book?** *(Some students might prefer the greater depth of a story in a book or the way a book allows the thoughts and feelings of a character to be described. Other students might prefer the graphic portrayal of a story or the characters in a movie.)*

Extend Tell students that the point of view of a movie can be changed by changing the camera angle. Show a short scene from a G-rated movie in which the camera angle shifts several times. Have students identify when and how the point of view shifts during the scene.

Language Arts Activity

Focus Help students appreciate the significance of point of view in how a story is told. Have them consider situations in which there is a clear difference in point of view, such as a school (student and teacher) or prison (prisoner and guard).

Teach If students have difficulty summarizing the plot advise them to describe fully what happens in the book and then reduce the length by deleting less important details or side plots.

Scoring Rubric
4 Exceeds criteria; includes a concise, engaging, and complete summary and a convincing explanation for choice of point of view
3 Meets criteria
2 Includes a summary and an explanation for choice of point of view but contains some errors
1 Includes an inadequate summary and/or does not explain choice of point of view

Explore Science Concepts

Discuss Explain that a motion picture is not displayed continuously. It actually flickers on and off, as each new frame is shown, 24 times a second. This is faster than the brain can comprehend, so we perceive the different frames as continuous motion. If we were able to register the individual frames that quickly, we would see a constant flicker, as one frame after another came into view. Ask students whether they have seen some of the earliest movies. If so, they may recall noticing that the movies flickered because the frame rate was slower.

Demonstrate Bring a "flip book" to class, or ask students to bring them for other students to see. By looking at the picture on each page of the book, students can see how similar one image is to the next. By flipping the pages, they can see how rapidly changing images appear as continuous motion.

Science Activity

Materials white paper, scissors, metric ruler, black construction paper, tape, record player or Lazy Susan

Focus Have students look at the illustration of the zoetrope. Tell students that a zoetrope is like a flip book. It is a way to show a series of images very rapidly.

Teach Ask students to read through the procedure, which explains how to make a zoetrope. Call their attention to the illustration at the bottom of the page, which shows them how to draw a series of images. Ask: **Why should the last image be almost the same as the first?** (*So the picture will not appear to jump between the last image and the first image when the zoetrope is rotated*) Make sure students use a ruler when they draw the images so that all the images are the same size and are equally spaced. Tell students that the taped white strip should fit inside the taped black construction paper and slide to the bottom, as in the illustration.

Expected Outcome When students look through the slits of the rotating zoetrope, the image should appear to be moving continuously from one drawing to the next.

How Pictures Seem to Move

The movie opens. The film rolls, and the action begins. What is happening? A movie is a fast-moving series of small photographs projected onto a screen. The pictures appear so fast—at about 24 pictures per second—that your eyes blend them together in continuous motion. But your eyes are tricking you. You are seeing an optical illusion.

When you watch a movie, your eyes see each picture for just a fraction of a second. Then the picture is replaced by the next one. The pictures move so fast that even when one image is gone, your brain continues to see it. Seeing this after-image is called "persistence of vision." It creates the illusion of motion.

Many discoveries and inventions in the 1800s combined to make the first motion picture. For example, in 1834, a toy called a zoetrope was invented. The zoetrope contained pictures inside a drumlike device with slits. People could spin the drum while looking through the slits. The motion of the zoetrope made the pictures appear to move.

By the late 1800s, American inventor Thomas Edison was working on a movie camera. It used a plastic called celluloid to coat film. Edison made the film 35 millimeters wide, a width still used today. In the late 1920s, moviemakers added another strip to the film that gave sound to movies.

Science Activity

Make your own moving picture by building a zoetrope.

- Cut a strip of white paper 45.5 cm by 7.5 cm. Mark the strip to make 8 equal picture frames.
- Near the center of the first frame, draw a picture. Your picture should be a simple outline of an object such as an animal or person.
- Draw your object again in the second frame, but change its position slightly. Repeat the step until you have drawn the object in every frame. Remember to change its position a bit each time, as shown in the illustration below.
- Cut a piece of black construction paper to measure 45.5 cm by 15 cm.
- Mark 8 vertical slits on the top half of the black paper, each 5.5 cm apart. Cut the slits, making each 4 mm wide and 7.5 cm deep.

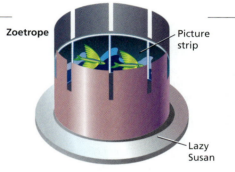

Zoetrope / Picture strip / Lazy Susan

- Tape the black paper into a circle with the slits on top.
- Tape the picture strip into a circle with the pictures on the inside. Slide the strip inside the black circle to create your zoetrope.
- Place your zoetrope on a record player or Lazy Susan. Center it. Look through the slits as you spin the zoetrope. What do you see?

Background

Integrating Science When a camera and projector both operate at a speed of 24 frames per second, the film is seen at the same rate as the event occurred when it was filmed. Occasionally, scenes are filmed at a faster or slower rate than the actual event.

When a scene is filmed faster than 24 frames a second and is projected at a normal rate later, the action appears in slow motion. This effect is useful for studying phenomena, such as a chameleon catching a fly, that occur too fast for the human eye to perceive. When a scene is filmed slower than 24 frames a second, the action appears speeded up when projected at a normal rate. This effect is useful for studying phenomena, such as plants growing, that occur very slowly.

Making Models

An immense fortress under attack, a sinking luxury liner, a fiery train crash—these scenes look real on the big screen. But moviemakers don't often stage actual catastrophes such as these. Increasingly they use computers or models. A movie may use several models in different sizes.

Models must be to scale so that every detail of the model appears in proper proportion. Scale is a ratio that compares the measurements of a model to the actual size of the object. For example, if a car is 3.5 meters (350 centimeters) long, a model at a scale of 1 : 16 would be almost 22 centimeters long. A larger model of the car, at 1 : 4, would be about 88 centimeters long.

The makers of the movie *The Lord of the Rings: The Two Towers* built full-size sections of Helm's Deep, a massive fortress that is an important location in the film. They built a second model one-quarter the size of the actual set, expressed as a scale of 1 : 4. They built a third model of the fortress in a scale of 1 : 35. This small-scale model was complete in every detail so that moviegoers would be convinced they were looking at Helm's Deep.

Helm's Deep
A movie frame from *Lord of the Rings: The Two Towers* shows Helm's Deep (top). A set designer puts the finishing touches on a small-scale model of the fortress (above).

Math Activity

Sketch a simple scene, such as a room interior or a city scene. Pick four objects in the scene and estimate or measure the actual size of each. The objects could include a chair, a person, a car, or a skyscraper. (**Note:** *The height of one story in a modern building equals about 4 meters.*) Decide on a scale for your model, such as 1 : 4, 1 : 12, or 1 : 16. After determining the actual sizes of the objects, calculate the size of each scale model.

O ◆ 145

Explore Mathematics Concepts

Use Math Skills Provide students with an opportunity to use a type of scale model that is already familiar to them. Give each student a copy of a road map that includes the scale. Have them use the scale to find a given distance on the map, such as the distance between two cities. (*Students should first find the distance on the map between the two locations and then convert the map distance to the actual distance using the scale.*)

Discuss Discuss models with which students are likely to be familiar: model cars. Ask: **Are these scale models?** (*Model cars typically are to scale.*) Point out that the scale-model props in movies that are described in the text are all smaller than the actual objects they represent. Ask: **What models used in movies might be larger than the actual objects they represent?** (*Students might mention props in movies, such as* Honey, I Shrunk the Kids, *in which people are supposed to be smaller than normal.*)

Math Activity

Materials metric ruler, meter stick, calculator, graph paper

Focus Tell students that when they draw something to scale, every dimension must be to scale. For example, if they draw a building that is 10 percent of its actual height, it must also be 10 percent of its actual width. Suggest that students use graph paper to draw their models and let one square represent a given distance, such as 1 meter.

Teach Explain that proportions are the basis of scale models. Review how to set up and solve proportions, using an example. Ask: **What is the length of a model of an object that has an actual length of 4 m if the scale of the model is 2 : 1?**
(*Let L equal length.*

Then $\frac{L}{4\text{ m}} = \frac{2}{1}$.

Solving for L gives: $L = \frac{(4\text{ m})(2)}{1}$, *or L = 8 m.*)

Answers Sizes of students' scale models will depend on the sizes of the actual objects and on the scales they used. Make sure that the actual objects have been measured accurately or estimated reasonably, that model dimensions have been calculated correctly, and that all of the dimensions are to scale.

Background

Integrating Science For the movie, *Mouse Hunt,* model makers and mechanical engineers used animatronics, or electronic puppets. The puppet mouse had to be about four times larger than a real mouse in order for all the mechanical components to fit inside the body. Because of the size of the model, the puppet designers found it difficult to make the fur look realistic. Hair technicians spent months experimenting with different kinds of fur to find one that made the puppet look realistic on film. When the mouse was finally finished, it took six puppeteers to operate it, one with a hand inside the mouse and five others using radio controls.

Explore Social Studies Concepts

Discuss Tell students that movies reflect changes in social behaviors and values as well as changes in technology. Give students an example of a significant social change, such as the role of females in society over the past several decades. Then, name movies that reflect this social change. (*Examples: Compare movies from the 1950s and movies from the 1990s in which women have roles in the work force.*)

Demonstrate Help students identify how movies of today differ from movies in the past by showing a brief scene from several movies, each representing a different decade. Describe any relevant technological advances that are reflected in the movies. If possible, invite a history teacher to share in this activity and identify any relevant historical events that are reflected in the movies.

Social Studies Activity

Focus Have students look at the pictures and read the captions on these two pages.

Teach Students may be surprised that audiences found the early movies convincing. Explain that audiences were not used to special effects in those days and were as impressed by the images in the films of their day as people today are with more technologically sophisticated special effects. Point out that advances in technology have not only influenced the special effects that are used in movies. They have also influenced the content of movies. For example, in the feature, they will read how the rapid rise in computers in the 1960s led to a fear of computers that was reflected in the 1968 movie, *2001: A Space Odyssey.*

Scoring Rubric

4 Exceeds criteria; includes a detailed, well-supported, and highly organized discussion of links between current events and movies
3 Meets criteria
2 Includes a discussion of links but may lack details, organization, and/or supporting evidence
1 Includes only general statements without organization and/or supporting evidence

Reflecting the Times

When moviemakers look for an idea for a new movie, they think first about what people are interested in seeing. Moviemakers want to know what's important to people. Advances in science and technology and recent events in history all influence people. Movies often reflect changes in people's lives.

In the early 1900s, people were just beginning to fly airplanes. Early science fiction movies of the 1920s and 1930s were pure fantasy.

By the 1950s, space flight technology was developing. In 1957, the Soviet Union sent the first satellite, *Sputnik I*, into orbit. Soon after, the United States and the Soviet Union were competing in space exploration. Both nations also were making powerful nuclear weapons. The idea of nuclear war frightened people. Many movies of the 1950s and 1960s reflected these fears. Giant insects and other monsters appeared on movie screens. Science fiction movies featured alien invasions.

The "space race" continued in the 1960s. American astronauts and Soviet cosmonauts orbited Earth. In July 1969, three American astronauts became the first people to reach the moon. Later, space probes sent back pictures of other planets. These space flights made people dream about space travel. About the same time, people began using computers. Some people were afraid the new machines would control them. In the 1968 movie *2001: A Space Odyssey*, the computer HAL did just that.

Interest in space kept science fiction movies popular in the 1980s and 1990s. By that time, computers were part of everyday life. They were not instruments to be feared.

Tension between the United States and the Soviet Union was relaxing. Movies seemed more optimistic about the future than in the 1950s.

***A Trip to the Moon,* 1902**
This early French movie represents an astronomer's dream. In the dream, men travel to the moon inside a capsule shot from a giant cannon.

***Them!,* 1954**
In this 1954 movie, nuclear tests in the American Southwest create mutant giant ants.

Background

Facts and Figures Listed below are the 10 top-grossing movies of all time (as of April 2004).
1. *Titanic* (1997) $1,835,300,000
2. *The Lord of the Rings: The Return of the King* (2003) $1,128,537,000
3. *Harry Potter and the Sorcerer's Stone* (2001) $968,600,000
4. *Star Wars: Episode I, The Phantom Menace* (1999) $922,300,000
5. *Jurassic Park* (1993) $919,700,000
6. *The Lord of the Rings: The Two Towers* (2002) $918,600,000
7. *Harry Potter and the Chamber of Secrets* (2002) $866,300,000
8. *The Lord of the Rings: The Fellowship of the Ring* (2001) $860,200,000
9. *Finding Nemo* (2003) $853,200,000
10. *Independence Day* (1996) $811,200,000

***E.T.,* 1982**
E.T. is an alien stranded on Earth. A group
of Earth children help him return home.

***Jurassic Park,* 1993**
In this movie, dinosaurs are on the rampage.
Here, *Tyrannosaurus rex* crushes a truck.

In popular movies such as *E.T.* and *Close Encounters of the Third Kind*, the human characters showed more curiosity than fear about aliens—even those that visited Earth. The movie *Men in Black* featured aliens who were more often humorous than threatening.

Social Studies Activity

Think of some recent movies that you and others may have seen. With your classmates, organize a panel discussion on the links between movies and current events. Consider changes that have occurred in the world around you. How have space probes, planet explorations, computers, video games, the Internet, and political events influenced these movies?

Tie It Together

Making a Movie

Put your movie ideas into action. With your classmates, plan a short (10–15 minute) movie. If possible, use a video camera to make your movie. Use what you've learned about point of view, the use of scale models, and editing.

- Think of a subject or event for your movie. As a class, outline the script for the movie.
- Work in small groups to make storyboards—drawings showing key scenes in the movie.

- Choose a director, actors, a camera operator, and a film editor.
- Assign groups to plan lights, sound effects, model-building, props, background painting, and photography.
- After shooting and editing your movie, present it for other students in your school.

O ◆ 147

Tie It Together

Making a Movie

Time 1 week (1 class period to outline the script and choose roles; 2 class periods to make storyboards and create props and scenery; 1 class period to rehearse; 1 class period to tape)

Tips Consider performing this activity as a whole class, because there are enough tasks for all students to be involved.

- Have students choose the subject of their video on the first day. Suggest that they depict in a 10–15 minute movie a story that they have all studied in school. Then, have students brainstorm a list of all the roles and tasks that will be needed. Record the roles and tasks on the board. To avoid conflict, assign roles and tasks to students using your best judgment of which job best suits each student. If students wish to exchange jobs, allow them to do so.
- Urge students to make their videos as simply and thriftily as possible. Discourage them from using excessively elaborate or costly props, backgrounds, or costumes.
- Urge each individual or group assigned to a particular task to check periodically with others to ensure that their goals are compatible in the areas in which they overlap. Lead students to appreciate how much communication and cooperation are required to make a feature-length film with a budget of millions of dollars.

Extend Invite a video producer to talk to the class about aspects of his or her work.

Think Like a Scientist

The Skills Handbook is designed as a reference for students to use whenever they need to review inquiry, reading, or math skills. You can use the activities in this part of the Skills Handbook to teach or reinforce inquiry skills.

Observing

Focus Remind students that an observation is what they can see, hear, smell, taste, or feel.

Teach Invite students to make observations of the classroom. List these observations on the board. Challenge students to identify the senses they used to make each observation. Then, ask: **Which senses will you use to make observations from the photograph on this page?** *(Sight is the only sense that can be used to make observations from the photograph.)*

Activity

Some observations that students might make include that the boy is skateboarding, wearing a white helmet, and flying in the air. Make sure that students' observations are confined to only things that they can actually see in the photograph.

Inferring

Focus Choose one or two of the classroom observations listed on the board, and challenge students to interpret them. Guide students by asking why something appears as it does.

Teach Encourage students to describe their thought processes in making their inferences. Point out where they used their knowledge and experience to interpret the observations. Then invite students to suggest other possible interpretations for the observations. Ask: **How can you find out whether an inference is correct?** *(By further investigation)*

Activity

One possible inference is that the boy just skated off a ramp at a skate park. Invite students to share their experiences that helped them make the inference.

Predicting

Focus Discuss the weather forecast for the next day. Point out that this prediction is an inference about what will happen in the

Think Like a Scientist

Scientists have a particular way of looking at the world, or scientific habits of mind. Whenever you ask a question and explore possible answers, you use many of the same skills that scientists do. Some of these skills are described on this page.

Observing

When you use one or more of your five senses to gather information about the world, you are **observing.** Hearing a dog bark, counting twelve green seeds, and smelling smoke are all observations. To increase the power of their senses, scientists sometimes use microscopes, telescopes, or other instruments that help them make more detailed observations.

An observation must be an accurate report of what your senses detect. It is important to keep careful records of your observations in science class by writing or drawing in a notebook. The information collected through observations is called evidence, or data.

Inferring

When you interpret an observation, you are **inferring,** or making an inference. For example, if you hear your dog barking, you may infer that someone is at your front door. To make this inference, you combine the evidence— the barking dog—and your experience or knowledge—you know that your dog barks when strangers approach—to reach a logical conclusion.

Notice that an inference is not a fact; it is only one of many possible interpretations for an observation. For example, your dog may be barking because it wants to go for a walk. An inference may turn out to be incorrect even if it is based on accurate observations and logical reasoning. The only way to find out if an inference is correct is to investigate further.

148 ◆ O

Predicting

When you listen to the weather forecast, you hear many predictions about the next day's weather—what the temperature will be, whether it will rain, and how windy it will be. Weather forecasters use observations and knowledge of weather patterns to predict the weather. The skill of **predicting** involves making an inference about a future event based on current evidence or past experience.

Because a prediction is an inference, it may prove to be false. In science class, you can test some of your predictions by doing experiments. For example, suppose you predict that larger paper airplanes can fly farther than smaller airplanes. How could you test your prediction?

Activity

Use the photograph to answer the questions below.

Observing Look closely at the photograph. List at least three observations.

Inferring Use your observations to make an inference about what has happened. What experience or knowledge did you use to make the inference?

Predicting Predict what will happen next. On what evidence or experience do you base your prediction?

future based on observations and experience.

Teach Help students differentiate between a prediction and an inference. You might organize the similarities and differences in a Venn diagram on the board. Both are interpretations of observations using experience and knowledge, and both can be incorrect. Inferences describe current or past events. Predictions describe future events.

Activity

Students might predict that the boy will land and skate to the other side. Others might predict that the boy will fall. Students should also describe the evidence or experience on which they based their predictions.

Classifying

Could you imagine searching for a book in the library if the books were shelved in no particular order? Your trip to the library would be an all-day event! Luckily, librarians group together books on similar topics or by the same author. Grouping together items that are alike in some way is called **classifying.** You can classify items in many ways: by size, by shape, by use, and by other important characteristics.

Like librarians, scientists use the skill of classifying to organize information and objects. When things are sorted into groups, the relationships among them become easier to understand.

Activity

Classify the objects in the photograph into two groups based on any characteristic you choose. Then use another characteristic to classify the objects into three groups.

Making Models

Have you ever drawn a picture to help someone understand what you were saying? Such a drawing is one type of model. A model is a picture, diagram, computer image, or other representation of a complex object or process. **Making models** helps people understand things that they cannot observe directly.

Scientists often use models to represent things that are either very large or very small, such as the planets in the solar system, or the parts of a cell. Such models are physical models—drawings or three-dimensional structures that look like the real thing. Other models are mental models—mathematical equations or words that describe how something works.

Activity

This student is using a model to demonstrate what causes day and night on Earth. What do the flashlight and the tennis ball in the model represent?

Communicating

Whenever you talk on the phone, write a report, or listen to your teacher at school, you are communicating. **Communicating** is the process of sharing ideas and information with other people. Communicating effectively requires many skills, including writing, reading, speaking, listening, and making models.

Scientists communicate to share results, information, and opinions. Scientists often communicate about their work in journals, over the telephone, in letters, and on the Internet.

They also attend scientific meetings where they share their ideas with one another in person.

Activity

On a sheet of paper, write out clear, detailed directions for tying your shoe. Then exchange directions with a partner. Follow your partner's directions exactly. How successful were you at tying your shoe? How could your partner have communicated more clearly?

Skills Handbook ◆ 149

Classifying

Focus Encourage students to think of common things that are classified.

Teach Ask: **What things at home are classified?** (*Clothing might be classified in order to place it in the appropriate dresser drawer; glasses, plates, and silverware are grouped in different parts of the kitchen; screws, nuts, bolts, washers, and nails might be separated into small containers.*) **What are some things that scientists classify?** (*Scientists classify many things they study, including organisms, geological features and processes, and kinds of machines.*)

Activity

Some characteristics students might use include color, pattern of color, use of balls, and size. Students' criteria for classification should clearly divide the balls into two, and then three, distinct groups.

Making Models

Focus Ask: **What are some models you have used to study science?** (*Students might have used human anatomical models, solar system models, maps, or stream tables.*) **How have these models helped you?** (*Models can help you learn about things that are difficult to study because they are very large, very small, or highly complex.*)

Teach Be sure students understand that a model does not have to be three-dimensional. For example, a map is a model, as is a mathematical equation. Have students look at the photograph of the student modeling the causes of day and night on Earth. Ask: **What quality of each item makes this a good model?** (*The flashlight gives off light, and the ball is round and can be rotated by the student.*)

Activity

The flashlight represents the sun and the ball represents Earth.

Communicating

Focus Have students identify the methods of communication they have used today.

Teach Ask: **How is the way you communicate with a friend similar to and different from the way scientists communicate about their work to other scientists?** (*Both may communicate using various methods, but scientists must be very detailed and precise, whereas communication between friends may be less detailed and precise.*) Encourage students to communicate like a scientist as they carry out the activity.

Activity

Students' answers will vary but should identify a step-by-step process for tying a shoe. Help students identify communication errors such as leaving out a step, putting steps in the wrong order, or disregarding the person's handedness.

SKILLS Handbook

Making Measurements

Students can refer to this part of the Skills Handbook whenever they need to review how to make measurements with SI units. You can use the activities here to teach or reinforce SI units.

Measuring in SI

Focus Review SI units with students. Begin by providing metric rulers, graduated cylinders, balances, and Celsius thermometers. Use these tools to reinforce that the meter is the unit of length, the liter is the unit of volume, the gram is the unit of mass, and the degree Celsius is the unit of temperature.

Teach Ask: **If you want to measure the length and the width of the classroom, which SI unit would you use?** *(Meter)* **Which unit would you use to measure the amount of mass in your textbook?** *(Gram)* **Which would you use to measure how much water a drinking glass holds?** *(Liter)* **When would you use the Celsius scale?** *(To measure the temperature of something)* Then use the measuring equipment to review SI prefixes. For example, ask: **What are the smallest units on the metric ruler?** *(Millimeters)* **How many millimeters are there in one centimeter?** *(10 millimeters)* **How many in 10 centimeters?** *(100 millimeters)* **How many centimeters are there in one meter?** *(100 centimeters)* **What does 1,000 meters equal?** *(One kilometer)*

Activity

Length The length of the shell is 7.8 centimeters, or 78 millimeters. If students need more practice measuring length, have them use meter sticks and metric rulers to measure various objects in the classroom.

Activity

Liquid Volume The volume of water in the graduated cylinder is 62 milliliters. If students need more practice, have them use a graduated cylinder to measure different volumes of water.

SKILLS Handbook

Making Measurements

By measuring, scientists can express their observations more precisely and communicate more information about what they observe.

Measuring in SI

The standard system of measurement used by scientists around the world is known as the International System of Units, which is abbreviated as SI (**Système International d'Unités,** in French). SI units are easy to use because they are based on multiples of 10. Each unit is ten times larger than the next smallest unit and one tenth the size of the next largest unit. The table lists the prefixes used to name the most common SI units.

Common SI Prefixes		
Prefix	**Symbol**	**Meaning**
kilo-	k	1,000
hecto-	h	100
deka-	da	10
deci-	d	0.1 (one tenth)
centi-	c	0.01 (one hundredth)
milli-	m	0.001 (one thousandth)

Length To measure length, or the distance between two points, the unit of measure is the **meter (m).** The distance from the floor to a doorknob is approximately one meter. Long distances, such as the distance between two cities, are measured in kilometers (km). Small lengths are measured in centimeters (cm) or millimeters (mm). Scientists use metric rulers and meter sticks to measure length.

Common Conversions	
1 km	= 1,000 m
1 m	= 100 cm
1 m	= 1,000 mm
1 cm	= 10 mm

Activity

The larger lines on the metric ruler in the picture show centimeter divisions, while the smaller, unnumbered lines show millimeter divisions. How many centimeters long is the shell? How many millimeters long is it?

150 ◆ O

Liquid Volume To measure the volume of a liquid, or the amount of space it takes up, you will use a unit of measure known as the **liter (L).** One liter is the approximate volume of a medium-size carton of milk. Smaller volumes are measured in milliliters (mL). Scientists use graduated cylinders to measure liquid volume.

Activity

The graduated cylinder in the picture is marked in milliliter divisions. Notice that the water in the cylinder has a curved surface. This curved surface is called the *meniscus.* To measure the volume, you must read the level at the lowest point of the meniscus. What is the volume of water in this graduated cylinder?

Common Conversion
1 L = 1,000 mL

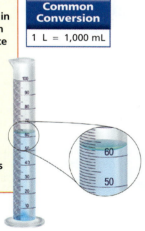

Mass To measure mass, or the amount of matter in an object, you will use a unit of measure known as the **gram (g).** One gram is approximately the mass of a paper clip. Larger masses are measured in kilograms (kg). Scientists use a balance to find the mass of an object.

> **Common Conversion**
>
> 1 kg = 1,000 g

Activity

The mass of the potato in the picture is measured in kilograms. What is the mass of the potato? Suppose a recipe for potato salad called for one kilogram of potatoes. About how many potatoes would you need?

Temperature To measure the temperature of a substance, you will use the **Celsius scale.** Temperature is measured in degrees Celsius (°C) using a Celsius thermometer. Water freezes at 0°C and boils at 100°C.

Time The unit scientists use to measure time is the **second (s).**

Activity

What is the temperature of the liquid in degrees Celsius?

Converting SI Units

To use the SI system, you must know how to convert between units. Converting from one unit to another involves the skill of **calculating,** or using mathematical operations. Converting between SI units is similar to converting between dollars and dimes because both systems are based on multiples of ten.

Suppose you want to convert a length of 80 centimeters to meters. Follow these steps to convert between units.

1. Begin by writing down the measurement you want to convert—in this example, 80 centimeters.

2. Write a conversion factor that represents the relationship between the two units you are converting. In this example, the relationship is 1 meter = 100 centimeters. Write this conversion factor as a fraction, making sure to place the units you are converting from (centimeters, in this example) in the denominator.

3. Multiply the measurement you want to convert by the fraction. When you do this, the units in the first measurement will cancel out with the units in the denominator. Your answer will be in the units you are converting to (meters, in this example).

Example

80 centimeters = ▇ meters

$$80 \text{ centimeters} \times \frac{1 \text{ meter}}{100 \text{ centimeters}} = \frac{80 \text{ meters}}{100}$$

$$= 0.8 \text{ meters}$$

Activity

Convert between the following units.
1. 600 millimeters = ▇ meters
2. 0.35 liters = ▇ milliliters
3. 1,050 grams = ▇ kilograms

Skills Handbook ◆ **151**

Activity

Mass The mass of the potato is 0.25 kilograms. You would need 4 potatoes to make one kilogram. If students need more practice, give them various objects, such as coins, paper clips, and books, to measure mass.

Activity

Temperature The temperature of the liquid is 35°C. Students who need more practice can measure the temperatures of various water samples.

Converting SI Units

Focus Review the steps for converting SI units, and work through the example with students.

Teach Ask: **How many millimeters are in 80 centimeters?** *(With the relationship 10 millimeters = 1 centimeter, students should follow the steps to calculate that 80 centimeters is equal to 800 millimeters.)* Have students do the conversion problems in the activity.

Activity

1. *600 millimeters = 0.6 meters*
2. *0.35 liters = 350 milliliters*
3. *1,050 grams = 1.05 kilograms*
If students need more practice converting SI units, have them make up conversion problems to trade with partners.

Conducting a Scientific Investigation

Students can refer to this part of the Skills Handbook whenever they need to review the steps of a scientific investigation. You can use the activities here to teach or reinforce these steps.

Posing Questions

Focus Ask: **What do you do when you want to learn about something?** (*Answers might include asking questions about it or looking for information in books or on the Internet.*) Explain that scientists go through the same process to learn about something.

Teach Tell students that the questions scientists ask may have no answers or many different answers. To answer their questions, scientists often conduct experiments. Ask: **Why is a scientific question important to a scientific investigation?** (*It helps the scientist decide if an experiment is necessary; the answer might already be known. It also helps focus the idea so that the scientist can form a hypothesis.*) **What is the scientific question in the activity on the next page?** (*Is a ball's bounce affected by the height from which it is dropped?*)

Developing a Hypothesis

Focus Emphasize that a hypothesis is one possible explanation for a set of observations. It is *not* a guess. It is often based on an inference.

Teach Ask: **On what information do scientists base their hypotheses?** (*Their observations and previous knowledge or experience*) Point out that a hypothesis does not always turn out to be correct. Ask: **When a hypothesis turns out to be incorrect, do you think the scientist wasted his or her time? Explain.** (*No. The scientist learned from the investigation and will develop another hypothesis that could prove to be correct.*)

Designing an Experiment

Focus Have a volunteer read the Experimental Procedure in the box. Invite students to identify the manipulated variable (*amount of salt*), the variables kept constant (*amount and temperature of water, location of containers*), the control (*Container 3*), and the responding variable (*time required for the water to freeze*).

Conducting a Scientific Investigation

In some ways, scientists are like detectives, piecing together clues to learn about a process or event. One way that scientists gather clues is by carrying out experiments. An experiment tests an idea in a careful, orderly manner. Although experiments do not all follow the same steps in the same order, many follow a pattern similar to the one described here.

Posing Questions

Experiments begin by asking a scientific question. A scientific question is one that can be answered by gathering evidence. For example, the question "Which freezes faster—fresh water or salt water?" is a scientific question because you can carry out an investigation and gather information to answer the question.

Developing a Hypothesis

The next step is to form a hypothesis. A **hypothesis** is a possible explanation for a set of observations or answer to a scientific question. In science, a hypothesis must be something that can be tested. A hypothesis can be worded as an *If . . . then . . .* statement. For example, a hypothesis might be *"If I add salt to fresh water, then the water will take longer to freeze."* A hypothesis worded this way serves as a rough outline of the experiment you should perform.

152 ◆ O

Teach Ask: **How might the experiment be affected if Container 1 had only 100 milliliters of water?** (*It wouldn't be an accurate comparison with the containers that have more water.*) Also make sure that students understand the importance of the control. Then, ask: **What operational definition is used in this experiment?** (*"Frozen" means the time at which a wooden stick can no longer move in a container.*)

Designing an Experiment

Next you need to plan a way to test your hypothesis. Your plan should be written out as a step-by-step procedure and should describe the observations or measurements you will make.

Two important steps involved in designing an experiment are controlling variables and forming operational definitions.

Controlling Variables In a well-designed experiment, you need to keep all variables the same except for one. A **variable** is any factor that can change in an experiment. The factor that you change is called the **manipulated variable**. In this experiment, the manipulated variable is the amount of salt added to the water. Other factors, such as the amount of water or the starting temperature, are kept constant.

The factor that changes as a result of the manipulated variable is called the **responding variable.** The responding variable is what you measure or observe to obtain your results. In this experiment, the responding variable is how long the water takes to freeze.

An experiment in which all factors except one are kept constant is called a **controlled experiment.** Most controlled experiments include a test called the control. In this experiment, Container 3 is the control. Because no salt is added to Container 3, you can compare the results from the other containers to it. Any difference in results must be due to the addition of salt alone.

Forming Operational Definitions Another important aspect of a well-designed experiment is having clear operational definitions. An **operational definition** is a statement that describes how a particular variable is to be measured or how a term is to be defined. For example, in this experiment, how will you determine if the water has frozen? You might decide to insert a stick in each container at the start of the experiment. Your operational definition of "frozen" would be the time at which the stick can no longer move.

Experimental Procedure

1. Fill 3 containers with 300 milliliters of cold tap water.

2. Add 10 grams of salt to Container 1; stir. Add 20 grams of salt to Container 2; stir. Add no salt to Container 3.

3. Place the 3 containers in a freezer.

4. Check the containers every 15 minutes. Record your observations.

Interpreting Data

The observations and measurements you make in an experiment are called **data.** At the end of an experiment, you need to analyze the data to look for any patterns or trends. Patterns often become clear if you organize your data in a data table or graph. Then think through what the data reveal. Do they support your hypothesis? Do they point out a flaw in your experiment? Do you need to collect more data?

Drawing Conclusions

A **conclusion** is a statement that sums up what you have learned from an experiment. When you draw a conclusion, you need to decide whether the data you collected support your hypothesis or not. You may need to repeat an experiment several times before you can draw any conclusions from it. Conclusions often lead you to pose new questions and plan new experiments to answer them.

Activity

Is a ball's bounce affected by the height from which it is dropped? Using the steps just described, plan a controlled experiment to investigate this problem.

Skills Handbook ◆ 153

Interpreting Data

Focus Ask: **What kind of data would you collect from the experiment with freezing salt water?** *(Time and state of the water)*

Teach Ask: **What if you forgot to record some data during an investigation?** *(You wouldn't be able to draw valid conclusions because some data are missing.)* Then, ask: **Why are data tables and graphs a good way to organize data?** *(They make it easier to record data accurately, as well as compare and analyze data.)* **What kind of data table and graph might you use for this experiment?** *(A table would have columns for each container with a row for each time interval in which the state of water is recorded. A bar graph would show the time elapsed until water froze for each container.)*

Drawing Conclusions

Focus Help students understand that a conclusion is not necessarily the end of a scientific investigation. A conclusion about one experiment may lead right into another experiment.

Teach Point out that in scientific investigations, a conclusion is a summary and explanation of the results of an experiment. For the Experimental Procedure described on this page, tell students to suppose that they obtained the following results: Container 1 froze in 45 minutes, Container 2 in 80 minutes, and Container 3 in 25 minutes. Ask: **What conclusions can you draw from this experiment?** *(Students might conclude that water takes longer to freeze as more salt is added to it. The hypothesis is supported, and the question of which freezes faster is answered—fresh water.)*

Activity

You might wish to have students work in pairs to plan the controlled experiment. Students should develop a hypothesis, such as, "If I increase the height from which a ball is dropped, then the height of its bounce will increase." They can test the hypothesis by dropping a ball from varying heights (the manipulated variable). All trials should be done with the same kind of ball and on the same surface (constants). For each trial, they should measure the height of the bounce (responding variable). After students have designed the experiment, provide rubber balls, and invite them to carry out the experiment so they can collect and interpret data and draw conclusions.

Technology Design Skills

Students can refer to this part of the Skills Handbook whenever they need to review the process of designing new technologies. You can use the activities here to teach or reinforce the steps in this process.

Identify a Need

Focus Solicit from students any situations in which they have thought that a tool, machine, or other object would be really helpful to them or others. Explain that this is the first step in the design of new products.

Teach Point out that identifying specific needs is very important to the design process. Ask: **If it was specified that the toy boat be wind-powered, how might that affect the design?** *(The boat would likely be designed with sails.)*

Research the Problem

Focus Explain that research focuses the problem so that the design is more specific.

Teach Ask: **What might happen if you didn't research the problem before designing the solution?** *(Answers include developing a design that has already been found to fail, using materials that aren't the best, or designing a solution that already exists.)* **What would you research before designing your toy boat?** *(Students might research designs and materials.)*

Design a Solution

Focus Emphasize the importance of a design team. Ask: **Why are brainstorming sessions important in product design?** *(A group will propose more new ideas than one person.)*

Teach Divide the class into teams to design the toy boat. Instruct them to brainstorm design ideas. Then, ask: **Why do you think engineers evaluate constraints after brainstorming?** *(Evaluating constraints while brainstorming often stops the flow of new ideas.)* **What design constraints do you have for your toy boat?** *(Materials must be readily available and teacher-approved. The boat must be 15 centimeters or less in length and must travel 2 meters in a straight line carrying a load of 20 pennies.)*

Technology Design Skills

Engineers are people who use scientific and technological knowledge to solve practical problems. To design new products, engineers usually follow the process described here, even though they may not follow these steps in the exact order. As you read the steps, think about how you might apply them in technology labs.

Identify a Need

Before engineers begin designing a new product, they must first identify the need they are trying to meet. For example, suppose you are a member of a design team in a company that makes toys. Your team has identified a need: a toy boat that is inexpensive and easy to assemble.

Research the Problem

Engineers often begin by gathering information that will help them with their new design. This research may include finding articles in books, magazines, or on the Internet. It may also include talking to other engineers who have solved similar problems. Engineers often perform experiments related to the product they want to design.

For your toy boat, you could look at toys that are similar to the one you want to design. You might do research on the Internet. You could also test some materials to see whether they will work well in a toy boat.

Drawing for a boat design ▼

154 ◆ O

Design a Solution

Research gives engineers information that helps them design a product. When engineers design new products, they usually work in teams.

Generating Ideas Often design teams hold brainstorming meetings in which any team member can contribute ideas. **Brainstorming** is a creative process in which one team member's suggestions often spark ideas in other group members. Brainstorming can lead to new approaches to solving a design problem.

Evaluating Constraints During brainstorming, a design team will often come up with several possible designs. The team must then evaluate each one.

As part of their evaluation, engineers consider constraints. **Constraints** are factors that limit or restrict a product design. Physical characteristics, such as the properties of materials used to make your toy boat, are constraints. Money and time are also constraints. If the materials in a product cost a lot, or if the product takes a long time to make, the design may be impractical.

Making Trade-offs Design teams usually need to make trade-offs. In a **trade-off,** engineers give up one benefit of a proposed design in order to obtain another. In designing your toy boat, you will have to make trade-offs. For example, suppose one material is sturdy but not fully waterproof. Another material is more waterproof, but breakable. You may decide to give up the benefit of sturdiness in order to obtain the benefit of waterproofing.

Build and Evaluate a Prototype

Once the team has chosen a design plan, the engineers build a prototype of the product. A **prototype** is a working model used to test a design. Engineers evaluate the prototype to see whether it works well, is easy to operate, is safe to use, and holds up to repeated use.

Think of your toy boat. What would the prototype be like? Of what materials would it be made? How would you test it?

Troubleshoot and Redesign

Few prototypes work perfectly, which is why they need to be tested. Once a design team has tested a prototype, the members analyze the results and identify any problems. The team then tries to **troubleshoot,** or fix the design problems. For example, if your toy boat leaks or wobbles, the boat should be redesigned to eliminate those problems.

Communicate the Solution

A team needs to communicate the final design to the people who will manufacture and use the product. To do this, teams may use sketches, detailed drawings, computer simulations, and word descriptions.

Activity

You can use the technology design process to design and build a toy boat.

Research and Investigate
1. Visit the library or go online to research toy boats.
2. Investigate how a toy boat can be powered, including wind, rubber bands, or baking soda and vinegar.
3. Brainstorm materials, shapes, and steering for your boat.

Design and Build
4. Based on your research, design a toy boat that
   • is made of readily available materials
   • is no larger than 15 cm long and 10 cm wide

   • includes a power system, a rudder, and an area for cargo
   • travels 2 meters in a straight line carrying a load of 20 pennies
5. Sketch your design and write a step-by-step plan for building your boat. After your teacher approves your plan, build your boat.

Evaluate and Redesign
6. Test your boat, evaluate the results, and troubleshoot any problems.
7. Based on your evaluation, redesign your toy boat so it performs better.

Skills Handbook ◆ 155

Build and Evaluate a Prototype

Focus Explain that building a prototype enables engineers to test design ideas.

Teach Relate building and testing a prototype to conducting an experiment. Explain that engineers set up controlled experiments to test the prototype. Ask: **Why do you think engineers set up controlled experiments?** (*From the data, they can determine which component of the design is working and which is failing.*) **How would you test your prototype of the toy boat**? (*Answers will vary depending on the toy boat's propulsion system.*)

Troubleshoot and Redesign

Focus Make sure students know what it means to troubleshoot. If necessary, give an example. One example is a stapler that isn't working. In that case, you would check to see if it is out of staples or if the staples are jammed. Then you would fix the problem and try stapling again. If it still didn't work, you might check the position of staples and try again.

Teach Explain that engineers often are not surprised if the prototype doesn't work. Ask: **Why isn't it a failure if the prototype doesn't work?** (*Engineers learn from the problems and make changes to address the problems. This process makes the design better.*) Emphasize that prototypes are completely tested before the product is made in the factory.

Communicate the Solution

Focus Inquire whether students have ever read the instruction manual that comes with a new toy or electronic device.

Teach Emphasize the importance of good communication in the design process. Ask: **What might happen if engineers did not communicate their design ideas clearly?** (*The product might not be manufactured correctly or used properly.*)

Activity

The design possibilities are endless. Students might use small plastic containers, wood, foil, or plastic drinking cups for the boat. Materials may also include toothpicks, straws, or small wooden dowels. Brainstorm with students the different ways in which a toy boat can be propelled. The boats may be any shape, but must be no longer than 15 centimeters.

As student groups follow the steps in the design process, have them record their sources, brainstorming ideas, and prototype design in a logbook. Also give them time to troubleshoot and redesign their boats. When students turn in their boats, they should include assembly directions with a diagram, as well as instructions for use.

Creating Data Tables and Graphs

Students can refer to this part of the Skills Handbook whenever they need to review the skills required to create data tables and graphs. You can use the activities provided here to teach or reinforce these skills.

Data Tables

Focus Emphasize the importance of organizing data. Ask: **What might happen if you didn't use a data table for an experiment?** *(Possible answers include that data might not be collected or they might be forgotten.)*

Teach Have students create a data table to show how much time they spend on different activities during one week. Suggest that students first list the main activities they do every week. Then they should determine the amount of time they spend on each activity each day. Remind students to give the data table a title. A sample data table is shown below.

Bar Graphs

Focus Have students compare and contrast the data table and the bar graph on this page. Ask: **Why would you make a bar graph if the data are already organized in a table?** *(The bar graph organizes the data in a visual way that makes them easier to interpret.)*

Teach Students can use the data from the data table they created to make a bar graph that shows the amount of time they spend on different activities during a week. The vertical axis should be divided into units of time, such as hours. Remind students to label both axes and give their graph a title. A sample bar graph is shown below.

Creating Data Tables and Graphs

**How can you make sense of the data in a science experiment?
The first step is to organize the data to help you understand them.
Data tables and graphs are helpful tools for organizing data.**

Data Tables

You have gathered your materials and set up your experiment. But before you start, you need to plan a way to record what happens during the experiment. By creating a data table, you can record your observations and measurements in an orderly way.

Suppose, for example, that a scientist conducted an experiment to find out how many Calories people of different body masses burn while doing various activities. The data table shows the results.

Notice in this data table that the manipulated variable (body mass) is the heading of one column. The responding variable (for

Calories Burned in 30 Minutes

Body Mass	Experiment 1: Bicycling	Experiment 2: Playing Basketball	Experiment 3: Watching Television
30 kg	60 Calories	120 Calories	21 Calories
40 kg	77 Calories	164 Calories	27 Calories
50 kg	95 Calories	206 Calories	33 Calories
60 kg	114 Calories	248 Calories	38 Calories

Experiment 1, the number of Calories burned while bicycling) is the heading of the next column. Additional columns were added for related experiments.

Bar Graphs

To compare how many Calories a person burns doing various activities, you could create a bar graph. A bar graph is used to display data in a number of separate, or distinct, categories. In this example, bicycling, playing basketball, and watching television are the three categories.

To create a bar graph, follow these steps.

1. On graph paper, draw a horizontal, or *x*-, axis and a vertical, or *y*-, axis.
2. Write the names of the categories to be graphed along the horizontal axis. Include an overall label for the axis as well.
3. Label the vertical axis with the name of the responding variable. Include units of measurement. Then create a scale along the axis by marking off equally spaced numbers that cover the range of the data collected.

4. For each category, draw a solid bar using the scale on the vertical axis to determine the height. Make all the bars the same width.
5. Add a title that describes the graph.

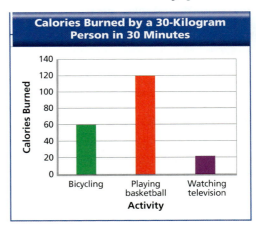

Time Spent on Different Activities in a Week

	Going to Classes	Eating Meals	Playing Soccer	Watching Television
Monday	6	2	2	0.5
Tuesday	6	1.5	1.5	1.5
Wednesday	6	2	1	2
Thursday	6	2	2	1.5
Friday	6	2	2	0.5
Saturday	0	2.5	2.5	1
Sunday	0	3	1	2

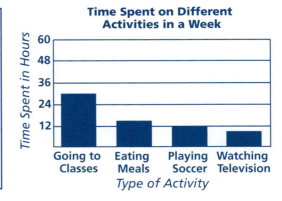

Line Graphs

To see whether a relationship exists between body mass and the number of Calories burned while bicycling, you could create a line graph. A line graph is used to display data that show how one variable (the responding variable) changes in response to another variable (the manipulated variable). You can use a line graph when your manipulated variable is **continuous,** that is, when there are other points between the ones that you tested. In this example, body mass is a continuous variable because there are other body masses between 30 and 40 kilograms (for example, 31 kilograms). Time is another example of a continuous variable.

Line graphs are powerful tools because they allow you to estimate values for conditions that you did not test in the experiment. For example, you can use the line graph to estimate that a 35-kilogram person would burn 68 Calories while bicycling.

To create a line graph, follow these steps.

1. On graph paper, draw a horizontal, or *x*-, axis and a vertical, or *y*-, axis.
2. Label the horizontal axis with the name of the manipulated variable. Label the vertical axis with the name of the responding variable. Include units of measurement.
3. Create a scale on each axis by marking off equally spaced numbers that cover the range of the data collected.
4. Plot a point on the graph for each piece of data. In the line graph above, the dotted lines show how to plot the first data point (30 kilograms and 60 Calories). Follow an imaginary vertical line extending up from the horizontal axis at the 30-kilogram mark. Then follow an imaginary horizontal line extending across from the vertical axis at the 60-Calorie mark. Plot the point where the two lines intersect.

Effect of Body Mass on Calories Burned While Bicycling

(graph: y-axis "Calories Burned in 30 Minutes" 0–120; x-axis "Body Mass (kg)" 0–70)

5. Connect the plotted points with a solid line. (In some cases, it may be more appropriate to draw a line that shows the general trend of the plotted points. In those cases, some of the points may fall above or below the line. Also, not all graphs are linear. It may be more appropriate to draw a curve to connect the points.)
6. Add a title that identifies the variables or relationship in the graph.

Activity

Create line graphs to display the data from Experiment 2 and Experiment 3 in the data table.

Activity

You read in the newspaper that a total of 4 centimeters of rain fell in your area in June, 2.5 centimeters fell in July, and 1.5 centimeters fell in August. What type of graph would you use to display these data? Use graph paper to create the graph.

Skills Handbook ◆ 157

Line Graphs

Focus Ask: **Would a bar graph show the relationship between body mass and the number of Calories burned in 30 minutes?** *(No. Bar graphs can only show data in distinct categories.)* Explain that line graphs are used to show how one variable changes in response to another variable.

Teach Walk students through the steps involved in creating a line graph using the example illustrated on the page. For example, ask: **What is the label on the horizontal axis? On the vertical axis?** *(Body Mass (kg); Calories Burned in 30 Minutes)* **What scale is used on each axis?** *(10 kg on the x-axis and 20 Calories on the y-axis)* **What does the second data point represent?** *(77 Calories burned for a body mass of 40 kg)* **What trend or pattern does the graph show?** *(The number of Calories burned in 30 minutes of cycling increases with body mass.)*

Activity

Students should make a different graph for each experiment. Each graph should have a different *x*-axis scale that is appropriate for the data. See sample graphs below.

Activity

Students should conclude that a bar graph would be best for displaying the data.

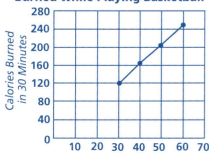

Effect of Body Mass on Calories Burned While Playing Basketball

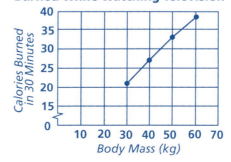

Effect of Body Mass on Calories Burned While Watching Television

Circle Graphs

Focus Emphasize that a circle graph must include 100 percent of the categories for the topic being graphed. For example, ask: **Could the data in the bar graph titled "Calories Burned by a 30-kilogram Person in Various Activities" (on the previous page) be shown in a circle graph? Why or why not?** (*No. It does not include all the possible ways a 30-kilogram person can burn Calories.*)

Teach Walk students through the steps for making a circle graph. If necessary, help them with the compass and the protractor. Use the protractor to illustrate that a circle has 360 degrees. Make sure students understand the mathematical calculations involved in making a circle graph.

Activity

You might have students work in pairs to complete the activity. Students' circle graphs should look like the graph below.

Ways Students Get to School

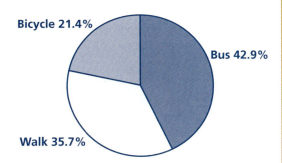

Bicycle 21.4%
Bus 42.9%
Walk 35.7%

Circle Graphs

Like bar graphs, circle graphs can be used to display data in a number of separate categories. Unlike bar graphs, however, circle graphs can only be used when you have data for *all* the categories that make up a given topic. A circle graph is sometimes called a pie chart. The pie represents the entire topic, while the slices represent the individual categories. The size of a slice indicates what percentage of the whole a particular category makes up.

The data table below shows the results of a survey in which 24 teenagers were asked to identify their favorite sport. The data were then used to create the circle graph at the right.

Favorite Sports

Sport	Students
Soccer	8
Basketball	6
Bicycling	6
Swimming	4

To create a circle graph, follow these steps.

1. Use a compass to draw a circle. Mark the center with a point. Then draw a line from the center point to the top of the circle.

2. Determine the size of each "slice" by setting up a proportion where *x* equals the number of degrees in a slice. (*Note:* A circle contains 360 degrees.) For example, to find the number of degrees in the "soccer" slice, set up the following proportion:

$$\frac{\text{Students who prefer soccer}}{\text{Total number of students}} = \frac{x}{\text{Total number of degrees in a circle}}$$

$$\frac{8}{24} = \frac{x}{360}$$

Cross-multiply and solve for x.

$$24x = 8 \times 360$$
$$x = 120$$

The "soccer" slice should contain 120 degrees.

158 ◆ O

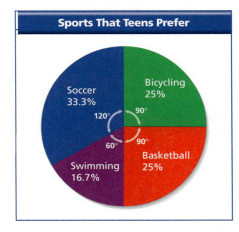

Sports That Teens Prefer

Soccer 33.3%, Bicycling 25%, Basketball 25%, Swimming 16.7%

3. Use a protractor to measure the angle of the first slice, using the line you drew to the top of the circle as the 0° line. Draw a line from the center of the circle to the edge for the angle you measured.

4. Continue around the circle by measuring the size of each slice with the protractor. Start measuring from the edge of the previous slice so the wedges do not overlap. When you are done, the entire circle should be filled in.

5. Determine the percentage of the whole circle that each slice represents. To do this, divide the number of degrees in a slice by the total number of degrees in a circle (360), and multiply by 100%. For the "soccer" slice, you can find the percentage as follows:

$$\frac{120}{360} \times 100\% = 33.3\%$$

6. Use a different color for each slice. Label each slice with the category and with the percentage of the whole it represents.

7. Add a title to the circle graph.

Activity

In a class of 28 students, 12 students take the bus to school, 10 students walk, and 6 students ride their bicycles. Create a circle graph to display these data.

158 ● O

Math Review

Scientists use math to organize, analyze, and present data. This appendix will help you review some basic math skills.

Mean, Median, and Mode

The **mean** is the average, or the sum of the data divided by the number of data items. The middle number in a set of ordered data is called the **median**. The **mode** is the number that appears most often in a set of data.

Example

A scientist counted the number of distinct songs sung by seven different male birds and collected the data shown below.

Male Bird Songs							
Bird	A	B	C	D	E	F	G
Number of Songs	36	29	40	35	28	36	27

To determine the mean number of songs, add the total number of songs and divide by the number of data items—in this case, the number of male birds.

$$\text{Mean} = \frac{231}{7} = 33 \text{ songs}$$

To find the median number of songs, arrange the data in numerical order and find the number in the middle of the series.

27 28 29 35 36 36 40

The number in the middle is 35, so the median number of songs is 35.

The mode is the value that appears most frequently. In the data, 36 appears twice, while each other item appears only once. Therefore, 36 songs is the mode.

Practice

Find out how many minutes it takes each student in your class to get to school. Then find the mean, median, and mode for the data.

Probability

Probability is the chance that an event will occur. Probability can be expressed as a ratio, a fraction, or a percentage. For example, when you flip a coin, the probability that the coin will land heads up is 1 in 2, or $\frac{1}{2}$, or 50 percent.

The probability that an event will happen can be expressed in the following formula.

$$P(\text{event}) = \frac{\text{Number of times the event can occur}}{\text{Total number of possible events}}$$

Example

A paper bag contains 25 blue marbles, 5 green marbles, 5 orange marbles, and 15 yellow marbles. If you close your eyes and pick a marble from the bag, what is the probability that it will be yellow?

$$P(\text{yellow marbles}) = \frac{15 \text{ yellow marbles}}{50 \text{ marbles total}}$$

$$P = \frac{15}{50}, \text{ or } \frac{3}{10}, \text{ or } 30\%$$

Practice

Each side of a cube has a letter on it. Two sides have *A*, three sides have *B*, and one side has *C*. If you roll the cube, what is the probability that *A* will land on top?

Math Review

Students can refer to this part of the Skills Handbook whenever they need to review some basic math skills. You can use the activities provided here to teach or reinforce these skills.

Mean, Median, and Mode

Focus Remind students that data from an experiment might consist of hundreds or thousands of numbers. Unless analyzed, the numbers likely will not be helpful.

Teach Work through the process of determining mean, median, and mode using the example in the book. Make sure students realize that these three numbers do not always equal each other. Point out that taken together, these three numbers give more information about the data than just one of the numbers alone.

Practice

Answers will vary based on class data. The mean should equal the total number of minutes divided by the number of students. The median should equal the number in the middle after arranging the data in numerical order. The mode should equal the number of minutes that is given most frequently.

Probability

Focus Show students a coin and ask: **What is the chance that I will get tails when I flip the coin?** (*Some students might know that there is a 1 in 2, or 50 percent, chance of getting tails.*)

Teach Set up a bag of marbles like the one in the example. Allow students to practice determining the probabilities of picking marbles of different colors. Then, encourage them to actually pick marbles and compare their actual results with those results predicted by probability.

Practice

$P(A) = 2$ sides with $\frac{A}{6}$ sides total
$P = \frac{2}{6}$, or $\frac{1}{3}$, or 33%

Area

Focus Ask: **Who knows what area is?** (*Area is equal to the number of square units needed to cover a certain shape or object.*) On the board, write the formulas for the area of a rectangle and a circle.

Teach Give students various objects of different shapes. Have them measure each object and determine its area based on the measurements. Point out that the units of the answer are squared because they are multiplied together. If students are interested, you might also explain that π is equal to the ratio of the circumference of a circle to its diameter. For circles of all sizes, π is approximately equal to the number 3.14, or $\frac{22}{7}$.

Practice

The area of the circle is equal to $21 \text{ m} \times 21 \text{ m} \times \frac{22}{7}$, or $1{,}386 \text{ m}^2$.

Circumference

Focus Draw a circle on the board. Then trace the outline with your finger and explain that this is the circumference of the circle, or the distance around it.

Teach Show students that the radius is equal to the distance from the center of the circle to any point on it. Point out that the diameter of a circle is equal to two times the radius. Give students paper circles of various sizes, and have them calculate the circumference of each.

Practice

The circumference is equal to $2 \times 28 \text{ m} \times \frac{22}{7}$, or 176 m.

Volume

Focus Fill a beaker with 100 milliliters of water. Ask: **What is the volume of water?** (*100 milliliters*) Explain that volume is the amount of space that something takes up. Then point out that one milliliter is equal to one cubic centimeter (cm³).

Teach Write on the board the formulas for calculating the volumes of a rectangle and a cylinder. Point out that volume is equal to the area of an object multiplied by its height. Then measure the beaker to show students the relationship between liquid volume (100 milliliters) and the number of cubic units it contains (100 cubic centimeters).

Area

The **area** of a surface is the number of square units that cover it. The front cover of your textbook has an area of about 600 cm².

Area of a Rectangle and a Square

To find the area of a rectangle, multiply its length times its width. The formula for the area of a rectangle is

$$A = \ell \times w, \text{ or } A = \ell w$$

Since all four sides of a square have the same length, the area of a square is the length of one side multiplied by itself, or squared.

$$A = s \times s, \text{ or } A = s^2$$

Example

A scientist is studying the plants in a field that measures 75 m × 45 m. What is the area of the field?

$$A = \ell \times w$$
$$A = 75 \text{ m} \times 45 \text{ m}$$
$$A = 3{,}375 \text{ m}^2$$

Area of a Circle

The formula for the area of a circle is

$$A = \pi \times r \times r, \text{ or } A = \pi r^2$$

The length of the radius is represented by r, and the value of π is approximately $\frac{22}{7}$.

Example

Find the area of a circle with a radius of 14 cm.

$$A = \pi r^2$$
$$A = 14 \times 14 \times \frac{22}{7}$$
$$A = 616 \text{ cm}^2$$

Practice

Find the area of a circle that has a radius of 21 m.

Circumference

The distance around a circle is called the circumference. The formula for finding the circumference of a circle is

$$C = 2 \times \pi \times r, \text{ or } C = 2\pi r$$

Example

The radius of a circle is 35 cm. What is its circumference?

$$C = 2\pi r$$
$$C = 2 \times 35 \times \frac{22}{7}$$
$$C = 220 \text{ cm}$$

Practice

What is the circumference of a circle with a radius of 28 m?

Volume

The volume of an object is the number of cubic units it contains. The volume of a wastebasket, for example, might be about 26,000 cm³.

Volume of a Rectangular Object To find the volume of a rectangular object, multiply the object's length times its width times its height.

$$V = \ell \times w \times h, \text{ or } V = \ell w h$$

Example

Find the volume of a box with length 24 cm, width 12 cm, and height 9 cm.

$$V = \ell w h$$
$$V = 24 \text{ cm} \times 12 \text{ cm} \times 9 \text{ cm}$$
$$V = 2{,}592 \text{ cm}^3$$

Practice

What is the volume of a rectangular object with length 17 cm, width 11 cm, and height 6 cm?

Practice

The volume of the rectangular object is equal to $17 \text{ cm} \times 11 \text{ cm} \times 6 \text{ cm}$, or $1{,}122 \text{ cm}^3$.

Fractions

A **fraction** is a way to express a part of a whole. In the fraction $\frac{4}{7}$, 4 is the numerator and 7 is the denominator.

Adding and Subtracting Fractions
To add or subtract two or more fractions that have a common denominator, first add or subtract the numerators. Then write the sum or difference over the common denominator.

To find the sum or difference of fractions with different denominators, first find the least common multiple of the denominators. This is known as the least common denominator. Then convert each fraction to equivalent fractions with the least common denominator. Add or subtract the numerators. Then write the sum or difference over the common denominator.

> **Example**
>
> $$\frac{5}{6} - \frac{3}{4} = \frac{10}{12} - \frac{9}{12} = \frac{10 - 9}{12} = \frac{1}{12}$$

Multiplying Fractions
To multiply two fractions, first multiply the two numerators, then multiply the two denominators.

> **Example**
>
> $$\frac{5}{6} \times \frac{2}{3} = \frac{5 \times 2}{6 \times 3} = \frac{10}{18} = \frac{5}{9}$$

Dividing Fractions
Dividing by a fraction is the same as multiplying by its reciprocal. Reciprocals are numbers whose numerators and denominators have been switched. To divide one fraction by another, first invert the fraction you are dividing by—in other words, turn it upside down. Then multiply the two fractions.

> **Example**
>
> $$\frac{2}{5} \div \frac{7}{8} = \frac{2}{5} \times \frac{8}{7} = \frac{2 \times 8}{5 \times 7} = \frac{16}{35}$$

> **Practice**
>
> Solve the following: $\frac{3}{7} \div \frac{4}{5}$.

Decimals

Fractions whose denominators are 10, 100, or some other power of 10 are often expressed as decimals. For example, the fraction $\frac{9}{10}$ can be expressed as the decimal 0.9, and the fraction $\frac{7}{100}$ can be written as 0.07.

Adding and Subtracting With Decimals
To add or subtract decimals, line up the decimal points before you carry out the operation.

> **Example**
>
> $$\begin{array}{r} 27.4 \\ + 6.19 \\ \hline 33.59 \end{array} \qquad \begin{array}{r} 278.635 \\ - 191.4 \\ \hline 87.235 \end{array}$$

Multiplying With Decimals
When you multiply two numbers with decimals, the number of decimal places in the product is equal to the total number of decimal places in each number being multiplied.

> **Example**
>
> $$\begin{array}{r} 46.2 \text{ (one decimal place)} \\ \times\ 2.37 \text{ (two decimal places)} \\ \hline 109.494 \text{ (three decimal places)} \end{array}$$

Dividing With Decimals
To divide a decimal by a whole number, put the decimal point in the quotient above the decimal point in the dividend.

> **Example**
>
> $$15.5 \div 5$$
> $$5)\overline{15.5} = 3.1$$

To divide a decimal by a decimal, you need to rewrite the divisor as a whole number. Do this by multiplying both the divisor and dividend by the same multiple of 10.

> **Example**
>
> $$1.68 \div 4.2 = 16.8 \div 42$$
> $$42)\overline{16.8} = 0.4$$

> **Practice**
>
> Multiply 6.21 by 8.5.

Fractions

Focus Draw a circle on the board, and divide it into eight equal sections. Shade in one of the sections, and explain that one out of eight, or one eighth, of the sections is shaded. Also use the circle to show that four eighths is the same as one half.

Teach Write the fraction $\frac{3}{4}$ on the board. Ask: **What is the numerator?** *(Three)* **What is the denominator?** *(Four)* Emphasize that when adding and subtracting fractions, the denominators of the two fractions must be the same. If necessary, review how to find the least common denominator. Remind students that when multiplying and dividing, the denominators do not have to be the same.

> **Practice**
>
> $$\frac{3}{7} \div \frac{4}{5} = \frac{3}{7} \times \frac{5}{4} = \frac{15}{28}$$

Decimals

Focus Write the number *129.835* on the board. Ask: **What number is in the ones position?** *(9)* **The tenths position?** *(8)* **The hundredths position?** *(3)* Make sure students know that 0.8 is equal to $\frac{8}{10}$ and 0.03 is equal to $\frac{3}{100}$.

Teach Use the examples in the book to review addition, subtraction, multiplication, and division with decimals. Make up a worksheet of similar problems to give students additional practice. Also show students how a fraction is converted to a decimal by dividing the numerator by the denominator. For example, $\frac{1}{2}$ is equal to 0.5.

> **Practice**
>
> $$6.21 \times 8.5 = 52.785$$

Ratio and Proportion

Focus Differentiate a ratio from a fraction. Remind students that a fraction tells how many parts of the whole. In contrast, a ratio compares two different numbers. For example, $\frac{12}{22}$, or $\frac{6}{11}$, of a class are girls. But the ratio of boys to girls in the class is 10 to 12, or $\frac{5}{6}$.

Teach Use the example in the book to explain how to use a proportion to find an unknown quantity. Provide students with additional practice problems, if needed.

Practice

$6 \times 49 = 7x$

$294 = 7x$

$294 \div 7 = x$

$x = 42$

Percentage

Focus On the board, write $50\% = \frac{50}{100}$. Explain that a percentage is a ratio that compares a number to 100.

Teach Point out that when calculating percentages, you are usually using numbers other than 100. In this case, you set up a proportion. Go over the example in the book. Emphasize that the number representing the total goes on the bottom of the ratio, as does the 100%.

Practice

Students should set up the proportion

$\frac{42 \text{ marbles}}{300 \text{ marbles}} = \frac{x\%}{100\%}$

$42 \times 100 = 300x$

$4200 = 300x$

$4200 \div 300 = 14\%$

Ratio and Proportion

A **ratio** compares two numbers by division. For example, suppose a scientist counts 800 wolves and 1,200 moose on an island. The ratio of wolves to moose can be written as a fraction, $\frac{800}{1,200}$, which can be reduced to $\frac{2}{3}$. The same ratio can also be expressed as 2 to 3 or 2 : 3.

A **proportion** is a mathematical sentence saying that two ratios are equivalent. For example, a proportion could state that $\frac{800 \text{ wolves}}{1,200 \text{ moose}} = \frac{2 \text{ wolves}}{3 \text{ moose}}$. You can sometimes set up a proportion to determine or estimate an unknown quantity. For example, suppose a scientist counts 25 beetles in an area of 10 square meters. The scientist wants to estimate the number of beetles in 100 square meters.

Example

1. Express the relationship between beetles and area as a ratio: $\frac{25}{10}$, simplified to $\frac{5}{2}$.
2. Set up a proportion, with x representing the number of beetles. The proportion can be stated as $\frac{5}{2} = \frac{x}{100}$.
3. Begin by cross-multiplying. In other words, multiply each fraction's numerator by the other fraction's denominator.

   $5 \times 100 = 2 \times x$, or $500 = 2x$

4. To find the value of x, divide both sides by 2. The result is 250, or 250 beetles in 100 square meters.

Practice

Find the value of x in the following proportion: $\frac{6}{7} = \frac{x}{49}$.

Percentage

A **percentage** is a ratio that compares a number to 100. For example, there are 37 granite rocks in a collection that consists of 100 rocks. The ratio $\frac{37}{100}$ can be written as 37%. Granite rocks make up 37% of the rock collection.

You can calculate percentages of numbers other than 100 by setting up a proportion.

Example

Rain falls on 9 days out of 30 in June. What percentage of the days in June were rainy?

$\frac{9 \text{ days}}{30 \text{ days}} = \frac{d\%}{100\%}$

To find the value of d, begin by cross-multiplying, as for any proportion:

$9 \times 100 = 30 \times d$ $d = \frac{900}{30}$ $d = 30$

Practice

There are 300 marbles in a jar, and 42 of those marbles are blue. What percentage of the marbles are blue?

Significant Figures

The **precision** of a measurement depends on the instrument you use to take the measurement. For example, if the smallest unit on the ruler is millimeters, then the most precise measurement you can make will be in millimeters.

The sum or difference of measurements can only be as precise as the least precise measurement being added or subtracted. Round your answer so that it has the same number of digits after the decimal as the least precise measurement. Round up if the last digit is 5 or more, and round down if the last digit is 4 or less.

Example

Subtract a temperature of 5.2°C from the temperature 75.46°C.

$$75.46 - 5.2 = 70.26$$

5.2 has the fewest digits after the decimal, so it is the least precise measurement. Since the last digit of the answer is 6, round up to 3. The most precise difference between the measurements is 70.3°C.

Practice

Add 26.4 m to 8.37 m. Round your answer according to the precision of the measurements.

Significant figures are the number of nonzero digits in a measurement. Zeroes between nonzero digits are also significant. For example, the measurements 12,500 L, 0.125 cm, and 2.05 kg all have three significant figures. When you multiply and divide measurements, the one with the fewest significant figures determines the number of significant figures in your answer.

Example

Multiply 110 g by 5.75 g.

$$110 \times 5.75 = 632.5$$

Because 110 has only two significant figures, round the answer to 630 g.

Scientific Notation

A **factor** is a number that divides into another number with no remainder. In the example, the number 3 is used as a factor four times.

An **exponent** tells how many times a number is used as a factor. For example, $3 \times 3 \times 3 \times 3$ can be written as 3^4. The exponent 4 indicates that the number 3 is used as a factor four times. Another way of expressing this is to say that 81 is equal to 3 to the fourth power.

Example

$$3^4 = 3 \times 3 \times 3 \times 3 = 81$$

Scientific notation uses exponents and powers of ten to write very large or very small numbers in shorter form. When you write a number in scientific notation, you write the number as two factors. The first factor is any number between 1 and 10. The second factor is a power of 10, such as 10^3 or 10^6.

Example

The average distance between the planet Mercury and the sun is 58,000,000 km. To write the first factor in scientific notation, insert a decimal point in the original number so that you have a number between 1 and 10. In the case of 58,000,000, the number is 5.8.

To determine the power of 10, count the number of places that the decimal point moved. In this case, it moved 7 places.

$$58{,}000{,}000 \text{ km} = 5.8 \times 10^7 \text{ km}$$

Practice

Express 6,590,000 in scientific notation.

Significant Figures

Focus Measure the length of a paper clip using two different rulers. Use one ruler that is less precise than the other. Compare the two measurements. Ask: **Which measurement is more precise?** (*The ruler with the smallest units will give the more precise measurement.*)

Teach Give students the opportunity to take measurements of an object using tools with different precision. Encourage students to add and subtract their measurements, making sure that they round the answers to reflect the precision of the instruments. Go over the example for significant digits. Check for understanding by asking: **How many significant digits are in the number 324,000?** (*Three*) **In the number 5,901?** (*Four*) **In the number 0.706?** (*Three*) If students need additional practice, create a worksheet with problems in multiplying and dividing numbers with various significant digits.

Practice

26.4 m + 8.37 m = 34.77 m
This answer should be rounded to 34.8 m because the least precise measurement has only one digit after the decimal. This number is rounded up to 8 because the last digit is more than 5.

Scientific Notation

Focus Write a very large number on the board, such as 100 million, using all the zeros. Then, write the number using scientific notation. Ask: **Why do you think scientists prefer to write very large numbers using scientific notation?** (*Possible answers include that it is easier to do calculations, convert units, and make comparisons with other numbers.*)

Teach Go over the examples, and ask: **In the second example, which numbers are the factors?** (*5.8 and 10^7*) **Which number is the exponent?** (*^{7}*) Explain that very small numbers have a negative exponent because the decimal point is moved to the right to produce the first factor. For example, 0.00000628 is equal to 6.28×10^{-6}.

Practice

$6{,}590{,}000 = 6.59 \times 10^6$

Reading Comprehension Skills

Students can refer to this part of the Skills Handbook whenever they need to review a reading skill. You can use the activities provided here to teach or reinforce these skills.

Learning From Science Textbooks

Reading in a content area presents challenges different from those encountered when reading fiction. Science texts often have more new vocabulary and more unfamiliar concepts that place greater emphasis on inferential reasoning. Students who can apply reading skills and information-organizing strategies will be more successful in reading and understanding a science textbook.

Activity

Turn with students to the first page of any section. Walk through the Reading Preview with students, showing them the Key Concepts that provide a guiding set of questions that students can answer from the text. Next, point out the Key Terms list, which highlights the science vocabulary. Last, have students find the Target Reading Skill with graphic organizer. Make the connection for students to the help in this Skills Handbook.

All in One Teaching Resources
• Target Reading Skills Handbook

Building Vocabulary

Focus Explain to students that knowing the definitions of key concept words can help them understand what they read.

Teach List on the board strategies to learn the definitions of new terms. Also solicit from students strategies that work for them—drawing a picture for the term, acting it out, or using it in conversation. Challenge students to choose a new strategy to learn the Key Terms in your next section.

Using Prior Knowledge

Focus Explain to students that using prior knowledge helps connect what they already know to what they are about to read.

Teach Point out that prior knowledge might not be accurate because memories have faded or perspectives have changed. Encourage students to ask questions to

Reading Comprehension Skills

Your textbook is an important source of science information. As you read your science textbook, you will find that the book has been written to assist you in understanding the science concepts.

Learning From Science Textbooks

As you study science in school, you will learn science concepts in a variety of ways. Sometimes you will do interesting activities and experiments to explore science ideas. To fully understand what you observe in experiments and activities, you will need to read your science textbook. To help you read, some of the important ideas are highlighted so that you can easily recognize what they are. In addition, a target reading skill in each section will help you understand what you read.

By using the target reading skills, you will improve your reading comprehension—that is, you will improve your ability to understand what you read. As you learn science, you will build knowledge that will help you understand even more of what you read. This knowledge will help you learn about all the topics presented in this textbook.

And—guess what?—these reading skills can be useful whenever you are reading. Reading to learn is important for your entire life. You have an opportunity to begin that process now.

The target reading skills that will improve your reading comprehension are described below.

Building Vocabulary

To understand the science concepts taught in this textbook, you need to remember the meanings of the Key Terms. One strategy consists of writing the definitions of these terms in your own words. You can also practice using the terms in sentences and make lists of words or phrases you associate with each term.

Using Prior Knowledge

Your prior knowledge is what you already know before you begin to read about a topic. Building on what you already know gives you a head start on learning new information. Before you begin a new assignment, think about what you know. You might page through your reading assignment, looking at the headings and the visuals to spark your memory. You can list what you know in the graphic organizer provided in the section opener. Then, as you read, consider questions like the ones below to connect what you learn to what you already know.

• How does what you learn relate to what you know?
• How did something you already know help you learn something new?
• Did your original ideas agree with what you have just learned? If not, how would you revise your original ideas?

Asking Questions

Asking yourself questions is an excellent way to focus on and remember new information in your textbook. You can learn how to ask good questions.

One way is to turn the text headings into questions. Then your questions can guide you to identify and remember the important information as you read. Look at these examples:

Heading: Using Seismographic Data
Question: How are seismographic data used?
Heading: Kinds of Faults
Question: What are the kinds of faults?

resolve discrepancies between their prior knowledge and what they have learned.

Asking Questions

Focus Demonstrate to students how to change a text heading into a question to help them anticipate the concepts, facts, and events they will read about.

Teach Encourage students to use this reading skill for the next section they read. Instruct them to turn the text headings into questions. Also challenge students to write at least four *what, how, why, who, when,* or *where* questions. Then, have students evaluate the skill. Ask: **Did asking questions about the text help you focus on the reading and remember what you read?** (*Answers will vary, but encourage honesty.*) If this reading skill didn't help, challenge them to assess why not.

You do not have to limit your questions to the text headings. Ask questions about anything that you need to clarify or that will help you understand the content. *What* and *how* are probably the most common question words, but you may also ask *why, who, when,* or *where* questions. Here is an example:

Properties of Waves

Question	Answer
What is amplitude?	Amplitude is . . .

Previewing Visuals

Visuals are photographs, graphs, tables, diagrams, and illustrations. Visuals, such as this diagram of a normal fault, contain important information. Look at visuals and their captions before you read. This will help you prepare for what you will be reading about.

Often you will be asked what you want to learn about a visual. For example, after you look at the normal fault diagram, you might ask: What is the movement along a normal fault? Questions about visuals give you a purpose for reading—to answer your questions. Previewing visuals also helps you see what you already know.

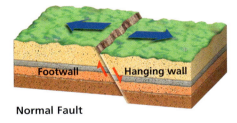

Footwall **Hanging wall**

Normal Fault

Outlining

An outline shows the relationship between main ideas and supporting ideas. An outline has a formal structure. You write the main ideas, called topics, next to Roman numerals. The supporting ideas, sometimes called subtopics, are written under the main ideas and labeled A, B, C, and so on. An outline looks like this:

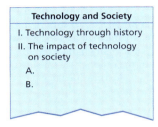

Technology and Society

I. Technology through history
II. The impact of technology on society
   A.
   B.

When you have completed an outline like this, you can see at a glance the structure of the section. You can use this outline as a study tool.

Identifying Main Ideas

When you are reading, it is important to try to understand the ideas and concepts that are in a passage. As you read science material, you will recognize that each paragraph has a lot of information and detail. Good readers try to identify the most important—or biggest—idea in every paragraph or section. That's the main idea. The other information in the paragraph supports or further explains the main idea.

Sometimes main ideas are stated directly. In this book, some main ideas are identified for you as key concepts. These are printed in boldface type. However, you must identify other main ideas yourself. In order to do this, you must identify all the ideas within a paragraph or section. Then ask yourself which idea is big enough to include all the other ideas.

Skills Handbook ♦ 165

Previewing Visuals

Focus Explain to students that looking at the visuals before reading will help them activate prior knowledge and predict what they are about to read.

Teach Assign a section for students to preview the visuals. First, instruct them to write a sentence describing what the section will be about. Then, encourage them to write one or two questions for each visual to give purpose to their reading. Also have them list any prior knowledge about the subject.

Outlining

Focus Explain that using an outline format helps organize information by main topic, subtopic, and details.

Teach Choose a section in the book, and demonstrate how to make an outline for it. Make sure students understand the structure of the outline by asking: **Is this a topic or a subtopic? Where does this information go in the outline? Would I write this heading next to a Roman numeral or a capital letter?** *(Answers depend on the section being outlined.)* Also show them how to indent and add details to the outline using numerals and lowercase letters.

Identifying Main Ideas

Focus Explain that identifying main ideas and details helps sort the facts from the information into groups. Each group can have a main topic, subtopics, and details.

Teach Tell students that paragraphs are often written so that the main idea is in the first or second sentence, or in the last sentence. Assign students a page in the book. Instruct them to write the main idea for each paragraph on that page. If students have difficulty finding the main idea, suggest that they list all of the ideas given in the paragraph, and then choose the idea that is big enough to include all the others.

Comparing and Contrasting

Focus Explain that comparing and contrasting information shows how concepts, facts, and events are similar or different. The results of the comparison can have importance.

Teach Point out that Venn diagrams work best when comparing two things. To compare more than two things, students should use a compare/contrast table. Have students make a Venn diagram or compare/contrast table using two or more different sports or other activities, such as playing musical instruments. Emphasize that students should select characteristics that highlight the similarities and differences in the activities.

Sequencing

Focus Tell students that organizing information from beginning to end will help them understand a step-by-step process.

Teach Encourage students to create a flowchart to show the things they did this morning to get ready for school. Remind students that a flowchart should show the correct order in which events occur. (*A typical flowchart might include: got up ➤ took a shower ➤ got dressed ➤ ate breakfast ➤ brushed teeth ➤ gathered books and homework ➤ put on jacket.*) Then explain that a cycle diagram shows a sequence of events that is continuous. Challenge students to create a cycle diagram that shows how the weather changes with the seasons where they live. (*Most cycle diagrams will include four steps, one for each season.*)

Comparing and Contrasting

When you compare and contrast, you examine the similarities and differences between things. You can compare and contrast in a Venn diagram or in a table. Your completed diagram or table shows you how the items are alike and how they are different.

Venn Diagram A Venn diagram consists of two overlapping circles. In the space where the circles overlap, you write the characteristics that the two items have in common. In one of the circles outside the area of overlap, you write the differing features or characteristics of one of the items. In the other circle outside the area of overlap, you write the differing characteristics of the other item.

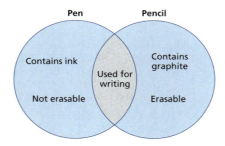

Table In a compare/contrast table, you list the items to be compared across the top of the table. Then list the characteristics or features to be compared in the left column. Complete the table by filling in information about each characteristic or feature.

Blood Vessel	Function	Structure of Wall
Artery	Carries blood away from heart	
Capillary		
Vein		

Sequencing

A sequence is the order in which a series of events occurs. Recognizing and remembering the sequence of events is important to understanding many processes in science. Sometimes the text uses words like *first, next, during,* and *after* to signal a sequence. A flowchart or a cycle diagram can help you visualize a sequence.

Flowchart To make a flowchart, write a brief description of each step or event in a box. Place the boxes in order, with the first event at the top of the page. Then draw an arrow to connect each step or event to the next.

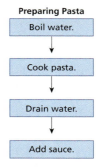

Cycle Diagram A cycle diagram shows a sequence that is continuous, or cyclical. A continuous sequence does not have an end because when the final event is over, the first event begins again. To create a cycle diagram, write the starting event in a box placed at the top of a page in the center. Then, moving in a clockwise direction around an imaginary circle, write each event in a box in its proper sequence. Draw arrows that connect each event to the one that occurs next, forming a continuous circle.

Identifying Supporting Evidence

A hypothesis is a possible explanation for observations made by scientists or an answer to a scientific question. A hypothesis is tested over and over again. The tests may produce evidence that supports the hypothesis. When enough supporting evidence is collected, a hypothesis may become a theory.

Identifying the supporting evidence for a hypothesis or theory can help you understand the hypothesis or theory. Evidence consists of facts—information whose accuracy can be confirmed by testing or observation.

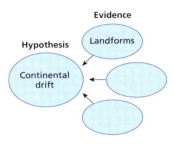

Science involves many cause-and-effect relationships. Seeing and understanding these relationships helps you understand science processes.

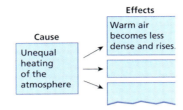

Concept Mapping

Concept maps are useful tools for organizing information on any topic. A concept map begins with a main idea or core concept and shows how the idea can be subdivided into related subconcepts or smaller ideas. In this way, relationships between concepts become clearer and easier to understand.

You construct a concept map by placing concepts (usually nouns) in ovals and connecting them with linking words. The biggest concept or idea is placed in an oval at the top of the map. Related concepts are arranged in ovals below the big idea. The linking words are often verbs and verb phrases and are written on the lines that connect the ovals.

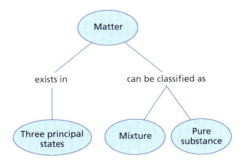

Relating Cause and Effect

Identifying causes and effects helps you understand relationships among events. A cause makes something happen. An effect is what happens. When you recognize that one event causes another, you are relating cause and effect. Words like *cause, because, effect, affect,* and *result* often signal a cause or an effect.

Sometimes an effect can have more than one cause, or a cause can produce several effects. For example, car exhaust and smoke from industrial plants are two causes of air pollution. Some effects of air pollution include breathing difficulties for some people, death of plants along some highways, and damage to some building surfaces.

Skills Handbook ◆ 167

Identifying Supporting Evidence

Focus Explain to students that identifying the supporting evidence will help them to understand the relationship between the facts and the hypothesis.

Teach Remind students that a hypothesis is neither right nor wrong, but it is either supported or not supported by the evidence from testing or observation. If evidence is found that does not support a hypothesis, the hypothesis can be changed to accommodate the new evidence, or it can be dropped.

Relating Cause and Effect

Focus Explain to students that cause is the reason for what happens. The effect is what happens in response to the cause. Relating cause and effect helps students relate the reason for what happens to what happens as a result.

Teach Emphasize that not all events that occur together have a cause-and-effect relationship. For example, tell students that you went to the grocery store and your car stalled. Ask: **Is there a cause-and-effect relationship in this situation? Explain.** *(No. Going to the grocery store could not cause a car to stall. There must be another cause to make the car stall.)*

Concept Mapping

Focus Elicit from students how a map shows the relationship of one geographic area to another. Connect this idea to how a concept map shows the relationship between terms and concepts.

Teach Challenge students to make a concept map with at least three levels of concepts to organize information about types of transportation. All students should start with the phrase *Types of transportation* at the top of the concept map. After that point, their concepts may vary. *(For example, some students might place* private transportation *and* public transportation *at the next level, while other students might choose* human-powered *and* gas-powered.*)* Make sure students connect the concepts with linking words.

- Complete student edition
- Video and audio
- Simulations and activities
- Section and chapter activities

Laboratory Safety

Laboratory safety is an essential element of a successful science class. Students need to understand exactly what is safe and unsafe behavior and what the rationale is behind each safety rule.

All in One Teaching Resources

- Laboratory Safety Teacher Notes
- Laboratory Safety Rules
- Laboratory Safety Symbols
- Laboratory Safety Contract

General Precautions

- Post safety rules in the classroom, and review them regularly with students before beginning every science activity.
- Familiarize yourself with the safety procedures for each activity before introducing it to your students.
- For open-ended activities like Chapter Projects, have students submit their procedures or design plans in writing and check them for safety considerations.
- Always act as an exemplary role model by displaying safe behavior.
- Know how to use safety equipment, such as fire extinguishers and fire blankets, and always have it accessible.
- Have students practice leaving the classroom quickly and orderly to prepare them for emergencies.
- Explain to students how to use the intercom or other available means of communication to get help during an emergency.
- Never leave students unattended while they are engaged in science activities.
- Provide enough space for students to safely carry out science activities.
- Instruct students to report all accidents and injuries to you immediately.

Safety Symbols

These symbols warn of possible dangers in the laboratory and remind you to work carefully.

 Safety Goggles Wear safety goggles to protect your eyes in any activity involving chemicals, flames or heating, or glassware.

 Lab Apron Wear a laboratory apron to protect your skin and clothing from damage.

 Breakage Handle breakable materials, such as glassware, with care. Do not touch broken glassware.

 Heat-Resistant Gloves Use an oven mitt or other hand protection when handling hot materials such as hot plates or hot glassware.

 Plastic Gloves Wear disposable plastic gloves when working with harmful chemicals and organisms. Keep your hands away from your face, and dispose of the gloves according to your teacher's instructions.

 Heating Use a clamp or tongs to pick up hot glassware. Do not touch hot objects with your bare hands.

 Flames Before you work with flames, tie back loose hair and clothing. Follow instructions from your teacher about lighting and extinguishing flames.

 No Flames When using flammable materials, make sure there are no flames, sparks, or other exposed heat sources present.

 Corrosive Chemical Avoid getting acid or other corrosive chemicals on your skin or clothing or in your eyes. Do not inhale the vapors. Wash your hands after the activity.

 Poison Do not let any poisonous chemical come into contact with your skin, and do not inhale its vapors. Wash your hands when you are finished with the activity.

168 ◆ O

 Fumes Work in a ventilated area when harmful vapors may be involved. Avoid inhaling vapors directly. Only test an odor when directed to do so by your teacher, and use a wafting motion to direct the vapor toward your nose.

 Sharp Object Scissors, scalpels, knives, needles, pins, and tacks can cut your skin. Always direct a sharp edge or point away from yourself and others.

 Animal Safety Treat live or preserved animals or animal parts with care to avoid harming the animals or yourself. Wash your hands when you are finished with the activity.

 Plant Safety Handle plants only as directed by your teacher. If you are allergic to certain plants, tell your teacher; do not do an activity involving those plants. Avoid touching harmful plants such as poison ivy. Wash your hands when you are finished with the activity.

 Electric Shock To avoid electric shock, never use electrical equipment around water, or when the equipment is wet or your hands are wet. Be sure cords are untangled and cannot trip anyone. Unplug equipment not in use.

 Physical Safety When an experiment involves physical activity, avoid injuring yourself or others. Alert your teacher if there is any reason you should not participate.

 Disposal Dispose of chemicals and other laboratory materials safely. Follow the instructions from your teacher.

 Hand Washing Wash your hands thoroughly when finished with the activity. Use antibacterial soap and warm water. Rinse well.

⚠ **General Safety Awareness** When this symbol appears, follow the instructions provided. When you are asked to develop your own procedure in a lab, have your teacher approve your plan before you go further.

End-of-Experiment Rules

- Always have students use warm water and soap for washing their hands.

Heating and Fire Safety

- No flammable substances should be in use around hot plates, light bulbs, or open flames.
- Test tubes should be heated only in water baths.

- Students should be permitted to strike matches to light candles or burners *only* with strict supervision. When possible, you should light the flames, especially when working with younger students.
- Be sure to have proper ventilation when fumes are produced during a procedure.
- All electrical equipment used in the lab should have GFI (Ground Fault Interrupter) switches.

Science Safety Rules

General Precautions

Follow all instructions. Never perform activities without the approval and supervision of your teacher. Do not engage in horseplay. Never eat or drink in the laboratory. Keep work areas clean and uncluttered.

Dress Code

Wear safety goggles whenever you work with chemicals, glassware, heat sources such as burners, or any substance that might get into your eyes. If you wear contact lenses, notify your teacher.

Wear a lab apron or coat whenever you work with corrosive chemicals or substances that can stain. Wear disposable plastic gloves when working with organisms and harmful chemicals. Tie back long hair. Remove or tie back any article of clothing or jewelry that can hang down and touch chemicals, flames, or equipment. Roll up long sleeves. Never wear open shoes or sandals.

First Aid

Report all accidents, injuries, or fires to your teacher, no matter how minor. Be aware of the location of the first-aid kit, emergency equipment such as the fire extinguisher and fire blanket, and the nearest telephone. Know whom to contact in an emergency.

Heating and Fire Safety

Keep all combustible materials away from flames. When heating a substance in a test tube, make sure that the mouth of the tube is not pointed at you or anyone else. Never heat a liquid in a closed container. Use an oven mitt to pick up a container that has been heated.

Using Chemicals Safely

Never put your face near the mouth of a container that holds chemicals. Never touch, taste, or smell a chemical unless your teacher tells you to.

Use only those chemicals needed in the activity. Keep all containers closed when chemicals are not being used. Pour all chemicals over the sink or a container, not over your work surface. Dispose of excess chemicals as instructed by your teacher.

Be extra careful when working with acids or bases. When mixing an acid and water, always pour the water into the container first and then add the acid to the water. Never pour water into an acid. Wash chemical spills and splashes immediately with plenty of water.

Using Glassware Safely

If glassware is broken or chipped, notify your teacher immediately. Never handle broken or chipped glass with your bare hands.

Never force glass tubing or thermometers into a rubber stopper or rubber tubing. Have your teacher insert the glass tubing or thermometer if required for an activity.

Using Sharp Instruments

Handle sharp instruments with extreme care. Never cut material toward you; cut away from you.

Animal and Plant Safety

Never perform experiments that cause pain, discomfort, or harm to animals. Only handle animals if absolutely necessary. If you know that you are allergic to certain plants, molds, or animals, tell your teacher before doing an activity in which these are used. Wash your hands thoroughly after any activity involving animals, animal parts, plants, plant parts, or soil.

During field work, wear long pants, long sleeves, socks, and closed shoes. Avoid poisonous plants and fungi as well as plants with thorns.

End-of-Experiment Rules

Unplug all electrical equipment. Clean up your work area. Dispose of waste materials as instructed by your teacher. Wash your hands after every experiment.

Handling Organisms Safely

- In an activity where students are directed to taste something, be sure to store the material in clean, *nonscience* containers. Distribute the material to students in *new* plastic or paper dispensables, which should be discarded after the tasting. Tasting or eating should never be done in a lab classroom.

- When growing bacterial cultures, use only disposable petri dishes. After streaking, the dishes should be sealed and not opened again by students. After the lab, students should return the unopened dishes to you.

- Two methods are recommended for the safe disposal of bacterial cultures. *First method:* Autoclave the petri dishes and discard them without opening. *Second method:* If no autoclave is available, carefully open the dishes (never have a student do this), pour full-strength bleach into the dishes, and let them stand for a day. Then pour the bleach from the petri dishes down a drain, and flush the drain with lots of water. Tape the petri dishes back together, and place them in a sealed plastic bag. Wrap the plastic bag with a brown paper bag or newspaper, and tape securely. Throw the sealed package in the trash. Thoroughly disinfect the work area with bleach.

- To grow mold, use a new, sealable plastic bag that is two to three times larger than the material to be placed inside. Seal the bag and tape it shut. After the bag is sealed, students should not open it. To dispose of the bag and mold culture, make a small cut near an edge of the bag, and cook the bag in a microwave oven on a high setting for at least one minute. Discard the bag according to local ordinance, usually in the trash.

- Students should wear disposable nitrile, latex, or food-handling gloves when handling live animals or nonliving specimens.

Using Glassware Safely

- Use plastic containers, graduated cylinders, and beakers whenever possible. If using glass, students should wear safety goggles.
- Use only nonmercury thermometers with anti-roll protectors.

Using Chemicals Safely

- When students use both chemicals and microscopes in one activity, microscopes should be in a separate part of the room from the chemicals so that when students remove their goggles to use the microscopes, their eyes are not at risk.

English and Spanish Glossary

A

acoustics The study of how sounds interact with each other and the environment. (p. 52)
acústica Estudio de cómo interactúan los sonidos entre ellos y con el medio ambiente.

amplitude The maximum distance the particles of a medium move away from their rest positions as a wave passes through the medium. (p. 12)
amplitud Distancia máxima a la que se separan las partículas de un medio de sus posiciones de reposo, cuando una onda atraviesa el medio.

amplitude modulation A method of transmitting signals by changing the amplitude of a wave. (p. 91)
amplitud modulada Método de transmisión de señales por el cual se cambia la amplitud de una onda.

antinode A point of maximum amplitude on a standing wave. (p. 22)
antinodo Punto de máxima amplitud en una onda estacionaria.

C

camera An optical instrument that uses lenses to focus light, and film to record an image of an object. (p. 131)
cámara Instrumento óptico que usa lentes para enfocar la luz, y película para grabar la imagen de un objeto.

cochlea A fluid-filled cavity in the inner ear that is shaped like a snail shell. (p. 55)
cóclea Cavidad llena de líquido en el oído interno que tiene forma de caracol.

complementary colors Any two colors that combine to form white light or black pigment. (p. 110)
colores complementarios Dos colores cualesquiera que se combinan para crear luz blanca o pigmento negro.

compression The part of a longitudinal wave where the particles of the medium are close together. (p. 9)
compresión Parte de una onda longitudinal donde las partículas del medio están muy juntas.

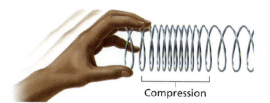

Compression

concave lens A lens that is thinner in the center than at the edges. (p. 123)
lente cóncava Lente que es más fina en el centro que en los extremos.

concave mirror A mirror with a surface that curves inward. (p. 116)
espejo cóncavo Espejo cuya superficie se curva hacia dentro.

cones Cells in the retina that respond to and detect color. (p. 126)
conos Células en la retina que responden y detectan el color.

constructive interference The interference that occurs when waves combine to make a wave with a larger amplitude. (p. 20)
interferencia constructiva Interferencia que ocurre cuando las ondas se combinan para crear una onda con una amplitud mayor.

convex lens A lens that is thicker in the center than at the edges. (p. 122)
lente convexa Lente que es más gruesa en el centro que en los extremos.

convex mirror A mirror with a surface that curves outward. (p. 118)
espejo convexo Espejo cuya superficie se curva hacia fuera.

cornea The transparent front surface of the eye. (p. 126)
córnea Superficie frontal transparente del ojo.

crest The highest part of a transverse wave. (p. 8)
cresta Parte más alta de una onda transversal.

D

decibel (dB) A unit used to compare the loudness of different sounds. (p. 44)
decibelio (dB) Unidad usada para comparar el volumen de diferentes sonidos.

density The ratio of the mass of a substance to its volume. (p. 40)
densidad Razón de la masa de una sustancia a su volumen.

destructive interference The interference that occurs when two waves combine to make a wave with a smaller amplitude. (p. 21)
interferencia destructiva Interferencia que ocurre cuando dos ondas se combinan para crear una onda con una amplitud más pequeña.

diffraction The bending of waves as they move around a barrier or pass through an opening. (p. 20)
difracción Cambio de dirección de las ondas cuando rodean una barrera o pasan por una abertura.

diffuse reflection Reflection that occurs when parallel rays of light hit a rough surface and all reflect at different angles. (p. 114)
reflexión difusa Reflexión que ocurre cuando rayos de luz paralelos tocan una superficie rugosa y se reflejan en diferentes ángulos.

Doppler effect The change in frequency of a wave as its source moves in relation to an observer. (p. 46)
efecto Doppler Cambio en la frecuencia de una onda a medida que se mueve su fuente en relación al observador.

E

ear canal A narrow region leading from the outside of the human ear to the eardrum. (p. 54)
canal auditivo Región estrecha que va desde el exterior del oído humano hasta el tímpano.

eardrum A small, tightly stretched, drumlike membrane in the ear. (p. 54)
tímpano Membrana pequeña muy tensa con forma de tambor que está en el oído.

echo A reflected sound wave. (p. 38)
eco Onda sonora reflejada.

echolocation The use of reflected sound waves to determine distances or to locate objects. (p. 61)
ecolocación Uso de ondas sonoras reflejadas para determinar distancias o para localizar objetos.

elasticity The ability of a material to bounce back after being disturbed. (p. 40)
elasticidad Capacidad de un material para volver a su forma original después de verse alterada.

electromagnetic radiation The energy transferred through space by electromagnetic waves. (p. 71)
radiación electromagnética Energía transferida por ondas electromagnéticas a través del espacio.

electromagnetic spectrum The complete range of electromagnetic waves placed in order of increasing frequency. (p. 75)
espectro electromagnético Gama completa de ondas electromagnéticas colocadas en orden de menor a mayor frecuencia.

electromagnetic wave Transverse waves that transfer electrical and magnetic energy. (p. 71)
ondas electromagnéticas Ondas transversales que transfieren energía eléctrica y magnética.

energy The ability to do work. (p. 7)
energía Capacidad para realizar trabajo.

eyepiece A lens that magnifies the image formed by the objective. (p. 130)
ocular Lente que aumenta la imagen formada por el objetivo.

F

farsightedness A condition that causes a person to see nearby objects as blurry. (p. 128)
hipermetropía Condición que causa que una persona vea borrosos los objetos cercanos.

fluorescent light Light bulb that glows when an electric current causes ultraviolet rays to strike a coating inside a tube. (p. 86)
luz fluorescente Lámpara que se ilumina cuando una corriente eléctrica causa que los rayos ultravioleta choquen con el recubrimiento interior de un tubo.

focal point The point at which light rays parallel to the optical axis meet, or appear to meet, after being reflected (or refracted) by a mirror (or a lens). (p. 116)
punto de enfoque Punto en el que se encuentran, o parecen encontrarse, los rayos de luz paralelos al eje óptico después de reflejarse (o refractarse) en un espejo (o lente).

frequency The number of complete waves that pass a given point in a certain amount of time. (p. 13)
frecuencia Número de ondas completas que pasan por un punto dado en cierto tiempo.

frequency modulation A method of transmitting signals by changing the frequency of a wave. (p. 91)
frecuencia modulada Método de transmisión de señales por el cual se cambia la frecuencia de una onda.

fundamental tone The lowest natural frequency of an object. (p. 49)
tono fundamental Frecuencia natural más baja de un objeto.

gamma rays Electromagnetic waves with the shortest wavelengths and highest frequencies. (p. 80)
rayos gamma Ondas electromagnéticas con la menor longitud de onda y la mayor frecuencia.

hertz (Hz) Unit of measurement for frequency. (p. 13)
Hercio (Hz) Unidad de media de frecuencia.

hologram A three-dimensional photograph created using lasers. (p. 134)
holograma Fotografía tridimensional creada usando rayos láser.

illuminated Word used to describe an object that can be seen because it reflects light. (p. 84)
iluminado Palabra que se usa para describir un objeto que se puede ver porque refleja la luz.

image A copy of an object formed by reflected or refracted rays of light. (p. 115)
imagen Copia de un objeto formado por rayos de luz que se reflejan y se refractan.

incandescent light Light bulb that glows when a filament inside it gets white hot. (p. 84)
luz incandescente Lámpara que se ilumina cuando un filamento interior se calienta tanto que se pone blanco.

index of refraction A measure of the amount a ray of light bends when it passes from one medium to another. (p. 120)
índice de refracción Medida de la inclinación de un rayo de luz cuando pasa de un medio a otro.

infrared rays Electromagnetic waves with wavelengths shorter than radio waves, but longer than visible light. (p. 77)
rayos infrarrojos Ondas electromagnéticas con longitud de onda menor que las ondas de radio, pero mayor que la de la luz visible.

infrasound Sound waves with frequencies below 20 Hz. (p. 45)
infrasonido Ondas sonoras con frecuencias menores de 20 Hz.

intensity The amount of energy per second carried through a unit area by a wave. (p. 43)
intensidad Cantidad de energía por segundo que lleva una onda a través de una unidad de área.

interference The interaction between waves that meet. (p. 20)
interferencia Interacción entre ondas que se encuentran.

iris The ring of muscle that controls the size of the pupil and gives the eye its color. (p. 126)
iris Anillo muscular que controla el tamaño de la pupila y da el color al ojo.

larynx Two folds of tissue that make up the human voice box. (p. 45)
laringe Dos pliegues de tejido que forman la caja sonora humana.

laser A device that producesa narrow beam of coherent light. (p. 132)
láser Aparato que produce un delgado rayo de luz coherente.

law of reflection The rule that the angle of reflection equals the angle of incidence. (p. 18)
ley de reflexión Regla que enuncia que el ángulo de reflexión es igual al ángulo de incidencia.

lens A curved piece of glass or other transparent material that is used to refract light. (p. 122)
lente Trozo de cristal u otro material transparente curvado que se usa para refractar la luz.

longitudinal wave A wave that moves the medium in a direction parallel to the direction in which the wave travels. (p. 9)
onda longitudinal Onda que mueve el medio en una dirección paralela a la dirección en la que viaja la onda.

loudness Perception of the energy of a sound. (p. 42)
volumen Percepción de la energía de un sonido.

luminous Word used to describe an object that can be seen because it emits light. (p. 84)
luminoso Palabra que se usa para describir un objeto que se puede ver porque emite luz.

mechanical wave A wave that requires a medium through which to travel. (p. 7)
onda mecánica Onda que necesita un medio por el cual viajar.

medium The material through which a wave travels. (p. 7)
medio Material a través del cual viaja una onda.

microscope An optical instrument that forms enlarged images of tiny objects. (p. 131)
microscopio Instrumento óptico que forma imágenes aumentadas de objetos diminutos.

microwaves Radio waves with the shortest wavelengths and the highest frequencies. (p. 76)
microondas Ondas de radio con la menor longitud de onda y la mayor frecuencia.

mirage An image of a distant object caused by refraction of light as it travels through air of varying temperature. (p. 121)
espejismo Imagen de un objeto distante causado por la refracción de la luz cuando viaja por el aire a temperaturas cambiantes.

music A set of tones and overtones combined in ways that are pleasing. (p. 48)
música Conjunto de tonos y sobretonos combinados de manera agradable.

nearsightedness A condition that causes a person to see distant objects as blurry. (p. 128)
miopía Condición que causa que una persona vea borrosos los objetos lejanos.

neon light Glass tube containing neon gas that produces light. (p. 87)
luz de neón Tubo de vidrio que contiene gas neón que produce luz.

node A point of zero amplitude on a standing wave. (p. 22)
nodo Punto de amplitud cero en una onda estacionaria.

objective A lens that gathers light from an object and forms a real image. (p. 130)
objetivo Lente que reúne la luz de un objeto y forma una imagen real.

opaque material A material that reflects or absorbs all of the light that strikes it. (p. 107)
material opaco Material que refleja o absorbe toda la luz que llega a él.

optic nerve Short, thick nerve that carries signals from the eye to the brain. (p. 126)
nervio óptico Nervio corto y grueso que lleva señales del ojo al cerebro.

optical axis An imaginary line that divides a mirror in half. (p. 116)
eje óptico Recta imaginaria que divide un espejo por la mitad.

optical fiber A long, thin strand of glass or plastic that can carry light for long distances without allowing the light to escape. (p. 136)
fibra óptico Filamento largo y delgado de vidrio o plástico que puede transportar luz a través de largas distancias sin dejarla escapar.

overtone A natural frequency that is a multiple of the fundamental tone's frequency. (p. 49)
armónico Frecuencia natural que es un múltiplo de la frecuencia del tono fundamental.

photoelectric effect The ejection of electrons from a substance when light is shined on it. (p. 73)
efecto fotoeléctrico Expulsión de electrones de una sustancia cuando le da la luz.

photon A tiny particle or packet of light energy. (p. 73)
fotón Partícula diminuta o paquete de energía luminosa.

pigment A colored substance used to color other materials. (p. 111)
pigmento Sustancia con color que se usa para colorear otros materiales.

pitch Perception of the frequency of a sound. (p. 44)
tono Percepción de la frecuencia de un sonido.

plane mirror A flat mirror that produces an upright, virtual image the same size as the object. (p. 115)
espejo plano Espejo liso que produce una imagen virtual vertical del mismo tamaño que el objeto.

polarized light Light that vibrates in only one direction. (p. 72)
luz polarizada Luz que vibra en una sola dirección.

primary colors Three colors that can be used to make any other color. (p. 110)
colores primarios Tres colores que se pueden usar para hacer cualquier color.

pupil The opening in the center of the iris through which light enters the inside of the eye. (p. 126)
pupila Abertura en el centro del iris a través de la cual entra la luz en el ojo.

P wave A longitudinal seismic wave. (p. 27)
onda P Onda sísmica longitudinal.

radar A system that uses reflected radio waves to detect objects and measure their distance and speed. (p. 76)
radar Sistema que usa ondas de radio reflejadas para detectar objetos y medir su distancia y velocidad.

radio waves Electromagnetic waves with the longest wavelengths and lowest frequencies. (p. 76)
ondas de radio Ondas electromagnéticas con la mayor longitud de onda y la menor frecuencia.

rarefaction The part of a longitudinal wave where the particles of the medium are far apart. (p. 9)
rarefacción Parte de una onda longitudinal donde las partículas del medio están alejadas.

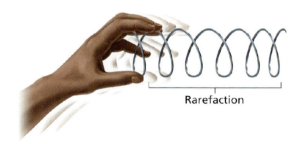

Rarefaction

ray A straight line used to represent a light wave. (p. 114)
rayo Línea recta que se usa para representar una onda de luz.

real image An upside-down image formed where rays of light meet. (p. 117)
imagen real Imagen invertida formada donde se encuentran los rayos de luz.

reflecting telescope A telescope that uses a concave mirror to gather light from distant objects. (p. 130)
telescopio de reflexión Telescopio que usa un espejo cóncavo para reunir luz de los objetos distantes.

reflection The bouncing back of an object or a wave when it hits a surface through which it cannot pass. (p. 18)
reflexión Rebote de un objeto o una onda cuando golpea una superficie por la cual no puede pasar.

refracting telescope A telescope that uses two convex lenses to form images. (p. 130)
telescopio refractor Telescopio que usa dos lentes convexas para formar imágenes.

refraction The bending of waves as they enter a new medium at an angle. (p. 19)
refracción Cambio de dirección de las ondas cuando entran en un nuevo medio a un determinado ángulo.

regular reflection Reflection that occurs when parallel rays of light hit a smooth surface and all reflect at the same angle. (p. 114)
reflexión regular Reflexión que ocurre cuando rayos de luz paralelos chocan contra una superficie lisa y se reflejan en el mismo ángulo.

resonance The increase in the amplitude of a vibration that occurs when external vibrations match an object's natural frequency. (p. 23)
resonancia Aumento en la amplitud de vibración que ocurre cuando vibraciones externas se corresponden con la frecuencia natural de un objeto.

retina The layer of cells that lines the inside of the eyeball. (p. 126)
retina Capa de células que recubre el interior del globo ocular.

reverberation The echoes of a sound that are heard after a sound source stops producing sound waves. (p. 52)
reverberación Ecos de un sonido que son oídos después de que la fuente sonora deja de producir ondas sonoras.

rods Cells in the retina that detect dim light. (p. 126)
bastones Células de la retina que detectan la luz tenue.

secondary color Any color produced by combining equal amounts of any two primary colors. (p. 110)
color secundario Color producido al combinar iguales cantidades de dos colores primarios cualesquiera.

seismic wave A wave produced by an earthquake. (p. 27)
onda sísmica Onda producida por un terremoto.

seismograph An instrument used to detect and measure earthquake waves. (p. 29)
sismógrafo Instrumento que se usa para detectar y medir ondas de terremotos.

sonar A system that uses reflected sound waves to detect and locate objects underwater. (p. 62)
sonar Sistema que usa ondas sonoras reflejadas para detectar y localizar objetos debajo del agua.

sonogram An image formed using reflected ultrasound waves. (p. 63)
sonograma Formación de una imagen usando ondas de ultrasonido reflejadas.

spectroscope An instrument used to view the different colors of light produced by different light sources. (p. 84)
espectroscopio Instrumento que se usa para ver los diferentes colores de la luz producidos por fuentes de luz diferentes.

standing wave A wave that appears to stand in one place, even though it is really two waves interfering as they pass through each other. (p. 22)
onda estacionaria Onda que parece que permanece en un lugar, aunque en realidad son dos ondas que interfieren cuando se cruzan.

surface wave A combination of a longitudinal wave and a transverse wave that travels along the surface of a medium. (p. 28)
onda superficial Combinación de una onda longitudinal con una onda transversal que viaja por la superficie de un medio.

S wave A transverse seismic wave. (p. 27)
onda S Onda sísmica transversal.

telescope An optical instrument that forms enlarged images of distant objects. (p. 130)
telescopio Instrumento óptico que forma imágenes aumentadas de los objetos lejanos.

thermogram An image that shows regions of different temperatures in different colors. (p. 77)
termograma Imagen que muestra regiones de diferentes temperaturas en diferentes colores.

total internal reflection The complete reflection of light by the inside surface of a medium. (p. 136)
reflexión interna total Reflexión completa de la luz en la superficie interna de un medio.

translucent material A material that scatters light as it passes through. (p. 107)
material traslúcido Material que dispersa la luz cuando ésta lo atraviesa.

transparent material A material that transmits light without scattering it. (p. 107)
material transparente Material que transmite luz sin dispersarla.

transverse wave A wave that moves the medium in a direction perpendicular to the direction in which the wave travels. (p. 8)
onda transversal Onda que mueve el medio en una dirección perpendicular a la dirección en la que viaja la onda.

trough The lowest part of a transverse wave. (p. 8)
valle Parte más baja de una onda transversal.

tsunami A huge surface wave on the ocean caused by an underwater earthquake. (p. 28)
tsunami Gran ola superficial del océano causado por un terremoto subterráneo.

tungsten-halogen bulb Incandescent light bulb containing a tungsten filament and a halogen gas. (p. 85)
lámpara de tungsteno-halógeno Lámpara de luz incandescente que contiene un filamento de tungsteno y gas halógeno.

 U

ultrasound Sound waves with frequencies above 20,000 Hz. (p. 45)
ultrasonido Ondas sonoras con frecuencias mayores de 20,000 Hz.

ultraviolet rays Electromagnetic waves with wavelengths shorter than visible light, but longer than X-rays. (p. 78)
rayos ultravioletas Ondas electromagnéticas con longitud de onda menor que la luz visible, pero mayor que la de los rayos X.

V

vapor light Light bulb containing neon or argon gas along with a small amount of solid sodium or mercury. (p. 86)
luz de vapor Lámpara que contiene gas neón o argón y una pequeña cantidad de sodio sólido o mercurio.

vibration A repeated back-and-forth or up-and-down motion. (p. 8)
vibración Movimiento repetido hacia delante y hacia atrás o hacia arriba y hacia abajo.

virtual image An upright image formed where rays of light appear to meet or come from. (p. 115)
imagen virtual Imagen vertical que se forma desde donde parecen provenir los rayos de luz.

visible light Electromagnetic waves that are visible to the human eye. (p. 78)
luz visible Ondas electromagnéticas visibles al ojo humano.

 W

wave A disturbance that transfers energy from place to place. (p. 7)
onda Perturbación que transfiere energía de un lugar a otro.

wavelength The distance between two corresponding parts of a wave. (p. 13)
longitud de onda Distancia entre dos partes correspondientes de una onda.

 X

X-rays Electromagnetic waves with wavelengths shorter than ultraviolet rays, but longer than gamma rays. (p. 79)
rayos X Ondas electromagnéticas con longitud de onda menor que los rayos ultravioleta, pero mayor que la de los rayos gamma.

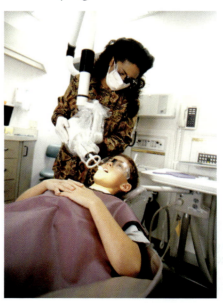

Page numbers for key terms are printed in **boldface** type.
Page numbers for illustrations, maps, and charts are printed in *italics*.

Index

Teacher's Edition entries appear in
blue type. The page on which a term is
defined is indicated in **boldface** type.

Index

Page numbers for key terms are printed in **boldface** type.
Page numbers for illustrations, maps, and charts are printed in *italics*.

Index

Page numbers for key terms are printed in **boldface** type.
Page numbers for illustrations, maps, and charts are printed in *italics*.

Acknowledgments

Staff Credits

Scott Andrews, Jennifer Angel, Laura Baselice, Carolyn Belanger, Barbara A. Bertell, Suzanne Biron, Peggy Bliss, Stephanie Bradley, James Brady, Anne M. Bray, Kerry Cashman, Jonathan Cheney, Joshua D. Clapper, Lisa J. Clark, Bob Craton, Patricia Cully, Patricia M. Dambry, Kathy Dempsey, Emily Ellen, Thomas Ferreira, Jonathan Fisher, Patricia Fromkin, Paul Gagnon, Robert Graham, Ellen Granter, Barbara Hollingdale, Etta Jacobs, Linda Johnson, Anne Jones, John Judge, Kevin Keane, Kelly Kelliher, Toby Klang, Russ Lappa, Carolyn Lock, Rebecca Loveys, Constance J. McCarty, Carolyn B. McGuire, Ranida Touranont McKneally, Anne McLaughlin, Eve Melnechuk, Tania Mlawer, Janet Morris, Francine Neumann, Marie Opera, Jill Ort, Joan Paley, Dorothy Preston, Rashid Ross, Siri Schwartzman, Laurel Smith, Emily Soltanoff, Jennifer A. Teece, Diane Walsh, Amanda M. Watters, Merce Wilczek, Amy Winchester, Char Lyn Yeakley. **Additional Credits** Tara Allamilla, Terence Hegarty, Louise Gachet, Andrea Golden, Stephanie Rogers, Kim Schmidt, Joan Tobin.

Illustration

David Corrente: 141; **John Edwards and Associates:** 18; **Ray Goudey:** 70; **Phillip Guzy:** 43, 45, 49, 50, 51l, 51r, 55, 79, 85, 86, 87, 110, 117, 121, 131, 132; **Matt Mayerchak:** 6, 8, 17, 24, 26, 28, 31, 36, 39, 42, 44, 48, 53, 54, 57, 60, 65, 89, 92, 101, 102, 113, 119, 120, 124, 125, 138; **Steve McEntee:** 8, 9, 10, 12–13, 19, 21, 30, 37t, 44, 61, 75, 93; **Richard McMahon:** 40, 50–51, 54, 71, 73, 90b, 94, 108, 109, 111, 114, 117, 123, 134–135, 136, 140l; **Robert Roper:** 38l, 38r, 46; **Roberta Warshaw:** 66l, 66r, 67.

Photography

Photo Research Paula Wehde

Cover Image bottom, Brian Sytnyk/Masterfile; **top,** Mark Lewis/Picturesque

Page iii, Washington University Photo Department; **vi,** E.R. Degginger/Color Pic; **vii,** Richard Haynes; **viii,** Richard Haynes; **x,** Courtesy of Christine Darden; **x-1,** NASA; **1b,** Courtesy of Christine Darden.; **2,** Matthew Pippen; **3,** Courtesy of Christine Darden.

Chapter 1
Pages 4–5, Paul Friedlander; **5 inset,** Lon C. Diehl/PhotoEdit; **6b,** Image Bank/Getty Images, Inc.; **6t,** Richard Haynes; **11b,** Chris Cole/Duomo; **11t,** Richard Haynes; **14,** Jim Zuckerman/Corbis; **16,** Richard Haynes; **17b,** Alese & Mort Pechter/Corbis; **17t,** Richard Haynes; **18,** Reno Tucillo; **19,** Fundamental Photographs; **20 both,** Coastal Inlets Research Program; **22 both,** Richard Megna/Fundamental Photographs; **23,** EERC; **24,** Richard Haynes; **25,** Richard Haynes; **26b,** Courtesy National Information Service for Earthquake Engineering, University of California, Berkeley; **29,** Getty Images, Inc.; **29 inset,** Getty Images, Inc.; **30,** Chris Cole/Duomo.

Chapter 2
Pages 34–35, Paul Arthur/Getty Images; **35 inset,** Jon Chomitz; **36b,** Corbis; **36t,** Richard Haynes; **37,** Richard Haynes; **40,** Richard Haynes; **41,** The Granger Collection, NY; **42,** Richard Haynes; **43 ear image,** Index Stock Imagery; **44 both,** Jack Vartoogian; **45,** Richard Haynes; **47,** Reuters/Corbis; **48b,** Michael Newman/PhotoEdit; **48t,** Richard Haynes; **50l,** Photo Disc/Getty Images, Inc.; **50–51m,** Doug Martin/Photo Researchers, Inc.; **51r,** Getty Images, Inc.; **52,** Ted Soqui/Corbis; **53,** Richard Haynes; **55,** Quest/Dorling Kindersley; **56l,** SPL/Photo Researchers, Inc.; **56r,** Russ Lappa; **58b,** Michael Newman/PhotoEdit; **58t,** Firefly Productions/Corbis; **59b,** David Madison/Getty Images, Inc.; **60b,** Dale Spartas/Corbis; **60t,** Getty Images, Inc.; **61l,** Minden Pictures; **61r,** Corbis; **63b,** Philippe Saada/Phototake; **63t,** CMSP; **64,** Reuters/Corbis.

Chapter 3
Pages 68–69, Roger Ressmeyer/Corbis; **69 inset,** Richard Haynes; **70,** Richard Haynes; **72l,** Clive Streeter/Dorling Kindersley; **72r,** Diane Schiumo/Fundamental Photographs; **74,** Richard Haynes; **76,** Corbis; **77,** Alfred Pasieska/SPL/Photo Researchers, Inc.; **78,** Peter A. Simon/Corbis; **79l,** Science VU/Visuals Unlimited; **79r,** Tom Stewart/Corbis; **82,** Richard Haynes; **84,** Photo Researchers, Inc.; **86,** Phil Degginger; **87,** Will & Deni McIntyre/Corbis; **89,** Richard Haynes; **90 TV,** TRBfoto/Getty Images, Inc.; **90 picture on TV,** Shaun Botterill/Getty Images, Inc.; **93,** Thinkstock/Index Stock Imagery, Inc.; **94l,** John Jenkins/American Museum of Radio & Electricity; **94r,** Science Photo Library; **95l,** AP/Wide World Photos; **95m,** David Ducros/SPL/Photo Researchers, Inc.; **95r,** Tony Freeman Photographs; **98,** Richard Haynes; **99,** Richard Haynes; **100b,** Alfred Pasieska/SPL/Photo Researchers, Inc.; **100t,** Photo Researchers.

Chapter 4
Pages 104–105, Dan McCoy/Rainbow; **105 inset,** Richard Haynes; **106b,** E.R. Degginger/Color Pic; **106t,** Richard Haynes; **107,** Richard Haynes; **108, 109,** PhotoDisc/Getty Images, Inc.; **110 parrot,** Getty Images, Inc.; **110 TV,** Russ Lappa; **110br,** Jerome Wexler/Photo Researchers, Inc.; **112,** Richard Haynes; **113b,** Tony Freeman/PhotoEdit; **113t,** Richard Haynes; **114,** Michael D. Gardner; **115 all,** Sergio Piumatti; **116,** Richard Haynes; **119b,** Russ Lappa; **119t,** Richard Haynes; **121b,** E.R. Degginger/Color Pic; **121t,** Getty Images, Inc.; **122b, all,** Getty Images, Inc.;

122t, David Parker/Photo Researchers, Inc.; **124,** Richard Haynes; **125,** David Young-Wolf/PhotoEdit; **127r,** Omnikron/Photo Researchers, Inc.; **127l,** Photo Researchers, Inc.; **129b,** NASA, Hui Yang University of Illinois Nursery of New Stars; **129t,** Richard Haynes; **133bl,** Tony Freeman/PhotoEdit; **133bm,** John Goell/The Picture Cube; **133br,** Getty Images, Inc.; **133tl,** Patrick Bennett/Corbis; **133tr,** Corbis; **134l,** Corbis; **134r,** Scala/Art Resource, NY; **135l,** Hulton-Deutsch Collection/Corbis; **135m,** Phototake; **135r,** Grant Heilman Photography, Inc.; **136,** Corbis; **137,** Custom Medical Stock Photo; **138,** Corbis.

Pages 142, Kobal Collection; **143,** Photofest; **145b,** "The Lord of the Rings: The Two Towers" (c) MMII, New Line Productions, Inc. TM Tolkien Ent. Licensed to New Line Productions, Inc. All rights Reserved, Photo appears courtesy of New Line Productions, Inc.; **145t,** Everett Collection; **146l,** The Kobal Collection; **146r,** Photofest; **147b,** Richard Haynes; **147tl,** Kobal Collection; **147tr,** Everett Collection; **148,** Tony Freeman/PhotoEdit; **149b,** Russ Lappa; **149m,** Richard Haynes; **149t,** Russ Lappa; **150,** Richard Haynes; **152,** Richard Haynes; **154,** Tanton Yachts; **155,** Richard Haynes; **157b,** Richard Haynes; **157t,** Dorling Kinderlsey; **159,** Image Stop/Phototake; **162,** Richard Haynes; **169,** Richard Haynes; **172,** Tony Freeman/PhotoEdit; **173,** Will & Deni McIntyre/Corbis; **175,** Philippe Saada/Phototake; **176l,** Dale Spartas/Corbis; **176r,** Tom Stewart/Corbis.